Heath's Modern Language Series

A
SHORTER FRENCH COURSE

BY

W. H. FRASER AND J. SQUAIR

PROFESSORS IN THE ROMANCE DEPARTMENT, UNIVERSITY OF TORONTO

D. C. HEATH & CO., PUBLISHERS

BOSTON   NEW YORK   CHICAGO

PREFACE

In preparing this book the authors have had particularly in mind the requirements of elementary classes in schools and colleges.

The amount of grammatical material in each lesson is small, and in nearly all cases the exercises are based on extracts of connected French illustrating the points of grammar under observation. These extracts cover a wide range of topics relating to every-day life. The vocabulary employed has been kept within moderate limits, and consists of words and expressions in common use.

The numerous oral exercises based on the French extracts are not intended to be exhaustive, but are designed rather to furnish suggestions for additional practice of a similar kind, to which the authors attach great importance. In most of the lessons oral or written practice is also provided in the continuation of tense-forms combined into connected phrases. Such exercises should be thoroughly studied and committed to memory, particularly since they often furnish additional examples of constructions which illustrate grammatical points contained in the lesson.

The English sentences in the exercises are provided for translation into French as a final test of knowledge. It is recommended that written tests of this nature should be required only after the translation has been mastered orally. Where two or more sets of English sentences are given, the first one is regularly based directly on the French above it, the additional set or sets being of a more difficult and general character suitable for extra drill and review.

For the convenience of teachers who prefer to begin with the spoken language rather than with the written language, a phonetic transcription of the French of the first ten lessons has been given at the end of the Introduction.

It is hoped that the exercises in general will prove suitable for the purposes of teachers who desire to combine in their class-work the advantages of the direct method with those of the grammatical method.

The book is not primarily intended to serve as a reference grammar, but the addition of a copious index and the prominent type of the section headings will render it easy of consultation for this purpose.

The authors take this opportunity of expressing their thanks to a large number of teachers for advice and criticism in the preparation of the work, and in particular to Professors Saint-Elme de Champ and W. C. Ferguson, of the University of Toronto, for assistance in the revision of the manuscript and proofs.

JANUARY, 1913

CONTENTS

INTRODUCTION

A. — The Alphabet

The letters of the alphabet, with their French names, are as follows:

a	*a*	h	*ache*	o	*o*	v	*vé*
b	*bé*	i	*i*	p	*pé*	w	*double vé*
c	*cé*	j	*ji*	q	*ku*	x	*iks*
d	*dé*	k	*ka*	r	*èr*	y	*i grec*
e	*é*	l	*èl*	s	*èss*	z	*zèd*
f	*èf*	m	*èm*	t	*té*		
g	*gé*	n	*èn*	u	*u*		

In addition to the letters, the following orthographic signs are employed: —

1. The acute accent (*accent aigu*), as in été.

2. The grave accent (*accent grave*), as in voilà, père, où.

3. The circumflex accent (*accent circonflexe*), as in âme, tête, île, côté, fût.

NOTE. — None of these marks serve to denote stress.

4. The cedilla (*cédille*), used under **c** to give it the sound of **s** before **a, o** or **u**, as in avançais, leçon, reçu.

5. The diæresis (*tréma*), to show that the vowel bearing it is to be pronounced separately from the preceding vowel, as in Noël.

NOTES. — 1. Words are commonly spelled orally by naming the letters as above, together with the other orthographic signs, if any, e.g. **bonté = bé-o-èn-té-é** *accent aigu;* when, however, **e** has no accent mark, it is often named by the sound which it has in **me, le,** etc. (cf. *H*, below), e.g. **mer = èm-e-èr.**

2. According to a newer method of spelling, employed by some, the letters are named thus: **a, be, ce, de, e, fe, gheu, heu, i, je, ke, le, me, ne, o, pe, ke, re, se, te, u, ve, double ve, kse, i, ze.**

3. The names of the letters are all masculine, according to some, while others make the names of **f, h, l, m, n, r, s,** feminine, thus: **un f** or **une f.**

B. — Pronunciation and Spelling

The pronunciation will be explained, as far as possible, by comparison with English sounds, but it must never be forgotten that the sounds of any two languages rarely correspond exactly. Moreover, the spelling of French, like that of English, is irregular and inconsistent; hence, to avoid confusion, a phonetic alphabet will be employed, in which each sound is represented by but one symbol, and each symbol represents but one sound.

C. — Phonetic Alphabet

[The examples are in ordinary spelling; the heavy type indicates the letters which correspond to the sounds of the symbols, and the phonetic transcription is given within brackets, as will be done wherever used throughout the book. The alphabet employed is that of the *Association Phonétique Internationale.*]

SYMBOLS	EXAMPLES	SYMBOLS	EXAMPLES
ː	(sign of length)	ɲ	agneau, digne [aɲo, diɲ]
a	patte, part [pat, paːr]	o	beau, nôtre [bo, noːtr]
ɑ	pas, passe [pɑ, pɑːs]	ɔ	note, fort [nɔt, fɔːr]
ɑ̃	tant, tante [tɑ̃, tɑ̃ːt]	ɔ̃	bon, oncle [bɔ̃, ɔ̃ːkl]
b	beau, robe [bo, rɔb]	œ	neuf, neuve [nœf, nœːv]
d	dame, fade [dam, fad]	œ̃	un, humble [œ̃, œ̃ːbl]
e	été [ete]	ø	peu, creuse [pø, krøːz]
ɛ	près, père [prɛ, pɛːr]	p	pas, attrape [pa, atrap]
ɛ̃	pin, mince [pɛ̃, mɛ̃ːs]	r	drap, rare [dra, raːr]
ə	le [lə]	s	si, pense [si, pɑ̃ːs]
f	fort, neuf [fɔːr, nœf]	ʃ	chou, vache [ʃu, vaʃ]
g	gant, longue [gɑ̃, lɔ̃ːg]	t	ta, patte [ta, pat]
h	aha! [a(h)a]	u	tout, tour [tu, tuːr]
i	ici, vive [isi, viːv]	y	tu, mur [ty, myːr]
j	hier, soleil [jɛːr, sɔlɛːj]	ɥ	huile [ɥil]
k	car, roc [kar, rɔk]	v	va, cave [va, kaːv]
l	la, cale [la, kal]	w	oui [wi]
m	mot, dame [mo, dam]	z	zone, rose [zoːn, roːz]
n	ni, une [ni, yn]	ʒ	je, rouge [ʒe, ruːʒ]

NOTE. — Before studying the pronunciation in detail, there are three important matters affecting it to be considered, namely, (1) syllabication, (2) stress, (3) vowel quantity.

D. — Syllabication

When consonants come between vowels in French the following rules are to be observed: —

1. A single consonant sound goes with the following vowel sound to form a syllable: a-mi, fi-nir, a-gneau, tâ-cher.

2. So also combinations of consonants which may be pronounced together, of which the last consonant is l or r (but not rl, lr): é-clai-rer, ou-vrir, pre-scrit.

3. Other combinations of consonants are divided: par-ler, mon-trer, per-du, fac-teur, mer-cre-di.

4. Final e (usually silent in prose) is regarded as forming a syllable: dou-z(e), bra-v(e), fi-n(e), u-n(e).

5. Doubled letters have regularly only a single sound, but are divided where necessary in writing: pa(s)-ser.

6. The prefix ex– is divided in speaking, but not in writing: ex-a-men (=eg-za-men).

NOTE. — Observe from the above that French syllables end in vowel sounds wherever possible, and hence that the consonantal ending of syllables, so frequent in English, must be carefully avoided. Compare in this respect ci-té, ta-bleau with 'cit-y,' 'tab-leau.'

E. — Stress

In French the syllables of words are uttered with almost equal force, a very slight additional force ("stress") being given to the last syllable, or to the last but one, in case the word ends in e, thus: che-**val**, par-**ler**, par-**lons**, fa-ta-li-**té**, **per**-dre, **ta**-ble.

NOTE. — Remember that accent marks have nothing to do with stress.

F. — Vowel Quantity

By vowel quantity is meant the length of time consumed in uttering a vowel sound. The following are the principal general rules: —

1. Final vowel sounds (including nasals) are short: fini, vie, parler, tableau, donner, tant, sapin.

2. All stressed vowels are long before the sounds [v], [z], [ʒ], [j], [r final]: cave [kaːv], amuse [amyːz], rouge [ruːʒ], feuille [fœːj], faire [fɛːr], livre [liːvr].

3. Of stressed vowels standing before other consonant sounds, nasals are long: grande [grɑ̃ːd], prince [prɛ̃ːs]; [o] and [ø] are long: faute [foːt], meute [møːt]; [ɑ] long (almost always): passe [pɑːs]; [ɛ] long or short: reine [rɛːn], vienne [vjɛn]; other vowels regularly short.

NOTE. — It is also possible to distinguish between "long" and "half-long" vowels in unstressed syllables, but for simplicity only long vowels will be indicated in the transcription.

G. — Pronunciation of Vowel Sounds

In pronouncing French vowel sounds the following general rules should be carefully observed: —

1. Never drawl a vowel sound or allow it to become a diphthong, as often happens in English; French vowels are uniform throughout their utterance, the position of the organs of speech remaining unchanged during the whole continuance of the sound.

2. Never slur over or clip out vowel sounds (except **e** in certain cases, see below), but give each its full value.

3. Lip rounding (as observed in 'who,' 'no,' 'law') and lip retraction, that is, drawing the corners of the mouth backward as in smiling (to be observed in 'let,' 'hat') are much more definite and energetic than in English.

NOTE. — Some vowel sounds are denoted by a single letter; others are denoted by two or more letters; see below.

H. — Single Letters denoting Vowel Sounds

a usually like **a** in 'pat,' but with wider mouth opening and definite lip retraction; the point of the tongue is against the lower teeth — Symbol [a]: patte [pat], part [paːr], chat [ʃa], malade [malad], papa [papa], mal [mal].

à always as above: là [la], voilà [vwala].

â usually like **a** in 'ah!' 'father,' but with the mouth well open, the lips neither rounded nor retracted, and the tongue not touching the lower teeth — Symbol [ɑ]: pâte [pɑːt], bâtir [bɑtiːr], bâton [bɑtɔ̃].

EXCEPTIONS: 1. **a** before final **s**, usually before medial **s**, and also in some rarer combinations (but with varying usage) = [ɑ]: pas [pɑ], passer [pɑse], gagner [gɑɲe], nation [nɑsjɔ̃], occasion [ɔkɑzjɔ̃], bataille [bɑtɑːj]. 2. **â** in verb-endings = [a]: nous donnâmes [dɔnam], vous donnâtes [dɔnat].

é almost always like **a** in 'patience,' but with definite lip retraction — Symbol [e]: été [ete], allé [ale], né [ne], déréglé [deregle].

è, ê always like **e** in 'let,' but with the mouth wider open and the lips definitely retracted — Symbol [ɛ]: près [prɛ], prêt [prɛ], père [pɛːr], espèce [ɛspɛs], fête [fɛːt], même [mɛːm], êtes [ɛːt].

e (1) like **e** in 'the boy,' but with slight lip rounding — Symbol [ə]. It is so pronounced in monosyllables and in any syllable not final before a single consonant sound (but see note, below): me [mə], le [lə], que [kə], cheval [ʃəval], tenir [təniːr], tu seras [səra], ceci [səsi], mercredi [mɛrkrədi], appartement [apartəmã]. This letter is commonly called e mute (e muet).

(2) but in the endings –er, –ez (r, z silent), in words like les, mes, etc., in et and a few other words, e = [e]: donner [dɔne], février [fevrje], avez [ave], chez [ʃe], les [le], ses [se], et [e], pied [pje], clef [kle], etc.

(3) it regularly has the sound of [ɛ] (cf. è, above), before a doubled consonant, or before two or more consonant sounds: cesser [sɛse], perdre [pɛrdr], espérer [ɛspere]; also before a final consonant sound, and before silent final t: avec [avɛk], cet [sɛt], fier [fjɛːr], jouet [ʒwɛ] (but not in et); also before il, ill: soleil [sɔlɛːj], abeille [abɛːj]; further, in tu es [ɛ], il est [ɛ].

EXCEPTIONS: Observe descendre [desãːdr], femme [fam], and adverbs in –emment, e.g., prudemment [prydamã]. Words in eff–, ex– (before vowel), dess– may be pronounced either with [ɛ] or [e]: effet [ɛfɛ or efɛ], example [ɛgzãːpl or egzãːpl], dessert [desɛːr or desɛːr], but observe dessus [dəsy], dessous [dəsu] and words like ressembler [rəsãble].

Silent e: The letter e is silent in prose (1) at the end of words: rue [ry], donnée [dɔne], place [plas], ai-je [ɛː ʒ], table [tabl], vendre [vãːdr]; (2) within words after a vowel sound: gaieté [gete], remercierons [rəmɛrsirɔ̃]; (3) in the verb-endings –es, –ent: tu donnes [dɔn], ils donnent [dɔn], ils donnaient [dɔnɛ].

NOTE. — In ordinary speech the [ə] sound is usually slighted or wholly omitted in most cases where consonantal combinations resulting therefrom can be readily pronounced, e.g. mad(e)moisell(e), ach(e)ter, maint(e)nant, am(e)ner; but mercredi, apercevant, lentement, etc.

i, î like i in 'machine,' with energetic lip retraction (never like i in 'city') — Symbol [i]: ici [isi], vive [viːv], vie [vi], il [il], île [il], famille [famiːj].

EXCEPTION: For i = [j], see Semi-Vowels, below.

o usually like o in 'not,' but with definite lip rounding — Symbol [ɔ]: note [nɔt], dot [dɔt], fort [fɔːr], robe [rɔb], école [ekɔl], votre [vɔtr], étoffe [etɔf], orner [ɔrne].

ô regularly like o in 'ocean,' but with much tenser lip rounding and protrusion, as for whistling — Symbol [o]: côté [kote], vôtre [voːtr], bientôt [bjẽto].

EXCEPTIONS: 1. o = [o] as a final sound, and in a few other words: mot [mo], nos [no], gros [gro]; rose [roːz], chose [ʃoːz],

grosse [groːs], fosse [fos], position [pozisjɔ̃], etc. 2. ô = [ɔ] in a
few words: hôtel [ɔtɛl], rôti [rɔti], etc.

u, û   has no English counterpart; the tongue position is the same as
for [i], but with tense lip rounding, without protrusion; best
acquired by prolonging the [i] sound, meanwhile rounding the
lips, or by rounding the lips and bringing the tongue to the
[i] position — Symbol [y]: tu [ty], mur [myːr], mûr [myːr],
vu [vy], rue [ry], utile [ytil], fût [fy], sur [syr].

EXCEPTION: For u = [ɥ], see Semi-Vowels, below.

y   when not beginning a syllable, y has the same sound as i —
Symbol [i]: syllabe [silab].

EXCEPTION: For y beginning a syllable, see Semi-Vowels,
below.

I. — Combinations denoting Vowel Sounds

ai, aî   usually = [ɛ], see è, above; aî always thus: mais [mɛ], faire
[fɛːr], j'aimais [ɛmɛ], j'aimerais [ɛmrɛ], maître [mɛːtr].

EXCEPTIONS: 1. ai = [e], as in été, when final in verb-endings: je donnai [dɔne], je donnerai [dɔnre], j'ai [e]; also in
gai [ge], and usually in je sais [se], il sait [se], maison [mezɔ̃].
2. ai = [ə], as in le, in –ais– of certain forms of the verb faire:
nous faisons [fəzɔ̃], je faisais [fəzɛ], faisant [fəzɑ̃], etc.

au, eau regularly = [o], see ô, above: autre [oːtr], aux [o], eau [o], chevaux [ʃəvo], sauter [sote], tableau [tablo], beau [bo].

EXCEPTIONS: au = [ɔ], see o above, in the future and conditional of avoir, and in a few other words: j'aurai [ɔre],
j'aurais [ɔrɛ], etc., Paul [pɔl], mauvais [mɔvɛ], etc.

ay, ey   when a final sound = [ɛ]: je paye [pɛ], Cambray [kɑ̃brɛ], Ney
[nɛ]; but a or e in this combination = [ɛ] when the y belongs
to the next syllable: ayez [ɛje], payer [pɛje], grasseyer
[grasɛje].

EXCEPTIONS: pays [pei], paysan [peizɑ̃].

ei   always = [ɛ]: reine [rɛːn], Seine [sɛːn].

eu, eû   (1) a sound which has no English counterpart; the tongue po-
œu   sition is the same as for [e], as in été, with tense lip rounding
and protrusion, as for whistling; to acquire the sound, pro-
long [e] and round the lips, or round the lips and bring the
tongue to the [e] position — Symbol [ø]. Thus pronounce
eu, œu as a final sound, and also eu before s and sometimes
t within a word: peu [pø], feu [fø], il veut [vø], heureux

[œrø], bœufs [bø], creuser [krøze], meute [møːt]; also, eû in
jeûne [ʒøːn], jeûner [ʒøne]; further, déjeuner [deʒøne].

EXCEPTIONS: eu, eû in tenses of avoir = [y], e being regarded
as silent: eu [y], nous eûmes [ym], ils eurent [yːr].

(2) also a sound which has no English counterpart; the tongue
position is the same as for [ɛ], as in près, with definite lip
rounding; best acquired by combining the two positions as
explained for (1) above — Symbol [œ]. Thus pronounce eu,
œu before a final consonant sound (not s), and before il, ill:
neuf [nœf], neuve [nœːv], fleur [flœːr], leur [lœːr], bœuf
[bœf], feuille [fœːj].

ue, œ   the same sound as eu (2), above: orgueil [ɔrgœːj], cueillir
[kœjiːr], œil [œːj].

ou, où   regularly like oo in 'boot,' but with much tenser lip rounding
oû   and protrusion, as for whistling — Symbol [u]: tout [tu],
doux [du], tour [tuːr], ou [u], où [u], goût [gu], goûter [gute],
rouge [ruːʒ]; observe août [u], a being silent.

NOTE. — For ou, oi, oî, oe, oê, see also Semi-Vowels, below.

K. — The Nasal Vowels

These sounds are quite foreign to English, and are formed
by uttering the French vowel sounds [ɑ], [ɛ], [ɔ], [œ], and at the
same time allowing the soft palate to hang freely as in breath-
ing, thus causing the breath to escape partly through the nose.
Control of the soft palate may be acquired by prolonging the
first part of the sound of **ang** as in 'sang,' but carefully avoiding
the completion of the sound. It must be especially noted that
there is absolutely no sound of **n**, **m** or **ng**, in French nasal
vowels, and hence great care must be taken neither to raise
the tongue nor close the lips until the sound is complete.

The sign of nasality orthographically is a single **n** or **m** in
the same syllable with the vowel; thus, nasal are: ta**n**t, se**m**-
bler, fi**n**, pei**n**dre, plei**n**, leço**n**, bo**n**, to**m**ber, chacu**n**; but if **n** or
m is followed by a vowel, or is doubled, or if **mn** occurs, there
is regularly no nasality; thus, non-nasal are: fine, commune,
pleine, ennemi, innocent, inutile, bonne, condamner.

NOTE. — The rule does not apply to certain words having **en-**, **enn-**, **emm-**, for
which see note, below.

an, am
en, em
like nasalized [ɑ] as described above — Symbol [ɑ̃]: tant [tɑ̃], tante [tɑ̃ːt], gant [gɑ̃], an [ɑ̃], viande [vjɑ̃ːd], champ [ʃɑ̃], en [ɑ̃], encre [ɑ̃ːkr], temps [tɑ̃], sembler [sɑ̃ble].

> EXCEPTIONS: en = [ɛ̃], see ain, etc., below, in some forms of tenir, venir, as a final sound, and in some other words: vient [vjɛ̃], tiendrai [tjɛ̃dre], bien [bjɛ̃], examen [ɛgzamɛ̃], chien [ʃjɛ̃], Benjamin [bɛ̃ʒamɛ̃].

> NOTE. — Observe ennui [ɑ̃nɥi], emmener [ɑ̃mne], with doubled n, m, and enivrer [ɑ̃nivre].

ain, aim
ein, eim
in, im
yn, ym
like nasalized [ɛ] as explained above — Symbol [ɛ̃]: pain [pɛ̃], faim [fɛ̃], plein [plɛ̃], peindre [pɛ̃ːdr], Reims [rɛ̃s], pin [pɛ̃], prince [prɛ̃ːs], jardin [ʒardɛ̃], simple [sɛ̃ːpl], impossible [ɛ̃pɔsibl], syntaxe [sɛ̃taks], symbole [sɛ̃bɔl].

> NOTE. — Observe also the same sound in tînmes [tɛ̃ːm], vînmes [vɛ̃ːm].

on, om
like nasalized [ɔ] as explained above — Symbol [ɔ̃]: bon [bɔ̃], oncle [ɔ̃ːkl], mon [mɔ̃], ont [ɔ̃], leçon [ləsɔ̃], tomber [tɔ̃be], ombre [ɔ̃ːbr], compter [kɔ̃te].

> EXCEPTION: on in monsieur = [ə]: monsieur [məsjø].

un, um
eun
like nasalized [œ] as explained above — Symbol [œ̃]: un [œ̃], chacun [ʃakœ̃], emprunter [ɑ̃prœ̃te], parfum [parfœ̃], à jeun [a ʒœ̃].

oin
for the sound of oin, see Semi-Vowels, below.

L. — Semi-Vowels

When **i, y, ou** do not of themselves form a syllable, but come before another vowel sound in the same syllable, they are pronounced with greater rapidity and tenseness of the vocal organs concerned, thus assuming a partially consonantal value, as described below, thus:

i, y
like very brief and forcible y in 'yes' — Symbol [j]: viande [vjɑ̃ːd], hier [jɛːr], fier [fjɛːr], bien [bjɛ̃], faïence [fajɑ̃ːs], yeux [jø], ayez [ɛje], payer [pɛje], Lyon [ljɔ̃].

ou
like very brief and tense w in 'we,' with close lip rounding and protrusion, as for whistling — Symbol [w]: oui [wi], jouer [ʒwe], louer [lwe], Louis [lwi].

> NOTE. — When u of gu, qu (usually silent) is pronounced, as it sometimes is, it has the sound [w] before a in some words: lingual [lɛ̃gwal], équateur, [ekwatœːr].

oi, oî
have the sound of [w] + [a] or [ɑ], the latter usually after r, and in a few other words: moi [mwa], voici [vwasi], boîte

[bwaːt], froid [frwɑ], roi [rwɑ], trois [trwɑ], croire [krwɑːr], le bois [bwɑ], le mois [mwɑ], pois [pwɑ], etc.

oê, oe   in a few words = [w]+[a]: poêle [pwal], moelle [mwal], etc.

oin   has the sound of [w]+[ɛ̃]: loin [lwɛ̃], joindre [ʒwɛ̃ːdr].

u   has no counterpart in English; best acquired by substituting [y] for it (as in tu, etc.), and gradually increasing the speed and force of utterance: lui [lɥi], suis [sɥi], puis [pɥi], fruit [frɥi], pluie [plɥi], tuile [tɥil], cuisine [kɥizin], nuance [nɥɑːs], aiguille [ɛgɥiːj or egɥiːj], questeur [kɥɛstœːr], Quirinal [kɥirinal].

> NOTE.— When u of gu, qu (usually silent) is pronounced, as it some-times is, it commonly has this sound before e, i, as in the last three examples.

M. — Consonants

The sounds of the consonants can be sufficiently described, for the most part, by noting the differences between their mode of formation and that of the nearest English sounds, and by observing the following general rules: —

1. The movements of the vocal organs are more prompt, definite and vigorous in uttering French consonants than for the corresponding English sounds.

2. Note the distinction of "voice," which means the hum-ming or droning sound produced by the vibration of the vocal chords (as observed in the v of 'vine' as compared with f of 'fine'), and remember that French voiced consonants are much more fully voiced than corresponding English sounds.

3. Final consonants are more usually silent, but final c, f, l and r in monosyllables are more usually sounded.

4. With slight exceptions, French doubled consonants have only a single sound.

> NOTE.— The doubling of consonant sounds is characteristic of very careful speech, and only some of the more striking cases are mentioned below.

b   regularly like b in 'bit,' 'tub,' fully voiced — Symbol [b]: beau [bo], robe [rɔb], bon [bɔ̃], table [tabl], là-bas [la bɑ], tomber [tɔ̃be], abbé [abe].

     EXCEPTION: b has the sound of p when next before a voice-less consonant: absolument [apsɔlymɑ̃], obtenir [ɔptəniːr], etc.

c (1) like **k** in 'take' — Symbol [k]. Thus **c** before **a**, **o**, **u** or a consonant, or when final: **c**ar [kar], é**c**ole [ekɔl], é**c**outer [ekute], **c**uré [kyre], **c**raie [krɛ], **c**lasse [klɑːs], ave**c** [avɛk], se**c** [sɛk].

(2) **c** has the same sound as **s** (1) below when standing before **e**, **i**, **y** — Symbol [s]: **c**e [sə], **c**eci [səsi], avan**c**er [avɑ̃se], **c**es [se], bi**c**yclette [bisiklɛt].

EXCEPTION: **c** = [g] in se**c**ond [səgɔ̃] and its derivatives.

ç always like **s** (1), below — Symbol [s]: j'avan**ç**ais [avɑ̃sɛ], avan**ç**ons [avɑ̃sɔ̃], le**ç**on [ləsɔ̃], re**ç**u [rəsy].

NOTE. — The letter **ç** is used only before **a**, **o**, **u** in order to denote the [s] sound.

ch usually like **sh** in 'show,' but is more energetically uttered — Symbol [ʃ]: **ch**ou [ʃu], va**ch**e [vaʃ], **ch**aise [ʃɛːz], **ch**er**ch**er [ʃɛrʃe], ar**ch**itecte [arʃitɛkt].

EXCEPTION: **ch** = [k], in some words from Greek: **ch**oléra [kɔlera], **ch**œur [kœːr], etc.

d like **d** in 'did,' fully voiced, with the point of the tongue thrust against the lower teeth, its upper surface forming a closure with the upper teeth, gums and palate; or with the tongue so far advanced that its point forms a closure with the upper teeth and gums — Symbol [d]: **d**ame [dam], mala**d**e [malad], **d**ans [dɑ̃], **d**onner [dɔne], **d**evant [dəvɑ̃], vian**d**e [vjɑ̃ːd], addi-tion [adisjɔ̃], su**d** [syd].

NOTE. — It must be observed that in forming English **d** (as also English **l**, **n**, **t**) the point of the tongue touches the roof of the mouth some little distance from the teeth, and that for corresponding French sounds the point of the tongue must be brought down and advanced to the teeth.

f like **f** in 'fife' — Symbol [f]: **f**ort [fɔːr], neu**f** [nœf], œu**f** [œf], **f**ine [fin], **f**rère [frɛːr], a**ff**aire [afɛːr].

g (1) like **g** in 'gig,' fully voiced — Symbol [g]. Thus **g** before **a**, **o**, **u** (but see **gu**) or a consonant: **g**are [gaːr], **g**ant [gɑ̃], **G**obelin [gɔblɛ̃], **g**oût [gu], ai**g**u [egy], **g**rand [grɑ̃], **g**lace [glas].

(2) like **s** in 'measure,' but more energetically uttered and fully voiced — Symbol [ʒ]. Thus **g** before **e**, **i**, **y**: **g**ens [ʒɑ̃], rou**g**e [ruːʒ], a**g**ir [aʒiːr], man**g**er [mɑ̃ʒe], **g**ymnase [ʒimnaːz].

gu before **e**, **i**, regularly like **g** (1): **gu**érir [geriːr], lon**gu**e [lɔ̃ːg], lan**gu**e [lɑ̃ːg], **gu**ide [gid], lan**gu**ir [lɑ̃giːr], **gu**ère [gɛːr].

ge always = [ʒ]: je man**ge**ais [mɑ̃ʒɛ], man**ge**ons [mɑ̃ʒɔ̃], je man**ge**ai [mɑ̃ʒe], **Ge**orges [ʒɔrʒ].

NOTE. — **ge** must be used to denote this sound before **a** or **o** in the con-jugation of verbs in –**ger**.

gn　regularly somewhat like **ni** in 'opinion'; it is formed by pressing the upper middle surface of the tongue against the roof of the mouth, the tip being at the same time thrust against the back surface of the lower front teeth — Symbol [ɲ]: agneau [aɲo], digne [diɲ], campagne [kɑ̃paɲ], gagner [gaɲe], accompagner [akɔ̃paɲe], magnifique [maɲifik], règne [rɛːɲ].

EXCEPTION: gn = [g]+[n] in some learned words: cognition [kɔgnisjɔ̃], etc.

h　when heard at all, which occurs only in hiatus, has a sound much weaker than **h** in 'hat' — Symbol [h]: aha! [a(h)a].

NOTE. — The letter h is known as h mute (*h muet*) when it gives rise to elision and liaison (cf. *N*, *O*, below), e.g. l'homme [l ɔm], les hommes [lez ɔm], and h aspirate (*h aspiré*) when it does not, e.g. le héros [lə ero], les héros [le ero]. The learner should regard h as absolutely silent.

j　always has the same sound as **g** (2), above — Symbol [ʒ]: je [ʒə], jeu [ʒø], jour [ʒuːr]; so also **je** (e being regarded as silent); Jean [ʒɑ̃].

k, ck　always like **k** in 'take' — Symbol [k]: kilogramme [kilogram], bifteck [biftɛk].

NOTE. — k is a rare letter in French.

l　regularly like **l** in 'law,' fully voiced, but with the tongue advanced as for [d] — Symbol [l]: la [la], cale [kal], aller [ale], table [tabl], oncle [ɔ̃ːkl], ils [il], village [vilaːʒ], fil [fil].

NOTES. — 1. The sound of l is frequently doubled when written double in initial syllable: illégal [illegal], illustre [illystr]; and by some in words like intelligent.
2. The l is silent in fils [fis].

ll　the letters **ll** after **i** (not initial), and **il** or **ill** after other vowels,
il(1)　have the same sound as that described for **i** as a semi-vowel (cf. *L*, above) — Symbol [j]: fille [fiːj], billet [bijɛ], briller [brije], soleil [sɔlɛːj], feuille [fœːj], fauteuil [fotœːj], écureuil [ekyrœːj], bataille [batɑːj], travail [travɑːj], travailler [travaje].

NOTE. — This sound of l is called *l mouillé*.

EXCEPTIONS: mille [mil], millier [milje], million [miljɔ̃], ville [vil], village [vilaːʒ], tranquille [trɑ̃kil], etc.

m　regularly like **m** in 'maim,' fully voiced — Symbol [m]: même [mɛːm], mot [mo], dame [dam], plume [plym], mon [mɔ̃], homme [ɔm], femme [fam].

EXCEPTIONS: m is silent in automne [otɔn], condamner [kɔ̃dɑne].

n   regularly like **n** in 'none,' fully voiced, and with the tongue advanced as for [d] — Symbol [n]: non [nɔ̃], ni [ni], lunettes [lynɛt], bonne [bɔn], donner [dɔne].

        EXCEPTION: **n** is silent in the 3d plural of verbs: ils parlent [parl], ils vendaient [vɑ̃dɛ].

p   regularly like **p** in 'pat,' 'rap' — Symbol [p]: patte [pat], attrape [atrap], père [pɛːr], papier [papje], plume [plym], apporter [apɔrte].

        EXCEPTIONS: **p** is silent in some words: sept [sɛt], compter [kɔ̃te], sculpter [skylte], etc.

ph   always like **f** — Symbol [f]: philosophe [filɔzɔf], Sophie [sɔfi].

q, qu   the letter **q** always and **qu** regularly = [k]: cinq [sɛ̃k], coq [kɔk], qui [ki], que [kə], quand [kɑ̃].

r   the sound of **r** has no English counterpart; it is formed by trilling the tip of the tongue against the upper gums, or even against the upper front teeth. The tongue must, of course, be well advanced, and never retracted or turned upward. The sound may be best practised at first in combinations with **d**, e.g. **d**ry, **d**rip, **d**rop (as in Scotch or Irish dialect) and afterwards in combinations in which it is less easily pronounced — Symbol [r]: drap [dra], très [trɛ], prêt [prɛ], rare [raːr], frère [frɛːr], sœur [sœːr], sur [syr], encre [ɑ̃ːkr], erreur [ɛrœːr]; **r** is doubled in the irregular future and conditional of certain verbs: je courrai [kurre], il mourrait [murrɛ].

        NOTE. — The above **r** is called "lingual" **r** (*r lingual*). Another **r** sound (called in French *r uvulaire* = "uvular" **r**), used especially in Paris and in other large cities and towns of France, is formed by drawing the tongue backward and elevating its root so as to cause a trilling of the uvula, but this **r** is usually more difficult for English-speaking people to acquire.

s   (1) like **s** in 'see,' but with the tongue advanced; sometimes the tip of the tongue is thrust against the lower teeth — Symbol [s]. Pronounce **s** thus when it begins a word (or a word in a compound) and in general when not between vowels; **ss** always: si [si], pense [pɑ̃ːs], son [sɔ̃], sœur [sœːr], vraisemblable [vrɛsɑ̃blabl], classe [klɑːs], laisser [lɛse], mars [mars], ours [urs], fils [fis].

    (2) like **z** in 'zone,' **s** in 'rose' with the tongue as for **s** (1), fully voiced — Symbol [z]. Pronounce **s** thus regularly between vowels: rose [roːz], chaise [ʃɛːz], maison [mezɔ̃], cousin [kuzɛ̃], amuser [amyze].

sc   always like **s** (1): science [sjãːs], scène [sɛːn].

t   (1) regularly like **t** in 'time,' but with the tongue advanced as for [d] — Symbol [t]: ta [ta], patte [pat], ton [tɔ̃], tes [te], tante [tãːt], écouter [ekute], lettre [lɛtr], sept [sɛt], huit [ɥit].

        (2) but in words whose English forms have the **sh** or **cy** sound **t** = [s]: nation [nɑsjɔ̃], patience [pasjãːs], prophétie [prɔfesi], etc.

        Note. — t is always silent in **et** (conjunction).

th   always like **t** (1): thé [te], théâtre [teɑːtr].

v   always like **v** in 'five,' fully voiced — Symbol [v]: va [va], cave [kav], voilà [vwala], vous [vu], pauvre [poːvr], trouver [truve].

w   (1) like [v], in some English and German words: wagon [vagɔ̃], Wagram [vagram], etc.

        (2) like [w], in some English words: tramway [tramwe], etc.

x   (1) usually = [ks]: extrême [ɛkstrɛːm], excellent [ɛksɛlã].

        (2) in **ex**– followed by a vowel **x** = [gz]: exemple [ɛgzãːpl *or* egzãːpl], exercice [ɛgzɛrsis *or* egzɛrsis].

        Exceptions: 1. **x** = [s] in dix [dis], six [sis], soixante [swasãːt] and rarer words. 2. **x** = [z] in deuxième {døzjɛm], sixième [sizjɛm], dixième [dizjɛm], dix-huit [diz ɥit], dix-neuf [diz nœf], etc.

z   like **s** (2) above: onze [ɔ̃ːz], zone [zoːn], gaz [gɑːz].

N. — Liaison

In a group of words closely connected grammatically, a final consonant sound is usually joined in pronunciation with a following word beginning with a vowel or **h** mute (*liaison* = "linking," "joining"):—

1. Certain consonants change their sound in liaison, thus: **d** = t, f (in neuf) = v, g = k, s or x = z; moreover, the n of a nasal is joined, and the nasal sometimes loses its nasality.

2. The groups requiring liaison are:

(*a*) Article, noun, adjective: un homme [œ̃ nɔm], les autres plumes [le zoːtr plym], bon ami [bɔ nami].

(*b*) Adjective, noun: petit enfant [pəti tãfã], petits enfants [pəti zãfã], dix ans [di zã], sang humain [sã kymɛ̃], des hommes aimables [de zɔm zɛmabl].

(*c*) Adverb, adjective or adverb: très âgé [trɛ zaʒe], fort habilement [fɔr tabilmã].

(*d*) Pronoun, verb: vous avez [vu zave], sont-ils [sɔ̃ til], vend-il [vɑ̃ til], nous y sommes [nu zi sɔm].

(*e*) Preposition and governed word: sans eux [sɑ̃ zø], chez un ami [ʃe zœ̃ nami].

(*f*) The **d** of **quand** (not interrogative): quand il parle [kɑ̃ til parl].

(*g*) Forms of **être** and **avoir**, especially as auxiliaries: ils sont ici [il sɔ̃ tisi], ils étaient arrivés [il zete tarive].

(*h*) A few common phrases, e.g. de temps en temps [də tɑ̃ zɑ̃ tɑ̃], etc.

3. The **t** of **et**, and the **m** of a nasal are never joined: lui et elle [lɥi e ɛl], le champ est à moi [lə ʃɑ̃ ɛ ta mwa].

NOTE. — The sounds joined belong in pronunciation to the following word, as shown above, but, for simplicity, they will be indicated in the transcriptions as final of the preceding word, e.g. les hommes [lez ɔm].

O. — Elision

The letters **a**, **e**, **i** are silent in certain cases before a vowel or **h** mute, and are replaced by an apostrophe (*apostrophe*): —

1. Thus **a** of **la** (article or pronoun): l'amie (=la amie), l'huile (=la huile), nous l'avons (=la avons).

2. Thus **e** of **le** (article or pronoun), of je, me, te, se, de, ce, ne, que (and some of its compounds): l'ami (=le ami), j'aime (=je aime), il m'écoute (=me écoute), d'un (=de un), c'est (=ce est), n'a-t-il (=ne a-t-il), qu'est-ce (=que est-ce), jusqu'à (=jusque à), etc.

3. Thus **i** of **si** before **il** or **ils** (not elsewhere): s'il (=si il).

P. — Punctuation

The same punctuation marks are used in French as in English.

1. Their French names are:

.	point	-	trait d'union	[ ]	crochets
,	virgule	—	tiret, *or* tiret de	{	accolade
;	point et virgule		séparation		
:	deux points	. . .	points suspensifs	*	astérisque
?	point d'interrogation	" "	guillemets	†	croix de renvoi
!	point d'exclamation	( )	parenthèse		

2. They are used as in English, but the *tiret* (dash) commonly serves to denote a change of speaker: Qui est là? dis-je. — Personne. — Quoi! personne! — Personne.

Q. — Capitals

Capitals (*lettres majuscules* or *capitales*) are used much as in English. Note however the following:

Un livre français.	*A French book.*
Cet Anglais parle français.	*That Englishman speaks French.*
Il arrivera le mardi 10 mai.	*He will come on Tuesday the 10th of May.*
Je dis ce que je pense.	*I say what I think.*

EXERCISES ON PRONUNCIATION

Note. — These exercises contain, for the most part, words chosen from the first twelve lessons, and should be frequently practised, selecting a paragraph or two at a time for this purpose, with a review of the phonetic principles involved. Pronouncing in unison, either for the whole class, or in groups, will be found of great advantage.

1. [a] and [ɑ]: la, ta, il a, là, avec, table, classe, pas, pâte, nous avons, Marie, femme, quatre, arbre, là-bas, dame, papa, moi, trois, ami, village, boîte, voilà, donnât, donnâmes, occasion, écraser.

2. [e] and [ɛ]: école, et, élève, chaise, crayon, Seine, fenêtre, papier, j'ai, avez, craie, église, mes, ses, elle, tu es, il est, cahier, vous êtes, derrière, grammaire, jouer, mère, mais, même, lunettes, français, lettre, donnai, il sait, abeille.

3. [ø] and [œ]: deux, peu, monsieur, sœur, leur, professeur, feu, il veut, heureux, neuf, bœuf, fleur, facteur, creuser, œufs, œil, il cueille.

4. [ə]: le, me, te, se, fenêtre, devant, maintenant, cheval, ceci, mercredi, monsieur, que, petit, promenade, leçon, donnes-tu, faisant, je faisais, faisons, venir, tenir, appeler.

5. [i] and [y]: livre, ils, Marie, une, plume, sur, ici, oui, qui, lunettes, amuser, étudier, église, diligent, fille, jolie, petite, amie, style, mûr, il fût, île, nous eûmes, ils eurent, eu.

6. [ɔ] and [o]: école, porte, homme, nos, vos, gros, encore, fort, joli, aussi, pauvre, chapeau, votre, vôtre, beau, alors, cocher, autre, bonne, donner, pomme.

7. [u]: nous, vous, cour, sous, ou, où, pour, cousin, tout, beaucoup, rouge, goût, goûter, le mois d'août.

8. [ɑ] and [ɑ̃]: bas, an, tas, tant, tâte, tante, encre, dans,

Jean, devant, ensemble, sembler, enfant, gant, champ, encore, content, grande, viande.

9. [ɛ] and [ɛ̃]: prêt, père, fait, fin, paix, pin, lait, lin, mais, main, jardin, plein, simple, peintre, plaindre, besoin, loin.

10. [ɔ] and [ɔ̃]: bonne, bon, personne, son, donne, donc, crayon, oncle, mon, ton, onze, maison, content, leçon, monter, accompagner, compter, tomber.

11. [œ] and [œ̃]: leur, un, peur, chacun, quelqu'un, parfum, emprunter.

12. [i] and [j]: vie, viande, si, sienne, vienne, fille, pièce, bille, papier, cahier, étudier, crayon, monsieur, ayez, travailler, travail, billet, abeille, vieil, œil, yeux.

13. [y] and [ɥ]: su, suis, lu, lui, tulle, tuile, saluer, nuage, pluie, cuisine, celui, minuit, juin, juillet.

14. [u] and [w]: où, oui, loue, louer, bout, boîte, Louis, voiture, mademoiselle, histoire, poire, moi, tramway.

15. [p] and [b]: pas, bas, papa, baba, père, peur, bon, bonne, porte, papier, pu, bu, pain, bain, obtenir, apporter, appeler.

16. [t] and [d]: ton, don, tant, dans, tout, doux, quatre, jardin, lettre, mettre, admettre, dame, diligent.

17. [f] and [v]: fin, vin, feu, il veut, livre, élève, frère, enfant, avec, affaire, géographie, devant, pauvre.

18 [k] and [g]: canne, gant, coup, goût, que, quatre, garçon, langue, craie, grand, grammaire, qui, expliquer, exemple.

19. [s] and [z]: son, sa, zone, onze, sous, sur, chaise, église, ici, garçon, dix, six, six hommes, dixième, sixième, maison, classe, passer, leçon, pièce, expliquer, examen.

20. [ʃ] and [ʒ]: champ, gens, chaise, joli, riche, image, poche, chapeau, chercher, jardin, Jean, Georges.

21. [l] and [n]: le, la, les, nous, nôtre, nos, leur, plume, table, non, canne, bonne, oncle, village, ville, tranquille, année, annoncer, automne, aller, allons, semblable.

22. [b] and [m]: bon, mon, bas, ma, homme, femme, Marie, madame, même, mère, grammaire, nous sommes.

23. [r]: drap, très, trois, près, grand, craie, crayon, porte, forte, riche, arbre, encre, derrière, jardin, sur, fleur, cour, sœur.

NOTE. — As an additional exercise, writing words chosen from the above, in phonetic symbols, is recommended.

PHONETIC TRANSCRIPTION OF LESSONS I–X

I

A. 1. yn sœːr. 2. œ frɛːr. 3. œ liːvr. 4. œ krejɔ̃. 5. yn plym.
6. yn tabl. 7. yn ʃɛːz. 8. yn fənɛːtr. 9. yn pɔrt. 10. yn ekɔl.
11. yn plym e œ krejɔ̃. 12. yn tabl e yn ʃɛːz.

II

A. 1. la krɛ. 2. l ãːkr. 3. la klaːs. 4. l ɔm. 5. lə prɔfesœːr.
6. l ɔ̃ːkl. 7. la fam. 8. la tãːt. 9. lə papje. 10. œn (*or* œn) ɔm e yn
fam. 11. lez ɔm e le fam. 12. œn elɛːv e œ prɔfesœːr. 13. lez elɛːv e
le prɔfesœːr. 14. l ãːkr e lə papje. 15. yn bwaːt.

III

A. 1. ʒ e yn bwaːt. 2. vuz ave dø krejɔ̃. 3. lez elɛːv ɔ̃t œ prɔfesœːr. 4. nuz avɔz œn ɔ̃ːkl e yn tãːt. 5. ʒã a le dø plym dãz yn bwaːt.
6. mari a trwa liːvr syr la tabl. 7. la klaːs a katr fənɛːtr. 8. lə prɔfesœːr a la krɛ e osi l ãːkr. 9. lə frɛːr e la sœːr ɔ̃ dø liːvr. 10. ty az œ
frɛːr e osi yn sœːr. 11. ʒã e mari ɔ̃ trwa frɛːr. 12. le fam ɔ̃ le dø
bwaːt. 13. nuz avɔ̃ le dø kle.

IV

A. 1. le liːvr sɔ̃ syr la tabl; il sɔ̃ syr la tabl. 2. lə prɔfesœːr e lez
elɛːv sɔ̃ dã la klaːs. 3. la kuːr ɛ dɛrjɛːr l ekɔl. 4. la klaːs a yn pɔrt; ɛl
a osi dø fənɛːtr. 5. nu sɔm dã la klaːs. 6. vuz ɛːt dã la kuːr. 7. l arbr
ɛ dəvã la pɔrt. 8. il ɛ dəvã la pɔrt. 9. ʒə sɥi dəvã la fənɛːtr. 10. ty
ɛ dɛrjɛːr la tabl. 11. l ɔ̃ːkl ɛ su l arbr. 12. la tãːt et avɛk l ɔ̃ːkl. 13. il
sɔ̃t ãsãːbl. 14. le fam sɔ̃ dã lə ʒardɛ̃. 15. ɛl sɔ̃t ãsãbl su lez arbr.
16. la gramɛːr e lə diksjɔnɛːr sɔ̃ syr la tabl.

V

A. 1. lə liːvr də ʒã e la plym də mari. 2. lə papje dy prɔfesœːr e
lə liːvr də l elɛːv. 3. la mɛːr dez ãfã. 4. lez ãfã də la fam.

C. 1. ʒã a t il le plym? 2. ki a le krejɔ̃? 3. ave vu le liːvr dy prɔfesœːr? 4. nɔ̃, məsjø, il sɔ̃ syr la tabl. 5. lez ãfã sɔ̃t il isi? 6. u sɔ̃ le
plym dez elɛːv? 7. mari, ɛ ty la? 8. u sɔm nu mɛ̃tnã? 9. mari et ɛl
dã la kuːr? 10. ɛː ʒ la plym də l elɛːv? 11. lez elɛːv ɔ̃t il le krejɔ̃?
12. lə pɛːr də l ãfã et il isi? 13. wi, madam, il ɛt isi. 14. u sɔ̃ le mɛːr
dez ãfã? 15. a ty la kan dy məsjø? 16. ki a le gã də la dam? 17. avɔ̃
nu le gã? 18. u ɛːt vu? 19. u sɥiːʒ? 20. k a t ɛl dã la bwaːt.

VI

A. Continue the following throughout the singular and plural: 1. ʒə. n e pa lə liːvr də l eleːv, ty n a pa lə liːvr də l eleːv, etc. 2. ʒə nə sɥi paz a l ekɔl ɔʒurdɥi, ty n ɛ paz, etc. 3. ɛː ʒ l ãːkr e le plym? etc.

B. 1. lez eleːv nə sɔ̃ paz a l ekɔl; u sɔ̃t il? 2. il sɔ̃t o ʃã. 3. la mezɔ̃ dy prɔfesœːr n ɛ paz isi. 4. ɛl ɛ la ba o vilaːʒ. 5. vu n ave pa le liːvr; u sɔ̃t il? 6. il sɔ̃t a la mezɔ̃. 7. nu n avɔ̃ pa le liːvr. 8. le dam nə sɔ̃ paz a l egliːz. 9. mari, ty n ɛ paz a l ekɔl ɔʒurdɥi. 10. ʒə nə sɥi paz o ʒardɛ̃. 11. la tãːt n ɛ paz a la kãpaɲ mɛtnã. 12. ɛl ɛt a la vil avɛk lez ãfã. 13. l eleːv n a pa la plym, mɛz il a lə krejɔ̃. 14. ʒə n e pa dø liːvr. 15. lez ãfã n ɔ̃ paz ãkɔːr l ãːkr.

VII

A. Continue, as in Exercise VI, A: 1. ʒə sɥi kɔ̃tã (*or* kɔ̃tãːt), ty ɛ, etc. 2. ʒə sɥi grã (*or* grãːd) e fɔːr (*or* fɔrt). 3. sɥiː ʒ diliʒã (*or* diliʒãːt)? 4. nə sɥiː ʒ pa riʃ? 5. n ɛː ʒ paz yn grãːd mezɔ̃?

B. Turn into negative interrogative: 1. ɛt ɛl riʃ? 2. sɔ̃ːt il isi? 3. l ɔ̃kl a t il yn ʒɔli mezɔ̃? 4. lez ãfã sɔ̃t il kɔ̃tã? 5. purkwa ɛːt vu kɔ̃tãːt, madam? 6. ave vuz yn grãːd mezɔ̃? 7. ɛː ʒ œ̃ ʒɔli liːvr? 8. a ty le gã də la dam?

C. Answer in the affirmative and also in the negative: 1. n ɛːt vu pa lez ãfã də məsjø ribo? 2. nə sɥiː ʒ pa grãːd e fɔrt? 3. məsjø ribo n ɛt il pa riʃ? 4. n ave vu pa dø pətit sœːr? 5. madam lədyk n a t ɛl paz yn grãːd mezɔ̃? 6. le pətit fiːj nə sɔ̃t ɛl paz isi? 7. le pəti garsɔ̃ n ɔ̃t il pa le plym? 8. n ɛː ʒ pa lə papje?

VIII

A. Continue: 1. ʒ e mɔ̃ livːr, ty a tɔ̃, etc. 2. u ɛ mɔ̃n ãːkr? u ɛ tɔ̃n ãːkr? etc. 3. ʒə n e pa ma plym, ty n a pa ta, etc. 4. n ɛː ʒ pa me krejɔ̃? n a ty pa te? etc.

C. 1. ʒə sɥi la fiːj də məsjø lənwaːr. 2. la mezɔ̃ də mɔ̃ peːr ɛt a kote də la mezɔ̃ də məsjø ribo. 3. sa mezɔ̃ ɛ trɛ ʒɔli. 4. nɔtr mezɔ̃ ɛ ʒɔli osi. 5. no mezɔ̃ sɔ̃ preskə sãblabl. 6. nɔtr mezɔ̃ a di pjɛs. 7. lœr mezɔ̃ a ɔ̃ːz pjɛs. 8. məsjø ribo ɛ mɔ̃n ɔ̃ːkl. 9. il ɛ lə frɛːr də ma mɛːr. 10. sa fam ɛ ma tãːt. 11. ɛl ɛ la sœːr də mɔ̃ peːr. 12. lœrz ãfã sɔ̃ no parã. 13. mari ribo ɛ ma pətit kuzin. 14. sɔ̃ frɛːr ɛ mɔ̃ kuzɛ̃. 15. nuz avɔ̃ le mɛːmz ami. 16. kleːr lədyk ɛ mɔn ami. 17. ɛl ɛt osi l ami də ma kuzin. 18. ʃarl lədyk ɛ mɔn ami. 19. il ɛt osi l ami də ʒã ribo.

D. (*Oral.*): 1. u ɛ la mezɔ̃ də vɔtr pɛːr? 2. vɔtr mezɔ̃ ɛt ɛl ʒɔli? 3. ki ɛ məsjø ribo? 4. də ki ɛt il lə frɛːr? 5. madam ribo ɛt ɛl vɔtr tɑ̃ːt? 6. ki sɔ̃ vo dø kuzɛ̃? 7. ki ɛ vɔtr ami? 8. ki ɛ l ami də vɔtr frɛːr? 9. u ɛ mɔn oːtr plym? etc.

IX

A. *Continue:* 1. ʒə l e, ty l a, etc. 2. ʒə lez e, etc. 3. ʒə nə l̃ e pɑ, etc. 4. ʒ e ma kan, ty a ta kan, etc. 5. ʒ e me gɑ̃, ty a te, etc. 6. n ɛ ː ʒ pɑ mɔ̃ pardəsy? n a ty pɑ tɔ̃? etc.

B. (məsjø dypɔ̃ e lwi) 1. lwi, u ɛ tɔ̃ pardəsy? — 2. ʒə l e, mɔ̃ pɛːr. — 3. a ty tɔ̃ ʃapo osi? — 4. wi, mɔ̃ pɛːr, lə vwasi. papa, a ty te gɑ̃? — 5. wi, mɔ̃ ɑ̃fɑ̃, ʒə lez e dɑ̃ ma poʃ. — 6. e tɔ̃ ʃapo? — 7. lə vwala syr la tabl la bɑ. — 8. mɛ ty n a pɑ te lynɛt. u sɔ̃t ɛl? — 9. le vwasi su mɔ̃ ʃapo. alɔːr nuz avɔ̃ tut noz afɛːr? e la vwatyːr ɛt ɛl prɛːt? — 10. wi, papa, la vwala a la pɔrt. — 11. e lə kɔʃe ɛt il la? — 12. lə vwala osi a kɔte də la vwatyːr. — 13. mɛ̃tnɑ̃ nu sɔm prɛ pur nɔtr prɔmnad.

C. (*Oral.*) 1. u ɛ vɔtr pardəsy? 2. ave vu vɔtr ʃapo? 3. ave vuz osi vo gɑ̃? 4. u sɔ̃ le lynɛt də vɔtr pɛːr? 5. ave vu tut voz afɛːr? 6. ɛːt vu prɛ mɛ̃tnɑ̃? 7. u ɛ la vwatyːr? 8. u ɛ lə kɔʃe? etc.

X

A. *Continue:* 1. ʒə lœr dɔn me plym, ty . . . te plym, etc. 2. ɛ s kə ʒə lɥi dɔn mɔ̃ kaje? ɛ s kə ty . . . tɔ̃ . . .? etc. 3. ʒə nə lɥi (*or* lœr) parl pɑ, etc. 4. ɛ s kə ʒə nə travaːj pɑ? nə travaːj ty pɑ? etc. 5. ʒə lə (*or* le) rəgard, etc. 6. ʒə nə l (*or* lez) ekut pɑ, etc.

B. 1. ɛ s kə vu travaje, mez ɑ̃fɑ̃? 2. wi, madmwazɛl, nu travajɔ̃. 3. parl ty lwi? 4. ɛ s kə ty parl, mari? 5. ʒɑ̃, ty parl? 6. wi, mad-mwazɛl, nu parlɔ̃. 7. mari dɔn lə liːvr a la dam. 8. ɛl lɥi dɔn lə papje osi. 9. lez ɑ̃fɑ̃ rəgard le ʒɔliz imaːʒ. 10. l ɛ̃stitytris lœr dɔn œ̃ gro liːvr. 11. ʒə travaːj boku.

C. 1. nu sɔmz a l ekɔl. 2. l ɛ̃stitytris dɔn le kaje oz elɛːv. 3. nu travajɔ̃. 4. ɛl ɛksplik la ləsɔ̃. 5. nu l ekutɔ̃. 6. ɛl parl boku oz elɛːv. 7. nu lɥi parlɔ̃ osi kəlkəfwa. 8. le pəti garsɔ̃ ʒu a prezɑ̃ dɑ̃ la kuːr. 9. il parl e kri boku. 10. le pətit fiːj sɔ̃ su lez arbr. 11. ɛl rəgard lez imaːʒ dɑ̃z œ̃ gro liːvr. 12. lez imaːʒ lez amyːz boku. 13. lez imaːʒ amyːz le pəti garsɔ̃z osi. 14. ɛl lœr dɔn lə liːvr.

LESSON I

1. **Indefinite Article**

MASCULINE	FEMININE	
un [œ̃]	une [yn]	*a, an,* (as numeral, *one*)

Un frère et une sœur.   *A brother and (a) sister.*
Un livre, une plume.   *A book, a pen.*

1. There are only two genders in French, the masculine and feminine, as seen in the examples above.

2. **Un** is used before masculine nouns and **une** before feminine nouns.

3. The indefinite article is repeated before each noun.

EXERCISE I

une chaise [ʃɛːz], *a chair*
un crayon [krɛjɔ̃], *a pencil*
une école [ekɔl], *a school*
et [e], *and*
une fenêtre [fənɛːtr], *a window*
un frère [frɛːr], *a brother*

un livre [liːvr], *a book*
une plume [plym], *a pen*
une porte [pɔrt], *a door*
une sœur [sœːr], *a sister*
une table [tabl], *a table*

A. 1. Une sœur. 2. Un frère. 3. Un livre. 4. Un crayon. 5. Une plume. 6. Une table. 7. Une chaise. 8. Une fenêtre. 9. Une porte. 10. Une école. 11. Une plume et un crayon. 12. Une table et une chaise.

B. 1. A book and (a)[1] pencil. 2. A school. 3. A pen and (a) book. 4. A chair and (a) table. 5. A window. 6. A door. 7. One pen. 8. A door and (a) window. 9. A table. 10. One book. 11. A brother and (a) sister.

[1] English words in parenthesis to be expressed in French.

1

LESSON II

2.   **Definite Article**

MASCULINE SINGULAR	FEMININE SINGULAR	PLURAL	
le, l' [lə, l]	la, l' [la, l]	les [le]	*the*

Le frère et la sœur.	*The brother and (the) sister.*
L'ami, l'homme, l'école.	*The friend, the man, the school.*
Les livres et les plumes.	*The books and (the) pens.*
Les amis, les hommes, les écoles.	*The friends, the men, the schools.*

1. **Le** is used before a masculine singular, and **la** before a feminine singular, beginning with a consonant; **l'** is used before any singular beginning with a vowel or **h** mute, i.e. the **e** or the **a** is elided (cf. Introd., O); **les** is used before any plural.

2. The definite article is repeated before each noun.

3. The plural of nouns is regularly formed by adding **s** to the singular.

EXERCISE II

NOTE. — The gender of nouns beginning with a vowel or **h** mute is indicated in the vocabularies by *m.* or *f.*; the gender of all other nouns is known by the article, which should be carefully learned along with the noun; for the gender of nouns denoting inanimate objects the rules in the Appendix may be found useful.

la boîte [bwaːt], *box*	l'homme [ɔm], *man*
la classe [klaːs], *classroom*	l'oncle [ɔ̃ːkl], *uncle*
la craie [krɛ], *chalk*	le papier [papje], *paper*
l'élève [eleːv], m. f., *pupil*	le professeur[1] [prɔfɛsœːr], *teacher*
l'encre [ãːkr], f., *ink*	la tante [tãːt], *aunt*
la femme [fam], *woman, wife*	

A. 1. La craie. 2. L'encre. 3. La classe. 4. L'homme. 5. Le professeur. 6. L'oncle. 7. La femme. 8. La tante. 9. Le papier. 10. Un homme et une femme. 11. Les hommes et les femmes. 12. Un élève et un professeur. 13. Les élèves et les professeurs. 14. L'encre et le papier. 15. Une boîte.

[1] A teacher in a secondary school, a college or university professor.

B. 1. The school. 2. The chairs. 3. The table. 4. The doors and (the) windows. 5. The teachers and (the) pupils. 6. The paper and (the) ink. 7. The uncles and (the) aunts. 8. The pencil and (the) chalk. 9. A man and (a) woman. 10. An uncle and (an) aunt.

C. 1. One sister and one brother. 2. The books and paper. 3. The pens and ink. 4. The school and classroom. 5. The women and men. 6. The tables and boxes. 7. The man and the pupil. 8. The schools and the classrooms. 9. A box and a table. 10. The brothers and sisters. 11. The schools and the teachers. 12. The pupils, the women, the uncles, the aunts.

NOTE. — For the use in classes of this and following English exercises, see Preface.

LESSON III

3.   Present Indicative of *avoir*, 'have'

j'ai [ʒ e], *I have*		**nous avons** [nuz avɔ̃], *we have*	
tu as [ty a], *thou hast, you have*		**vous avez** [vuz ave], *you have*	
il a [il a], *he (it) has*		**ils ont** [ilz ɔ̃], *they* (m.) *have*	
elle a [ɛl a], *she (it) has*		**elles ont** [ɛlz ɔ̃], *they* (f.) *have*	

NOTE. — Observe the elision of **e** in **je** (cf. Introd., *O*). A knowledge of this principle will be taken for granted henceforth.

4. Verb and subject agree in number and person:

L'élève a un livre.   *The pupil has a book.*
Les élèves ont les plumes.   *The pupils have the pens.*

5. Pronouns in Address. — 1. In ordinary formal address **vous** = *you*, whether singular or plural.

2. But *you* = **tu** in familiar or affectionate address, as usually between members of a family, very intimate friends, children; usually also by grown persons to children, and always in addressing animals and things.

NOTE. — **Vous** is to be used in the exercises, unless rule 2 is clearly applicable. Foreigners in speaking French will rarely require to use any other form than **vous**.

EXERCISE III

aussi [osi], *too, also*	**Marie** [mari], *Mary*
la clef [kle], *key*	**quatre** [katr], *four*
dans [dɑ̃], *in, within*	**sur** [syr], *on, upon*
deux [dø], *two*	**trois** [trwɑ], *three*
Jean [ʒɑ̃], *John*	

A. 1. J'ai une boîte. 2. Vous avez deux crayons. 3. Les élèves ont un professeur. 4. Nous avons un oncle et une tante. 5. Jean a les deux plumes dans une boîte. 6. Marie a trois livres sur la table. 7. La classe a quatre fenêtres. 8. Le professeur a la craie et aussi l'encre. 9. Le frère et la sœur ont deux livres. 10. Tu as un frère et aussi une sœur. 11. Jean et Marie ont trois frères. 12. Les femmes ont les deux boîtes. 13. Nous avons les deux clefs.

B. 1. The teacher has three pupils. 2. We have the ink and (the) pens. 3. I have the chalk in a box. 4. You have the books and papers. 5. The school has three doors. 6. You have the paper and the pen. 7. John and Mary have the pencils. 8. The women have four chairs and two tables. 9. We have two boxes on the table. 10. Mary has an uncle and an aunt.

C. 1. She has also a brother and two sisters. 2. The men have three brothers. 3. The classroom has two doors and four windows. 4. He has one uncle and one aunt. 5. The teachers have the books. 6. The pupils have three teachers. 7. They (*m.*) have the pen and the ink. 8. You (*tu*) have four pens in the box. 9. I have also four pens on the table. 10. We have the pencils and the chalk. 11. The women have the keys.

LESSON IV

6.   **Present Indicative of *être*, 'be'**

je **suis** [ʒə sɥi], *I am*	nous **sommes** [nu sɔm], *we are*
tu **es** [ty ɛ], *thou art, you are*	vous **êtes** [vuz ɛːt], *you are*
il **est** [il ɛ], *he (it) is*	ils **sont** [il sɔ̃], *they* (m.) *are*
elle **est** [ɛl ɛ], *she (it) is*	elles **sont** [ɛl sɔ̃], *they* (f.) *are*

7. Agreement. — 1. The personal pronoun regularly agrees with its antecedent in gender, number and person; hence, in the third person **il(s)** and **elle(s)** will stand both for persons and things:

Où est la plume? — **Elle** est sur la table.	*Where is the pen? — It is on the table.*

2. A pronoun referring to two or more antecedents of different gender is masculine plural:

Ils (= Jean et Marie) sont là.	*They (= John and Mary) are there.*
Ils (= livre et plume) sont ici.	*They (= book and pen) are here.*

EXERCISE IV

l'arbre [arbr], m., *tree*
avec [avɛk], *with*
la cour [ku:r], *yard, court(yard)*
derrière [dɛrjɛ:r], *behind*
devant [dəvã], *before, in front of*

le dictionnaire [diksjɔnɛ:r], *dictionary*
ensemble [ãsã:bl], adv., *together*
la grammaire [gramɛ:r], *grammar*
le jardin [ʒardɛ̃], *garden*
sous [su], *under, below*

A. 1. Les livres sont sur la table; ils sont sur la table. 2. Le professeur et les élèves sont dans la classe. 3. La cour est derrière l'école. 4. La classe a une porte; elle a aussi deux fenêtres. 5. Nous sommes dans la classe. 6. Vous êtes dans la cour. 7. L'arbre est devant la porte. 8. Il est devant la porte. 9. Je suis devant la fenêtre. 10. Tu es derrière la table. 11. L'oncle est sous l'arbre. 12. La tante est avec l'oncle. 13. Ils sont ensemble. 14. Les femmes sont dans le jardin. 15. Elles sont ensemble sous les arbres. 16. La grammaire et le dictionnaire sont sur la table.

B. 1. The tree is in front of the door. 2. The pupils are in the yard. 3. The yard has three trees. 4. We are in the garden. 5. It is in front of the school. 6. The chair is behind the door. 7. The pupils are together under the trees. 8. You are in the classroom. 9. The aunt is with the uncle. 10. They are together in the garden. 11. The grammars are on the table.

C. 1. You (*tu*) are a pupil. 2. I am with the teacher. 3. We have three books and you have two books. 4. They are on the table. 5. I am the teacher; I am with the pupils. 6. I have three

sisters; they are in the classroom.   7. The teacher has a pen; it
is on the table.   8. The pens are on the table; they are in a box.
9. John and Mary are in the yard. 1(. They are under the trees.
11. The dictionary is on the chair.

LESSON V

8.   Present Indicative Interrogative of *avoir* and *être*

ai-je?	[ɛː ʒ], *have I?*	**suis-je?**	[sɥiː ʒ], *am I?*
as-tu?	[a ty], *have you?*	**es-tu?**	[ɛ ty], *are you?*
a-t-il?	[a t il], *has he?*	**est-il?**	[ɛt il], *is he?*
a-t-elle?	[a t ɛl], *has she?*	**est-elle?**	[ɛt ɛl], *is she?*
avons-nous?	[avɔ̃ nu], *have we?*	**sommes-nous?**	[sɔm nu], *are we?*
avez-vous?	[ave vu], *have you?*	**êtes-vous?**	[ɛːt vu], *are you?*
ont-ils?	[ɔ̃t il], *have they?*	**sont-ils?**	[sɔ̃t il], *are they?*
ont-elles?	[ɔ̃t ɛl], *have they?*	**sont-elles?**	[sɔ̃t ɛl], *are they?*

1. In a question the personal pronoun subject follows the
verb and is joined to it by a hyphen.

2. When the third person singular ends in a vowel, -t- is in-
serted.

9. Remarks on Interrogation. — 1. When the subject of an
interrogative sentence is a noun, this noun usually comes before the verb, and is repeated after it in the form of a pronoun:

> L'**élève** a-t-il les plumes?   *Has the pupil* (lit. *the pupil has he*)
> *the pens?*

2. Questions may also be asked by means of interrogative
words, as in English:

> **Qui** a l'encre et les plumes?   *Who has the ink and the pens?*
> **Où** sont les plumes?   *Where are the pens?*

3. These two forms of interrogation may be combined:

> **Où** le professeur est-il?   *Where is the teacher?*

4. *What?* = **que**, as direct object or predicate:

> **Qu'**avez-vous là?   *What have you there?*

10. Possessive. — 1. Possession is denoted by **de** = *of:*

Le livre **de** Marie.   *Mary's book.*

2. **De** is repeated before each noun:

Les amis **de** Jean et **d'**Albert.   *The friends of John and Albert.*

3. **De** + **le** (article) is always contracted to **du**, and **de** + **les** to **des**, but **de la, de l'** are not contracted:

La plume **du** frère.   *The brother's pen.*
Les plumes **des** sœurs.   *The pens of the sisters.*
But: La plume **de la** sœur, **de l'**élève, etc.

EXERCISE V

la **canne** [kan], *cane, stick*
la **dame** [dam], *lady*
l'**enfant** [ãfã], m. f., *child, boy, girl*
le **gant** [gã], *glove*
ici [isi], *here*
là [la], *there*
madame [madam], *madam, Mrs.*
maintenant [mɛ̃tnã], *now*
la **mère** [mɛːr], *mother*

le **monsieur** [məsjø], *gentleman, Sir, Mr.*
non [nɔ̃], *no*
où [u], *where?*
oui [wi], *yes*
le **père** [pɛːr], *father*
qui [ki], invar., *who? whom?*
que, qu' [kə, k], invar., *what?*

A. 1. Le livre de Jean et la plume de Marie. 2. Le papier du professeur et le livre de l'élève. 3. La mère des enfants. 4. Les enfants de la femme.

B. 1. John's father. 2. Mary's mother. 3. The windows of the school. 4. The child's father. 5. The children's mother.

C. 1. Jean a-t-il les plumes? 2. Qui a les crayons? 3. Avez-vous les livres du professeur? 4. Non, monsieur, ils sont sur la table. 5. Les enfants sont-ils ici? 6. Où sont les plumes des élèves? 7. Marie, es-tu là? 8. Où sommes-nous maintenant? 9. Marie est-elle dans la cour? 10. Ai-je la plume de l'élève? 11. Les élèves ont-ils les crayons? 12. Le père de l'enfant est-il ici? 13. Oui, madame, il est ici. 14. Où sont les mères des enfants? 15. As-tu la canne du monsieur? 16. Qui a les gants de la dame? 17. Avons-nous les gants? 18. Où êtes-vous? 19. Où suis-je? 20. Qu'a-t-elle dans la boîte?

D. 1. *Turn orally into interrogative form all the sentences in Exercises III, A, and IV, A.* 2. *Form answers to the questions in part C of this exercise.*

E. 1. Have you the teacher's cane? 2. What have you there? 3. Is Mary here now? 4. Where is she? 5. Where is Mary's mother? 6. Are the boy's pens and pencils in the box? 7. Yes, madam, and the box is on the chair. 8. Have the pupils (*m.* or *f.*) the books?

F. 1. Have we the pupils' books now? 2. Who has the lady's gloves? 3. Mary, have you the child's box? 4. Have I the gentleman's paper? 5. John, where are you (*tu*)? 6. Are you the teacher's uncle? 7. No, sir, I am the teacher's brother. 8. Are the ladies' gloves here?

LESSON VI

11. **Present Indicative Negative of *avoir* and *être***

I have not, etc.		*I am not, etc.*	
je n'ai pas	[ʒə n e pɑ]	je ne suis pas	[ʒə nə sɥi pɑ]
tu n'as pas	[ty n a pɑ]	tu n'es pas	[ty n ɛ pɑ]
il n'a pas	[il n a pɑ]	il n'est pas	[il n ɛ pɑ]
nous n'avons pas	[nu n avɔ̃ pɑ]	nous ne sommes pas	[nu nə sɔm pɑ]
vous n'avez pas	[vu n ave pɑ]	vous n'êtes pas	[vu n ɛːt pɑ]
ils n'ont pas	[il n ɔ̃ pɑ]	ils ne sont pas	[il nə sɔ̃ pɑ]

NOTE.—Elle(s) will henceforth be omitted from the paradigms.

1. With verbs, *not* = **ne . . . pas**, the verb being placed between them.

12. Place. — 1. The preposition **à** = *to, at, in*, often denotes place, and must be repeated before each noun:

Il est **à** Paris ou **à** Rome.   *He is in Paris or* (*in*) *Rome.*

2. **À + le** (article) is always contracted to **au** and à + **les** to **aux**, but **à la, à l'** are not contracted:

Les enfants sont **au** jardin.	*The children are in the garden.*
Les hommes sont **aux** champs.	*The men are in the fields.*
But: **à la** porte, **à l'**école, etc.	

NOTE. — The preposition **dans**, *in, within*, denotes place in a more definite and restricted sense than **à**.

EXERCISE VI

aujourd'hui [oʒurdɥi], *to-day*	**là-bas** [la bɑ], *over there, yonder*
la campagne [kãpaɲ], *country*	**mais** [mɛ], *but*
le champ [ʃã], *field*	**la maison** [mezɔ̃], *house*
l'église [egliːz], f., *church*	**le village** [vilaːʒ], *village*
encore [ãkɔːr], *yet, still, again*	**la ville** [vil], *town, city*

à la campagne, *in the country;* **à l'école,** *at (the) school;* **à l'église,** *at (the) church;* **à la maison,** *at the house, at home, home;* **à la ville,** *at or in the town, in town, in the city*

A. Continue the following throughout the singular and plural:
1. Je n'ai pas le livre de l'élève, tu n'as pas le livre de l'élève, etc.
2. Je ne suis pas à l'école aujourd'hui, tu n'es pas, etc. 3. Ai-je l'encre et les plumes? etc.

B. 1. Les élèves ne sont pas à l'école; où sont-ils? 2. Ils sont aux champs. 3. La maison du professeur n'est pas ici. 4. Elle est là-bas au village. 5. Vous n'avez pas les livres; où sont-ils? 6. Ils sont à la maison. 7. Nous n'avons pas les livres. 8. Les dames ne sont pas à l'église. 9. Marie, tu n'es pas à l'école aujourd'hui. 10. Je ne suis pas au jardin. 11. La tante n'est pas à la campagne maintenant. 12. Elle est à la ville avec les enfants. 13. L'élève n'a pas la plume, mais il a le crayon. 14. Je n'ai pas deux livres. 15. Les enfants n'ont pas encore l'encre.

C. Turn into negative form: 1. Ils sont aux champs. 2. Elle est au village. 3. Les dames sont à la maison. 4. L'école a trois portes. 5. Les élèves ont les papiers. 6. Nous sommes à la campagne. 7. Vous êtes à l'école. 8. Tu as les crayons. 9. Vous avez les livres. 10. Les enfants sont au jardin.

D. 1. Mary is not at home; she is at school. 2. The uncle and aunt are not in the country. 3. I haven't (have not) the pencils. 4. You haven't the book, but you have the paper. 5. I am not yet at home. 6. You are not at church to-day. 7. You haven't the lady's gloves. 8. The teacher's house is not in the village. 9. We are not yet home. 10. John hasn't the teacher's chalk. 11. Who is at the door? 12. The man is at the door.

E. 1. We haven't the children's boxes. 2. The pupils haven't the chairs. 3. The children are not in the city. 4. They are in the country to-day. 5. Are the pupils at school? 6. No, sir, they are not at school. 7. I haven't the books; they are not here. 8. We are not yet in the country. 9. The children are not yet here. 10. John, have you (*tu*) not the teacher's chalk? 11. The teacher's chalk is in the box.

LESSON VII

13.   Present Indicative Interrogative Negative of
avoir and *être*

Have I not? etc.		*Am I not?* etc.	
n'ai-je pas?	[n ɛː ʒ pɑ]	ne suis-je pas?	[nə sɥiː ʒ pɑ]
n'as-tu pas?	[n a ty pɑ]	n'es-tu pas?	[n ɛ ty pɑ]
n'a-t-il pas?	[n a t il pɑ]	n'est-il pas?	[n ɛt il pɑ]
n'avons-nous pas?	[n avɔ̃ nu pɑ]	ne sommes-nous pas?	[nə sɔm nu pɑ]
n'avez-vous pas?	[n ave vu pɑ]	n'êtes-vous pas?	[n ɛːt vu pɑ]
n'ont-ils pas?	[n ɔ̃t il pɑ]	ne sont-ils pas?	[nə sɔ̃t il pɑ]

14. Agreement of Adjectives. — 1. The feminine of adjectives is regularly formed by adding **e** to the masculine, but adjectives in **–e** do not change; the plural is regularly formed by adding **s** to the singular, as for nouns:

Masc.	Fem.	Masc. Plur.	Fem. Plur.	
petit	petite	petits	petites	*small*
riche	riche	riches	riches	*rich*

2. The adjective agrees in gender and number with the word qualified:

Un petit livre; une petite maison.	*A small book; a small house.*
Les livres sont jolis.	*The books are pretty.*
Les maisons sont jolies.	*The houses are pretty.*
Ils (elles) sont jolis (jolies).	*They are pretty.*

3. An adjective qualifying two (or more) words must be plural masculine if both words are masculine or of different gender, and plural feminine if both are feminine:

Le père et le fils sont forts.	*The father and son are strong.*
La sœur et le frère sont grands.	*The sister and brother are tall.*
La mère et la fille sont jolies.	*The mother and daughter are pretty.*

4. Agreement with **je, tu, nous, vous** is according to sense:

Nous sommes contents (*or* contentes). *We are satisfied.*

EXERCISE VII

content [kɔ̃tɑ̃], *satisfied, pleased, glad*	**grand** [grɑ̃], *great, large, tall*
diligent [diliʒɑ̃], *diligent, industrious*	**joli** [ʒɔli], *pretty*
la fille [fiːj], *daughter, girl*	**pauvre,** [poːvr], *poor*
fort [fɔːr], *strong*	**petit** [pəti], *small, little*
le garçon [garsɔ̃], *boy*	**pourquoi** [purkwa], *why?*
	riche [riʃ], *rich*
	très [trɛ], *very*

A. Continue, as in Exercise VI, A: 1. Je suis content(e), tu es, etc. 2. Je suis grand(e) et fort(e). 3. Suis-je diligent(e)? 4. Ne suis-je pas riche? 5. N'ai-je pas une grande maison?

B. Turn into negative interrogative: 1. Est-elle riche? 2. Sont-ils ici? 3. L'oncle a-t-il une jolie maison? 4. Les enfants sont-ils contents? 5. Pourquoi êtes-vous contente, madame? 6. Avez-vous une grande maison? 7. Ai-je un joli livre? 8. As-tu les gants de la dame?

C. Answer in the affirmative and also in the negative: 1. N'êtes-vous pas les enfants de M. (= monsieur) Ribot? 2. Ne suis-je pas grande et forte? 3. M. Ribot n'est-il pas riche? 4. N'avez-vous pas deux petites sœurs? 5. Mme (= madame) Leduc n'a-t-elle

pas une grande maison? 6. Les petites filles ne sont-elles pas ici?
7. Les petits garçons n'ont-ils pas les plumes? 8. N'ai-je pas le
papier? etc.

D. 1. Are you not satisfied? 2. Why is she not satisfied? 3. The
little girls are not very industrious. 4. Are John's aunts not
rich? 5. Are you (*tu*) not Mrs. Ribot's little daughter? 6. Hasn't
Mr. Leduc a large house in the village? 7. Haven't you the little
boy's pencil? 8. Haven't Mr. and Mrs. Ribot a pretty house in the
country? 9. Haven't I a large garden? 10. Mary, haven't you
the poor girl's book?

E. 1. The women are very poor. 2. Mr. Ribot's wife is very
rich. 3. Isn't Mary's sister very tall? 4. She is tall and strong.
5. Why are you not satisfied, madam? 6. Are the ladies not satisfied? 7. They are satisfied now. 8. Are we not industrious?
9. You are not very industrious. 10. Isn't Mary's little box very
pretty?

LESSON VIII

15.   The Possessive Adjective

Masc. Sing.	Fem. Sing.	Masc. or Fem. Plur.	
mon [mɔ̃]	ma [ma]	mes [me]	*my*
ton [tɔ̃]	ta [ta]	tes [te]	*thy, your*
son [sɔ̃]	sa [sa]	ses [se]	*his, her, its, one's*
notre [nɔtr]	notre [nɔtr]	nos [no]	*our*
votre [vɔtr]	votre [vɔtr]	vos [vo]	*your*
leur [lœːr]	leur [lœːr]	leurs [lœːr]	*their*

16. Agreement. — 1. The possessive adjective agrees in gender and number with the noun denoting the object possessed,
and must be repeated before each noun:

    Mon oncle et **ma** tante.   *My uncle and (my) aunt.*
    Votre plume et **vos** crayons.   *Your pen and (your) pencils.*

2. **Mon, ton, son** are used instead of **ma, ta, sa** before feminines beginning with a vowel or **h** mute:

    Mon amie (*f.*); **ton** histoire (*f.*).   *My friend; your history.*
    Son autre plume.   *His (her) other pen.*

3. Since **son** (**sa, ses**) = *his, her, its,* it can be known only from the context which is meant:

Jean (Marie) a **son** livre.　　　*John (Mary) has his (her) book.*
Chaque jour a **ses** peines.　　　*Each day has its troubles.*

EXERCISE VIII

l'ami [ami], m., *friend*
l'amie [ami], f., *friend*
autre [oːtr], adj., *other*
Charles [ʃarl], *Charles*
Claire [klɛːr], *Clara, Claire*
le côté [kote], *side*
le cousin [kuzɛ̃], m., *cousin*
la cousine [kuzin], f., *cousin*

dix [dis], *ten*
même [mɛːm], *same*
onze [ɔ̃ːz], *eleven*
les parents [parɑ̃], *relatives, rela-tions, parents*
la pièce [pjɛs], *room*
presque [prɛsk], *almost*
semblable [sɑ̃blabl], *like, alike*

à côté de, *by the side of, beside;* **de qui?** *whose? of whom?*

A. Continue: 1. J'ai mon livre, tu as ton, etc. 2. Où est mon encre? où est ton encre? etc. 3. Je n'ai pas ma plume, tu n'as pas ta, etc. 4. N'ai-je pas mes crayons? n'as-tu pas tes? etc.

B. Make the possessive adjectives agree: 1. Le professeur a *son* canne (craie, papiers). 2. Les élèves ont *leur* livres (plumes). 3. J'ai *mon* plume (encre, papier). 4. Nous avons *notre* gants (chaises, tables). 5. Vous avez *votre* plumes (canne, papier). 6. Marie a *son* boîte (boîtes). 7. As-tu *ton* plume (encre, livres)?

C. 1. Je suis la fille de M. Lenoir. 2. La maison de mon père est à côté de la maison de M. Ribot. 3. Sa maison est très jolie. 4. Notre maison est jolie aussi. 5. Nos maisons sont presque semblables. 6. Notre maison a dix pièces. 7. Leur maison a onze pièces. 8. M. Ribot est mon oncle. 9. Il est le frère de ma mère. 10. Sa femme est ma tante. 11. Elle est la sœur de mon père. 12. Leurs enfants sont nos parents. 13. Marie Ribot est ma petite cousine. 14. Son frère est mon cousin. 15. Nous avons les mêmes amis. 16. Claire Leduc est mon amie. 17. Elle est aussi l'amie de ma cousine. 18. Charles Leduc est mon ami. 19. Il est aussi l'ami de Jean Ribot.

D. (*Oral.*) 1. Où est la maison de votre père? 2. Votre maison est-elle jolie? 3. Qui est M. Ribot? 4. De qui est-il le frère?

5. Mme Ribot est-elle votre tante? 6. Qui sont vos deux cousins? 7. Qui est votre amie? 8. Qui est l'ami de votre frère? 9. Où est mon autre plume? etc.

E. 1. Our house is in the country. 2. Your house is beside our house. 3. Is their house not very large? 4. Are our houses not very pretty? 5. His house has ten rooms. 6. My house has eleven rooms. 7. Your (thy) aunt has a house in the village. 8. Our relatives are in (the) town. 9. My mother's brother is my uncle. 10. My little sisters have the same books.

F. 1. Your father's sister is your aunt. 2. John Ribot is my cousin. 3. Charles Leduc is my friend's (*f.*) brother. 4. Who is your friend? 5. Are your friends not yet here? 6. Mary Ribot is my cousin. 7. Where is your (thy) ink? 8. Where is her other pen? 9. Where are their other pens? 10. The two rooms are almost alike.

LESSON IX

17. *Voici, voilà.* — When objects are pointed out by look, gesture or the like, *here is, here are* = **voici** [vwasi], and *there is, there are* = **voilà** [vwala], *here* and *there* being stressed:

Voici mon ami.	*Here is my friend.*
Voilà mes plumes.	*There are my pens.*

NOTE. — **Voici** (= vois + ici) means literally *see here*, **voilà** (= vois + là), *see there*.

18. **Some Personal Pronoun Objects**

MASC. SING.	FEM. SING.	MASC. OR FEM. PLUR.
le, l' [lǝ, l], *him* or *it*	**la, l'** [la, l], *her* or *it*	**les** [le], *them*

Je **le** blâme; je **l'**admire.	*I blame him; I admire him (her).*
Je **la** donne; nous **l'**avons.	*I give it; we have it* (e.g. *pen*).
Vous ne **les** avez pas.	*You haven't them* (e.g. *books, pens*).
Où est Marie? — **La** voilà.	*Where is Mary? — There she is.*

1. These pronouns denote the direct object in the third person, and have the same forms as the definite article.

2. They are placed before the verb (but see § 72), and before **voici** and **voilà**.

EXERCISE IX

l'affaire [afɛːr], f., *affair, business, thing*
alors [alɔːr], *then*
le chapeau [ʃapo], *hat*
le cocher [kɔʃe], *coachman, driver*
Louis [lwi], *Louis*
les lunettes [lynɛt], f., *spectacles, glasses*
papa [papa], *papa*

le pardessus [pardəsy], *overcoat*
la poche [pɔʃ], *pocket*
pour [pur], *for*
prêt [prɛ], *ready*
la promenade [prɔmnad], *walk, drive*
tout [tu], f. **toute**, *all, every*
la voiture [vwatyːr], *carriage*

A. Continue: 1. Je l'ai, tu l'as, etc. 2. Je les ai, etc. 3. Je ne l'ai pas, etc. 4. J'ai ma canne, tu as ta canne, etc. 5. J'ai mes gants, tu as tes, etc. 6. N'ai-je pas mon pardessus? n'as-tu pas ton, etc.

B. (*Monsieur Dupont et Louis*) 1. Louis, où est ton pardessus? — 2. Je l'ai, mon père. — 3. As-tu ton chapeau aussi? — 4. Oui, mon père, le voici. Papa, as-tu tes gants? — 5. Oui, mon enfant, je les ai dans ma poche. — 6. Et ton chapeau? — 7. Le voilà sur la table là-bas. — 8. Mais tu n'as pas tes lunettes. Où sont-elles? — 9. Les voici sous mon chapeau. Alors nous avons toutes nos affaires? Et la voiture est-elle prête? — 10. Oui, papa, la voilà à la porte. — 11. Et le cocher est-il là? — 12. Le voilà aussi à côté de la voiture. — 13. Maintenant nous sommes prêts pour notre promenade.

C. (*Oral.*) 1. Où est votre pardessus? 2. Avez-vous votre chapeau? 3. Avez-vous aussi vos gants? 4. Où sont les lunettes de votre père? 5. Avez-vous toutes vos affaires? 6. Êtes-vous prêts maintenant? 7. Où est la voiture? 8. Où est le cocher? etc.

D. 1. Have you my overcoat? 2. Yes, sir, here it is. 3. Where are my gloves? 4. There they are on the table. 5. Have you your hat? 6. Yes, sir, I have it. 7. Where are your glasses? 8. I haven't them. 9. Where is the carriage? 10. There it is at the door. 11. Where is the coachman? 12. There he is beside the carriage. 13. Have we all our things? 14. Yes, papa, we have them. 15. Are we ready for our drive? 16. We are ready.

E. 1. Who has my ink? 2. Haven't you it? 3. I haven't it.
4. John hasn't it. 5. Here it is; I have it now. 6. Where are
your books? 7. Haven't you them here? 8. We haven't them
here to-day. 9. There they are on the table. 10. The teacher's
chalk is here; here it is. 11. There is his cane; there it is. 12. My
pens are in my box; here they are.

LESSON X

19.   **Present Indicative of *donner*, 'give'**

1. AFFIRMATIVE

I give, am giving, do give, etc.

je donne	[ʒə dɔn]
tu donnes	[ty dɔn]
il donne	[il dɔn]
nous donn**ons**	[nu dɔnɔ̃]
vous donn**ez**	[vu dɔne]
ils donn**ent**	[il dɔn]

2. NEGATIVE

I do not give, am not giving, etc.

je ne donne pas	[ʒə nə dɔn pɑ]
tu ne donnes pas	[ty nə dɔn pɑ]
il ne donne pas	[il nə dɔn pɑ]
nous ne donn**ons** pas	[nu nə dɔnɔ̃ pɑ]
vous ne donn**ez** pas	[vu nə dɔne pɑ]
ils ne donn**ent** pas	[il nə dɔn pɑ]

3. INTERROGATIVE

Am I giving? do I give? etc.

donné-je?	[dɔnɛː ʒ]
donnes-tu?	[dɔn ty]
donne-t-il?	[dɔn t il]
donnons-nous?	[dɔnɔ̃ nu]
donnez-vous?	[dɔne vu]
donnent-ils?	[dɔnt il]

4. NEGATIVE INTERROGATIVE

Am I not giving? do I not give? etc.

ne donné-je pas?	[nə dɔnɛː ʒ pɑ]
ne donnes-tu pas?	[nə dɔn ty pɑ]
ne donne-t-il pas?	[nə dɔn t il pɑ]
ne donnons-nous pas?	[nə dɔnɔ̃ nu pɑ]
ne donnez-vous pas?	[nə dɔne vu pɑ]
ne donnent-ils pas?	[nə dɔnt il pɑ]

·1. Conjugate as above all regular verbs in **–er**.

2. Observe particularly that most English tenses have various forms, e.g. *I give, I am giving, I do give*, while French
tenses have only one form (in this case, je **donne**); so also for
interrogative and negative forms, e.g. *does he give? is he giving?*
(= **donne**-t-il), *they are not giving, they do not give* (= ils ne
donnent pas).

20. Interrogation. — 1. By prefixing **est-ce que** [ɛ s kə] (lit. *is it that?*), any statement may be turned into a question:

Il a ses gants.	*He has his gloves.*
Est-ce qu'il a ses gants?	*Has he his gloves?*

NOTE. — This form usually replaces the 1st sing. interrog., e.g. **est-ce que** je donne? = donné-je?

2. An interrogative word, if used, precedes **est-ce que**:

Qu'est-ce qu'il désire?	*What does he wish?*
Où est-ce qu'ils demeurent?	*Where do they live?*

3. Inflection of the voice may serve to indicate interrogation:

Vous demeurez ici?	*Do you live here?*

21. Indirect Object. — 1. The indirect object is denoted by **à**:

Je donne une plume **à** Jean.	*I give John a pen (a pen to John).*
Je parle **aux** élèves.	*I am speaking to the pupils.*

2. With a verb, *to him, to her* = **lui** [lɥi], *to them* = **leur** [lœ:r]; they precede the verb:

Je **lui** (leur) parle.	*I speak to him or her (to them).*

EXERCISE X

amuser [amyze], *amuse*
beaucoup [boku], *much, very much, a great deal*
le cahier [kaje], *exercise book*
crier [krie], *cry out, shout*
donner [dɔne], *give, give away*
écouter [ekute], *listen (to)*
expliquer [ɛksplike], *explain*
gros [gro], *large, big*

l'image [ima:ʒ], f., *image, picture*
l'institutrice [ẽstitytris], f., *teacher*
jouer [ʒwe], *play*
la leçon [ləsɔ̃], *lesson*
mademoiselle [madmwazɛl], *Miss*
parler [parle], *speak*
quelquefois [kɛlkəfwa], *sometimes*
regarder [rəgarde], *look at*
travailler [travaje], *work*

à présent [prezɑ̃], *at present, now*

A. Continue: 1. Je leur donne mes plumes, tu . . . tes plumes, etc. 2. Est-ce que je lui donne mon cahier? est-ce que tu . . . ton . . .? etc. 3. Je ne lui (*or* leur) parle pas, etc. 4. Est-ce que je ne travaille pas? ne travailles-tu pas? etc. 5. Je le (*or* les) regarde, etc. 6. Je ne l' (*or* les) écoute pas, etc.

B. 1. Est-ce que vous travaillez, mes enfants? 2. Oui, mademoiselle, nous travaillons. 3. Parles-tu, Louis? 4. Est-ce que tu
parles, Marie? 5. Jean, tu parles? 6. Oui, mademoiselle, nous
parlons. 7. Marie donne le livre à la dame. 8. Elle lui donne le
papier aussi. 9. Les enfants regardent les jolies images. 10. L'institutrice leur donne un gros livre. 11. Je travaille beaucoup.
12. *Turn sentences* 1–11 *into negative form*.

C. 1. Nous sommes à l'école. 2. L'institutrice donne les cahiers
aux élèves. 3. Nous travaillons. 4. Elle explique la leçon. 5. Nous
l'écoutons. 6. Elle parle beaucoup aux élèves. 7. Nous lui parlons
aussi quelquefois. 8. Les petits garçons jouent à présent dans la
cour. 9. Ils parlent et crient beaucoup. 10. Les petites filles sont
sous les arbres. 11. Elles regardent les images dans un gros livre.
12. Les images les amusent beaucoup. 13. Les images amusent les
petits garçons aussi. 14. Elles leur donnent le livre.

D. 1. I am speaking. 2. You are not working. 3. John is
not listening. 4. Doesn't the pupil listen? 5. The pupils speak
to the teacher; they speak to her. 6. She speaks to them. 7. Are
you not working? 8. We work a great deal. 9. We give the little
boys our book. 10. Where are you? 11. What are you looking
at? 12. We are looking at our exercise books. 13. What are
the little girls looking at? 14. They are looking at the pictures.
15. We are listening to the children. 16. They are playing in
the yard.

E. 1. Who is speaking to the pupils? 2. The teacher (*f*.) is
speaking to them. 3. Are the children playing in the yard now?
4. Yes, miss, they are playing under the trees. 5. The teacher is
explaining our lessons. 6. We are listening to her. 7. Are the boys
not shouting a great deal? 8. We are amusing the little boys.
9. We give them our pictures. 10. Are the little boys not working?
11. No, sir, they are not working. 12. Do the men work much?
13. Yes, sir, they work in the fields. 14. Are the grammars not
on the table? 15. Yes, they are on the table with the dictionary.

LESSON XI

22.   Conjunctive Personal Pronouns

SINGULAR

me [mə], *me, (to) me*
te [tə], *thee, you, (to) thee, (to) you*
le [lə], m., *him, it* }
la [la], f., *her, it* }
lui [lɥi], m. f., *(to) him, (to) her*
se [sə], m. f., *himself, herself, itself, (to) himself, etc.*

PLURAL

nous [nu], *us, (to) us*
vous [vu], *you, (to) you*
les [le], m. f., *them*
leur [lœːr], m. f., *(to) them*
se [sə], m. f., *themselves, (to) themselves*

(*a*) These forms are called "conjunctive" because they are used along with verbs as objects.

(*b*) Le, la, les (§ 18), lui, leur (§ 21, 2) are repeated here for completeness.

23.   Use of Conjunctive Objects

Il **me** (te, nous, vous) frappe.
Il **me** (te, nous, vous) parle.
Ma mère **m'**aime (t'aime).
Il **se** coupe; il **se** dit.

He strikes me (you, us, you).
He speaks to me (to you, etc.).
My mother loves me (loves you).
He cuts himself; he says to himself.

1. **Me, te, se, nous, vous** serve both as direct and as indirect objects of verbs.

2. All conjunctive personal pronoun objects precede the verb, unless it be an imperative affirmative (§ 72).

EXERCISE XI

accompagner [akɔ̃paɲe], *accompany, go (come) with*
aimable [emabl], *amiable, kind*
apporter [apɔrte], *bring*
la bonne [bɔn], *servant, maid*
la carte [kart], *map*
chercher [ʃerʃe], *seek, look for*
le facteur [faktœːr], *postman, letter-carrier*

laisser [lese], *let, leave*
la lettre [letr], *letter*
montrer [mɔ̃tre], *show*
prêter [prete], *lend*
quand [kɑ̃], *when*
remercier [rəmɛrsje], *thank*
rencontrer [rɑ̃kɔ̃tre], *meet*
saluer [salɥe], *salute, bow to, etc.*
souvent [suvɑ̃], *often*
trouver [truve], *find*

A. Continue: 1. Il me cherche, il te, etc. 2. Les images m'a-musent, . . . t'amusent, etc. 3. Mon frère me prête ses livres, . . . te prête ses livres, etc. 4. Mes amis m'accompagnent à l'école, . . . t'accompagnent, etc. 5. Le professeur m'explique la leçon, . . . t'explique, etc.

B. 1. Mon frère m'apporte le gros livre. 2. Il me montre les images. 3. Les images du livre t'amusent-elles? 4. Elles m'a-musent beaucoup. 5. Votre père nous cherche. 6. Il nous accom-pagne à l'école. 7. Le professeur vous montre la carte. 8. Je salue le professeur quand je le rencontre. 9. Il me salue aussi. 10. Louis me prête souvent ses livres. 11. Il est très aimable. 12. Vous prête-t-il ses livres aussi? 13. Oui, et je lui prête mes plumes et mon encre. 14. Le facteur apporte les lettres. 15. Il les laisse dans la boîte à la porte. 16. La bonne les trouve dans la boîte et les apporte à mon père. 17. Il la remercie. 18. Les enfants s'amusent dans le jardin.

C. (Oral.) 1. Qui m'apporte le gros livre? 2. Qui nous montre les images? 3. Qu'est-ce qu'il vous montre? 4. Saluez-vous votre professeur? 5. Quand est-ce qu'il nous salue? 6. Qu'est-ce que tu prêtes à Louis? 7. Qui m'apporte les lettres? 8. À qui les donne-t-elle? 9. Votre père la remercie-t-il? 10. Est-elle contente? 11. Où les enfants s'amusent-ils? etc.

D. 1. I bring him the big book. 2. Who is showing us the pic-tures? 3. Don't the pictures amuse you? 4. Yes, Miss Ribot, they amuse me [very][1] much. 5. My brother is looking for you (thee). 6. The teacher is explaining the map to us. 7. He explains the map to them also. 8. I bow to him when I meet him. 9. He bows to me when he meets me.

E. 1. I am lending you (thee) my books. 2. What does the postman bring us? 3. He brings the letters and leaves them on the table at the door. 4. Here are your letters on the table. 5. The maid brings us the letters. 6. We thank her. 7. Are the children not amusing themselves? 8. Do we not bring her the book? 9. There are our sisters; we bring them the pictures.

---

[1] Words in brackets to be omitted in translating.

LESSON XII

24. The General Noun. — A noun used in a general sense regularly takes the definite article in French, though not usually in English:

La vie est courte.	*Life is short.*
L'homme est mortel.	*Man is mortal.*
J'aime **les** Français.	*I like Frenchmen (the French).*
Le fer est dur.	*Iron is hard.*
Le cheval est très utile.	*The horse is very useful.*

25. The Partitive Noun. — 1. *Some, any,* either expressed or understood with a noun = **de** + the definite article:

J'ai **de la** craie, **du** papier.	*I have (some) chalk, (some) paper.*
Avez-vous **de** l'encre?	*Have you (any) ink?*
A-t-il **des** frères (amis)?	*Has he any brothers (friends)?*

2. Thus is formed the plural of a noun with **un(e):**

Un livre; **des** livres.	*A book; (some) books.*

3. The general and partitive sense must be distinguished:

Les arbres ont **des** feuilles.	*Trees (gen.) have leaves (part.).*
Les chiens sont **des** animaux.	*Dogs are animals.*

EXERCISE XII

aimer [ɛme], *love, like, be fond of*
l'amusement [amyzmã], m., *amusement*
l'argent [arʒã], m., *silver, money*
la bille [biːj], *marble* (plaything)
étudier [etydje], *study*
facilement [fasilmã], *easily, readily*
le français [frãsɛ], *(the) French* (*language*)
la géographie [ʒeografi], *geography*
l'histoire [istwaːr], f., *history, story*
la langue [lãːg], *tongue, language*
la lecture [lɛktyːr], *reading*
la poire [pwaːr], *pear*
la pomme [pɔm], *apple*
la toupie [tupi], *top*
la viande [vjãːd], *meat*

j'aime le français, *I am fond of (like) French;* but note: **parlez-vous français?** *do you speak French?*

A. Continue: 1. J'aime la lecture, tu . . . etc. 2. Est-ce que je parle français? parles-tu . . . etc. 3. Je ne parle pas français, tu ne . . . etc. 4. Je leur donne des cahiers et des plumes, tu leur donnes . . . etc. 5. J'aime les pommes et les poires, tu . . . etc. 6. J'ai de l'encre et du papier, tu as . . . etc. 7. J'aime l'argent, tu aimes . . . etc. 8. J'ai de l'argent dans ma poche, tu as . . . dans ta, etc.

B. 1. J'aime la viande. 2. Avez-vous de la viande? 3. Aimez-vous les pommes? 4. Je les aime beaucoup. 5. Les hommes aiment-ils l'argent? 6. Ils l'aiment. 7. Avez-vous de l'argent dans votre poche? 8. Je lui prête de l'argent. 9. Les enfants étudient-ils la géographie et l'histoire? 10. N'aiment-ils pas la lecture? 11. Ils l'aiment beaucoup. 12. Avez-vous des pommes? 13. Non, monsieur, mais nous avons des poires.

C. Complete the partitive form: 1. J'ai d . . . encre, d . . . plumes et d . . . papier. 2. A-t-il d . . . craie et d . . . crayons? 3. Nous avons d . . . frères et d . . . sœurs. 4. Elle a d . . . argent. 5. Ils ont d . . . pommes. 6. A-t-elle d . . . viande? 7. Nous avons d . . . arbres dans notre cour.

D. 1. Mes frères et mes sœurs étudient leurs leçons. 2. Ils aiment beaucoup l'histoire et la géographie. 3. Ils aiment aussi le français. 4. À l'école nous parlons français. 5. Les enfants parlent facilement les langues quand le professeur les parle. 6. Les élèves ont des amusements à l'école. 7. Les petits garçons ont des billes et des toupies. 8. Les petites filles ont des livres. 9. Elles aiment beaucoup la lecture. 10. Elles trouvent aussi des images dans les livres. 11. Les images amusent les enfants.

E. 1. Have you any apples? 2. Do you like apples? 3. I don't like them. 4. We like reading. 5. We are studying history and geography. 6. I have some money in my pocket. 7. Are you fond of money? 8. I am giving them some money. 9. Children like apples. 10. Has John any apples? 11. Has he any ink? 12. No, madam, but I am lending him some paper and ink.

F. 1. We like reading. 2. Little boys like marbles. 3. They have marbles and tops. 4. Our teacher speaks French. 5. Do you speak French? 6. Don't you like French? 7. Have you any amuse-

ments at school? 8. Little girls like books. 9. The little girls have
books. 10. Books amuse them. 11. Do not men love money?
12. Have you any money in your pocket? 13. Are you studying
history and the languages?

LESSON XIII

26. Quantity. — 1. The word limited by a noun or adverb of
quantity is preceded by **de**, usually without article:

Une livre **de** viande.	*A pound of meat.*
Beaucoup **de** thé.	*A great deal of tea (much tea).*
Beaucoup **de** pommes (**d'**amis).	*A great many apples (friends).*
Un peu **de** pain; trop **de** pain.	*A little bread; too much bread.*
Assez **d'**argent.	*Enough (of) money or money enough.*

2. But observe the following expressions:

La plupart **des** hommes.	*(The) most (of the) men.*
J'ai bien **des** amis ici.	*I have many friends here.*
Désire-t-il encore **des** pommes?	*Does he wish some more apples?*

27. Use of en. — 1. *Some* or *any*, as a pronoun = **en** [ã] (lit.
of it, of them); it must be used to replace a partitive noun, even
though *some, any*, be omitted in English:

A-t-il de l'encre? — Il **en** a.	*Has he any ink? —He has (some).*
Désire-t-il du thé? — Il **en** désire.	*Does he wish tea? — He does.*

2. Similarly **en** must replace a noun preceded by a numeral,
or the governed word of an expression of quantity:

A-t-elle une plume?	*Has she a pen?*
Elle **en** a une (deux, etc.).	*She has one (two, etc.).*
Elle **en** a beaucoup.	*She has a great many.*

3. Besides the above uses, observe that **en** in general has the
force of **de** (= *of, from, with, etc.*) + a noun or pronoun:

J'**en** suis content.	*I am pleased with (glad of) it or them.*

4. **En** has the same position as a conjunctive pronoun object
(cf. § 23, 2).

EXERCISE XIII

assez [ase], *enough*

l'automne [otɔn], m. or f., *autumn*

cent [sã], *a hundred*

combien [kɔ̃bjɛ̃], *how much (many)*?

désirer [dezire], *desire, wish, want*

l'écureuil [ekyrœːj], m., *squirrel*

en [ã], *in*

la faîne [fɛːn], *beechnut*

la feuille [fœːj], *leaf*

la livre [liːvr], *pound*

ramasser [ramɑse], *pick up, gather*

rester [reste], *remain, stay*

le sac [sak], *bag, sack*

souffler [sufle], *blow*

le thé [te], *tea*

tomber [tɔ̃be], *fall*

le vent [vã], *wind*

le verger [vɛrʒe], *orchard*

(un) peu [pø], (a) *little, few;* en automne [ãn otɔn], *in autumn*

NOTE. — Forms like *I do, I have*, with a verb understood, must not be used in French; the sentence must be complete.

A. Continue: 1. J'ai beaucoup de pommes, tu, etc. 2. J'en ai beaucoup, etc. 3. Je n'en ai pas beaucoup, etc. 4. J'en ai dix, etc. 5. J'ai peu d'argent, etc. 6. J'en ai peu, etc. 7. J'ai encore de l'argent, etc. 8. J'ai bien de l'argent, etc. 9. J'en ai encore beaucoup, etc. 10. J'ai bien des amis, etc.

B. 1. Avez-vous assez d'argent? 2. J'en ai assez. 3. Que désirez-vous? 4. Je désire une livre de thé. 5. Avez-vous beaucoup de pommes? 6. Nous n'en avons pas beaucoup. 7. Nous avons peu de pommes. 8. Nous en avons très peu. 9. Combien en avez-vous? 10. J'en ai trois. 11. Désirez-vous encore des pommes? 12. J'en désire encore.

C. 1. Nous sommes en automne. 2. Peu de feuilles restent sur les arbres. 3. Le vent souffle et beaucoup de faînes tombent. 4. Les écureuils en ramassent beaucoup. 5. Les enfants aiment les faînes et en ramassent aussi. 6. Dans son verger M. Dupont a cent sacs de pommes. 7. Il en donne dix sacs à son frère. 8. Son frère en donne à ses enfants. 9. La plupart des enfants aiment les pommes. 10. Les autres enfants en désirent aussi. 11. Les enfants de M. Dupont en donnent à leurs petits amis.

D. (Oral.) 1. Quand les feuilles tombent-elles? 2. Qu'est-ce que les écureuils ramassent? 3. Est-ce que les enfants ramassent des faînes? 4. Qu'est-ce que vous avez dans votre verger? 5. En avez-vous beaucoup? 6. À qui en donnez-vous? 7. Êtes-vous contents de votre verger? 8. Combien de pommes avez-vous? etc.

E. 1. Have you many apples?   2. We have a great many. 3. Have you any more apples?   4. Yes, sir, we have some more. 5. What do the squirrels pick up in autumn?   6. They pick up a great many beechnuts.   7. Our friends have four sacks of apples. 8. We have a great many also.   9. Have your friends much money? 10. They have (= they have much of it).   11. Has the little boy any pears?   12. He has.   13. We are picking up pears in the orchard.   14. Are you picking up any?   15. Do you give any [away] to your relatives?   16. We give some away to our cousins.

F. 1. Do you wish any money?   2. No, sir, I have some.   3. Have you much?   4. I have enough.   5. Has Louis enough?   6. He has (enough of it).   7. How many apples have you?   8. How many has John?   9. I have one; John has two.   10. You haven't enough; you have very few.   11. Here are some more.   12. Here are some on the table.   13. Do most men love money?   14. They do (= they love it).

LESSON XIV

28. Omission of Article. — With a partitive noun (§ 25) the definite article is omitted, and **de** alone is used: —

1. In a general negation, complete absence of the object in question being implied:

Je n'ai pas **de** pain.	*I have no (haven't any) bread.*
Il n'a pas **d'**amis ici.	*He has no friends here.*
Je n'ai pas **de** plume.	*I have no pen.*

2. When an adjective precedes the noun, and likewise when a noun is understood after an adjective:

Marie a **de** jolies fleurs.	*Mary has (some) pretty flowers.*
J'ai **de** votre argent.	*I have some of your money.*
De grands arbres et **de** petits.	*Large trees and small (ones).*
But: **Des** pommes mûres.	*Ripe apples (adj. following).*

NOTE. — For exceptions and special cases, see Lesson LXXX.

29. Observe the omission of a partitive sign in the following:

Il n'a ni pommes ni poires.	*He has neither apples nor pears.*
Sans amis et sans argent.	*Without friends and without money.*
Le panier est plein de pommes.	*The basket is full of apples.*

30. Observe the use of **de** in the following expressions:

Une robe de soie.	*A silk dress (dress of silk).*
Une leçon de français.	*A French lesson.*
Une salle de classe.	*A classroom.*

31. *Il y a.* — *There is, there are,* are rendered thus when no stress rests on the word *there,* and when the expression is not accompanied by look or gesture (cf. § 17):

Il y a un livre sur la table.	*There is a book on the table.*
Y a-t-il des livres ici?	*Are there any books here?*
Il n'y a pas de plumes ici.	*There are no pens here.*
N'y a-t-il pas de plumes ici?	*Are there no pens here?*
Il y en a.	*There is (are) some.*
Il n'y en a pas.	*There is (are) none.*
Y en a-t-il?	*Is (are) there any?*
N'y en a-t-il pas?	*Is (are) there none (not any)?*

(*a*) Observe that **en** follows **y.**

EXERCISE XIV

brouter [brute], *browse, crop*	**partout** [partu], *everywhere*
déjà [deʒa], *already*	**plein** [plɛ̃], *full (of, de)*
la fleur [flœːr], *flower*	**pousser** [puse], *grow*
la glace [glas], *ice*	**le printemps** [prɛ̃tɑ̃], *spring*
l'herbe [ɛrb], f., *grass*	**la salle** [sal], *hall, room*
la joie [ʒwa], *joy, happiness*	**sans** [sɑ̃], *without*
même [mɛːm], adv., *even*	**le sud** [syd], *south*
le mouton [mutɔ̃], *sheep*	**la vache** [vaʃ], *cow*
la neige [nɛːʒ], *snow*	**vert** [vɛːr], *green*
le pain [pɛ̃], *bread*	

ne . . . ni . . . ni [nə ni ni], *neither . . . nor;* **au printemps,** *in spring*

A. Continue: 1. Je n'ai ni plumes ni encre, tu, etc. 2. J'ai de jolis livres, etc. 3. Je n'ai pas d'argent, etc. 4. Je suis sans gants et sans chapeau, etc. 5. J'étudie ma leçon de français, tu . . . ta, etc. 6. Je suis dans la salle de classe, etc. 7. Il y a de grands arbres dans ma cour, . . . dans ta, etc. 8. Y a-t-il de jolies fleurs dans mon jardin? . . . dans ton, etc. 9. Il y en a dans mon jardin, . . . dans ton, etc. 10. N'y en a-t-il pas dans mon jardin? . . . dans ton, etc.

B. 1. Avez-vous du pain? 2. Je n'ai pas de pain. 3. Nous n'avons ni pain ni viande. 4. Vous avez là de jolies fleurs. 5. Nous avons beaucoup de jolies fleurs. 6. À la ville il y a de grandes maisons et de petites. 7. Avez-vous beaucoup d'amis? 8. Nous n'en avons pas ici. 9. Y a-t-il de jolies maisons à la campagne? 10. As-tu de mon papier? 11. J'en ai. 12. Y a-t-il des livres sur la table? 13. N'y en a-t-il pas? 14. Il n'y en a pas.

C. 1. Voici maintenant le printemps. 2. Il n'y a ni neige ni glace. 3. Le vent du sud souffle. 4. Les arbres sont déjà verts. 5. L'herbe pousse aux champs. 6. Les vaches et les moutons la broutent. 7. Partout il y a de jolies fleurs. 8. Nous en trouvons dans les champs et dans les jardins. 9. Les arbres des vergers en sont pleins. 10. Il y a de la joie partout. 11. Même sans amis et sans argent les hommes sont contents.

D. (*Oral.*) 1. Y a-t-il de la neige au printemps? 2. Où trouvons-nous de jolies fleurs? 3. Y a-t-il de la joie partout? 4. Les arbres sont-ils pleins de fleurs? 5. Où sont les moutons et les vaches? 6. Qu'est-ce qu'ils broutent? 7. N'avez-vous pas de fleurs? 8. Qui a de jolies fleurs? 9. Qui nous donne une leçon de français? 10. Où nous donne-t-il notre leçon de français? 11. Qu'est-ce qu'il y a sur la table? 12. Y a-t-il des plumes dans votre boîte? etc.

E. 1. I have no flowers. 2. We have no French lesson to-day. 3. Have you no large trees in your yard? 4. John has some of my paper. 5. There are some pretty flowers in our garden. 6. There are large houses and small houses in the city. 7. I have neither ink nor pens here. 8. The poor boy is without money. 9. The teacher is giving us a French lesson in the classroom. 10. There are a great many books on the table. 11. Are there any large houses in the village? 12. There are some very large [ones].

F. 1. Are there any pretty flowers in the fields? 2. There are already some in the fields and gardens. 3. Do the cows crop grass? 4. Yes, sir, and the sheep crop it too. 5. Sheep and cows like grass. 6. Sometimes there is snow in spring. 7. But there isn't much. 8. We have neither ice nor snow now. 9. The grass is already green. 10. The south wind is blowing. 11. There is no ice to-day. 12. Flowers grow in spring. 13. The gardens are full of them.

LESSON XV

32. Irregular Plurals. — Observe the following exceptions to the general rule of adding **s** to the singular (cf. § 2, 3): —

1. Nouns in **–s, –x, –z**, and adjectives in **–s, –x**, are unchanged:

bois, *wood(s)*   nez, *nose(s)*   bas   bas, *low*
voix, *voice(s)*   heureux, heureux, *happy*

2. Nouns in **–au, –eu**, and a few in **–ou**, add **x**:

chapeau(**x**), *hat(s)*   jeu(**x**), *game(s)*   bijou(**x**), *jewel(s)*

(*a*) Also in **–ou**: caillou(**x**), *pebble*, chou(**x**), *cabbage*, genou(**x**), *knee*, hibou(**x**), *owl*, joujou(**x**), *toy*, but sou(**s**), *cent, halfpenny*, etc.

3. Adjectives in **–eau** also add **x**:

beau(**x**), *fine*   nouveau(**x**), *new*

4. Nouns, and the commoner adjectives, in **–al** take **–aux**:

animal   animaux, *animal*   égal   égaux, *equal*

(*a*) Bal(**s**), *ball*, carnaval(**s**), *carnival*, and some rarer nouns are regular.

5. Seven nouns in **–ail** take **–aux**; the commonest are:

travail   travaux, *work(s)*   corail   coraux, *coral(s)*

6. Note also:

œil   yeux, *eye(s)*   ciel   cieux, *sky, skies, heaven(s)*

33. Position of Adjectives. — Qualifying adjectives, used with nouns, regularly follow, especially when denoting: —

1. Physical quality, such as colour, shape, heat, cold, etc.:

De l'encre **noire**; de l'eau **froide**.   *Black ink; cold water.*
Une pierre **dure** (ronde).   *A hard (round) stone.*
Du vin **doux** (aigre).   *Sweet (sour) wine.*

2. Nationality, religion and the like:

Le droit **anglais**; l'église **catholique**.   *(The) English law; the Catholic church.*

3. So also participles used as adjectives:

La cruche **cassée**.   *The broken pitcher.*
Un tableau **frappant**.   *A striking picture.*

4. But certain adjectives of frequent use generally precede:

beau, *fine*	long, *long*	jeune, *young*
joli, *pretty*	court, *short*	vieux, *old*
vilain, *ugly*	gros, *big*	nouveau, *new*
bon, *good*	grand, *large*	
mauvais, *bad*	petit, *small*	

NOTES. — 1. Adjectives used figuratively, unemphatically or when merged in sense with the noun, often precede, irrespective of the above rules, e.g. une **étroite** amitié, *an intimate* (lit. *narrow*) *friendship;* but une rue **étroite**, *a narrow street.*

2. Many adjectives vary in meaning, before or after the noun, e.g. mon **cher** enfant, *my dear child;* une robe **chère**, *a costly dress.*

EXERCISE XV

abondant [abɔ̃dɑ̃], *abundant*
l'animal [animal], m., *animal*
beau [bo], *fine, beautiful, hand-some, good-looking*
bleu [blø], *blue*
le bois [bwɑ], *wood*
le bruit [brɥi], *sound, noise*
la cerise [sɔriːz], *cherry*
le chant [ʃɑ̃], *song, singing*
chargé [ʃarʒe], *laden*
le cheval [ʃəval], *horse*
le clou [klu], *nail*
l'été [ete], m., *summer*

le feuillage [fœjaːʒ], *leaves, foliage*
la fraise [frɛːz], *strawberry*
habiter [abite], *inhabit, live in*
intéressant [ɛ̃teresɑ̃], *interesting*
mûr [myːr], *ripe, mature*
noir [nwaːr], *black*
l'œil [œːj], m., pl. yeux [jø], *eye*
l'oiseau [wazo], m., *bird*
la paille [paːj], *straw*
le pommier [pɔmje], *apple tree*
la soie [swa], *silk*
tendre [tɑ̃ːdr], *tender*

en été [ɑ̃n ete], *in summer*

A. Continue: 1. Je regarde les beaux chevaux noirs, tu, etc. 2. J'ai deux chapeaux de paille, etc. 3. Je n'en ai pas de soie, etc. 4. Je suis sous les beaux arbres, etc. 5. J'ai deux gros livres intéressants, etc. 6. J'ai un sac de pommes mûres, etc. 7. J'ai des yeux bleus, etc. 8. J'ai deux gros clous, etc.

B. 1. En été nous sommes souvent aux bois. 2. Ils sont beaux et très intéressants. 3. Nous regardons souvent les beaux arbres. 4. Nous écoutons aussi le bruit des feuilles et le chant des oiseaux. 5. Beaucoup de petits oiseaux habitent les bois. 6. Nous aimons leur chant. 7. Il y a aussi de petits animaux dans le feuillage.

8. Ils nous amusent quand ils jouent ensemble. 9. Aux champs l'herbe est tendre et abondante. 10. Les vaches et les chevaux l'aiment beaucoup. 11. Dans le verger les pommiers sont chargés de petites pommes. 12. Elles ne sont pas encore mûres. 13. Mais les cerises et les fraises sont presque mûres. 14. Il y a deux beaux enfants sous les pommiers. 15. Ils ont de très beaux yeux bleus. 16. Ils ont de beaux chapeaux de paille. 17. Mon père a un chapeau de soie.

C. (*Oral.*) 1. Qu'est-ce que vous regardez dans les bois? 2. Qu'est-ce que nous écoutons aux bois? 3. Que trouvez-vous aux bois? 4. Est-ce que les petits animaux vous amusent? 5. Y a-t-il beaucoup de fraises mûres au jardin? 6. Où trouvons-nous de l'herbe tendre? 7. Combien d'enfants y a-t-il sous les arbres? 8. Avez-vous un joli chapeau de paille? etc.

D. 1. Beautiful woods. 2. Interesting books. 3. A pretty blue bird. 4. Beautiful blue eyes. 5. Fine black horses. 6. The little animals of the woods. 7. The tender and abundant grass. 8. Ripe apples; green apples. 9. A straw hat; a silk hat. 10. Black ink; blue paper. 11. A strong man; strong men. 12. Ripe cherries; ripe strawberries. (*For* 13 *and* 14, *see* § 32.) 13. Games, jewels, works, pebbles, voices. 14. New books, toys and games, pretty corals.

E. 1. How many hats have you? 2. I have two. 3. I have a straw hat and a silk hat. 4. Do you like straw hats? 5. I do (= I like them), in summer. 6. There are three beautiful children under the apple trees. 7. The children's eyes are blue. 8. They are playing together. 9. We like the singing of the birds. 10. When the little animals play they amuse us very much. 11. Do the horses like the tender grass? 12. They do.

F. 1. Are there many apples in the orchard? 2. The apple trees are laden with (*de*) apples. 3. But they are still small. 4. There are no ripe apples yet. 5. Most men like fine horses. 6. My uncle has two beautiful apple trees in his garden. 7. We listen to the singing of the little birds in the woods. 8. When the wind blows there is a sound in the leaves. 9. The sounds of the woods are very interesting. 10. Many interesting little animals live in the woods.

LESSON XVI

34. Irregular Feminine Adjectives. — The stem of certain adjectives is modified on adding the ending –e (cf. § 14), thus: —

1. By change of final consonant (**f = v, g = gu, x = s, c = ch**, sometimes **qu**):

actif	active, *active*	blanc	blanche, *white*
long	longue, *long*	public	publique, *public*
heureux	heureuse, *happy*		

(a) But observe: doux, douce, *sweet;* faux, fausse, *false.*

2. By doubling the final consonant of **–el, –eil, –en, –on**, and commonly also final **–s** and **–t**:

cruel	cruelle, *cruel*	bon	bonne, *good*
pareil	pareille, *like*	gros	grosse, *big*
ancien	ancienne, *ancient, former*	muet	muette, *dumb*

(a) Similarly gentil, gentille, *nice.*

(b) Regular are: gris(e), *grey,* prêt(e), *ready,* and some others; six in –et have –ète, e.g. complet, complète, *complete;* observe also frais, fraîche, *fresh, cool.*

3. Adjectives in **–er**, and a few others, change **e** to **è**:

léger	légère, *light*	sec	sèche, *dry* (cf. 1, above)
cher	chère, *dear*	complet	complète, *complete* (cf.
bref	brève, *brief* (cf. 1, above)		2, *b*, above)

4. Five adjectives have two masculine forms in the singular, the form in **–l** standing always before a vowel or **h** mute, and serving to form the feminine, like 2 above:

beau *or* bel	belle, *fine*	nouveau *or* nouvel	nouvelle, *new*
fou *or* fol	folle, *foolish*	vieux *or* vieil	vieille, *old*
mou *or* mol	molle, *soft*		

EXERCISE XVI

la branche [brãːʃ], *branch*	**jaune** [ʒoːn], *yellow*
la cave [kaːv], *cellar*	**nu** [ny], *bare*
couper [kupe], *cut, cut down*	**rouge** [ruːʒ], *red*
court [kuːr], *short*	**le traîneau** [trɛno], *sleigh*
le flocon [flɔkɔ̃], *flake (of snow)*	**transporter** [trãspɔrte], *bring*
l'hiver [ivɛːr], m., *winter*	

en hiver [ãn ivɛːr], *in winter*

NOTE. — The adjectives of § 34, above, are not given in the vocabulary.

A. Turn the English words into French with proper order and agreement: 1. Nous avons (*good*) poires. 2. Aimez-vous (*fine, sweet*) pommes? 3. Avez-vous (*good, red*) pommes? 4. Je leur donne (*big, sweet*) pommes. 5. Nous avons (*fine, white*) chevaux. 6. Il y a (*little, blue*) oiseaux aux bois. 7. Il y a (*good*) vaches aux champs. 8. Le monsieur a (*a fine, silk*) chapeau.

B. 1. Voici maintenant l'hiver. 2. Le bel arbre qui (*which*) est devant notre maison n'a pas de feuilles vertes. 3. Il en a de jaunes. 4. Mais ses longues branches sont presque nues. 5. Il n'y a pas de pommes au verger. 6. Mais nous avons de grosses belles pommes rouges à la cave. 7. Il y a aussi de jolies poires douces à la cave. 8. Peu de petits animaux sont aux bois. 9. Il y a de la neige partout. 10. Les champs sont blancs. 11. Les maisons sont blanches. 12. De gros flocons de neige tombent encore. 13. Deux hommes forts coupent de gros arbres là-bas. 14. Ils ont un traîneau et deux chevaux. 15. Avec le traîneau ils transportent le bois à la maison.

C. 1. The big flakes of white snow are falling. 2. The branches of the fine tree are almost bare. 3. We find no little animals in the woods. 4. There are no squirrels in the woods. 5. They do not like the winter. 6. Are the fields white in winter? 7. The fields are white, and the houses are white too. 8. There is white snow everywhere. 9. What are the men cutting yonder? 10. They are cutting big trees. 11. They bring home the wood with the sleigh.

D. 1. A long letter; long letters. 2. Are you happy, (my) children? 3. Mary is not happy; the other little girls are happy. 4. Our house is very old. 5. Are the ladies not yet ready? 6. Clara is a dear little girl; is she not very nice? 7. Mr. Dupont is a handsome man. 8. His wife is a fine-looking lady. 9. There is an old tree before the old house. 10. Old trees; old houses. 11. We have a new lesson to-day. 12. Public affairs are interesting. 13. My letter is short.

LESSON XVII

35. Use of *ce*. — Observe the English use of *it*, with the verb *to be*, to anticipate a real subject following the verb, e.g. *it* is my brother, *it* is they. The indeclinable demonstrative **ce** is similarly used with **être** when the real subject follows, and stands not only for *it*, but also for *he* (*she, they*), *this* (*that, these, those*), according to the context:

C'est Marie, et sa mère.   *It is Mary, and her mother.*
C'est une jolie dame.   *She (that) is a pretty lady.*
Ce sont des amis de Jean.   *They (these) are friends of John.*

36. Some Relative Pronouns. — 1. The relative pronouns of most frequent use are **qui** [ki] = *who, which, that*, as subject, and **que** [kə] = *whom, which, that*, as direct object of a verb:

La dame **qui** parle.   *The lady who is speaking.*
Les livres **qui** sont ici.   *The books which are here.*
Les parents **que** nous aimons. *The relatives whom we love.*
Les lettres **que** j'apporte.   *The letters that I bring.*

(*a*) All relative pronouns are considered as having the gender, number and person of the antecedent.

2. The relative pronoun (direct object), often omitted in English, is never omitted in French:

Le papier **qu'il** me donne.   *The paper he gives me.*

37. Observe the following interrogative forms involving the use of a relative pronoun:

Qui est-ce **qui** parle?   *Who (is it who) speaks?*
Qui est-ce **que** vous désirez? *Whom do you wish?*
Qu'est-ce **qui** vous amuse?   *What amuses you?*
Qu'est-ce **que** vous désirez?   *What do you wish?*

(*a*) The use of **qu'est-ce qui** is obligatory; the use of the others is optional (cf. § 91).

EXERCISE XVII

demeurer [dəmœre], *live, dwell*   **George(s)** [ʒɔrʒ], *George*
difficile [difisil], *difficult, hard*   **intéresser** [ɛ̃terese], *interest*
facile [fasil], *easy* .   **le tableau noir** [tablo nwaːr], *blackboard*
frapper [frape], *strike, knock*   **toujours** [tuʒuːr], *always, still*

A. 1. C'est une longue leçon; elle n'est pas facile; elle est sur le tableau noir. 2. Qui est là? Est-ce Marie? 3. Non, c'est sa sœur. 4. C'est le facteur qui nous apporte toujours les lettres. 5. Où sont les lettres qu'il nous apporte? 6. Les voilà. 7. Qu'y a-t-il (*or* qu'est-ce qu'il y a) sur la table? 8. Ce sont nos lettres. 9. Les pommiers de notre verger sont grands. 10. Ils sont très grands. 11. Ce sont de grands pommiers. 12. Est-ce votre ami qui frappe à la porte? 13. Non, c'est un monsieur qui cherche M. Leduc. 14. Qui demeure ici? 15. C'est M. Dupont. 16. Ce n'est pas M. Dupont que je cherche, c'est M. Leduc.

B. 1. Marie et Claire sont très diligentes. 2. Ce sont des élèves diligentes. 3. Ce sont des amies de ma sœur. 4. Qu'est-ce qui vous intéresse dans ce livre? 5. Ce sont les jolies images qui m'intéressent. 6. Qu'est-ce que vous désirez? 7. Je désire les fleurs que vous avez là. 8. La maison de mon oncle est très vieille. 9. Elle est très vieille, mais c'est une maison que j'aime beaucoup. 10. Qui est-ce qui nous explique la leçon au tableau noir? 11. C'est notre professeur. 12. Qui est-ce que vous accompagnez à l'école? 13. J'accompagne Georges et Louis. 14. Ce sont des amis que j'aime beaucoup.

C. 1. Our French lesson is difficult. 2. It is a very difficult lesson. 3. What do you wish? 4. I wish the pens that are in your box. 5. Is Mrs. Dupont very old? 6. She is a very old lady. 7. Are your friends at the door? 8. No, sir, those are some friends of my brother. 9. Who lives here? 10. It is Mr. Leduc who lives here. 11. The trees which are in our garden are large. 12. They are very large trees. 13. The flowers you have there are pretty. 14. Our lesson is on the blackboard.

D. 1. What is amusing you now? 2. It is the little animals playing (which play) in the trees. 3. What is the postman giving to your father? 4. He is giving him some letters. 5. Here are the letters which he brings us. 6. The lessons we have to-day are not easy. 7. This is a book which I do not like. 8. These are the books which interest us. 9. Who is knocking at the door? 10. They are some friends (*f.*) of my mother. 11. It is George Dupont who always goes with me to school. 12. We are good friends. 13. He is a friend whom I like very much. 14. The teacher is at the blackboard.

LESSON XVIII

38. An Indefinite Pronoun. — 1. The form **on** = *one, some one, we, you, they, people;* its verb is always third singular:

On [õ] parle de Jean.   *We (you, they, etc.) speak of John.*

2. When following a verb with final vowel, **on** is joined to it by -t-, like **il**, etc. (cf. § 8):

Que désire-t-on?   *What do they (etc.) wish?*

3. A construction with **on** often corresponds to an English passive, especially when the agent is not mentioned:

Ici on parle français.   *French (is) spoken here.*

(*a*) **on** = **l'on** optionally after certain words, e.g. **et, où, si, que,** etc., to avoid hiatus.

39. Use of y. — 1. The pronominal adverb **y** [i] = **à** (**dans, sur,** etc.) + a noun or pronoun and means *to (at, in, on, etc.) it* or *them:*

Je laisse la lettre sur la table.   *I leave the letter on the table.*
J'y laisse la lettre.   *I leave the letter on it.*

2. **Y** = *there,* of a place previously referred to; it is less emphatic than **là,** which regularly denotes a place not previously referred to:

Il est au jardin.   *He is in the garden.*
Il y est encore.   *He is still there (in it).*
But: Qu'avez-vous là?   *What have you there?*

3. **Y** precedes the verb like a conjunctive pronoun (cf. § 23).

40. *Tout.* — *Every, all, whole* = **tout,** which serves either as an adjective or a pronoun; its forms are:

m. s. **tout** [tu], f. s. **toute** [tut], m. pl. **tous** [tu(s)], f. pl. **toutes** [tut]

Tout homme, **toute** femme.   *Every man, every woman.*
Tous les livres, **toutes** les plumes. *All the books, all the pens.*
Toute la journée.   *The whole (all the) day.*
Je les ai **tous** [tus].   *I have them all.*

(*a*) The article, when present, always follows **tout.**
(*b*) The s of **tous,** used pronominally, is sounded.

EXERCISE XVIII

admirer [admire], *admire*
animé [anime], *animated, lively*
danser [dɑ̃se], *dance*
le groupe [grup], *group*
joyeux [ʒwajø], *joyous, merry*
le mérite [merit], *merit*
le monde [mɔ̃ːd], *world, people*
patiner [patine], *skate*
le paysage [peizaːʒ], *landscape*
le pin [pɛ̃], *pine tree, pine*
plusieurs [plyzjœːr], pl. adj. *or* pron., invar., *several*

remarquer [rəmarke], *remark, observe, notice*
représenter [rəprezɑ̃te], *represent*
le salon [salɔ̃], *drawing-room, parlour*
sembler [sɑ̃ble], *seem, appear*
surtout [syrtu], *above all, especially*
le tableau [tablo], *picture, painting*
tout [tu], absol., *everything*
tranquille [trɑ̃kil], *tranquil, quiet*

on voit [vwa], irreg., *one sees;* tout le monde [tu l mɔ̃ːd], *everybody*

A. Continue: 1. On admire tous mes tableaux, . . . tous tes, etc. (*also interrogatively*). 2. Toutes mes fleurs sont jolies, toutes tes, etc. 3. Je suis au jardin, j'y suis, tu es au jardin, tu y es, etc. 4. Est-ce que j'y suis? etc. 5. Je les admire tous, tu, etc.

B. 1. Dans notre salon il y a plusieurs tableaux. 2. On en admire surtout deux qui représentent des paysages. 3. Dans l'un on trouve des vaches qui broutent l'herbe. 4. On y remarque aussi plusieurs moutons. 5. Tous les animaux semblent tranquilles et contents. 6. On y voit aussi des enfants qui dansent sous les arbres. 7. C'est un tableau de beaucoup de mérite. 8. L'autre tableau représente un paysage d'hiver. 9. Presque tout y est blanc. 10. Mais il y a un groupe de pins qui sont très verts. 11. À côté des pins on voit des enfants joyeux qui patinent sur la glace. 12. D'autres enfants y jouent avec leurs traîneaux. 13. C'est un tableau très animé. 14. Tout le monde l'aime.

C. (Oral.) 1. Qu'y a-t-il dans le salon? 2. Admire-t-on vos tableaux? 3. Tous vos tableaux sont-ils beaux? 4. Y voit-on des vaches? 5. Y remarque-t-on d'autres animaux? 6. Les animaux qu'on y voit sont-ils tous tranquilles? 7. Où dansent les enfants qu'on y voit? 8. Est-ce un beau tableau? etc.

D. 1. Here are two pictures. 2. We have several pictures in our drawing-room. 3. Everybody admires two of them especially.

4. The pictures that they (*on*) admire are landscapes. 5. In (the) one we (you, etc.) observe many trees. 6. You notice in it also cows and sheep. 7. All the animals that one sees in it are quiet and they seem happy. 8. We observe also children dancing (who dance). 9. (Some) other children are playing under the trees. 10. Those (*ce*) are my little sisters who are playing there.

E. 1. In the other picture we (you, etc.) see snow. 2. Everything is white (*m.*). 3. There is snow everywhere. 4. There is some snow even on the green pines. 5. Almost the whole landscape is white. 6. All the houses are white. 7. We observe yonder some children (who are) skating. 8. Several other children are there also. 9. They are playing there with their sleighs. 10. People play a great deal on the ice in winter. 11. The pictures are much admired (use *on*). 12. Everybody admires good pictures.

LESSON XIX

41. The Regular Conjugations. — 1. French verbs are conveniently divided into three conjugations, according to the infinitive endings –**er**, –**ir**, –**re**:

I	II	III
Donner, *to give*	Finir, *to finish*	Vendre, *to sell*

2. Like these are conjugated all regular verbs with corresponding infinitive endings.

42.　　Present Indicative of *donner, finir, vendre*

I give, I am giving, I do give, etc.	*I finish, I am finishing, I do finish, etc.*	*I sell, I am selling, I do sell, etc.*
je donne [dɔn]	finis [fini]	vends [vã]
tu donnes [dɔn]	finis [fini]	vends [vã]
il donne [dɔn]	finit [fini]	vend[1] [vã]
nous donnons [dɔnɔ̃]	finissons [finisɔ̃]	vendons [vãdɔ̃]
vous donnez [dɔne]	finissez [finise]	vendez [vãde]
ils donnent [dɔn]	finissent [finis]	vendent [vãːd]

Learn also negative and interrogative forms (cf. § 19).

[1] **Vendre** is irregular in this single form; the only wholly regular verb of this conjugation is **rompre**, which has **rompt**, but **vendre** is here given as being more useful for practice.

43.   **The Demonstrative Adjective**

SINGULAR	PLURAL

m. **ce** [sə], **cet** [set] ⎱
f. **cette** [set]   ⎰ *this* or *that*   m. *or* f. **ces** [se], *these* or *those.*

Ce livre, cet ami, cet homme.   *This book, this friend, this man.*
Cet autre livre.   *This (that) other book.*
Cette plume et **cette** encre.   *This pen and (this) ink.*
Ces plumes, ces hommes.   *These pens, these men.*
Cet arbre-**ci** et cet arbre-**là**.   *This tree and that tree.*

1. **Ce** becomes **cet** before a vowel or **h** mute.
2. The demonstrative adjective is repeated before each noun.
3. For emphasis, or to distinguish *this* (*these*) from *that* (*those*), **-ci, -là**, respectively, are added to the noun.

EXERCISE XIX

les **bénéfices** [benefis], m., *profit(s)*
le **bout** [bu], *end*
fleurir [flœriːr], *blossom, be in bloom*
grossir [grosiːr], *grow larger*
longtemps [lɔ̃tã], *a long time, long*
le **marchand** [marʃã], *merchant, dealer*
mûrir [myriːr], *ripen*
pendant [pãdã], prep., *during*
perdre [pɛrdr], *lose*
pourrir [puriːr], *decay*
le **public** [pyblik], *the public*
quelque [kɛlk(ə)], adj., *some*
rendre [rãːdr], *render, do, make*
le **service** [sɛrvis], *service*
le **temps** [tã], *time*
tirer [tire], *draw, derive, get*
trop [trɔ *or* tro], *too much, too*

en même temps, *at the same time;* au bout de quelque temps, *after some time*

A. Continue: 1. Je vends ces pommes au marchand, tu, etc. 2. Je n'en vends pas beaucoup, tu, etc.   3. Je finis cette longue leçon, tu, etc.   4. Je ne finis pas la leçon d'histoire, tu, etc. (*also interrogatively*).   5. Est-ce que je perds du temps? est-ce que tu? etc.

B. Supply the proper form of ce: 1. C ... marchand; c ... marchands.   2. C ... élève (*m.*); c ... élève (*f.*); c ... élèves.   3. C ... autre livre; c ... autres hommes.   4. C ... autre plume; c ... autres amies.   5. C ... arbre-ci; c ... arbres-là.

C. 1. Mon père a beaucoup de pommiers dans son verger. 2. Les pommiers fleurissent au printemps. 3. Au bout de quelque temps on voit de petites pommes sur les branches. 4. Pendant l'été les pommes grossissent. 5. En automne elles mûrissent. 6. Quand on les laisse trop longtemps sur les pommiers elles tombent. 7. Alors elles pourrissent. 8. Quand nos pommes sont mûres nous les vendons aux marchands. 9. Les marchands les transportent à la ville. 10. Et là on les vend au public. 11. Mon père et les marchands en tirent des bénéfices, et en même temps ils rendent un grand service au public.

D. (*Oral.*) 1. Quand ces pommiers fleurissent-ils? 2. Que voit-on sur les branches des pommiers? 3. Quand est-ce que les petites pommes grossissent? 4. Quand mûrissent-elles? 5. Les pommes tombent-elles en automne? 6. À qui vendons-nous les pommes? 7. Ces marchands vendent-ils beaucoup de pommes? 8. À qui en vendent-ils? 9. Qui en tire des bénéfices? etc.

E. 1. When do apples ripen? 2. Are these apples already ripe? 3. No, those apples are still green, but these apples are ripe. 4. Those apples are growing larger. 5. They are ripening already. 6. The ripe apples are falling. 7. The apples which fall decay. 8. I sell my apples to the dealer. 9. He derives profit (*pl.*) from them. 10. I do (render) him a service. 11. He does the public a service. 12. We do the public a great service. 13. Are my father and the dealer not doing the public a service? 14. They are.

F. 1. These pupils often lose (lose often) their books. 2. Do you often lose your books? 3. This little girl often loses her gloves. 4. We lose our time when we do not listen to the teacher. 5. I am finishing this French lesson. 6. Mary is finishing a long letter. 7. Why do you not finish your lessons? 8. We are finishing them now. 9. Those dealers sell us apples. 10. Are you selling those apples? 11. I am not; they are not yet ripe. 12. We sell our apples when they are ripe. 13. Our cherries and strawberries ripen in summer.

LESSON XX

44.   **Past Participles**

Given	*Finished*	*Sold*	*Had*	*Been*
donné [dɔne]	fini [fini]	vendu [vãdy]	eu [y]	été [ete]

45. Compound Tenses. — The compound tenses of a verb are formed by adding its past participle to the various simple tenses of an auxiliary verb (usually **avoir**, sometimes **être**, cf. § 51).

46.   **The Past Indefinite**

I have given (finished, etc.) or I gave (I finished, etc.)

j'ai	donné (fini, vendu, eu, été)
tu as	donné (fini, vendu, eu, été)
il a	donné (fini, vendu, eu, été)
nous avons	donné (fini, vendu, eu, été)
vous avez	donné (fini, vendu, eu, été)
ils ont	donné (fini, vendu, eu, été)

47. Use of Past Indefinite. — It denotes not only what has happened or has been happening, as in English, but also what happened (= English past tense):

J'ai fini mon ouvrage.	*I have finished my work.*
Il a travaillé au jardin.	*He has been working in the garden.*
Elle a été ici hier.	*She was here yesterday.*
Nous avons quitté Paris en hiver.	*We left Paris in (the) winter.*

NOTE. — The past indefinite is the ordinary past tense of French. For the past tense of narrative in the literary style, see § 152.

48. Word-Order. — 1. In compound tenses, rules of word-order (cf. §§ 8, 11, 23) regularly apply to the auxiliary:

Nous **ne** l'avons **pas** fini.	*We have not finished it.*
N'a-t-elle **pas** été diligente?	*Has she not been industrious?*

2. No adverb (except **ne**) may come between the subject and the verb:

Je perds **souvent** mon temps.	*I often lose my time.*

3. As may be learned from observation, certain adverbs, such as **bien**, **déjà**, **pas**, **plus**, **jamais**, etc., regularly come between the auxiliary and the participle:

> Il a **bien** parlé.　　　　　　　*He has spoken well.*

(*a*) But **aujourd'hui**, **hier**, **demain**, **autrefois**, **tard**, **ici**, **là**, may not come between auxiliary and participle.

NOTE. — Great variety is found in the position of adverbs and adverbial phrases, but the above rules should be observed in the following exercises.

EXERCISE XX

abord (d') [d abɔːr], (*at*) *first*

battre [batr], *beat, thresh*

bien [bjɛ̃], *well, very, very well*

bientôt [bjɛ̃to], *soon*

le blé [ble], *wheat*

le boulanger [bulɑ̃ʒe], *baker*

ensuite [ɑ̃sɥit], *then, next, afterwards*

l'épi [epi], m., *ear (of grain), head*

la farine [farin], *flour*

la grange [grɑ̃ːʒ], *barn*

jaunir [ʒoniːr], *grow (become) yellow*

labourer [labure], *plough*

manger [mɑ̃ʒe], *eat*

le meunier [mønje], *miller*

le moissonneur [mwasɔnœːr], *harvester*

la plupart [plypaːr], *the most part*

pour [pur], prep., *for, in order to, to*

puis [pɥi], *then, next, afterwards*

la récolte [rekɔlt], *harvest, crop*

semer [səme], *sow*

vite [vit], *quickly*

vu [vy], p. part. of **voir** (irreg.), *seen*

A. Continue: 1. J'ai déjà coupé mon blé, tu . . . ton, etc. 2. Je l'ai déjà coupé, etc. 3. Je n'ai pas encore labouré mon champ, tu . . . ton, etc. 4. Je n'ai pas été à l'école aujourd'hui, etc. 5. Je n'y ai pas été, etc. 6. Est-ce que j'ai vendu du pain? as-tu vendu? etc. 7. Je n'en ai pas vendu, etc. 8. Je n'en ai pas eu, etc.

B. 1. D'abord on a labouré les champs. 2. Puis on y a semé le blé. 3. Les oiseaux n'en ont pas beaucoup mangé (*or* mangé beaucoup). 4. Pour la plupart il a bien poussé. 5. Bientôt on a vu les beaux épis. 6. Ensuite les champs ont jauni. 7. Au bout de quelque temps les moissonneurs ont coupé le blé. 8. Ils l'ont transporté à la grange, et puis ils l'ont battu. 9. Nous avons eu une bonne récolte. 10. On a vendu beaucoup de blé au meunier. 11. Le meunier a vendu sa farine au boulanger. 12. Le boulanger a vendu son pain au public. 13. Et tout le monde a été content.

C. (*Oral.*) 1. Avez-vous déjà labouré votre champ? 2. Qu'est-ce que vous y avez semé? 3. Les oiseaux en ont-ils mangé? 4. Le blé a-t-il bien poussé? 5. Les champs ont-ils jauni très vite? 6. Jaunissent-ils au printemps? 7. Qui a coupé le blé? 8. Quand l'a-t-on coupé? 9. Où l'a-t-on transporté? 10. Qui l'a battu? 11. À qui l'avez-vous vendu? 12. À qui le meunier a-t-il vendu la farine? etc.

D. 1. We ploughed our fields in spring. 2. Then we sowed wheat in them. 3. Did the birds eat much of it? 4. They didn't eat much of it. 5. The wheat grew well. 6. It grew very quickly. 7. And we admired the fine heads. 8. Soon these heads became yellow. 9. They became yellow during the summer. 10. Wheat becomes yellow when it ripens. 11. The harvesters have cut all our wheat. 12. They have been threshing it to-day.

E. 1. The wheat has been taken (use *on*) to the barn. 2. We had a great deal of it (put *beaucoup* last). 3. After some time it was threshed (use *on*). 4. The harvesters threshed it. 5. Then we sold some of it to the miller. 6. But he didn't get (= have) all our wheat. 7. We left some of it in the barn. 8. We gave the straw to the cows and sheep. 9. The miller sold his flour to the baker. 10. The baker sold good bread to the public. 11. Everybody ate some of it. 12. Did you have some of it?

LESSON XXI

49. Agreement of Past Participle. — 1. When a direct object, noun or pronoun, precedes the auxiliary **avoir** in a compound tense, the past participle agrees in gender and number with that direct object:

Quels **livres** a-t-il achetés?	*What books has he bought?*
J'ai vendu mes pommes.	*I have sold my apples.*
Je **les** ai vendues.	*I have sold them.*
La viande **que** j'ai achetée.	*The meat that I have bought.*
En avez-vous acheté?	*Have you bought any (of it)?*

(*a*) **En** is not a direct object; hence, no agreement.

2. When used as an adjective, the past participle agrees like an adjective (cf. § 14).

L'année passée.   *Last year.*

50.   Interrogative Adjective

SINGULAR   PLURAL

m. **quel?** [kɛl], f. **quelle?** [kɛl]   m. **quels?** [kɛl], f. **quelles?** [kɛl]
which? what?   *which? what?*

Quel livre?   **Quelle** plume?   *Which (what) book?   Which (what) pen?*

Quels sont vos livres?   *Which are your books?*

(a) In exclamations **quel** = *what a!* (sing.), *what!* (plur.).

Quelle belle vue! **Quels** crimes! *What a fine view!   What crimes!*

EXERCISE XXI

acheter [aʃte], *buy*
aigre [ɛːgr], *sour*
l'an [ã], m., *year*
l'année [ane], f., *year*
le client [kliã], *client, customer, patient*
cueillir [kœjiːr], *pluck, gather*
donner [dɔne], *yield*
l'échelle [eʃɛl], f., *ladder*

l'espèce [ɛspɛs], f., *species, kind*
l'heure [œːr], f., *hour*
le panier [panje], *basket*
passer [pɑse], *pass, spend* (time)
la perte [pɛrt], *loss*
le poirier [pwarje], *pear tree*
revendre [rəvãːdr], *sell again*
tard [taːr], *late*

l'année passée, *last year;* de bonne heure, *early;* tous les ans (jours), *every year (day)*

A. Continue: 1. Voici les livres que j'ai achetés, . . . que tu . . ., etc.   2. Quelles sont les langues que j'ai étudiées? . . . que tu . . ., etc.   3. Voilà la maison que j'ai vendue, . . . que tu . . ., etc.   4. Les leçons que j'ai finies, . . . que tu . . ., etc.   5. Le livre qui m'a amusé(e), . . . qui t'a . . ., etc.

B. 1. Dans notre verger il y a cent poiriers.   2. Ils nous ont donné beaucoup de poires cette année.   3. Ils en donnent beaucoup tous les ans.   4. Quelles espèces de poires avez-vous?   5. Nous en avons plusieurs.   6. Nous en avons de douces et d'aigres.   7. Nous en avons qui mûrissent de bonne heure et d'autres qui mûrissent

tard. 8. On les a déjà toutes cueillies sans perte. 9. Pour les
cueillir on a des échelles et des paniers. 10. Nous les avons toutes
vendues dans la ville. 11. M. Liard les a achetées. 12. C'est le
même marchand qui a acheté nos poires l'année passée. 13. Les
poires sont chères cette année. 14. M. Liard les a revendues à ses
clients. 15. Il en a tiré de gros bénéfices.

C. (*Oral.*) 1. Combien de poiriers avez-vous? 2. Est-ce qu'ils
ont donné beaucoup de poires? 3. Quelles espèces de poires avez-
vous? 4. Mûrissent-elles de bonne heure? 5. Les avez-vous déjà
cueillies? 6. Qu'a-t-on pour les cueillir? 7. En avez-vous perdu
beaucoup? 8. A-t-on cueilli les poires vertes? 9. Où a-t-on vendu
les poires? 10. À qui les avez-vous vendues? 11. Qui est M.
Liard? 12. À qui vend-il des poires? etc.

D. 1. Our pear trees yield us a great many pears. 2. We have
a good crop of them every year. 3. We have had many kinds of
pears this year. 4. We have gathered them already. 5. They were
gathered (use *on*) in autumn. 6. We didn't lose any of them.
7. The pears ripened early this year. 8. Last year they ripened
late. 9. We have sold them all. 10. We sold them to our customers.
11. What pears did you not sell? 12. We didn't sell the pears which
ripened late. 13. The pears we didn't sell are in the cellar.
14. Dealers make large profits from our apples and pears.

E. 1. Where are the letters which the postman brought me?
2. I have found the pen which you lost. 3. Here are the gloves I
bought you. 4. The lessons we had to-day are too long. 5. What
lessons have you been studying? 6. What books have you brought
me? 7. What pens have you given him? 8. What pupils went
with you to school? 9. What trees have been cut down (use *on*)?
10. John has found the papers which you have been looking for.
11. These are interesting books which you have given me. 12. These
apples that I have bought are very sour. 13. We have baskets
and ladders for gathering pears.

LESSON XXII

51. Compound Tenses with *être*. — 1. From **être** + the past participle are formed the compound tenses of some intransitive verbs denoting motion or change of condition; such are:

aller, *go*	**monter**, *go up*	**retourner**, *go back*
arriver, *arrive*	**mourir**, *die*	**revenir**, *come back*
descendre, *descend*	**naître**, *be born*	**sortir**, *go (come) out*
devenir, *become*	**partir**, *set out*	**tomber**, *fall*
entrer, *enter*	**rentrer**, *go in again*	**venir**, *come*

(a) Irregular past participles: **mort** (mourir), **né** (naître), **venu** (venir); e.g. **Il est mort**, *He died* (or *is dead*); **Il est né**, *He was born.*

2. The past participle of such verbs must agree with the subject, like an adjective (cf. § 14):

I have arrived (*I arrived*), etc.

je suis arrivé *or* ée	nous sommes arrivés *or* ées
tu es arrivé *or* ée	vous êtes arrivés *or* ées
il est arrivé	ils sont arrivés
elle est arrivée	elles sont arrivées

(a) The auxiliary is to be translated by *have.*

EXERCISE XXII

arriver [arive], *arrive, come*
la beauté [bote], *beauty, fine sight (thing)*
chez [ʃe], *at the house (etc.) of*
la chose [ʃoːz], *thing*
entrer [ɑ̃tre] **dans**, *enter, go into*
faire [fɛːr], *do, make*
fait [fɛ], p. part. of **faire**
hier [jeːr], *yesterday*
lointain [lwɛ̃tɛ̃], *distant*
Louise [lwiːz], *Louisa*

le magasin [magazɛ̃], *shop, store*
magnifique [maɲifik], *magnificent*
le matin [matɛ̃], *morning*
par [par], *by, through*
le parc [park], *park*
partir [partiːr], *set out, start, leave*
rentrer [rɑ̃tre], *go (come) in again, go (come) home*
la rue [ry], *street*
le soir [swaːr], *evening*
sortir [sortiːr], *go (come) out*

chez mon père, *at the house (place of business, etc.) of my father, at my father's;* **faire une promenade**, *take a walk (drive, etc.).*

A. Continue: 1. Je suis arrivé(e) ce matin, etc. 2. Je suis parti(e) hier, etc. 3. Je ne suis pas entré(e) dans la salle, etc. 4. Je n'y suis pas entré(e), etc. 5. Est-ce que je suis sorti(e) de l'église? es-tu . . . etc. 6. Je n'en suis pas sorti(e), etc.

B. Put into the past indefinite, supplying proper auxiliary and past participle: 1. Ces dames . . . *sortir.* 2. Quand . . . -vous *arriver,* mademoiselle? 3. Je . . . *arriver* hier. 4. Est-ce que vos sœurs . . . *partir?* 5. *Form additional examples employing the verbs in* § 51.

C. 1. Nous sommes arrivés hier soir chez nos cousins qui demeurent dans une ville lointaine. 2. Ce matin nous sommes partis de bonne heure pour faire une promenade. 3. Nos cousins nous ont accompagnés pour nous montrer les beautés de la ville. 4. Il y a un très beau parc dans cette ville. 5. Nous y avons passé quelque temps, et ensuite nous sommes entrés dans une belle église qui nous a beaucoup intéressés. 6. Quand nous sommes sortis de l'église nous sommes entrés dans un grand magasin. 7. Nous n'y avons pas acheté beaucoup de choses. 8. Mais nous avons admiré les belles choses que nous y avons vues. 9. Puis nous sommes sortis du magasin et nous sommes rentrés chez nos cousins par une rue magnifique.

D. (Oral.) 1. Où demeurent vos cousins? 2. Quand êtes-vous partis? 3. Quand êtes-vous arrivés? 4. Est-ce une belle ville que vous avez vue? 5. Êtes-vous sortis? 6. Pourquoi? 7. Qui vous a accompagnés? 8. Êtes-vous partis de bonne heure? 9. Les rues de cette ville sont-elles belles? 10. Les avez-vous admirées? 11. Où êtes-vous entrés? 12. Qu'est-ce que vous avez fait ensuite? 13. Et alors qu'avez-vous fait? etc.

E. 1. Our cousins arrived this morning. 2. This morning they went out to (*pour*) take a walk. 3. My brother accompanied them. 4. They set out together. 5. He showed them the fine sights of the city. 6. First they went into a magnificent park. 7. They didn't spend much time there. 8. Then they went into the old church which you (*on*) see beside the park. 9. It is a very beautiful church. 10. My cousins admired it very much. 11. When they came out of the church they went into one of the fine stores. 12. Afterwards they went home.

F. 1. Have your cousins arrived? 2. Louisa arrived yesterday, but Charles and his brother haven't come yet. 3. My mother has gone out with my cousin (*f.*) to show her the city. 4. They went out together this morning. 5. They set out early. 6. They went into one of the large stores. 7. Have they come home yet (*déjà*)? 8. Yes, they returned home through one of our magnificent streets. 9. My mother has been showing us the fine things that they bought. 10. We admired them very much. 11. Charles and his brother are here now. 12. They arrived this evening very late. 13. We are all glad to (*de*) see them. 14. My aunt was born and she died in this city.

LESSON XXIII

52.   Disjunctive Personal Pronouns

Singular	Plural
moi [mwa], *I, me*	**nous** [nu], *we, us*
toi [twa], *thou, thee, you*	**vous** [vu], *you*
lui [lɥi], *he, him*	**eux** [ø], *they* (m.), *them* (m.)
elle [ɛl], *she, her*	**elles** [ɛl], *they* (f.), *them* (f.)
soi [swa], *oneself, himself, etc.*	

(*a*) These forms regularly denote persons, and are called "disjunctive" because they may be used apart from the verb.

(*b*) The ordinary rule of agreement applies (cf. § 7).

53. Disjunctives with Prepositions. — A personal pronoun governed by a preposition takes the disjunctive form:

Il parle de **moi** (toi, eux, etc.).   *He speaks of me (you, them, etc.).*

EXERCISE XXIII

Alice [alis], *Alice*	**avant** [avɑ̃], prep., *before* (of time)
après [aprɛ], prep., *after*	**le voisin** [vwazɛ̃], *neighbour*

à qui est cette maison? *to whom does that house belong?* or *whose house is that?* **elle est à mon père,** *it belongs to my father* (*is my father's*); **elle est à lui,** *it belongs to him* (*it is his*); **mon cousin est chez nous,** *my cousin is at our house;* **notre voisin n'est pas chez lui** (or **à la maison**) **aujourd'hui,** *our neighbour is not at home to-day;* **je suis arrivé tard chez moi** (or **à la maison**), *I arrived home late;* **tout le monde est chez soi,** *everybody is at home*

A. Continue: 1. Mes amis sont chez moi, . . . chez toi, etc. 2. Je ne suis pas chez moi, tu . . . toi, etc. 3. Ce livre est-il à moi, . . . à toi? etc. 4. Il n'est pas à moi, . . . à toi, etc. 5. Ce matin on a parlé de moi, . . . de toi, etc. 6. Charles est arrivé avant moi, . . . toi, etc.

B. 1. Our neighbours are not at home to-day. 2. My mother is not at home. 3. Our cousins are at our house. 4. My little sisters are playing with them. 5. Alice is playing with Louisa. 6. She is playing with her. 7. Why do you not play with me? 8. This picture is for you (thee). 9. This pencil is mine. 10. Those pencils are theirs (*f.*). 11. Have you been at your uncle's? 12. We haven't been at his house this summer. 13. Whose keys are these?

C. 1. There is our teacher. 2. We have been speaking of him. 3. He spoke of you (thee) and me in school to-day. 4. He is not pleased with (*de*) me. 5. Charles arrived before me. 6. I arrived after him. 7. We arrived after them (*f.*). 8. Are these letters for them? 9. Do these pens belong to Louisa? 10. Yes, they are hers. 11. They are not mine. 12. Does Mr. Liard live here? 13. He does, but he is not at home.

LESSON XXIV

54. Disjunctives continued. — In addition to their use after prepositions (§ 53), they are employed as follows: —

1. As the real (or logical) subject with **ce** (cf. § 35):

C'est **moi** (toi, lui, elle, nous, vous), ce sont **eux** (elles).	*It is I (thou, he, she, we, you), it is they.*
Est-ce **moi** (toi, lui, elle, nous, vous), sont-ce **eux** (elles)?	*Is it I (thou, he, she, we, you), is it they?*

(*a*) In the third plural c'est eux (elles), **est**-ce eux (elles)? are often found.

2. When a verb is implied, but not expressed:

Qui est là? — **Moi** (eux, elle).	*Who is there? — I (they, she).*
Qui as-tu vu? — **Lui** (elles).	*Whom did you see? — Him (them).*

3. In comparisons, and after **ne . . . que:**

Il est plus grand que **moi.**	*He is taller than I.*
Il ne chante pas comme **eux.**	*He does not sing as they do.*
Je n'ai vu que **lui.**	*I saw him only.*

4. In appositions, often with the emphatic addition of **même**:

Moi je l'ai entendu aussi.	*I heard it too.*
Vous l'avez vu **vous-même(s).**	*You saw it yourself(-selves).*

5. When the subject or object is compound:

Vous et **lui** (vous) l'avez fait.	*You and he have done it.*
Son **ami** et **lui** sont ici.	*His friend and he are here.*
Je vous vois, **toi** et ton **frère.**	*I see you and your brother.*

6. Soi regularly has indefinite or general force:

Chacun pour **soi.**	*Everybody for himself.*
But: Il est content de **lui**(-même).	*He is satisfied with himself.*

55. Present Indicative of *voir* (irreg.), 'see'

I see, I am seeing, I do see, etc.

je vois [vwa]	nous voyons [vwajɔ̃]
tu vois [vwa]	vous voyez [vwaje]
il voit [vwa]	ils voient [vwa]

EXERCISE XXIV

l'auteur [otœːr], m., *author*	**oh** [o], *oh*
bien [bjɛ̃], *indeed, truly*	**penser** [pɑ̃se], *think*
le colonel [kɔlɔnɛl], *colonel*	**la pièce** [pjɛs], *play* (theatre)
comme [kɔm], *as, like*	**près de** [prɛ də], *near*
la comtesse [kɔ̃tɛs], *countess*	**le rôle** [roːl], *rôle, part*
la connaissance [kɔnɛsɑ̃ːs], *ac-*	**le théâtre** [teɑːtr], *theatre*
quaintance	**vrai** [vrɛ], *true*
la loge [lɔːʒ], *box* (theatre)	

en effet [ɛfɛ], *in fact, indeed, it is true;* **de l'autre côté,** *on the other side, over there;* **c'est vrai,** *it (that) is true;* **c'est votre ami, n'est-ce pas?** *it is your friend, is it not?* **mais non,** *no, no!*

A. Continue: 1. C'est moi qui l'ai trouvé, c'est toi qui l'as . . . etc. 2. Est-ce moi qui l'ai perdu? etc. 3. Ce n'est pas moi, ce n'est pas toi, etc. 4. N'est-ce pas moi? etc.

B. (*Un frère et une sœur au théâtre*) 1. C'est une pièce de (*by*) Labiche, n'est-ce pas? — 2. Oui, c'est lui qui en est l'auteur. — 3. C'est Coquelin qui joue le rôle de M. Perrichon? — 4. Oui, c'est lui. — 5. Y a-t-il de nos connaissances au théâtre ce soir? — 6. Oh oui; voilà là-bas deux de mes amies. — 7. En effet ce sont elles. —

8. Et voilà de l'autre côté trois de tes amis. — 9. C'est vrai; ce sont eux. Ils nous regardent. Ils nous saluent. Derrière eux dans une loge on voit [le] colonel D. — 10. Oui, c'est bien lui. Près de lui dans cette autre loge je vois la comtesse de B. — 11. Mais non, ce n'est pas elle, je pense. — 12. Qui est-ce alors? — 13. C'est la dame que nous avons rencontrée chez la comtesse. — 14. Son frère est avec elle, n'est-ce pas? — 15. Oui, elle et lui sont toujours ensemble comme toi et moi.

C. (*Oral on B, above.*)

D. 1. Is Augier the author of this play? 2. He is not (= it is not he). 3. It is Labiche. 4. It is not he who plays the rôle of Perrichon. 5. That is Coquelin. 6. Is it (the) countess (of) B. whom we (*on*) see in that box? 7. It is. 8. Who is that lady beside her? 9. It is Mrs. D. whom we saw at her house. 10. Did I not see her at your house? 11. It was (is) her sister whom you saw at my house. 12. (The) Colonel B. is in the other box. 13. His wife is with him. 14. It is they who live near us.

E. 1. It is I. 2. It is they (*m.*). 3. It is they (*f.*) isn't it? 4. Is it they (*m.*)? 5. Is that you? 6. It is. 7. I was there myself. 8. You saw him yourselves. 9. This book is mine. 10. It belongs to me. 11. I bought it myself in the city. 12. Mary and her brother are here. 13. She and her brother are playing with us. 14. She and he are always together. 15. It is they who are going with us. 16. Who has seen that play by Labiche? 17. I [have].

LESSON XXV

56. Comparatives. — 1. To form comparatives, **plus** = *more*, **moins** = *less*, or **aussi** = *as*, is placed before the adjective, and **que** = *than* or *as* after it:

Il est **plus** grand **que** Jean.	*He is taller than John.*
Il est **moins** grand **que** moi.	*He is not so tall as I.*
Il est **aussi** grand **qu'**elle.	*He is as tall as she.*

2. With a negative, **aussi** generally becomes **si**:

Il n'est pas **si** grand (*or* il est moins grand) que moi.	*He is not so tall as I.*

57. Superlatives. — 1. To form superlatives, the definite article or a possessive adjective precedes **plus, moins**:

Elle est **la** plus (moins) aimable.   *She is the most (least) amiable.*
C'est **mon** meilleur ami.   *He is my best friend.*

OBSERVE. — La plus jeune des deux. *The younger of the two.*

2. The definite article must not be omitted when the adjective follows the noun:

La leçon **la** plus difficile.   *The most difficult lesson.*

3. After a superlative, *in* = **de** in such sentences as:

La plus jeune **de** la classe.   *The youngest (girl) in the class.*

58. Irregular Comparison. — Observe the following:

bon, *good*	meilleur, *better*	le meilleur, *the best*
mauvais, *bad*	pire, *worse*	le pire, *the worst*
petit, *small*	moindre, *less*	le moindre, *the least*

(*a*) **Pire** is less common than **plus mauvais**, and serves also as a comparative to **méchant**, *bad, evil, wicked*.

(*b*) In general, **moindre** = *less* (in importance), **plus petit** = *smaller, less* (in size).

59. Comparison of Adverbs. — 1. They are regularly compared like adjectives, but **le** of the superlative is invariable:

Plus (moins, aussi) facilement.   *More (less, as) easily.*
Le plus (moins) souvent.   *(The) most (least) frequently.*

2. But observe the irregular forms:

bien, *well*	mieux, *better*	beaucoup, *much*	plus, *more*
mal, *badly* { pis or plus mal, *worse*		peu, *little*	moins, *less*

3. **Plus** (**moins**), as adverb of quantity, requires **de** (= *than*) before a numeral:

Il en a plus **de** dix livres.   *He has more than ten pounds of it.*

EXERCISE XXV

A. Continue: 1. Je suis plus grand que Jean, tu . . . etc. 2. Il est moins fort que moi, . . . toi, etc. 3. Est-ce que je suis plus petite qu'elle? es-tu . . .? etc. 4. Je suis la meilleure élève de la classe, tu, etc. 5. N'ai-je pas la leçon là plus difficile? etc. 6. J'ai vendu mes meilleures pommes, tu . . . tes, etc.   7. Est-ce que j'aime mieux les fleurs rouges? aimes-tu . . . ? etc.   8. J'en ai moins de deux livres, tu, etc.

B.   1. I am as tall as you.   2. But I am not so strong as you. 3. You are taller than your brother, are you not?   4. John is as tall and as strong as he.   5. The pears are not so ripe as the apples. 6. John's lesson is very difficult.   7. He has the most difficult lesson.   8. His lesson is the most difficult of all the lessons.   9. Alice is the most industrious pupil in our class.   10. George skates better than I.   11. He doesn't skate as well as you.   12. He skates very badly, in fact.   13. But we skate oftener than he.   14. He skates very little.

C.   1. The grass is less abundant in this field.   2. Your house is the oldest house in the town.   3. Our house is much better; we like it better.   4. Our neighbours' house is larger.   5. This picture is still worse than the other.   6. It is a picture without the least merit.   7. Charles always arrives at school later than I.   8. Here is the most interesting of my books.   9. These pens are very bad. 10. Those pens are still worse.   11. I have bought more than four pounds of meat.   12. I wish two pounds of your best tea.   13. You always arrive later than the others.   14. And you work still less than they.   15. I have more friends than you.   16. I have fewer (= less) friends, but I have more money.

LESSON XXVI

60. The Infinitive. — The commoner uses of the infinitive are: —

1. Following directly after certain verbs, such as:

aller, *go*	**faire**, *make, cause*	**savoir**, *know how to*
désirer, *desire*	**falloir**, *be necessary*	**voir**, *see*
devoir, *owe*	**laisser**, *let*	**vouloir**, *will, wish*
espérer, *hope*	**pouvoir**, *be able, can*	

Pouvez-vous me prêter de l'encre?	*Can you lend me some ink?*
Nous allons acheter du thé.	*We are going to buy some tea.*
Désire-t-il nous parler?	*Does he wish to speak to us?*
Il faut acheter de la viande.	*We (you, etc.) must buy some meat.*

2. Preceded by **de** after many verbs, such as:

cesser, *cease*   ordonner, *order*   refuser, *refuse*
dire, *tell*   prier, *beg, request*   tâcher, *attempt, try*
éviter, *avoid*

Elle a cessé **de** chanter.   *She has ceased singing.*
Je vous prie **de** m'écouter.   *I beg you to listen to me.*

3. Preceded by **de** after nouns and some adjectives:

Le crime **de** voler.   *The crime of stealing.*
Je suis content **de** vous voir.   *I am glad to see you.*

4. Preceded by **à** after many verbs, such as:

aimer, *like*   enseigner, *teach*   réussir, *succeed*
apprendre, *learn*   inviter, *invite*

Je les ai invités **à** rester.   *I invited them to stay.*
J'aime (**à**) patiner.   *I like to skate.*

(*a*) **à** after **aimer** is sometimes omitted.

5. Preceded by **à** after some adjectives:

Je suis prêt **à** partir.   *I am ready to set out (go).*
Cet ouvrage est facile **à** faire.   *That work is easy to do.*

6. Preceded by prepositions other than **de** or **à**:

J'ai parlé **sans** penser.   *I spoke without thinking.*
Il écoute **pour** apprendre.   *He listens in order to learn.*

7. Observe its use to render English forms in *–ing:*

Il parle de **partir**.   *He speaks of going.*
Il est parti sans nous **parler**.   *He went without speaking to us.*

61.   **Present Indicative of *aller* (irreg.)**

I go, I am going, I do go, etc.

je vais [ve]	nous allons [alɔ̃]
tu vas [va]	vous allez [ale]
il va [va]	ils vont [vɔ̃]

62.   **Present Indicative of *pouvoir* (irreg.)**

I am able to, I can, I may, etc.

je peux *or* puis [pø, pɥi]	nous pouvons [puvɔ̃]
tu peux [pø]	vous pouvez [puve]
il peut [pø]	ils peuvent [pœːv]

(*a*) In questions: **puis-je?** or **est-ce que je peux (puis)?**

EXERCISE XXVI

dîner [dine], vb., *dine*
le dîner [dine], *dinner*
il faut [fo], pres. indic. of falloir,
　it is necessary
le fruit [frui], *fruit*
l'intention [ɛ̃tɑ̃sjɔ̃], f., *intention*
inviter [ɛ̃vite], *invite*
le légume [legym], *vegetable*
le marché [marʃe], *market*

le morceau [mɔrso], *piece, bit*
l'œuf [œf], m., pl. œufs [ø], *egg*
offrir [ɔfriːr], *offer*
l'omelette [ɔmlɛt], f., *omelet*
orner [ɔrne], *ornament, decorate*
réussir [reysiːr], *succeed*
six [sis], *six*
tâcher [taʃe], *attempt, try*
venir [vəniːr], *come*

avoir l'intention de, *intend to;* il faut acheter, *one (we, you, they, etc.)
must buy;* il lui (nous, etc.) faut acheter, *he (we, etc.) must buy*

A. Continue: 1. Je vais acheter de bons légumes, tu . . ., etc.
2. Je ne peux pas en trouver. 3. Je suis rentré(e) sans en acheter. 4. Puis-je trouver des fruits au marché? 5. J'ai réussi à en
trouver de très bons. 6. Je tâche de faire une bonne omelette.
7. J'ai l'intention d'inviter des amis à dîner. 8. Je suis con-
tent(e) de les voir. 9. Je ne suis pas prêt(e) à partir. 10. Je les
vois venir.

B. (Madame X. et sa bonne) 1. Nous avons invité des amis à
dîner ce soir. 2. Nous allons en avoir six. 3. Je vais au marché
et vous allez m'accompagner, Louise. — 4. Bien, madame, j'ai mon
panier. 5. Je suis prête à partir. — 6. Pouvons-nous trouver maintenant de bons légumes au marché? — 7. Oh, oui, on peut en avoir
(*get*) de très bons, je pense. — 8. J'ai aussi l'intention d'acheter des
œufs pour faire une omelette. — 9. Les bons œufs sont souvent
difficiles à trouver, mais on réussit quelquefois à en avoir. — 10. Il
faut chercher aussi un bon morceau de viande. 11. Les bons morceaux ne sont pas toujours faciles à trouver. 12. Mais nous allons
tâcher d'en avoir. — 13. Il faut acheter des fruits et aussi des fleurs
pour orner la table. 14. Nous sommes contents de voir nos amis
quand nous avons un bon dîner à leur offrir.

C. (Oral.) 1. Votre mère invite-t-elle des amis à dîner? 2. Combien d'amis va-t-elle avoir à table ce soir? 3. Qui va l'accompagner
au marché? 4. Sont-elles prêtes à partir? 5. Sont-elles déjà parties?
6. Que cherchent-elles d'abord au marché? 7. Peut-on trouver de

bons légumes au marché? 8. Pourquoi va-t-elle acheter des œufs?
9. Les bons œufs sont-ils faciles à trouver? 10. A-t-elle réussi à
en trouver? 11. Pourquoi va-t-elle acheter des fleurs? etc.

D. 1. I am going to invite some friends to dinner (to dine).
2. Are you going to the market? 3. Yes, I am (going there). 4. You
can go with me, can't you? 5. Here is my basket; I am ready to go.
6. Can we (*on*) find good vegetables in the market to-day? 7. Yes,
I saw some very good ones. 8. Do you not intend to buy some eggs?
9. Are you going to make an omelet? 10. An omelet is easy to
make when one has good eggs. 11. Good eggs are not always easy
to find. 12. I am trying to find some. 13. I have succeeded in
finding some. 14. We must buy a good piece of meat. 15. I
intend to have cherries or strawberries.

E. 1. Good meat is hard to find. 2. You (*on*) can always find
good meat at Mr. Liard's. 3. Have you bought the flowers? 4. We
must have some to decorate the table. 5. I am not going to buy
any. 6. Can we not gather some in the garden? 7. Now we are
going to look for some fruit (*plur.*). 8. We must buy some fruit.
9. I intend to buy a great deal of it. 10. Are you glad to see your
friends? 11. Yes, I am glad to see them. 12. Have you a good
dinner to offer them? 13. Yes, we are going to give (*offrir*) them a
good dinner. 14. We have invited them to come early. 15. We
see them coming. 16. You can't speak French without studying a
great deal.

LESSON XXVII

63.   Imperfect Indicative of *donner*, *finir*, *vendre*

I was giving, etc.		*I was finishing, etc.*		*I was selling, etc.*	
je donnais	[dɔnɛ]	finissais	[finisɛ]	vendais	[vãdɛ]
tu donnais	[dɔnɛ]	finissais	[finisɛ]	vendais	[vãdɛ]
il donnait	[dɔnɛ]	finissait	[finisɛ]	vendait	[vãdɛ]
nous donnions	[dɔnjɔ̃]	finissions	[finisjɔ̃]	vendions	[vãdjɔ̃]
vous donniez	[dɔnje]	finissiez	[finisje]	vendiez	[vãdje]
ils donnaient	[dɔnɛ]	finissaient	[finisɛ]	vendaient	[vãdɛ]

64. Imperfect Indicative of *avoir* and *être*

I had, used to have, etc. *I was, used to be, etc.*

j'avais [avɛ] j'étais [etɛ]
tu avais [avɛ] tu étais [etɛ]
il avait [avɛ] il était [etɛ]

nous avions [avjɔ̃] nous étions [etjɔ̃]
vous aviez [avje] vous étiez [etje]
ils avaient [avɛ] ils étaient [etɛ]

65. Use of Imperfect. — 1. It denotes what used to happen or continued to happen:

Nous **parlions** souvent de vous. *We often used to speak of you.*
Il **perdait** souvent sa plume. *He would often lose his pen.*
Mon oncle **était** très vieux. *My uncle was very old.*

2. It denotes what was happening when something else happened (cf. § 47) or was happening:

On **chantait** quand je suis venu. *They were singing when I came.*
Il **parlait** pendant que nous *He was speaking while we sang*
chantions. *(were singing).*

66. Present and Imperfect Indicative of *faire* (irreg.)

I do, am doing, etc. *I was doing, etc.*

je fais [fɛ] je faisais [fəzɛ]
tu fais [fɛ] tu faisais [fəzɛ]
il fait [fɛ] il faisait [fəzɛ]

nous faisons [fəzɔ̃] nous faisions [fəzjɔ̃]
vous faites [fɛt] vous faisiez [fəzje]
ils font [fɔ̃] ils faisaient [fəzɛ]

67. The Pluperfect. — The pluperfect of a verb is formed by adding its past participle to the imperfect of **avoir** or **être** (cf. §§ 45, 51), thus:

I had given, etc. *I had arrived, etc.*

j'avais donné j'étais arrivé(e)
tu avais donné, etc. tu étais arrivé(e), etc.

EXERCISE XXVII

l'abeille [abɛːj], f., *bee*
arracher [araʃe], *tear out (up)*
attraper [atrape], *catch, capture*
chanter [ʃɑ̃te], *sing*
clair [klɛːr], *clear, bright*
commencer [kɔmɑ̃se], *begin*
couler [kule], *run (of liquids)*
l'eau [o], f., *water*
hors de [ɔːr də], prep., *out of*
jamais [ʒamɛ], *ever*
le jour [ʒuːr], *day*
ne . . . jamais [nə . . . ʒamɛ], *never*

le miel [mjɛl], *honey*
la mouche [muʃ], *fly*
le nid [ni], *nest*
la nuance [nɥɑ̃ːs], *shade (of colour)*
l'ouvrage [uvraːʒ], m., *work*
pendant que [pɑ̃dɑ̃ kə], *while, whilst*
le poisson [pwasɔ̃], *fish*
le ruisseau [rɥiso], *brook, stream*
sauter [sote], *leap, jump*
sauvage [sovaːʒ], *wild*
terminer [tɛrmine], *finish, complete*
voler [vɔle], *fly*

être en fleur(s), *be in flower, blossom, bloom;* de branche en branche, *from branch to branch;* de temps en temps, *from time to time, now and then, occasionally;* il y avait, *there was, there were.*

A. Continue: 1. Je jouais et chantais tout le temps, tu, etc. 2. Je faisais souvent une promenade. 3. Est-ce que je ne finissais pas mes leçons? 4. J'étais chez moi alors. 5. J'étais arrivé avant lui. 6. Je vendais mes pommes aux marchands. 7. J'avais terminé mon ouvrage quand ils sont arrivés. 8. N'y avait-il pas de plumes dans ma boîte? 9. Qu'est-ce que je fais (faisais)?

B. 1. J'ai fait l'autre jour une promenade aux bois. 2. C'était un beau jour de printemps. 3. Les feuilles avaient commencé à pousser. 4. Elles étaient de toutes les nuances. 5. Il y avait même des arbres qui étaient en fleur(s). 6. Les écureuils sautaient de branche en branche. 7. Les oiseaux volaient d'arbre en arbre. 8. Ils chantaient pendant qu'ils faisaient leurs nids. 9. J'ai trouvé de jolies petites fleurs sauvages. 10. Je n'en ai pas cueilli. 11. Je n'arrache jamais les fleurs sauvages. 12. Il y avait aussi des abeilles qui cherchaient du miel de fleur en fleur. 13. L'eau du ruisseau coulait claire et abondante. 14. Les poissons y jouaient et sautaient hors de l'eau de temps en temps pour attraper les mouches.

C. (*Oral exercise on B, above.*)

(Be careful to distinguish between the imperfect and past indefinite in *D* and *E*.)

D. 1. What were you doing the other day? 2. I was taking a walk in the woods. 3. I spent some (*quelque*) time in the fields also. 4. It was a beautiful spring day. 5. I saw many little animals. 6. The squirrels were playing in the trees. 7. They were jumping from tree to tree. 8. The woods were full of wild flowers. 9. There were flowers of all (the) shades. 10. The birds were very merry. 11. They had begun to make their nests. 12. And they sang while they were building (*faire*) them. 13. The bees were flying from flower to flower. 14. The clear water was flowing in the streams. 15. Now and then a fish would jump out of the water. 16. It was trying to catch the flies.

E. 1. When I was at school I used to play a great deal. 2. I was very fond of skating. 3. We were speaking of you this morning. 4. I had finished my work when the postman came. 5. I had completed it already. 6. We used to sell all our apples to Mr. Liard. 7. He made large profits from them. 8. But we didn't sell him any apples this autumn. 9. We were at the door of the house when you were passing in the street. 10. You were playing while we were working. 11. The apples were ripening, but the pears were still green. 12. Robert never used to lose his books. 13. He would never come (*arriver*) late to school. 14. The teacher was not pleased with him. 15. Did you arrive before the others? 16. No, sir, they arrived before me.

LESSON XXVIII

68. Position of Pronoun Objects. — 1. Conjunctive personal pronoun objects (§ 23) and pronominal adverbs (namely **en** and **y**) come next before the verb, unless it be imperative affirmative (§ 72).

2. When two of these forms come together before the verb, their relative position is as follows:

me te se nous vous	before	le la les	before	lui leur	before **y**	before **en**

Il **me** (te, nous, vous) **les** donne.	*He gives them to me (you, us, etc.).*
Elle **se les** achète.	*She buys them for herself.*
Je ne **les lui** (leur) donne pas.	*I don't give them to him (them).*
Je **l'y** ai envoyé pour **le lui** dire.	*I sent him there to tell him it.*
Il **y en** avait au marché.	*There was (were) some at the market.*

(*a*) Pronouns of the first and second persons (**me, te, nous, vous**) and **se** of the third person precede all others.

(*b*) The direct object of the third person precedes the indirect (except **se**, as above).

(*c*) **Y** and **en** come last, **y** preceding **en**.

(*d*) **Ne** precedes all pronoun objects.

NOTE. — When the conjunctive direct object is **me, te, nous, vous, se**, the indirect object with **à** follows the verb, e.g. Il *me* présente *à vous*, *He introduces me to you;* Il *vous* présente *à lui*, *He introduces you to him.*

EXERCISE XXVIII

l'article, m., *article, thing*	**ordinaire**, *ordinary*
autrefois, *formerly*	**ou**, *or*
le besoin, *need, necessity*	**l'outil**, m., *tool*
certain, *certain*	**le patin**, *skate*
constamment, *constantly*	**quelconque**, adj., *some, any (whatever)*
différent, *different*	
emprunter, *borrow (from, à)*	**raconter**, *relate, tell*
le fils, *son*	**la réception**, *reception*
l'intelligence, f., *intelligence, understanding*	**la vaisselle**, *dishes (collectively)*
le lait, *milk*	**la vie**, *life, living*
mener, *lead, take, bring*	**vivre**, *live*

avoir besoin de, *to have need of, need;* **en bonne intelligence**, *on good terms.*

A. Continue: 1. Il me les donne, il te, etc. 2. Il ne me l'avait pas donné, . . . te . . . etc. 3. Ne me les a-t-il pas prêtés? ne te les . . . ? etc. 4. Je lui en ai prêté quelquefois, tu, etc. 5. J'y en ai cherché, tu, etc. 6. Je les leur ai empruntés, tu, etc. 7. Je ne peux pas la leur prêter, tu, etc. 8. Je vais lui en acheter, tu, etc.

B. Substitute pronouns for the expressions in italics: 1. On me raconte *l'histoire.* 2. Je prête *mes plumes à Louise.* 3. Les avez-vous rencontrés *dans la rue?* 4. J'ai apporté *la lettre à mon père.*

5. Pourquoi n'a-t-il pas donné *de l'argent aux pauvres?*   6. Je vais prêter *mes livres aux élèves.*   7. Je ne trouve pas *de plumes dans cette boîte.*

C. 1. Il faut vivre en bonne intelligence avec ses (*one's*) voisins. 2. Nous habitions autrefois à la campagne et nous prêtions constamment à nos voisins les différents articles de la vie ordinaire. 3. Ma mère avait souvent besoin d'un article quelconque et Mme Lebrun le lui prêtait. 4. Moi je prêtais à son fils mes patins ou mon traîneau. 5. Quand les filles de Mme Lebrun n'avaient pas un certain livre mes sœurs le leur prêtaient. 6. Quelquefois nous n'avions pas de vache pour nous donner du lait; alors nos voisins nous en donnaient. 7. Quand nous avions besoin d'outils pour travailler au jardin nous leur en empruntions. 8. Quand Mme Lebrun n'avait pas assez de vaisselle pour son jour de réception, ma mère lui en prêtait. 9. Quand il y avait du monde chez eux et quand il n'y en avait pas chez nous ils nous invitaient à danser. 10. Quand M. et Mme Lebrun désiraient aller à la ville mon père les y menait souvent.

D. (*Oral.*) 1. Qui étaient vos voisins à la campagne? 2. Étaient-ce de bons voisins? 3. Votre mère leur prêtait-elle beaucoup d'articles? 4. Leur en empruntait-elle souvent? 5. Est-ce que Charles Lebrun vous prêtait jamais ses patins? 6. Lui prêtiez-vous souvent votre traîneau? 7. Votre père empruntait-il des outils à M. Lebrun? 8. Vos sœurs désirent-elles aller à la ville? 9. Qui va les mener à la ville? 10. Pouvez-vous les accompagner à la ville? etc.

E. 1. We had good neighbours in the country. 2. They used to lend us many articles. 3. And we often lent them some. 4. They used to borrow many things from us. 5. Can you lend me your skates? 6. I cannot lend them to you to-day. 7. Robert Lebrun has borrowed them from me. 8. I lent them to him this morning; he needed them. 9. My mother has lent some dishes to Mrs. Lebrun. 10. She often lends her some. 11. Does your father often borrow tools or nails from (à) Mr. Lebrun? 12. He borrows some from him sometimes. 13. When we wished to go to the city our neighbour took us there in his carriage.

F. 1. Charles often lends me books. 2. Does he lend you (thee) any? 3. He doesn't lend me any. 4. He cannot lend me any to-day. 5. He has lent them to George; he has lent them to him. 6. He has lent him some. 7. He cannot lend you any. 8. We met our friends at the church door. 9. We met them there. 10. Here are some pretty flowers; we are going to give her them. 11. Who brought us the letters? 12. The postman brought them to us. 13. He used to bring us some every day.

LESSON XXIX

69.   Imperative Mood of *donner*, *finir*, *vendre*

Give, let us give, etc.	*Finish, let us finish, etc.*	*Sell, let us sell, etc.*
2d Sing. donne	finis	vends
1st Plur. donnons	finissons	vendons
2d Plur. donnez	finissez	vendez

(*a*) The second person singular of the first conjugation adds **s** before **y** or **en**, e.g. donnes-en.

70.   Imperative of *avoir* and *être*

2d Sing. aie, *have*	sois, *be*
1st Plur. ayons, *let us have*	soyons, *let us be*
2d Plur. ayez, *have*	soyez, *be*

71.   Imperative Negative

ne donne pas   ne donnons pas   ne donnez pas

72. Pronominal Objects. — 1. Conjunctive personal pronoun objects and pronominal adverbs follow the imperative affirmative, and are joined to it and to one another by hyphens:

Donnez-lui la plume.	*Give him the pen.*
Donnez-la-lui.	*Give it to him.*
Donnons-leur-en.	*Let us give them some (of it).*

2. But if the imperative be negative, the general rules of position (§ 68) hold good:

Ne **me la** donnez pas.   *Do not give it to me.*

3. **Moi** for **me** and **toi** for **te** are used after an imperative, unless before **en**, in which case an apostrophe replaces the hyphen:

Donnez-**moi** l'argent.   *Give me the money.*
Donnez-le-**moi**; donnez-**m'en**.   *Give me it; give me some.*
Amuse-**toi**; va-**t'en**.   *Enjoy yourself; go away.*

4. After an imperative, the direct object precedes the indirect; **y** and **en** come last, **y** preceding **en**:

Donnez-**les-moi** (leur).   *Give them to me (to them).*
Menez-**nous-y**.   *Take us there.*

73.   Imperative of *aller* (irreg.) and *faire* (irreg.)

2d Sing. **va**	1st Plur. allons	2d Sing. **fais**	1st Plur. fais**ons**
	2d Plur. allez		2d Plur. **faites**

(*a*) Before **y**, **va** becomes **vas**, e.g. Vas-y, *Go there.*

EXERCISE XXIX

attendre, *wait for*	**la minute**, *minute*
le biscuit, *biscuit*	**l'obligeance**, f., *kindness*
cela, invar., *that*	**plaît**, from **plaire**, irreg., (*it*) *pleases*
l'employé, m., *employee, clerk*	**le prix**, *price*
envoyer, *send*	**quinze**, *fifteen*
l'épicier, m., *grocer*	**le sou**, *sou* (= *one cent*)
le fromage, *cheese*	**le sucre**, *sugar*
goûter (à), *taste*	**la suite**, *continuation*
mesdames, pl. of **madame**, *ladies*	

et avec cela? *what next?* (lit. *and with that?*); **tout de suite**, *at once, immediately;* **s'il vous plaît**, *if you please;* **trois sous la livre**, *three cents a pound*

A. Give orally the imperative affirmative and negative of: 1. Parler. 2. Finir. 3. Vendre. 4. Attendre. 5. Être. 6. Aller. 7. Avoir. 8. Faire. 9. *Turn into the negative form:* donnez-la-moi; parlez-leur-en; vendez-les-lui; allez-y.

B. (*Chez l'épicier*) Je vais chez l'épicier. — J'y vais aussi tout de suite. Attendez-moi. — Oui, je vais vous attendre à la porte du magasin. Soyez-y dans quinze minutes. Ne perdons pas de temps. (*On y arrive*) Entrons. Parlons à cet employé-là.—Vous désirez, mesdames? — Du sucre, s'il vous plaît. — Oui, mesdames. — Montrez-nous-en. — En voilà, mesdames, et du bon. — Quel en est le prix? — Six sous la livre. — Donnez-m'en quatre livres, et donnez-en deux livres à mon amie. — Et avec cela, mesdames? — Montrez-moi du thé. — En voilà. — Ce thé n'est pas bon, je pense. Ne m'en donnez pas. — Ayez l'obligeance d'attendre une minute, madame, en voici du bon. — Vous avez du fromage? — Oui, mesdames. — Montrez-le-nous. — Il est très bon. Goûtez-y. — Où peut-on trouver des biscuits? — Là-bas, mesdames. — Menez-nous-y, monsieur, s'il vous plaît. — Bien, mesdames.

C. (1) *Translate the following sentences;* (2) *substitute pronouns for the italics;* (3) *turn into negative form:* 1. Bring me *the cane*, please. 2. Explain *the lesson* to them. 3. Let us give him *some money*. 4. Pass me *the bread*. 5. Lend us *your books*. 6. Let us speak to him *of his school*. 7. Pick up *the pencils* for her. 8. Show me *some tea*. 9. Accompany us *to the city*. 10. Go and buy (*imperative + infinitive*) *some fruit*. 11. Notice the beauty *of the landscape*. 12. Take us *to the city*.

D. 1. Are you going to the grocer's? 2. We are going (there) at once. 3. Wait for us at the door. 4. Come in, please; what do you wish, ladies? 5. Have you any good tea? 6. Show me some. 7. Give me two pounds of it, please. 8. My friend (*f.*) wishes some too. 9. Give her a pound of it. 10. What next, ladies? 11. I wish some good cheese. 12. Here is some good cheese. 13. Taste it (*see B, l.* 12). 14. I don't like it. 15. Don't give me any of it. 16. Have the kindness to wait a little, madam, here is some of another kind.

E. *Translate both affirmatively and negatively:* 1. Speak to that clerk; speak to him. 2. Show me some sugar, please; show me some. 3. Give my friend some; give her four pounds of it. 4. Give me some also; give me two pounds. 5. Show me the tea, please; show me it. 6. Show me some biscuits. 7. Send these articles to my father's. 8. Send them there before (the) dinner. 9. Let us go home at once. 10. Go (thou) there at once. 11. Let us be satisfied. 12. Let us wait for her. 13. Make me an omelet, please.

LESSON XXX

74.   Future Indicative of *donner*, *finir*, *vendre*

I shall give, etc.	*I shall finish, etc.*	*I shall sell, etc.*
je donnerai	finirai	vendrai
tu donneras	finiras	vendras
il donnera	finira	vendra
nous donnerons	finirons	vendrons
vous donnerez	finirez	vendrez
ils donneront	finiront	vendront

75.   Future Indicative of *avoir* and *être*

I shall have, etc.		*I shall be, etc.*	
j'aurai	nous aurons	je serai	nous serons
tu auras	vous aurez	tu seras	vous serez
il aura	ils auront	il sera	ils seront

76. Use of the Future. — It is used in general as in English, but must also be employed when futurity is implied, e.g. after **quand** or **lorsque**, *when*, **aussitôt que**, *as soon as:*

Quand il **arrivera** je partirai.   *When he comes I shall go.*

77.   Future Indicative of *aller* (**irreg.**) and *faire* (**irreg.**)

I shall go, etc.		*I shall do, etc.*	
j'irai	nous irons	je ferai	nous ferons
tu iras	vous irez	tu feras	vous ferez
il ira	ils iront	il fera	ils feront

78. Future Anterior. — It is formed by adding the past participle to the future of **avoir** or **être**:

j'aurai donné, *I shall have given, etc.*
je serai arrivé(e), *I shall have arrived, etc.*

EXERCISE XXX

l'architecte, m., *architect*
le bain, *bath*
bâtir, *build*
la bibliothèque, *library*
la boiserie, *wainscoting*
la chambre, *room*
choisir, *choose, select*
coucher, *lie down, sleep*
la cuisine, *kitchen*
épais, *thick*
espérer, *hope*
l'étage, m., *story, flat, floor*
étroit, *narrow*
large, *wide, broad*
le maçon, *mason*

la menuiserie, *woodwork*
le menuisier, *joiner, carpenter*
mince, *thin*
le mur, *wall*
neuf, *new*
l'ouvrier, m., *workman*
le parquet, *floor*
peindre, *paint*
le peintre, *painter*
le plan, *plan*
prochain, *next*
que, conj., *that*
la semaine, *week*
surveiller, *superintend*
le terrain, (*building*) *lot*

la chambre à coucher, *bedroom;* la salle à manger, *dining room;* la salle de bains, *bathroom;* être bien, *be comfortable;* il y aura, *there will be* .

A. Continue: 1. J'aurai une belle maison dans cette rue, tu, etc. 2. J'y serai bien. 3. J'habiterai cette maison au printemps. 4. Je ne perdrai pas de temps. 5. Je ne sortirai pas ce matin. 6. Il y aura dix pièces dans ma maison, . . . ta. 7. Je ferai de bons plans. 8. Je n'irai pas les voir.

B. 1. Nous aurons une maison neuve l'année prochaine. 2. Elle sera dans une belle rue. 3. Nous avons déjà choisi le terrain. 4. Nous aurons un bon architecte qui fera les plans. 5. Il surveillera les ouvriers. 6. Il y en aura beaucoup. 7. Les maçons bâtiront les murs. 8. Les murs seront très épais; mon père n'aime pas les murs minces. 9. Les menuisiers feront les portes, les fenêtres, les parquets et la boiserie. 10. Les peintres peindront la menuiserie. 11. La maison aura trois étages. 12. Elle aura dix pièces. 13. Il y aura le salon, la salle à manger, la cuisine, la bibliothèque, la salle de bains et plusieurs chambres à coucher. 14. Espérons que nous y serons bien.

C. (*Oral.*) 1. Aurez-vous bientôt une maison neuve? 2. Qui choisira le terrain? 3. Où sera votre maison? 4. Ferez-vous les plans vous-même? 5. Que fera l'architecte? 6. Combien d'étages y aura-t-il? 7. Combien de pièces aurez-vous? 8. La salle à manger sera-t-elle à côté de la cuisine? 9. Que feront les menuisiers? 10. Qui bâtira les murs? 11. Quelles sont les différentes pièces d'une maison? etc.

D. 1. You will soon have a new house. 2. It will be in a fine street. 3. We shall soon choose the lot. 4. My father will select the plan next week. 5. There will be many workmen. 6. There will be masons, joiners and painters. 7. The masons will build the walls. 8. When the doors and windows are ready, the joiners will bring them. 9. The painters will paint them. 10. How many rooms will there be? 11. We shall have ten or eleven of them. 12. We shall have a kitchen, a dining room and a library. 13. There will also be several large bedrooms. 14. The cellar too will be very large. 15. Shall you be comfortable in your new house? 16. Let us hope so (*le*). 17. You will be very comfortable in it, I think.

E. 1. I shall go out when my sister is ready. 2. Let us go to town when we have (the) time (for it). 3. We shall go to the grocer's at once. 4. The architect will make the plans. 5. When he has made (*fut. ant.*) them, he will bring them to us. 6. We shall show them to you when he brings them. 7. When you go to the grocer's bring me some good tea. 8. I shall do so (*le*). 9. When you take a walk I shall go with you. 10. Shall we go to see you when you are in the country? 11. They will go to skate when they have finished. 12. When the house is ready we shall live in it. 13. The dining room will be wider than the parlour. 14. The bedrooms are narrower.

LESSON XXXI

79.   **Demonstrative Pronouns**

ce, invar., *this, that, it, etc.*
ceci, invar., *this*
cela, invar., *that*
celui, m., **celle,** f., *this* or *that* (*one*), *the one, he* (*she*)
ceux, m. plur., **celles,** f. plur., *these, those, the ones*

(*a*) **Cela** is sometimes contracted to **ça** [sa], colloquially.

80. Use of *ce*. — 1. For its use as anticipatory subject with être, see §§ 35, 54.

2. **Ce** = *this* (*that*), *it*, is also used as the real subject of **être**:

C'est facile (vrai, bien). *It (that) is easy (true, well).*

81. Use of *ceci*, *cela*. — Ceci = *this* (the nearer) and **cela** = *that* (the more remote) are·used to denote something indicated but not named:

Cela est joli mais j'aime **ceci**. *That is pretty, but I like this.*
J'ai parlé de **cela**. *I spoke of that.*

(*a*) If the object referred to has been named, or if the name is fully implied, **celui-ci** (**-là**) must be used.

82. Use of *celui*. — 1. The form **celui** (**celle**, etc.) = *this* or *that* (*one*), *the one*, *he*, refers to persons or things:

Cet ami et **celui** qu'il cherche. *This friend and the one he seeks.*
Mes plumes et **celles** de Marie. *My pens and Mary's (those of M.).*
Celles que vous aimez. *The ones (e.g. flowers) you like.*
Celui qui cherche trouve. *He who seeks finds.*

2. The particles **-ci** and **-là** are added to **celui** (**celle**, etc.) to contrast the nearer with the more remote, of persons or things already mentioned:

Voici les deux chaînes; gardez *Here are the two chains; keep this*
celle-ci et donnez-moi **celle-là**. *(one) and give me that (one).*

3. **Celui-ci** = *the latter* and **celui-là** = *the former*:

Cicéron et Virgile étaient célèbres; *Cicero and Virgil were celebrated;*
celui-ci était poète et **celui-là** *the former was an orator and the*
orateur. *latter a poet.*

(*a*) The order is reversed as compared with English.

EXERCISE XXXI

aller, *fit, suit, become* (of clothing)
le carton, *cardboard box*
la cravate, *necktie*
demander, *ask*
essayer, *try, try on*
la main, *hand*

le fond, *bottom, back part, end* (of a room, etc.).
merci, *thank you, thanks*
prendre, *take, get, catch*
le rayon, *shelf, department* (of a store), *counter*

monsieur désire? *what do you wish (sir)?* **ce chapeau me va bien,** *this hat fits (suits, becomes) me;* **avoir à la main,** *to have (hold) in one's hand*

A. Supply a suitable demonstrative pronoun: 1. Ces pommes-ci sont mûres; c . . . sont vertes. 2. Donnez-moi ceci; ne me donnez pas c . . . 3. Ces gants-ci sont trop grands; c . . . sont trop petits. 4. Nos plumes et c . . . des autres élèves. 5. Cette poire-là est douce, mais c . . . est aigre. 6. C . . . qui nous salue est ma cousine. 7. C . . . est Robert qui arrive.

B. J'ai perdu ma canne et celle de mon frère. Je vais à un grand magasin pour en acheter deux. (*Un employé demande*) Monsieur désire? — Des cannes, s'il vous plaît. — Vous les trouverez là-bas au fond. (*J'y vais*) — Montrez-moi des cannes. — En voilà. Aimez-vous celles-ci ou celles-là? — Je prendrai deux de celles-ci. (*Je vais au rayon des gants*) — Je désire des gants. — De ceux qu'on vous a montrés hier? — Oui. — Des gants blancs, n'est-ce pas? Essayez ceux-ci. — Ils ne me vont pas. Montrez-moi ceux qui sont dans ce carton-là. — Ceux-ci vous vont bien. (*Je cherche une cravate*) — Avez-vous de jolies cravates bleues? — En voici. Prendrez-vous celle-ci ou celle-là? — Je prendrai celle que vous avez à la main. — Et avec ça? — Merci, c'est tout pour aujourd'hui.

C. (*Oral.*) 1. Quelles cannes avez-vous perdues? 2. Qui vous montre des cannes? 3. Où sont celles que vous cherchez? 4. Aimez-vous mieux celle-ci ou celle-là? 5. Prendrez-vous celle-ci? 6. Vous désirez des gants, n'est-ce pas? 7. Ceux-ci vous vont-ils bien? 8. Ceux-là sont-ils trop grands? 9. Désirez-vous une cravate blanche? 10. Celle qui est dans le carton vous plaît-elle? 11. Celle-ci est très jolie, n'est-ce pas? etc.

D. 1. I have lost my gloves and my brother's also. 2. The ones I lost were very fine. 3. The glove department is at the back of the store. 4. The clerk shows us some gloves. 5. He asks: "Do you wish these gloves or those?" 6. These don't fit me. 7. These are too large. 8. Those are not too small. 9. Give me the ones you have in your hand. 10. Have you tried on these? 11. You are going to try them on, are you not? 12. Do you like black gloves or white gloves? 13. We like the latter. 14. What pretty neckties! 15. Robert's is pretty too. 16. You are speaking of the one he bought last week, are you not? 17. The one he bought is blue; this one is white. 18. Those I bought yesterday have come.

E. 1. Which necktie do you wish? 2. Don't you like the one
I have in my hand? 3. No, I like the one which I see in that box.
4. I shall take that one. 5. I shall not take this one. 6. Is that
(*ce*) all? 7. Thanks, that is all. 8. Those who seek find. 9. I
like this; I don't like that. 10. Did you speak of that to the teacher?
11. Gather up all this; leave all that on the table. 12. Our house
is beside Mr. Leduc's. 13. Our house is very old; Mr. Leduc's is
new. 14. Do you like to play with John or with Robert? 15. With
the latter. 16. Give me two pounds of this tea and one pound of
that. 17. Did you buy this picture yesterday? 18. No, it isn't
this one; it is the one which you see near the window.

LESSON XXXII

83.　　　　　The Possessive Pronouns

Singular	Plural	
le mien, m.	les miens, m.	
la mienne, f.	les miennes, f.	} *mine*
le tien, m.	les tiens, m.	
la tienne, f.	les tiennes, f.	} *thine, yours*
le sien, m.	les siens, m.	
la sienne, f.	les siennes, f.	} *his, hers, its, one's*
le nôtre, m.		
la nôtre, f.	les nôtres, m., f., *ours*	
le vôtre, m.		
la vôtre, f.	les vôtres, m., f., *yours*	
le leur, m.		
la leur, f.	les leurs, m., f., *theirs*	

Contractions: **de + le = du, de + les = des; à + le = au, à + les =
aux**, e.g. **du** mien, **des** siennes, **au** vôtre, **aux** leurs, etc.

84. Agreement. — They agree in gender and number with the
noun denoting the object possessed:

　　Ses amis et **les miens** (i.e. amis).　　*His friends and mine.*

85. Use of Possessive Pronouns. — 1. With **être**, the preposition **à + a** disjunctive pronoun denotes mere ownership

(cf. Lesson XXIII), whereas the use of a possessive pronoun denotes distinction of ownership:

Cette plume est **à moi.**   *This pen belongs to me (is mine).*
Cette plume est **la mienne.**   *This pen is mine (not yours, etc.).*

2. Since **le sien** (**la sienne**, etc.) = *his, hers, its, one's,* the
meaning is determined by the context:

J'ai mes livres; elle a **les siens.**   *I have my books; she has hers.*

3. Observe the idioms:

Un de mes amis.   *A friend of mine (one of my friends).*
Un Français de mes amis. *A Frenchman, a friend of mine.*

86.   **Present Indicative of *vouloir* (irreg.), 'will,'**
'wish,' 'like,' etc.

I will, wish, desire, want (to), etc.

je veux   nous voulons
tu veux   vous voulez
il veut   ils veulent

EXERCISE XXXII

la brosse, *brush*   propre, *clean*
les cheveux, m., *hair*   la toilette, *toilet*
la dent, *tooth*   le savon, *soap*
eh bien! *well then*   la serviette, *towel, napkin*
enfin, *at last*   toucher à, *touch, meddle with*
la maman, *mamma*   vouloir, irreg., *will, wish, want*
oublier, *forget*   *to, etc.*
le peigne, *comb*

faire sa toilette, *make one's toilet, dress (intr. vb.)*; brosse à dents, *toothbrush*

A. Substitute possessive pronouns for the expressions in italics:
1. Voulez-vous voir *mes lettres?* 2. Veux-tu me prêter *tes livres?*
3. Je veux chercher *ma brosse.* 4. Je parle *de votre tableau.* 5. Je
parlais *à vos sœurs.* 6. A-t-il fait *sa toilette?* 7. J'admire *leur
maison.* 8. Marie a perdu *ses patins.* 9. Nous avons cueilli *nos
pommes.* 10. Ils ont vendu *leurs pommes.* 11. Voici *mon chapeau;*
voilà *ton chapeau.* 12. Elle veut étudier *son livre.*

B. (Deux frères font leur toilette) As-tu vu ma serviette? —
Oui, la voilà. — Mais non, ce n'est pas la mienne, c'est la tienne. —

Oui, c'est vrai. Celle-ci est à moi et celle-là est à toi. — Et où est
le savon? — Voici mon savon, voilà le tien. — Donne-moi un morceau du tien, s'il te plaît; le mien n'est pas bon. — Eh bien, je t'en
donne. — Je ne trouve pas ma brosse à dents. — La voilà. — Mais
non, c'est celle de papa. Et celle-là est à maman. Les leurs sont
meilleures que les nôtres. Mais il ne faut pas y toucher. Enfin
voici la mienne. — Maintenant ma toilette est faite.— Et tes cheveux? — C'est vrai. J'ai oublié cela, mais où est mon peigne?
Veux-tu me prêter le tien? Je ne peux pas trouver le mien. — On
ne prête pas ses articles de toilette. Ce n'est pas propre.

C. (*Oral.*) · 1. Que voulez-vous faire? 2. Que vont faire les
deux frères? 3. Cette serviette est-elle la mienne? 4. Est-elle à
vous? 5. N'est-elle pas à moi? 6. Où est la mienne? 7. Quel
peigne est celui-là? 8. De quel peigne parlez-vous? 9. Les brosses
de papa sont-elles meilleures que les miennes? 10. Les nôtres
sont-elles moins bonnes que les siennes? 11. Ce peigne-ci est-il le
mien? 12. À qui est celui-là? 13. Votre toilette est-elle déjà
faite? etc.

D. 1. We are dressing. 2. Have you found your towel? 3. I
have not. 4. What towel have you in your hand? 5. Is it mine?
6. This one is not yours, it is mine. 7. Yours is larger, isn't it?
8. Have you my soap or your own (= yours)? 9. I haven't seen
yours; I have my own. 10. Will you give me a piece of yours?
11. Papa's brushes are better than ours. 12. Yes, but don't touch
his. 13. Lend me your comb, please; I can't find mine. 14. Look
for yours; look for it everywhere. 15. Here it is, at last I have
found it. 16. We are dressed (*see B, l.* 9).

E. 1. This house is ours. 2. That one is our neighbour's. 3. His
is larger than ours. 4. My uncle has his gloves and my aunt
has hers. 5. Have you forgotten yours? 6. Here is your toothbrush, but where is mine? 7. We speak of our lessons, he speaks
of his. 8. Have you Mary's pens? 9. Here are hers. 10. The
other pupils have lost theirs. 11. This necktie is mine. 12. Those
are John's; he bought them yesterday. 13. Our lessons are longer
than theirs. 14. Theirs are easier than ours. 15. Mrs. Dupont is a
friend of ours. 16. I lend my friends money; do you lend yours any?

LESSON XXXIII

87. Interrogative Pronouns

SINGULAR	PLURAL

qui? invar., *who, whom?*
que? invar., *what?*
quoi? invar., *what?*
lequel? m.   lesquels? m. } *which? which* or
laquelle? f.   lesquelles? f. } *what one(s)?*

Contractions: **du**quel, **des**quel(le)s, **au**quel, **aux**quel(le)s

88. *Qui?* — 1. This form regularly denotes persons only:

Qui parle?   Qui a-t-il vu?   *Who speaks?   Whom did he see?*
De qui (à qui) parle-t-il?   *Of (to) whom is he speaking?*
Dites-moi de qui il parle.   *Tell me of whom he is speaking.*

2. With **être**, quel? is often used for qui?

Quelle est cette dame?   *Who is that lady (what lady is that)?*

3. *Whose?* denoting ownership = à qui? otherwise de qui?:

À qui est cette maison?   *Whose house is this?*
De qui êtes-vous (le) fils?   *Whose son are you?*

89. *Que?* and *quoi?* — 1. *What?* as direct object or predicate of a verb = que? but only in direct questions:

Qu'avez-vous trouvé?   *What have you found?*
Que sont-ils devenus?   *What has become of them?*

2. *What?* as a subject is regularly qu'est-ce qui?:

Qu'est-ce qui fait ce bruit?   *What is making that noise?*

3. *What?* after a preposition, or absolutely = quoi?:

De quoi parlez-vous?   *Of what are you speaking?*
Il a répondu. — Quoi?   *He has answered. — What?*

90. *Quel?* and *lequel?* — 1. Distinguish the adjective quel? = *which, what?* immediately preceding its noun (cf. § 50) from

the pronoun **lequel?** = *which (one)? what (one)?* used apart from
a noun:

Quelle dame est arrivée?	*Which (what) lady has come?*
Laquelle des dames est arrivée?	*Which of the ladies has come?*
Auxquelles parle-t-il?	*To which (ones) is he speaking?*
Quels livres a-t-il?	*What (which) books has he?*
Je demande **lesquels** il cherche.	*I ask which (ones) he seeks.*

91. Interrogative Locutions. — Certain expressions formed
with **est-ce + qui** or **que** are frequently used instead of the
simpler interrogative forms, thus:

Qui est-ce qui parle?	for	Qui parle?
Qui est-ce que vous saluez?	"	Qui saluez-vous?
À qui est-ce que vous parlez?	"	À qui parlez-vous?
Qu'est-ce que cela montre?	"	Que montre cela?
Qu'est-ce que c'est?	"	Qu'est-ce?
Qu'est-ce que c'est que cela?	"	Qu'est-ce que cela?
De quoi est-ce qu'il parle?	"	De quoi parle-t-il?

(*a*) Observe the use of **que** to introduce the real subject: **Qu'est-ce que**
c'est *que* **cela?** *What is that?* **Qu'est-ce que c'est** *que* **la gloire?** *What
is glory?*

EXERCISE XXXIII

l'air, m., *air, atmosphere*	**Marie de Médicis** [medisis], *Marie*
ancien, *old, ancient, former*	**le marronnier**, *chestnut* [*de' Medici*
anglais, *English*	**la musique**, *music*
le cours, *course of lectures, lecture*	**le palais**, *palace, large edifice*
coûter, *cost*	**Paris**, *Paris*
entendre, *hear*	**la partie**, *part, portion*
la France, *France*	**la place**, *place, seat*
Guignol, m., *Punch and Judy*	**le sénat**, *senate*
important, *important*	**la Sorbonne**, *Sorbonne*
le jardin, *garden(s), park*	**le tambour**, *drum*
loin, adv., *far, distant*	**les Tuileries**, f., *Tuileries*
Luxembourg, m., *Luxembourg*	**l'université**, f., *university*

faire son cours, *deliver his lecture;* **chevaux de bois**, *merry-go-round;* **en**
plein air, *in the open air;* **qu'est-ce que cela veut dire?** *what does that*
mean?

A. (*Au jardin du Luxembourg*) Qu'est-ce que c'est que le Luxembourg? — C'est l'ancien palais de Marie de Médicis. C'est aujourd'hui le palais du Sénat de France. — Lequel est le plus beau, le jardin des Tuileries ou le jardin du Luxembourg? — J'aime mieux celui-ci. — Qui avez-vous salué? — C'est un professeur de mes amis qui va faire son cours à la Sorbonne. — Qu'est-ce que c'est que la Sorbonne? — C'est une partie importante de l'Université de Paris. Elle n'est pas loin d'ici. — Quelle est la musique que nous entendons? — C'est la musique des chevaux de bois. — Et maintenant, qu'est-ce que c'est que ça? — Quoi? — Ce bruit qu'on entend là-bas. — Ça, c'est le tambour de Guignol. C'est le théâtre des enfants. C'est un théâtre en plein air. C'est le théâtre le moins cher de Paris. Les bonnes places coûtent deux sous.

B. (*Oral.*) 1. Auquel des jardins allez-vous? 2. Quel palais est celui-là? 3. Lequel de ces deux jardins aimez-vous le mieux? 4. Qui est-ce que vous avez salué? 5. Qui est-ce qui nous a salués? 6. Où va-t-il? 7. Qu'est-ce qu'il va faire? 8. De quelle université la Sorbonne fait-elle partie? 9. Quelle musique entendons-nous? 10. Qu'est-ce que veut dire en anglais "chevaux de bois"? 11. Qu'est-ce que c'est que Guignol? 12. Combien les places coûtent-elles? etc.

C. 1. What park is this? 2. What is the Luxembourg? 3. Whose palace was it formerly? 4. What beautiful trees! 5. What trees are these? 6. They are chestnuts. 7. Which is the more important of the two parks? 8. Who was (is) that gentleman who saluted us? 9. He is a professor of the Sorbonne. 10. He is going to deliver his lecture. 11. What sound is that? 12. It is music, isn't it? 13. What is that yonder? 14. It is (are) the merry-go-round. 15. What (how much) do the seats cost in the children's theatre? 16. You can have good seats in it for two sous. 17. Of which ancient palace are you speaking?

D. 1. What lady is that? 2. Whose children are those? 3. Whose daughter are you? 4. What are you speaking of? 5. What are you listening to? 6. What do I hear? 7. I hear Punch and Judy's drum. 8. What has fallen? 9. Whose garden is this? 10. For whom are you waiting? 11. For what are you waiting? 12. Which

seats cost the least?   13. Which of the children is your brother?
14. Which of those ladies are your aunts?   15. Which part of the
field do you wish to buy?   16. What books have you there?   17. To
which of the dealers did your father sell his vegetables?   18. From
which of your friends did you borrow the money?   19. What pictures do you want to buy?   20. Ask (à) the dealer which ones he
wants to sell.

. LESSON XXXIV

92.   **The Relative Pronouns**

> **qui**, invar., *who, which, that;* (after prep.) *whom*
> **que**, invar., *whom, which, that*
> **dont**, invar., *whose, of whom, of which*
> **où**, invar., *to (in, at, etc.) which; where*
> **lequel**, m. sing., **lesquels**, m. plur. } *who, whom, which, that*
> **laquelle**, f. sing., **lesquelles**, f. plur. }
> **quoi**, invar., *what, which*

Contractions: **du**quel, **des**quel(le)s, **au**quel, **aux**quel(le)s

(a) For agreement and rule regarding omission, see § 36.

93. *Qui, que.* — 1. For the general use of these forms, see § 36.
2. **Qui** = *whom* may stand after a preposition:

L'ami de (à) **qui** je parle.   *The friend of (to) whom I speak.*

94. *Dont.* — 1. This form is much used with the force of **de**
+ a relative = *of* or *from whom (which), whose:*

Les amis **dont** je parle.   *The friends of whom I speak.*
L'église **dont** je vois la tour.   *The church whose tower I see.*

2. But *whose*, depending on a noun governed by a preposition, must be rendered by **duquel**, etc., or **de qui**, placed after
the governed noun:

La dame au fils **de laquelle** (*or* de   *The lady to whose son I give lessons.*
   qui) je donne des leçons.

95. *Lequel.* — 1. In general, this form is rather sparingly used, except for emphasis, or to avoid ambiguity:

Le livre **lequel** (que) je te montre.	*The book which I show you.*
L'ami **auquel** (à qui) je parle.	*The friend to whom I speak.*
La lettre **de laquelle** (dont), etc.	*The letter of which, etc.*
Une édition de ce livre, **laquelle** on vend fort bon marché.	*An edition of this book, which (sc. edition) is sold very cheap.*

2. After a preposition, however, a **lequel** form should be used if the antecedent is an animal or thing:

Le chien **auquel** je donne l'os.	*The dog to which I give the bone.*
La salle dans **laquelle** il est.	*The room in which he is.*

96. *Où.*— The adverb **où**, *where*, has the value of **dans** (**à**, etc.) + a relative, to denote place or time:

La maison **où** (dans laquelle) je loge.	*The house in which (where) I lodge.*
Le siècle **où** nous vivons.	*The age in which we live.*
L'endroit d'**où** il vient.	*The place from which he comes.*

97. *Quoi.* — This form = *what, which*, without definite antecedent, stands after a preposition, rarely otherwise:

Voilà **de quoi** j'avais besoin.	*That is what I needed.*

98. 1. *What* meaning *that which* = **ce** + a relative:

Ce qui m'amuse.	*What (subj.) amuses me.*
Ce que je dis; **ce dont** je parle.	*What (obj.) I say; what I speak of.*

2. Similarly *which* summing up a sentence:

Il est pauvre, **ce qui** est triste.	*He is poor, which is sad.*

3. Observe the recapitulatory use of **ce**:

Ce que je crains **c'**est sa colère.	*What I fear is his anger.*

(*a*) For indefinite relative pronouns, see Lesson LXXXVIII.

99. Conjunction *que.* — *That* (conjunction) = **que**, is never omitted in French, as *that* often is in English:

Je crois **que** cela est vrai.	*I think (that) that is true.*

EXERCISE XXXIV

chasser, *hunt*
le cours d'eau, *stream*
frais, *fresh, cool*
l'ombre, f., *shade*
par, *for*
la pêche, *fishing*
la perdrix, *partridge*
la propriété, *property, estate*

remarquable, *remarkable*
rendre, *render, make*
la rivière, *river*
la source, *spring*
traverser, *cross, go (run, etc.)*
  through
la truite, *trout*
venu, p. part. of **venir**, *came*

aller à la pêche, *go fishing;* chasser la perdrix, *hunt partridges*

A. Supply suitable relative pronoun forms: 1. L'église . . . nous sommes entrés. 2. La table . . . il laisse les lettres. 3. L'élève . . . j'ai prêté ce livre. 4. Ce . . . nous avons besoin. 5. Les marchands . . . je vendais mes pommes. 6. Ce . . . nous a amusés. 7. L'oncle chez . . . je demeurais. 8. La lettre de mon ami . . . est arrivée ce matin. 9. La ville de . . . nous sommes venus. 10. Voilà ce . . . il demande. 11. La maison . . . on voit les fenêtres. 12. Nous aimons ceux . . . nous aiment.

B. 1. Aimez-vous la pêche? — 2. Oui, où voulez-vous aller à la pêche? — 3. Il y a une petite rivière près d'ici où on prend de bons poissons. 4. C'est la jolie petite rivière dont je vous ai déjà parlé. 5. C'est un cours d'eau qui traverse la propriété de M. Durand laquelle est remarquable par sa beauté. 6. M. Durand est le monsieur dont nous avons vu le fils hier. 7. C'est le monsieur dans les bois duquel nous avons chassé la perdrix. 8. C'est une rivière de laquelle l'eau est claire et fraîche. 9. C'est une eau de source, et ce qui la rend encore plus fraîche c'est qu'elle coule toujours à l'ombre. 10. Voilà ce qui fait que les truites y sont abondantes.

C. (Oral.) 1. Quel amusement aimez-vous le mieux? 2. Que voulez-vous faire ce matin? 3. Où est la rivière dont vous parliez hier? 4. De qui traverse-t-elle la propriété? 5. Qui est ce M. Durand dont vous parlez? 6. Est-ce le monsieur dans les bois duquel nous avons chassé la perdrix? 7. La rivière de laquelle vous parlez est-elle belle? 8. Qu'est-ce qui en rend l'eau bien fraîche? 9. Est-ce un cours d'eau où on trouve beaucoup de truites? etc.

D. 1. There is a small stream yonder which crosses our property. 2. It is the stream of which I have often spoken to you. 3. Mr. Durand's house which you saw this morning is near the river. 4. He is the gentleman whose daughter dined at our house yesterday. 5. We hunt partridges sometimes in his woods, where there are a great many of them. 6. Here is a little river which runs in the shade. 7. That is (*voilà* or *c'est*) what makes the water so cool. 8. It is a river in which one can always catch trout. 9. It is also a river which is remarkable for its beauty. 10. What makes it so beautiful (it) is the clear (and) cool water and the abundant shade. 11. It is there that we shall go fishing. 12. Very well, that is what we shall do.

E. 1. What I spoke of is true. 2. What amuses you? 3. This is what amuses me. 4. That is what the postman has brought. 5. John has studied well, which pleases (*plaît à*) his teacher. 6. The house in which we were living last year. 7. The park in which I am going to take a walk. 8. The bird to which I give the piece of sugar. 9. The letter of which I was speaking. 10. The friends to whom I have lent my books. 11. The books which I have lent them. 12. The lady whose daughter is at my mother's. 13. The neighbours with whose child we often play. 14. The spring from which this river flows is cool. 15. Have you any of the thin paper of which I was speaking?

LESSON XXXV

100. Indefinite Adjectives and Pronouns. — In the following sections are explained the uses of the commoner words of this class. For the use of **on**, see § 38; for the use of **tout**, see § 40.

101. *Autre* and *autrui*. — 1. The various senses of *other*, (*an-*)*other*, (*the*) *other*, *others* are regularly rendered by **autre**:

Une **autre** fois; d'**autres** arbres.	*Another time; other trees.*
D'**autres** sont arrivé(e)s.	*Others have come.*
Les autres ne sont pas ici.	*The others are not here.*

2. **L'un**, **l'autre** (as also the feminine and plural) are combined into various phrases:

Elles se flattent **l'une l'autre.**	*They flatter each other.*
Ils parlent **les uns des autres.**	*They speak of one another.*
Ils sont morts **l'un et l'autre** (or **tous deux** or **tous les deux**).	*They are both dead.*

3. Distinguish **un autre** from **encore un**:

Une autre plume.	*Another (a different) pen.*
Encore une plume.	*Another (an additional) pen.*

4. **Autrui** = *others, other people*, stands regularly after a preposition, and is somewhat rarely used:

Les biens **d'autrui** (or **des autres**).	*Other people's goods.*

102. *Quelqu'un*. — The singular = *somebody, some (any) one;* the plural = *some, some people, any, a few:*

Il y a **quelqu'un**(e) à la porte.	*There is somebody at the door.*
Voilà **quelques-unes** de vos amies.	*There are some of your friends.*
J'en ai **quelques-uns** (e.g. livres).	*I have some (a few).*

103. *Quelque chose* = *something, anything:*

Quelque chose est tombé.	*Something has fallen.*
J'ai vu **quelque chose** de beau.	*I have seen something fine.*

(*a*) This form is masculine, though **chose** as a noun is feminine.

104. Negative Forms. — 1. **Personne, rien, aucun, nul, pas un**, have negative force when the verb is preceded by **ne**, or when no verb is expressed.

2. Thus used, **personne** = *nobody, no one, not anybody*, and **rien** = *nothing, not anything:*

Personne n'est venu; je n'ai vu **personne**; ne parlez à **personne**.	*Nobody has come; I saw nobody; don't speak to anybody.*
Rien ne me fait peur; je n'ai **rien** vu.	*Nothing frightens me; I have seen nothing (not anything).*
Que dit-il? — **Rien** (de nouveau).	*What does he say? — Nothing (new).*
Personne ici! — **Personne.**	*Nobody here! — Nobody.*

(*a*) Observe that **personne** as a pronoun is masculine, while **personne** as a noun is feminine.

3. Similarly **aucun, nul, pas un** = *no, not any* (as adjectives), and *none, no one, not one* (as pronouns):

Aucun auteur **ne** dit cela.	*No author says that.*
A-t-il de l'espoir? — **Aucun.**	*Has he any hope? — None.*
Nulle espérance **ne** me reste.	*No hope remains to me.*

4. If, however, the context contains or implies a negative, **personne, rien, aucun** (not **nul** or **pas un**) are rendered in English by an affirmative:

Il n'a rien dit à **personne.**	*He said nothing to anybody.*
Il refuse de **rien** dire.	*He refuses to say anything.*
Sans **aucune** cause.	*Without any cause.*
Sans **rien** faire.	*Without doing anything.*

5. Observe the following summary of negative forms and note that in these, as well as in the indefinites used negatively, the negation is expressed by **ne** + a completing word:

ne . . . **pas,** *not*	**ne** . . . **jamais,** *never*	**ne** . . . **plus,** *no longer*
ne . . . **point,** *not*	**ne** . . . **guère,** *hardly*	**ne** . . . **que,** *only*

105. Tel. — *Such a* = **un tel** (observe the word-order):

Une telle maison.	*Such a house.*

EXERCISE XXXV

attacher, *attach, tie*	**la loutre,** *otter*
auparavant, *before*	**mauvais,** *bad*
la bête, *animal, beast*	**méchant,** *wicked, cross*
bon, *kind* (to = **pour**), *gentle*	**parce que,** *because*
le castor, *beaver*	**la plante,** *plant*
le chameau, *camel*	**porter,** *bear, carry; wear*
le dos, *back*	**refuser,** *refuse*
l'éléphant, m., *elephant*	**le rhinocéros,** *rhinoceros*
exister, *exist, live*	**taquiner,** *tease*
la fois, *time* (repeated)	

jardin des plantes, *Botanical* (in Paris also *Zoological*) *Gardens*

A. Continue: 1. Je n'ai guère vu de bêtes sauvages, tu. 2. Je n'ai jamais rien vu de si bon. 3. Je lui donnais quelque chose de bon. 4. Je n'y ai vu personne. 5. Je n'y ai rien vu. 6. Est-ce que j'y ai jamais été? 7. Je ne lui ai rien donné de mauvais.

B. 1. Nous avons été hier au jardin des plantes avec nos cousins.
2. Il y a là beaucoup d'animaux aussi bien que beaucoup de plantes.
3. Nous n'y avions jamais été auparavant. 4. Et nous n'avions
guère vu de bêtes sauvages. 5. Nous n'avons jamais rien vu de
plus intéressant. 6. Il y avait plusieurs éléphants. 7. On en avait
attaché quelques-uns, parce qu'ils étaient méchants. 8. D'autres
étaient très bons et portaient des enfants sur leur dos. 9. Quand
on leur donnait quelque chose de bon à manger ils étaient très
contents. 10. Ils refusaient de rien manger de mauvais. 11. Mais
personne ne les taquinait. 12. Tout le monde était bon pour eux.
13. L'année passée mes cousins y avaient vu un rhinocéros, mais il
n'existait plus. 14. Un vieux chameau était mort aussi. 15. Il
n'y en avait que deux petits. 16. Il n'y avait plus ni castors ni
loutres. 17. Mais il y avait beaucoup d'autres animaux intéressants.

C. (*Oral.*) 1. Où avez-vous été hier? 2. Que veut dire "jardin
des plantes"? 3. Y aviez-vous été auparavant? 4. Qu'avez-vous
vu d'intéressant? 5. Pourquoi avait-on attaché quelques-uns des
éléphants? 6. Pourquoi les éléphants étaient-ils contents? 7. Leur
a-t-on donné quelque chose de mauvais? 8. Quelqu'un les taqui-
nait-il? 9. Pourquoi n'avez-vous pas vu le rhinocéros? 10. Avez-
vous vu beaucoup d'autres bêtes sauvages? etc.

D. 1. Do you never go to the Botanical Gardens? 2. I go there
sometimes. 3. I have been there several times this summer.
4. Some of my cousins went with me. 5. It is something very interesting. 6. There is nothing more interesting for children. 7. Yesterday we saw some elephants that we hadn't seen before. 8. Some
of these elephants had been tied [up] (use *on*), because they were
cross. 9. Others were very gentle (*bon*), and were carrying children
on their backs. 10. Let us give the beavers something good to eat.
11. Let us not give them anything bad. 12. They will refuse to
eat anything bad. 13. Did anybody tease them? 14. Nobody.
15. The otters were no longer in existence. 16. We saw only two
camels. 17. There were no others. 18. We didn't see any other
animals.

E. 1. A certain author relates this story. 2. We have a few good friends, but not (*pas*) many. 3. The others have not come yet. 4. Somebody is knocking at the door; who is it? 5. It is Mr. Durand's son; he has brought you something. 6. I haven't seen anybody. 7. We have not spoken to anybody. 8. Nobody has spoken to us. 9. Has the postman brought me no letters? 10. Not one. 11. I have seen none (*aucun*) of our neighbours to-day. 12. Who told you such a story? 13. Has anybody ever caught trout in that stream? 14. Yes, I have caught some in it.

F. 1. Give me my other spectacles, because these are not good. 2. Others can do the same thing. 3. This pen is bad; give me another. 4. I have never liked (*de*) such amusements. 5. Nobody met us in the street. 6. There was nobody at home when I arrived. 7. We haven't done anything wrong (*mauvais*). 8. Do you wish anything? 9. Nothing, thank you. 10. No letter for me to-day! 11. None. 12. Nobody can paint (*de*) such pictures. 13. Such is the story he has told us. 14. Is your soap not as good as mine? 15. My brother's toothbrush is much better than my sister's.

LESSON XXXVI

106. Orthographical Peculiarities. — Verbs of the first conjugation in –**cer**, –**ger** and –**yer**, as also those with **e** or **é** in the syllable next before the infinitive ending, are conjugated like **donner**, but have certain peculiarities of orthography which may best be observed by referring to Appendix, *D*, where all these irregularities are shown.

(*a*) The models avancer, manger, payer, mener, espérer, appeler, jeter, acheter, should be studied before doing the following exercise.

107.　　　**Present Indicative of *dire* (irreg.), 'say,' 'tell'**

I say, etc.

je dis	nous disons
tu dis	vous dites
il dit	ils disent

EXERCISE XXXVI

amener, *bring, take*
appeler, *call*
avancer, *advance, go on*
avidement, *greedily*
les bonbons, m., *sweetmeats, candy*
la carotte, *carrot*
le chat, *cat*
comment, *how?*
l'entrée, f., *entrance, admission (fee)*
la fosse, *ditch, pit*
le gardien, *keeper*
habile, *clever*

habilement, *cleverly*
jeter, *throw (away)*
lancer, *throw, fling, toss*
libre, *free*
le lion, *lion*
le moment, *moment, time*
l'ours, m., *bear*
payer, *pay (for)*
ressembler à, *resemble*
le roi, *king*
le rugissement, *roar(ing)*
le singe, *monkey*
vers, *towards*

donner à manger à, *to feed;* fosse aux ours, *bear pit;* palais des singes, *monkey house*

A. Continue: 1. Je ne paie (paye) rien, tu. 2. J'achète (achèterai) des bonbons. 3. J'avance (avançais) vers l'entrée. 4. Je jette (jetterai) du pain aux ours. 5. J'espère qu'il arrivera bientôt. 6. Je mange (mangeais) de la viande. 7. J'appelle (appellerai) les autres.

B. (Au jardin des plantes — suite) 1. Ce sont toujours nos cousins qui nous y amènent. 2. L'entrée est libre. 3. On ne paie rien. 4. À l'entrée on achète plusieurs choses pour donner aux animaux. 5. Puis nous avançons vers la fosse aux ours. 6. On leur jette du pain et des carottes. 7. Ils les attrapent très habilement. 8. On avance encore et on arrive au palais des singes. 9. Nous mangeons des bonbons et nous leur en lançons. 10. Ils les mangent très avidement. 11. Ensuite nous entrons chez les lions. 12. C'est au moment où on leur donne à manger. 13. Les gardiens leur jettent de gros morceaux de viande. 14. Ils les attrapent avec des rugissements. 15. Le lion ressemble beaucoup à un gros chat sauvage. 16. On l'appelle souvent le roi des animaux.

C. (Oral.) 1. Qui est-ce que vous amenez avec vous? 2. Combien paie-t-on à l'entrée? 3. Qu'est-ce que vous achetez à l'entrée? 4. Pourquoi achète-t-on ces choses? 5. Vers quelle partie du jardin avançons-nous? 6. Que ferons-nous des (*with the*) carottes? 7. L'ours est-il très habile? 8. Pourquoi dites-vous cela? 9. Qu'est-ce

que c'est que le palais des singes? 10. Que jetez-vous aux singes?
11. Que faisaient les gardiens des lions? 12. Comment appelle-t-on
le lion? etc.

D. 1. Here we are again (*encore une fois*) in the home of (*chez*)
the animals. 2. Our cousins take us there. 3. They pay [for] the
price of admission. 4. The entrance is not free to-day. 5. Everybody buys something to feed the animals. 6. I am buying candy for
the monkeys. 7. I shall buy some bread and carrots for the bears.
8. Let us go on now towards the bears. 9. Here is what they call
the bear pit. 10. We shall throw the bears some carrots. 11. Let
us toss some candy to the monkeys. 12. They catch it (*les*) cleverly
and eat it greedily. 13. What were the lions doing when you saw
them? 14. They were eating big pieces of meat which the keepers
were throwing them. 15. What (how) do people call the lion?
16. Do lions resemble cats? 17. I hope to see these interesting
animals another day.

E. 1. We are beginning to speak French. 2. I was beginning my
lessons when you came. 3. He will bring his brother. 4. Who is
calling me? 5. John, call your (thy) brother. 6. Throw [away]
that apple; it isn't ripe. 7. Very well, I shall throw it away. 8. Give
me another (of them). 9. Let us go on now, we are losing our time.
10. I was advancing towards the entrance of the park. 11. The
children were eating candy. 12. Let us not eat this candy; I don't
like it. 13. Let us go in; I shall pay [for] the seats. 14. How much
do we pay (use *on*)? 15. I shall buy this picture because I like it
(it pleases me). 16. The lions were eating the meat greedily.

LESSON XXXVII

108. Article with Place-Names. — 1. Names of continents,
countries, provinces, and of most large islands near Europe,
regularly take the definite article, and always so as subject or
direct object of a verb:

L'Asie est un grand continent.   *Asia is a large continent.*
Ils habitent le Mexique.   *They live in Mexico.*
Nous parlons de la France.   *We are speaking of France.*

2. With such names **en** denotes *where, to where,* and the article is omitted; but if the name be plural, or be the masculine name of a country outside of Europe, **à** + the definite article is used:

Il est **en** (va **en**) Europe.	*He is in (is going to) Europe.*
Il voyage **en** France (Portugal, *m.*)	*He travels in France (Portugal).*
Il est **aux** États-Unis.	*He is in the United States.*
Il est **au** (va **au**) Japon.	*He is in (goes to) Japan.*

3. The article is usually omitted in adjectival phrases formed with **de,** unless the name of the country be plural or be that of a masculine country outside of Europe; and similarly for **de** denoting mere point of departure:

Les vins **d'**Italie; le roi **d'**Espagne.	*Italian wines; the king of Spain.*
Il revient **d'**Italie (**de** Portugal).	*He returns from Italy (Portugal).*
But: La faïence **des** Indes (**du** Japon).	*Indian (Japanese) porcelain.*
Il est revenu **du** Canada.	*He has returned from Canada.*

4. *To, at, in* = **à,** without article, before names of cities, towns, villages:

À Rome (Berlin, Sèvres).	*To, at or in Rome (Berlin, Sèvres).*

5. Any place-name having a qualifying adjunct requires the definite article:

Dans **l'**Amérique du Nord.	*In North America.*
La Rome de ce siècle.	*Rome of this century.*

(*a*) The definite article forms a part of some names of cities, e.g. **le** Caire, *Cairo,* **le** Havre, *Havre,* **la** Nouvelle-Orléans, *New Orleans,* **la** Havane, *Havana.*

6. Names of mountains always, and names of rivers regularly, have the definite article:

Les Alpes; **le** Nil; **le** mont Blanc.	*The Alps; the Nile; Mt. Blanc.*

109. Present Indicative of *partir* (irreg.), 'set out,' 'start,' 'leave,' 'go'

I set out, go, etc.

je pars	nous partons
tu pars	vous partez
il part	ils partent

EXERCISE XXXVII

l'**Américain**,[1] m., *American*
l'**Anglais**,[1] m., *Englishman*
l'**Angleterre**, f., *England*
le **Canadien**,[1] *Canadian*
la **capitale**, *capital*
le **fleuve**, *river* (falling into the sea)
haut, *high*
importer, *import*
le **lac**, *lake*
les **lainages**, m., *woollen goods, woollens*
la **Loire**, *Loire*
Londres, *London*
Lyon, *Lyons*
la **Manche**, *English Channel*

la **mer**, *sea*
le **Mississipi**, *the Mississippi*
la **montagne**, *mountain*
le **nord**, *north*
l'**ouest**, m., *west*
le **pays**, *country*
le **port**, *port, wharf*
le **Rhône**, *Rhone*
le **Saint-Laurent**, *St. Lawrence*
la **Seine**, *Seine*
séparer, *separate*
situer, *situate*
la **Tamise**, *Thames*
le **vin**, *wine*

A. Continue: 1. Je suis en France, tu.   2. Je demeure aux États-Unis.   3. J'irai en Europe l'été prochain.   4. Je passerai quelques jours à Paris.   5. Je ne vais pas au Canada.   6. J'aime le thé du Japon.   7. J'habite l'Amérique du Nord.   8. Je pars du Havre.

B. 1. La France est un pays situé dans l'ouest de l'Europe. 2. Paris est la capitale de la France.   3. Quelques grands fleuves de la France sont la Seine, le Rhône et la Loire.   4. Paris est sur la Seine.   5. Lyon est sur le Rhône.   6. La plus haute montagne de la France c'est le mont Blanc.   7. Il n'y a pas de grands lacs en France.   8. On en trouve dans l'Amérique du Nord.   9. Les fleuves des États-Unis et du Canada sont très importants.   10. Le Saint-Laurent et le Mississipi sont plus grands que le Rhône et la Loire. 11. L'Angleterre n'est pas loin de la France.   12. Londres, sur la Tamise, en est la capitale.   13. La Manche sépare les deux pays. 14. Les Anglais vont souvent en France et les Français en Angleterre.   15. On trouve des Anglais à Paris et des Français à Londres. 16. Les Anglais importent les vins de France (*or* français); les Français importent les lainages d'Angleterre (*or* anglais).   17. Le Havre est un port de mer sur la Manche.   18. C'est du Havre qu'on part

---

[1] Adjectives of nationality used as proper nouns require a capital.

pour les États-Unis et le Canada.   19. Il y a beaucoup de Français
aux États-Unis et au Canada.   20. Les Américains et les Canadiens
vont souvent en France.

C. (Oral Exercise on B.)

D. Supply the prepositional form: 1. Nos parents demeurent
. . . France, . . . Paris, . . . Europe, . . . États-Unis, . . . Canada,
. . . Angleterre, . . . l'Amérique du Nord. 2. Je suis allé . . . Europe,
. . . Londres, . . . Angleterre, . . . États-Unis, . . . la Nouvelle-
Orléans, . . . Paris.

E. 1. Where is France?   2. France is in the west of Europe.
3. The Seine is one of the great rivers of France.   4. The Rhone is
another of its great rivers. 5. Paris is on the former. 6. Lyons
is on the latter. 7. Mt. Blanc is in France. 8. It is the high-
est mountain in Europe. 9. There are no large lakes in France.
10. Some of the largest lakes are in North America. 11. England
is near France. 12. Have you ever been in London? 13. It is a
seaport and the capital of England. 14. The English Channel
separates France from England. 15. Englishmen cross the
English Channel to go to France. 16. Frenchmen cross it to go
to England. 17. They sometimes start from Havre.

F. 1. There are many Englishmen in Paris. 2. We (*on*) find
also many Frenchmen in London. 3. Englishmen like French wines.
4. Frenchmen like English woollens. 5. Have you ever been in
Havre? 6. People (*on*) start from Havre to go to the United States
and Canada. 7. Canada and the United States are very large
countries. 8. The rivers of North America are much longer than
those of Europe. 9. The St. Lawrence is larger than the Seine.
10. Americans like to pass the winter in Europe. 11. They set
out in autumn to pass the winter in England or in France. 12. There
are many Frenchmen in the United States. 13. There are many
Americans and Canadians in Paris. 14. Are you not going to Paris
this winter? 15. Have you any of the thick paper I gave you?

LESSON XXXVIII

110.   The Conditional of *donner*, *finir*, *vendre*

I should give, etc.	*I should finish, etc.*	*I should sell, etc.*
je donner**ais**	finir**ais**	vendr**ais**
tu donner**ais**	finir**ais**	vendr**ais**
il donner**ait**	finir**ait**	vendr**ait**
nous donner**ions**	finir**ions**	vendr**ions**
vous donner**iez**	finir**iez**	vendr**iez**
ils donner**aient**	finir**aient**	vendr**aient**

(*a*) In *all* verbs the conditional has the same stem as the future (cf. § 74); the conditional endings are the same as those of the imperfect indicative (cf. § 63).

111.   The Conditional of *avoir* and *être*

I should have, etc.

j'aur**ais**	nous aur**ions**
tu aur**ais**	vous aur**iez**
il aur**ait**	ils aur**aient**

I should be, etc.

je ser**ais**	nous ser**ions**
tu ser**ais**	vous ser**iez**
il ser**ait**	ils ser**aient**

112. Conditional Anterior. — It is formed by adding the past participle to the above as auxiliaries (cf. § 44):

j'aurais vendu, etc., *I should have sold, etc.*
je serais arrivé(e), etc., *I should have arrived, etc.*

113. Conditional Sentences. — 1. The conditional is used to express what would happen (result) in case something else were to happen (condition):

S'il avait le temps (*condition*) il   *If he had time, he would play.*
    jouerait (*result*).

(*a*) **si** elides the **i** only before **il** or **ils**.

2. A *result* clause in the conditional (English *should* or *would*) regularly has the *if* clause in the imperfect indicative, whatever be the corresponding English form:

Si j'étudiais bien (*condition*), mon   *If I studied (if I were to study, were*
   père serait content (*result*).   *I to study, if I should study,*
                                 should I study) well, my father
                                 would be glad.

3. A *result* clause in the present, the imperative, or the future, requires the *if* clause to be in the present indicative, whatever be the corresponding English form:

Il joue s'il a le temps.   *He plays if he has time.*
Jouez si vous avez le temps.   *Play if you have time.*
S'il est ici demain, je lui parlerai.   *If he is (be, should be, should he be)*
                                 here to-morrow, I shall (or will)
                                 speak to him.

(*a*) Contrast the tense after **si** in the last example with § 76: Quand il arrivera, je partirai, *but* s'il arrive, je partirai.

4. The auxiliary is considered as the verb in compound tenses, and the above rules apply to it:

Si j'**avais** fini plus tôt, j'**aurais**   *If I had finished sooner, I should*
   fait une promenade.   *have taken a walk.*

5. The tense following **si** = *whether* (*if*), is not restricted as above:

Je demande s'il **partira**.   *I ask whether (if) he will go.*
J'ai demandé s'il **partirait**.   *I asked whether he would go.*

EXERCISE XXXVIII

la cascade, *cascade, waterfall*
le col, (*mountain*) *pass*
demain, *to-morrow*
descendre, *descend, go down*
l'état, m., *state, condition*
l'excursion, f., *excursion*
la forêt, *forest*
le glacier, *glacier*
la gorge, *gorge, ravine*
jusqu'à, *as far as, to*

monter, *go up, ascend, get into* (*carriage, etc.*)
la saison, *season*
le sapin, *fir, spruce*
la scierie, *sawmill*
le sentier, *path(way)*
si, *if, whether*
la station, *station*
tant, *so much, so many*
le torrent, *torrent.*

la station d'été, *summer resort;* **je voudrais** (**bien**), *I should like to*

Imperfect Indicative of aller, pouvoir, vouloir

j'allais	je pouvais	je voulais
tu allais, etc.	tu pouvais, etc.	tu voulais, etc.

Future Indicative of pouvoir, vouloir

je pourrai	je voudrai
tu pourras, etc.	tu voudras, etc.

Conditional of aller, faire, pouvoir, vouloir

j'irais	je ferais	je pourrais	je voudrais
tu irais, etc.	tu ferais, etc.	tu pourrais, etc.	tu voudrais, etc.

A. Continue: 1. Si j'ai le temps, je ferai une promenade, si tu ... tu ... 2. J'aurais fait une promenade si j'avais eu le temps, tu ... si tu ... 3. S'il était arrivé, je serais parti, ... tu ... 4. Je lui prêterais le livre si je l'avais, tu ... si tu ... 5. Je ne vendrais pas mes pommes à ce marchand, tu ... tes ... 6. J'irai au lac si je peux, tu ... si tu ... 7. Je voudrais y aller si je pouvais, tu ... si tu ... 8. Je pourrai y aller si je veux, tu ... si tu ...

B. 1. Nous sommes arrivés de bonne heure au village de Beaulieu. 2. C'est une jolie petite station d'été. 3. S'il n'y a pas trop de neige aux cols et aux bois, nous ferons bientôt des excursions. 4. Si les sentiers étaient assez bons, nous prendrions celui qui passe par la forêt de sapins. 5. Il nous mènerait jusqu'à la cascade. 6. Si nous pouvions, nous irions jusqu'au petit lac. 7. Nous voudrions bien le voir en cette saison. 8. Si nous étions arrivés plus tard, les sentiers auraient été en meilleur état. 9. Nous serions allés jusqu'au glacier. 10. Nous aurions vu le torrent qui en coule. 11. Et nous serions descendus dans la gorge où il passe. 12. Si nous voulions, nous pourrions monter demain jusqu'à la scierie.

C. (Oral.) 1. Qu'est-ce que c'est que le village de Beaulieu? 2. Que veut dire en anglais "station d'été"? 3. Qu'allez-vous faire si les sentiers sont en bon état? 4. Où irait-on s'il n'y avait pas tant de neige? 5. Si on prend ce sentier-ci où arrivera-t-on? 6. Et celui-là où nous mènerait-il? 7. Pourrait-on y aller ce matin? 8. Où voudriez-vous aller? 9. Êtes-vous monté jusqu'au glacier? 10. Qu'est-ce que vous auriez vu si vous y étiez monté? 11. Descendrez-vous dans la gorge si vous pouvez? 12. Pourrait-on monter aujourd'hui jusqu'à la scierie? etc.

D. Change the infinitives into the proper forms: 1. Si vous (*avoir*) ma plume donnez-la-moi. 2. Si vous voulez ce livre je vous le (*donner*). 3. Si je (*pouvoir*), j'irai patiner. 4. S'ils (*être arrivé*) je serais déjà parti. 5. J'irais au marché si je (*pouvoir*). 6. Voudriez-vous y aller si vous (*pouvoir*)? 7. Nous jetterons ces pommes si elles ne (*être*) pas bonnes. 8. J'(*avoir acheté*) ce tableau s'il n'avait pas été si cher.

E. 1. Are you going to the summer resort near the village of Beaulieu? 2. Are you going there if you have time enough and money enough? 3. If we were at Beaulieu, we should make an excursion in the mountains. 4. If there were not so much snow, we should go as far as the spruce forest. 5. If this path led to the forest, I should take it. 6. Our friends would accompany us there. 7. I should go as far as the pass if I could. 8. Should you like to see the little lake at this season? 9. Yes, I should like to go there if the paths were in good condition. 10. They would be in better condition if there were less snow. 11. If you had gone as far as the glacier, you would have seen something very beautiful. 12. If we should be able, we shall go down into the gorge or to the waterfall. 13. Had we gone down there, we should have seen the torrent. 14. You can go up to the sawmill now if you like. 15. Ask (*à*) your friend if he will be here early to-morrow.

F. 1. If you wish to see the letter, here it is. 2. If he is here to-morrow, show it to him. 3. We shall wait if we can. 4. I should have waited for him had I had time. 5. We should have lent him some money if we had had any. 6. Had I not left my books at school, I should study this evening. 7. If I were to leave my books at school, my father would not be pleased at it (*en*). 8. Had he been there, I should have spoken to him of it. 9. Should he be there to-morrow, I shall speak to him. 10. I should be very glad if you went with me. 11. We should be glad if he were to arrive before us. 12. If you should go to the market, buy me some flowers, if you please. 13. If there are any flowers at the market, I shall buy you some. 14. When you find any, bring me some.

LESSON XXXIX

114. Impersonal Verbs. — 1. Such verbs are conjugated in the third person singular only, with the subject **il** = *it:*

Il faut (fallait, faudra).   *It is (was, will be) necessary.*

(*a*) **Il** is omitted in certain phrases, e.g. **N'importe** (= il n'importe), *It doesn't matter.*

2. Many verbs may be used both personally and impersonally, some having a special meaning as impersonals:

Nous arriverons de bonne heure.   *We shall arrive early.*
Il arrive souvent que, etc.   *It often happens that, etc.*

3. Conditions of the weather, etc., are denoted by impersonal verbs, and by **faire** used impersonally:

Il neige; il pleuvra.   *It is snowing; it will rain.*
Il fait beau (temps).   *It is fine (weather).*
Il fait chaud; il fait du vent.   *It is hot; it is windy.*

(*a*) Distinguish from constructions with a personal subject, e.g. **Le temps est beau** (froid), *The weather is fine (cold).*

4. For impersonal **il y a** (avait, etc.), see § 31; for **il faut** (fallait, etc.), see § 60, 1.

5. Observe **il y a** = *ago:*

Il est arrivé **il y a** une heure.   *He arrived an hour ago.*

6. Further, an indirect object with **il faut** denotes (1) the person who *lacks*, *needs* (= **avoir besoin de**), or (2) the person concerned in the action expressed by an infinitive:

Il faut un chapeau **à Jean.**   *John needs a hat.*
Il **leur** faudra cent francs.   *They will need a hundred francs.*
Il **lui** faudra étudier davantage. *He will have to (must) study more.*

EXERCISE XXXIX

assez, *rather, quite*	**geler**, *freeze*
la boue, *mud*	**malade**, *ill, sick*
le cas, *case*	**neiger**, *snow*
le climat, *climate*	**pleuvoir**, irreg., *rain*
davantage, *more, still more*	**sec**, *dry*
dégeler, *thaw*	**le soleil**, *sun*
doux, *soft, mild*	**le sport**, *sport*
fort, adv., *heavily, hard*	**superbe**, *superb, splendid*
froid, *cold*	**le temps**, *weather*

quel temps fait-il? *what kind of weather is it?* **il fait beau (temps),** *it is fine (weather)*; **le temps est très beau,** *the weather is very fine;* **il fait du soleil (du vent, de la boue),** *it is sunny (windy, muddy)*; **il pleut (a plu, pleuvait, pleuvra, pleuvrait, etc.),** *it is raining (rained, was raining, will rain, would rain, etc.)*

A. (*Station d'hiver*) 1. Il a neigé il y a quelques jours. 2. Puis il a plu un peu. 3. Ensuite il a gelé assez fort. 4. Ce matin il gèle encore, mais il fait beau (temps). 5. Il fait du soleil et presque pas de (*hardly any*) vent. 6. Il fait un temps superbe. 7. Il y aura bientôt beaucoup d'amusements sur la montagne. 8. S'il neigeait et s'il gelait encore plus fort, il y en aurait davantage. 9. On est ici pour les sports d'hiver, et on ne serait pas content s'il faisait trop doux. 10. S'il faisait moins froid, il dégèlerait. 11. Il y aurait de l'eau et de la boue partout. 12. En ce cas on ne pourrait pas patiner. 13. Ce qu'il faut dans les stations d'hiver c'est un air sec et froid. 14. Un tel climat est bon pour les malades et aussi pour ceux qui aiment les sports.

B. (*Oral.*) 1. Neige-t-il? 2. Neigeait-il hier? 3. Quand a-t-il neigé? 4. Qu'est-ce qu'il a fait ensuite? 5. Quel temps fait-il ce matin? 6. Le temps n'est-il pas beau pour la saison? 7. Faisait-il du vent hier? 8. Fera-t-il du soleil aujourd'hui? 9. Pourrions-nous sortir s'il neigeait? 10. Y aurait-il beaucoup d'amusements s'il gelait bien fort? 11. Pourquoi n'êtes-vous pas venu à la station d'hiver? 12. Seriez-vous content s'il faisait doux? 13. Qu'est-ce qui arriverait s'il faisait un temps plus doux? 14. Y aurait-il de la boue? 15. Ne pouvons-nous pas patiner quand il dégèle? 16. Quel temps nous faut-il dans les stations d'hiver? etc.

C. 1. We are here for the winter sports. 2. We arrived two days ago. 3. The weather is splendid. 4. Last week it snowed heavily. 5. Then it rained. 6. This morning it is freezing quite hard, but it is fine. 7. It is windy, but at the same time it is sunny. 8. There will be a great many people (*monde*) on the mountain to-day. 9. We should not be pleased if the weather were mild. 10. If it snowed still more, we should be better (more) pleased. 11. If it should rain, we shall have no ice. 12. Then it will be muddy. 13. There will be mud on all the paths. 14. Should we be able to

skate if it thawed? 15. To (*pour*) skate we must have good ice.
16. What we need (it) is a cold climate.

D. 1. What kind of weather will it be this evening? 2. Is it
not going to rain? 3. It will not rain; it is too windy. 4. It
would rain if it were not so (use *tant*) windy. 5. It was very cold
yesterday. 6. It will be milder to-day. 7. In that case, we shall
take a walk. 8. We can't go out when it is raining. 9. The weather
is always bad at this season. 10. If it were fine to-day, we should
be glad. 11. It has been raining, but it is dry at present. 12. If it
freezes, we are going to skate. 13. It was mild yesterday, but now
we have (a) cold weather. 14. It was muddy because it had rained.
15. We shall have to (use *faudra*) wait for him. 16. He hasn't
come yet.

LESSON XL

115. Reflexive Verbs. — A reflexive verb is one whose subject is represented as acting on itself. Some verbs are always
reflexive, but any transitive verb may be so used.

116. Present Indicative and Imperative of *se cacher*

I hide myself, etc.

je **me** cache	nous **nous** cachons
tu **te** caches	vous **vous** cachez
il (elle) **se** cache	ils (elles) **se** cachent

(*a*) These same pronoun forms (**me**, **te**, etc.) are used also as indirect
objects, e.g. Je **me** rappelle cela, *I remember that* (lit. *recall that to myself*).

(*b*) Observe the imperative: cache-**toi**, cachons-**nous**, cachez-**vous**, and
negatively: ne **te** cache pas, ne **nous** cachons pas, ne **vous** cachez pas.

117. Use of Reflexives. — 1. A French reflexive often renders
an English non-reflexive (generally intransitive):

Il **s'arrête**; il **s'écrie**.   *He stops; he exclaims.*

2. Or a reflexive + a preposition has the value of an English
transitive verb:

Je **m'approchais** de la ville.   *I was approaching the town.*
Vous souvenez-vous de cela?   *Do you remember that?*

3. The reflexive often translates the English passive, especially when the agent is not specified:

Ce livre **se publie** à Paris.   *This book is published in Paris.*
Cela **se dit** partout.   *That is said everywhere.*

4. When the verb is plural, the meaning may be either reflexive or reciprocal, ambiguity being avoided, where necessary, by some modifying expression:

Nous nous flattons.   *We flatter ourselves* (or *each other*).
Ils se font mal **l'un à l'autre.** *They hurt one another.*

5. Observe the use of the definite article along with an indirect reflexive object to denote possession, especially of parts of the body, clothing, etc.:

Je **me** lave **les** mains.   *I am washing my hands.*

EXERCISE XL

l'abri, m., *shelter*
s'amuser, *enjoy oneself*
s'approcher (de), *approach, come near, go near*
la baie, *bay*
se baigner, *bathe* (intr.)
balnéaire, *bathing* (as adj.)
le bateau, *boat*
le bord, *border, shore*
le café-restaurant, *restaurant*
le casino, *casino*
le concert, *concert*
déranger, *disturb*
s'embarquer, *go on board*

l'endroit, m., *place*
excellent, *excellent*
gêner, *restrain, confine, etc.*
nager, *swim*
le pied, *foot*
la plage, *beach*
plonger, *plunge, dive*
se promener, *take a walk, etc.*
se rappeler, *remember*
la route, *way, road*
le trottoir, *sidewalk, pavement*
se trouver, *find oneself, be*
la vapeur, *steam*

bains de mer, *sea-bathing;* **station balnéaire**, *seaside resort;* **à l'abri de,** *sheltered from;* **se promener** or **faire une promenade à pied** (**à cheval, en voiture, en bateau, etc.**), *to take* or *go for a walk* (*ride, drive, sail, row, etc.*); **bateau à vapeur**, *steamer, steamboat;* **se donner la main**, *shake hands;* **comment vous appelez-vous?** *what is your name?* **comment vous portez-vous?** *how are you?* **je me porte bien, merci**, *I am well, thank you;* **ne vous dérangez pas**, *don't disturb yourself;* **ne vous gênez pas**, *make yourself at home*

A. (*La station balnéaire*) 1. C'est une ville qui se trouve au bord de la mer. 2. On s'y amuse beaucoup. 3. On y trouve des bains de mer excellents. 4. La plage où on se baigne est très belle. 5. Tout (*quite*) près se trouve une jolie petite baie à l'abri des vents. 6. Là on peut se promener en bateau. 7. Il y a aussi un endroit où on peut nager et plonger. 8. Au port nous nous embarquons sur le bateau à vapeur pour faire des excursions. 9. Près de la plage il y a une route avec un trottoir où on se promène à pied, à cheval ou en voiture. 10. Le casino se trouve au bout du trottoir. 11. Des concerts s'y donnent tous les jours. 12. Les salons de lecture et le café-restaurant s'y trouvent aussi.

B. Continue: 1. Je me trouve très bien ici, tu. 2. Je m'amusais beaucoup. 3. Est-ce que je me baignerai aujourd'hui? te baigneras-tu? 4. Je ne m'embarquerai pas sur le bateau. 5. Je ne vais pas m'y embarquer. 6. Je me porte bien. 7. Je ne me rappelle pas cela. 8. *Give the imperative affirmative and negative of:* se promener, s'embarquer, se rappeler.

C. (*Oral.*) 1. Qu'est-ce que c'est qu'une station balnéaire? 2. Où se trouve la station dont vous parlez? 3. Espérez-vous vous y amuser beaucoup? 4. Où allez-vous vous baigner? 5. Aimez-vous à vous promener en bateau? 6. Où peut-on s'embarquer? 7. Voulez-vous vous embarquer à présent? 8. Où se promène-t-on à pied? 9. N'allez-vous pas vous promener à cheval ce matin? 10. Ne vous portez-vous pas bien? 11. Où se donnent les concerts? etc.

D. 1. We are going to an excellent seaside resort. 2. It is[1] on the seashore near a village. 3. It is[1] on a pretty little bay. 4. I shall enjoy myself very much there. 5. Don't you admire the beautiful beach? 6. We are going to bathe there this morning. 7. Do you like to go boating sometimes? 8. Let us go boating. 9. We can swim and dive here if we wish. 10. Let us go on board the steamer now. 11. I shall take a walk first. 12. I am not very well. 13. If you wish to go for a ride, I will accompany you. 14. A concert will be given in the casino this evening. 15. The reading room was[1] formerly in the casino at the end of the road. 16. Shall you

[1] Use se **trouver**.

be in the reading room when we arrive there?   17. Will you take
my chair?   18. Don't disturb yourself, I'll take this one.

E. 1. Let us not hide (ourselves).   2. We shall not hide.   3. We
salute each other when we meet (each other).   4. We always shook
hands when we met (each other).   5. What is his name?   6. What
is your name?   7. How are you to-day?   8. What is the name of
that village to which the sidewalk leads?   9. It is called Belleroche.
10. Do you remember that story?   11. People are telling it at all
the seaside resorts.   12. Don't go near the water.   13. Don't cut
yourself (*2d sing.*).   14. I shall buy myself a fine house.   15. These
two sisters love one another very much.   16. This is my chair;
take it; make yourself at home.

LESSON XLI

118. The Passive Voice. — 1. The passive voice of a transitive verb is formed by adding its past participle to the auxiliary verb **être**, thus:

Present Indicative		Past Indefinite Indicative	
I am loved, etc.		*I have been loved, etc.*	
je suis	aimé(e)	j'ai	été aimé(e)
tu es	aimé(e)	tu as	été aimé(e)
il (elle) est	aimé(e)	il (elle) a	été aimé(e)
nous sommes	aimé(e)s	nous avons	été aimé(e)s
vous êtes	aimé(e)s	vous avez	été aimé(e)s
ils (elles) sont	aimé(e)s	ils (elles) ont	été aimé(e)s

(*a*) The past participle **été** is always invariable, but the participle of
the passive verb agrees with the subject in gender and number, like an
adjective (cf. § 14); for other tenses of the passive, see Appendix, *C*, 4.

2. After a passive, *by* = **par**, usually when a definite intention on the part of the agent is implied; otherwise by **de**:

Elle a été tuée **par** les voleurs.	*She was killed by the robbers.*
La dame était suivie **de** son fils.	*The lady was followed by her son.*
Ils seront aimés **de** tous.	*They will be loved by everybody.*

3. The English passive is frequently translated into French
by using **on** (cf. § 38, 3) with an active verb, or by a reflexive con-

struction (cf. § 117, 3), unless the agent is specified (cf. 2, above), or unless the passive denotes merely a resultant condition:

On m'a trompé.	*I have been deceived.*
On a répondu à ma question.	*My question has been answered.*
Ce livre **se publie** à Paris.	*This book is published in Paris.*
But: Les salles sont fermées.	*The halls are closed.*

EXERCISE XLI

célèbre, *celebrated, famous*
le château, *castle*
la décoration, *decoration*
s'élever, *rise, stand*
équestre, *equestrian*
exécuter, *execute*
fermer, *close, shut*
généralement, *generally*
l'intérieur, m., *interior*
italien, *Italian*

Marc-Aurèle, *Marcus Aurelius*
les meubles, m., *furniture*
Napoléon, *Napoleon*
ouvert, p. part. of **ouvrir,** *open*
la reine, *queen*
restaurer, *restore*
la scène, *scene*
la statue, *statue*
la tapisserie, *tapestry*
visiter, *visit*

de nos jours, *in our day(s), nowadays*

A. 1. Nous avons visité aujourd'hui un château célèbre. 2. Il a été bâti par un des rois de France et restauré par Napoléon. 3. La décoration a été exécutée par des peintres italiens et français. 4. La plus grande partie du château est ouverte au public. 5. Mais il y a des salles qui sont toujours fermées. 6. Une des cours s'appelle la cour du Cheval-Blanc. 7. Une statue équestre de Marc-Aurèle s'y élevait autrefois. 8. À l'intérieur se voient beaucoup de tableaux et de tapisseries. 9. Les scènes de ces tableaux sont quelquefois empruntées aux vies des rois et des reines. 10. On y voit aussi de beaux meubles. 11. Ils sont généralement plus beaux que ceux qui se font de nos jours.

B. (*Oral.*) 1. Qu'avez-vous fait ce matin? 2. Le public peut-il voir ce château? 3. Par qui ce château a-t-il été bâti? 4. Par qui a-t-il été restauré? 5. La grande salle est-elle fermée aujourd'hui? 6. Comment s'appelle cette cour-là? 7. Pourquoi s'appelle-t-elle comme cela? 8. Qu'est-ce qu'on voit à l'intérieur de cette salle? 9. Fait-on de beaux meubles de nos jours? 10. Sont-ils aussi beaux que ceux qui se faisaient autrefois? etc.

C. 1. The castles that we have visited are very famous. 2. We visited one yesterday. 3. By whom was it built? 4. By whom was it restored? 5. It was built by an ancient French king and restored by Napoleon. 6. Some of the halls are closed to the public. 7. They will be open next week. 8. The decoration of this castle is much admired. 9. By whom was it executed? 10. What is the name of this courtyard? 11. It is called the court of the White Horse. 12. Many tapestries are [to be] seen in the halls of the castle. 13. The scenes of the most part of the tapestries have been borrowed from the lives of the kings. 14. The furniture which is made in our days is not always beautiful.

D. 1. This castle was formerly inhabited by the kings of France. 2. It was built when there were kings and queens in France. 3. There are none now (*plus*). 4. The decoration was done by Italian painters. 5. Italian painters have always been famous. 6. Their pictures are to be seen (use *on*) in all the cities of Europe. 7. Such pictures are not [to be] found nowadays. 8. The most important halls of the castle are closed. 9. These halls are generally open to the public. 10. They are closed now because the walls are being restored. 11. They can be seen next week. 12. The beautiful statue no longer stands in the court. 13. Did you find the nails you lost? 14. Do you remember where you left the keys?

LESSON XLII

119. Reflexive Compound Tenses. — They are always formed with the auxiliary **être** + the past participle, thus:

Past Indefinite

I have hidden myself, etc.

je me suis caché(e)			nous nous sommes caché(e)s	
tu t'es caché(e)			vous vous êtes caché(e)s	
il (elle) s'est caché(e)			ils (elles) se sont caché(e)s	

(a) For other tenses and for **s'en aller**, see Appendix, *C*, 5.

120. Agreement of Past Participle. — 1. In compound tenses
the past participle agrees only with a preceding *direct* object,
whether such object be the reflexive object or not:

Elle s'est excusée.	*She excused herself.*
Elle s'est acheté des gants.	*She bought herself some gloves.*
Les gants qu'il s'est achetés.	*The gloves that he bought himself.*
Elles se le sont rappelé. ⎫	*They remembered it.*
Elles s'en sont souvenues. ⎭	

(a) The principle of agreement is the same as that of the past participle
in tenses formed with **avoir** (cf. § 49).

2. If **me, te, nous, vous** refer to a feminine noun, the agreement will be feminine:

Vous vous êtes trompée, madame. *You were mistaken, madam.*

EXERCISE XLII

s'en aller, *go away*	**s'habiller,** *dress (oneself)*
s'arrêter, *stop*	**se laver,** *wash oneself*
le billet, *ticket, note*	**se lever,** *rise, get up*
le branle, *movement*	**mettre,** irreg., *put, place*
le café, *coffee, (first) breakfast*	**mis,** p. part. of **mettre**
se coucher, *lie down, go to bed, retire (to rest)*	**le paquebot,** *packet, steamer*
	se précipiter, *rush*
débarquer, *disembark, go on shore, land*	**prendre,** irreg. *take, get, buy*
	pris, p. part. of **prendre**
se dépêcher, *make haste, hasten*	**réveiller,** *waken (tr.)*
s'écrier, *exclaim*	**se réveiller,** *waken (intr.)*
la figure, *figure, face*	**se souvenir de,** irreg., *remember*
la gare, *station* (railway), *depot*	**le train,** *train*

se mettre en branle, *begin to move, get started;* **de grand matin,** *very early
(in the morning)*

PRESENT INDICATIVE OF **prendre,** *take;* **venir,** *come*

je prends	nous prenons	je viens	nous venons
tu prends	vous prenez	tu viens	vous venez
il prend	ils prennent	il vient	ils viennent

A. Continue: 1. Je me suis couché(e) de bonne heure, tu. 2. Je
ne me suis levé(e) que très tard. 3. Si je m'étais habillé(e), si tu,
etc. 4. Je ne me serais pas arrêté(e) pour cela. 5. Est-ce que je
ne me suis pas vite habillé(e)? 6. Je voulais m'en aller de grand

matin. 7. Je m'en suis allé(e) avant lui. 8. Je m'en suis souvenu(e).

B. Turn into the past indefinite: 1. Elles s'y amusent beaucoup. 2. Ils se couchent toujours de bonne heure. 3. Ne vous couchez-vous pas de bonne heure? 4. Les gants qu'elle s'achète. 5. Elle ne s'achète pas de gants. 6. Vous en allez-vous? 7. Mon frère et ma sœur s'arrêtent. 8. Nous nous lavons les mains. 9. N'y vont-elles pas? 10. Ils se donnent la main.

C. 1. Mon frère et moi nous nous sommes couchés de bonne heure hier (au) soir. 2. Nous voulions nous en aller de bonne heure ce matin. 3. Si nous ne nous étions pas couchés de bonne heure, nous nous serions réveillés trop tard pour partir aujourd'hui. 4. Je me suis réveillé de grand matin. 5. J'ai réveillé mon frère. 6. Nous nous sommes levés tout de suite. 7. Nous nous sommes lavé la figure et les mains. 8. Nous nous sommes vite habillés. 9. Mon frère s'est écrié: "Dépêchons-nous." 10. Nous nous sommes précipités dans la salle à manger. 11. Nous prenons notre café et nous partons. 12. À la gare nous prenons nos billets et nous voilà dans le train. 13. Le train s'est mis en branle. 14. Il ne s'arrête qu'au port de mer. 15. Nous nous sommes embarqués sur le paquebot. 16. Dans quelques jours nous débarquerons en Amérique.

D. (Oral.) 1. Votre frère s'est-il déjà couché? 2. Vous êtes-vous couchés tard? 3. Pourquoi pas (*not*)? 4. Vos frères se sont-ils réveillés tard? 5. Qui vous a réveillés? 6. Vous êtes-vous levés tout de suite? 7. Êtes-vous déjà habillé? 8. Votre frère s'est-il déjà lavé les mains? 9. Pourquoi vous êtes-vous dépêchés? 10. Pourquoi êtes-vous allés dans la salle à manger? 11. Où avez-vous pris vos billets? 12. Où le train s'est-il arrêté? 13. Où vous êtes-vous embarqués? 14. Où avez-vous débarqué? etc.

E. 1. Have your brothers gone to bed yet (*déjà*)? 2. Yes, they wanted to rise early to-morrow. 3. Waken your brothers. 4. They woke [up] an hour ago. 5. They have risen. 6. They have dressed (themselves). 7. They are coming now. 8. Let us make haste. 9. We hastened. 10. They rushed into the dining room. 11. Their coffee was ready. 12. They took it at once. 13. They get their tickets at the station. 14. We are getting our tickets. 15. They

went on board (*monter*) at once.　16. The train has begun to move.
17. After some days they landed in America.

F. 1. The gloves that I have bought myself are too small.　2. All
our friends are going away.　3. They have gone away.　4. We
remember our friends.　5. We don't forget them.　6. My brothers
are washing their hands.　7. They have washed their hands.　8. My
sisters have dressed (themselves).　9. They (*f.*) rushed into the
carriage.　10. They (*f.*) went on board the steamer.　11. The train
is coming.　12. Has the train stopped?　13. It has not stopped yet.
14. We went on board the steamer.　15. Let us go on shore now.

LESSON XLIII

121.　　　　　　　　**Cardinal Numerals**

1	un, une	[œ̃, yn]	21	vingt et un	[vɛ̃t e œ̃]
2	deux	[dø]	22	vingt-deux	[vɛ̃d dø]
3	trois	[trwɑ]	30	trente	[trɑ̃:t]
4	quatre	[katr]	31	trente et un	[trɑ̃t e œ̃]
5	cinq	[sɛ̃:k]	40	quarante	[karɑ̃:t]
6	six	[sis]	50	cinquante	[sɛ̃kɑ̃:t]
7	sept	[sɛt]	60	soixante	[swasɑ̃:t]
8	huit	[ɥit]	70	soixante-dix	[swasɑ̃:t dis]
9	neuf	[nœf]	71	soixante et onze	[swasɑ̃:t e ɔ̃:z]
10	dix	[dis]	80	quatre-vingts	[katrə vɛ̃]
11	onze	[ɔ̃:z]	81	quatre-vingt-un	[katrə vɛ̃ œ̃]
12	douze	[du:z]	90	quatre-vingt-dix	[katrə vɛ̃ dis]
13	treize	[trɛ:z]	91	quatre-vingt-onze	[katrə vɛ̃ ɔ̃:z]
14	quatorze	[katɔrz]	100	cent	[sɑ̃]
15	quinze	[kɛ̃:z]	101	cent un	[sɑ̃ œ̃]
16	seize	[sɛ:z]	200	deux cents	[dø sɑ̃]
17	dix-sept	[dis sɛt]	201	deux cent un	[dø sɑ̃ œ̃]
18	dix-huit	[diz ɥit]	1000	mille	[mil]
19	dix-neuf	[diz nœf]	1001	mille un	[mil œ̃]
20	vingt	[vɛ̃]	2000	deux mille	[dø mil]

Nouns of Number: 1,000,000 = **un million**; 2,000,000 = **deux millions**;
1,000,000,000 = **un milliard**.

Et serves as a connective in 21, 31, 41, 51, 61, 71; otherwise, compounds *under* 100 take hyphens, whether standing alone or forming
part of a larger number.

From 61 to 99 counting is by twenties.

Quatre-vingt and multiples of **cent** (200, etc.) require a plural –s, except (1) when followed by a *numeral* (not a noun of number), e.g. deux cent quatre-vingt-six francs; (2) in dates, e.g. l'an quatre cent; (3) as ordinals, e.g. page trois cent.

Cent = *a* (or *one*) *hundred;* **mille** = *a* (or *one*) *thousand.*

Million and **milliard** take –s, if plural, and require **de** before a noun: deux millions **de** francs.

NOTES ON PRONUNCIATION: 1. The final consonant of 5, 6, 7, 8, 9, 10, 17, 18, 19, is silent before initial consonant or **h** aspirate of a word multiplied by them, not elsewhere: 'Cinq livres' [sɛ̃ liːvr] but 'le cinq mai' [lə sɛ̃ːk me].

2. No elision or liaison occurs before **huit, onze:** Le huit [lə ɥit]; les huit livres [le ɥi liːvr]; le onze [lə ɔ̃ːz]; les onze francs [le ɔ̃ːz frɑ̃].

3. The **t** is sounded in **vingt** in 21, 23, 24, 25, 26, 27, 28, 29, becomes **d** in 22, is silent from 81 to 99, is silent in **cent un, deux cent un**, etc.

122. Multiplicatives. — *Once* = **une fois** (lit. *time*), *twice* = **deux fois**, *three times* = **trois fois**, etc.:

Deux fois deux font quatre.	*Twice two are four.*
Dix fois dix font cent.	*Ten times ten make a hundred.*

123. Money, Weights, Measures. — In France these are all according to the decimal system; observe the following:

le franc = about 20 cents, *or* 10 pence (English money).

le centime = $\frac{1}{100}$ franc (100 centimes = 1 fr.).

le gramme = about $\frac{1}{28}$ ounce avoirdupois (454 gr. = 1 lb.).

le kilogramme (1000 gr.) = about $2\frac{1}{5}$ lbs. ($\frac{1}{2}$ kg. = slightly over 1 lb.).

le mètre = 3 ft. $3\frac{2}{5}$ in. (about 40 inches).

le centimètre = $\frac{1}{100}$ metre (5 cm. = about 2 inches).

le kilomètre (1000 m.) = about $\frac{5}{8}$ mile.

le litre = about $1\frac{3}{4}$ pints ($4\frac{1}{2}$ litres = about 1 imperial gallon).

(*a*) Popularly un **sou** is used for 5 centimes; un **kilo** for un kilogramme; une **livre** for $\frac{1}{2}$ kilogramme (un demi-kilo).

124. Article Distributively. — 1. The English *a, an*, used with a weight, measure or number, in referring to *price*, is rendered by the French definite article; elsewhere generally by **par:**

Deux francs **la** livre (**le** mètre).	*Two francs a pound (a metre).*
Dix sous **la** douzaine (**la** pièce).	*Ten cents a dozen (apiece).*
Trois francs **par** jour (leçon).	*Three francs a day (a lesson).*
Cent kilomètres **par** *or* **à** l'heure.	*A hundred kilometres an hour.*

2. The definite article is also used distributively with expressions of time:

Il vient **le** dimanche.	*He comes on Sunday(s)*
Le vapeur part tous **les** lundis.	*The steamer starts every Monday.*
Tous **les** mois.	*Every month* or *once a month.*

EXERCISE XLIII

les asperges, f., *asparagus*	**l'étoffe**, f., *stuff, material, cloth*
l'automobile, f., *automobile*	**la femme de chambre**, *housemaid*
la botte, *bunch*	**se figurer**, *imagine, fancy*
le chou, *cabbage*	**les gages**, m., *wages*
la comparaison, *comparison*	**gagner**, *gain, earn*
compter, *count*	**le mois**, *month*
la cuisinière, *cook*	**la pomme de terre**, *potato*
dépenser, *spend*	**la robe**, *dress*
la douzaine, *dozen*	**le veau**, *calf, veal*
économiser, *save*	

je les ai payés cher, *I paid dear for them;* **figurez-vous!** *just imagine (fancy)!* (à) **bon marché**, *cheap* or *cheaply;* (à) **meilleur marché**, *cheaper*

A. 1. La vie est très chère à présent. 2. On vivait à meilleur marché il y a trente ans. 3. Maintenant on gagne plus et on dépense plus. 4. Regardez ce morceau de veau. 5. Je l'ai payé quatre francs vingt (centimes) (4 fr. 20) le kilo(-gramme). 6. Ces œufs m'ont coûté un franc soixante-quinze (centimes) la douzaine. 7. En comparaison les légumes se vendent bon marché. 8. J'ai payé les pommes de terre dix centimes (*or* deux sous) le demi-kilo (*or* la livre). 9. Les asperges coûtent maintenant trente centimes (*or* six sous) la botte. 10. Je paie les choux vingt-cinq centimes (*or* cinq sous) la pièce. 11. Et les gages des bonnes! 12. Je donne à ma cuisinière quatre-vingts francs et à ma femme de chambre soixante-dix francs par mois. 13. Elles pourraient (*could*) bien économiser de quatre à cinq cents francs par an. 14. Mais elles ne veulent plus porter de robes bon marché. 15. Elles paient cher tout ce qu'elles achètent. 16. Figurez-vous! Ma cuisinière porte une robe dont l'étoffe a coûté dix francs le mètre. 17. Tout va vite de nos jours. 18. C'est comme les automobiles qui vont (à) cinquante kilomètres à l'heure.

B. (*Oral.*) 1. *Count in French from* 1 *to* 10; *from* 10 *to* 20; *from* 20 *to* 35; *from* 60 *to* 70; *from* 70 *to* 80. 2. *Read aloud in French:* 40, 41, 42, 45, 50, 51, 53, 55, 60, 61, 64, 65, 70, 71, 75, 80, 81, 85, 86, 90, 91, 92, 95, 97, 98, 99, 100, 101, 102, 112, 115, 119, 189, 200, 201, 225, 1000, 2002, 80,025, 2,000,990. 3. *Recite the multiplication table* (*or parts of it*), *thus:* Deux fois un font deux; deux fois deux font quatre, etc. 4. Combien font 2 fois 7; 8 fois 6? etc.

C. (*Oral.*) 1. Le veau est-il bon marché? 2. Combien avez-vous payé ce morceau-là? 3. Les œufs sont-ils chers? 4. Combien coûtent-ils à présent? 5. Combien paie-t-on le kilo de pommes de terre? 6. Peut-on en avoir à meilleur marché? 7. M. Liard a-t-il de belles asperges? 8. Combien coûtent-elles chez lui? 9. Combien est-ce qu'il vend ses choux? 10. Comptez jusqu'à vingt. Etc.

D. 1. Everything cost less (dear) thirty years ago. 2. People used to live cheaply formerly. 3. We used to buy veal [at] one franc seventy-five centimes a kilo. 4. Now it costs from four francs twenty centimes to four francs fifty. 5. Ten years ago eggs used to cost 85 centimes a dozen. 6. Now we pay (from) 1 franc 15 to 1 franc 75 for them. 7. Vegetables are (sold, *reflex.*) cheaper. 8. A half kilo of potatoes costs two or three sous. 9. One can buy cabbage(s) [at] 25 or 30 centimes apiece. 10. Our cook earns 85 francs a month. 11. That makes 1020 francs a year. 12. How much did the material for (*de*) your dress cost you? 13. I paid 5 francs 25 a metre for it. 14. You paid too dear for it. 15. Mr. Dupont's automobile goes 60 kilometres an hour.

E. *Give in francs and centimes the equivalents of:* 1. One cent; 5, 7, 10, 12, 15, 17, 20, 25, 35, 50, 75, 85, 90 cents. 2. One dollar, $1.25, $1.35, $1.70, $1.85, $2.00, $75.00, $1500.00, $400,000.00. 3. *Give in dollars and cents in English the equivalents of:* 1 fr., 0 fr. 85, 0 fr. 75, 1 fr. 25, 1 fr. 55, 65 fr., 55 fr. 15, 1000 fr., 2,000,000 fr.

F. 1. Living was not so dear formerly. 2. People spend twice as much (*plus*) now. 3. Here is a piece of veal which cost me 4 francs 80 a kilo. 4. There are 3 kilos of it, and I paid 14 francs 40 centimes. 5. Asparagus costs 35 centimes a bunch. 6. In France you buy potatoes by (*à*) the pound. 7. You pay 2 or 3 cents a pound for them when they are cheap. 8. They were dear

last winter, but they are cheaper now. 9. Wages too are much
higher (*plus élevés*). 10. A good housemaid earns from 60 to 75
francs a month. 11. She can save 300 or 400 francs a year.
12. People earn a great deal and spend a great deal. 13. Our cook
bought cloth for a dress the other day. 14. Just imagine! She paid
9 francs 80 a yard (*mètre*) for it. 15. The cloth was very heavy
(= thick).

LESSON XLIV

125.   Ordinal Numerals

1st	premier	[prəmje]	7th septième		[sɛtjɛm]
2d {	second	[səgɔ̃]	8th huitième		[ɥitjɛm]
	deuxième	[døzjɛm]	9th neuvième		[nœvjɛm]
3d	troisième	[trwɑzjɛm]	10th dixième		[dizjɛm]
4th	quatrième	[katriɛm]	11th onzième		[ɔ̃zjɛm]
5th	cinquième	[sɛ̃kjɛm]	21st vingt et unième	[vɛ̃t e ynjɛm]
6th	sixième	[sizjɛm]	22d vingt-deuxième	[vɛ̃d døzjɛm]

(*a*) Except **premier** and **second**, they are formed by adding –**ième** to the
last consonant of the corresponding cardinal, **cinq** adding **u**, and **f** of **neuf**
becoming **v** before –**ième**.

(*b*) The use of **deuxième** for **second** generally implies a series of more than
two, but it is always used in compounds.

126.   Fractions

$\frac{1}{2}$ {	un demi	$\frac{1}{5}$	un cinquième
	une moitié	$\frac{1}{11}$	un onzième
$\frac{1}{3}$ {	un tiers	$\frac{3}{16}$	trois seizièmes
	un troisième	$\frac{7}{100}$	sept centièmes
$\frac{1}{4}$ {	un quart	$\frac{10}{101}$	dix cent-unièmes
	un quatrième	$\frac{11}{1000}$	onze millièmes, etc.

Une demi-heure.	*Half an hour.*
Une heure et demie.	*An hour and a half.*
La moitié (les trois quarts) du temps.	*Half (three quarters of) the time.*

(*a*) For denominators above 4 ordinals only are used, but note the special
forms in $\frac{1}{2}$, $\frac{1}{3}$, $\frac{1}{4}$; fractional expressions with **partie** (*part*) are also common: la troisième partie = $\frac{1}{3}$.

(*b*) **Demi** before a noun is invariable and joined to it by a hyphen, but
elsewhere agrees.

(*c*) Note the use of the article in the various examples.

127. Numeral Adverbs. — They are formed from the ordinals by –ment, according to rule (cf. § 216):

premièrement, *first, firstly*   troisièmement, *thirdly*

secondement   } *secondly*   etc.   etc.
deuxièmement }

128. Collectives. — Certain nouns are used with collective force:

Une **paire** de gants.   *A pair of gloves.*
Une **trentaine** d'élèves.   *Some thirty (about 30) pupils.*

(a) Those ending in –aine, added to the last consonant of a cardinal, denote usually an approximate number: Une hui**taine**, diz**aine** (di**x** becomes diz), douz**aine**, quinz**aine**, vingt**aine**, cent**aine**, etc. = *about* 8, 10, 12, 15, 20 (*a score*), 100, etc.; so also un **millier** = *about* 1000.

129. Year Dates. — The year in dates is expressed by a cardinal, as in English, but **mil** replaces **mille**:

L'an quatre cent.   *The year four hundred.*
En (*or* l'an) mil neuf cent onze. }
En dix-neuf cent onze.   } *In (the year) 1911.*

(a) For the year 1000, A.D., and for dates other than those of the Christian era, **mille** is commonly used.

130. Numerical Titles. — 1. Titles of rulers are denoted by cardinal numerals, except **premier** = *first*:

Napoléon **premier** (**trois**).   *Napoleon the First (Third).*

(a) *The* in such titles is untranslated.

2. Other numerical titles are expressed as in English:

La **sixième** scène du **second** acte.   *The sixth scene of the second act.*
Acte **deux**(**-ième**), scène **six**(**-ième**). *Act two (2d), scene six (6th).*
Tome **troisième** (**trois**).   *Volume third (three).*
Au **vingtième** (XXe) siècle.   *In the 20th century.*

131. Dimensions. — The following are some typical expressions:

Cette salle est longue de 8 m.   *This room is 8 metres long.*
Elle a 8 m. de longueur (*or* de long) *It is 8 metres long by 5 metres wide.*
  sur 5 m. de largeur (*or* de large).
Elle est plus longue de 2 m.   *It is longer by 2 metres.*

(a) *By* = **sur** or **de** according to meaning; see examples.

EXERCISE XLIV

appris, p. part., *learned*

la Bible, *Bible*

calculer, *calculate*

carré, *square*

le chapitre, *chapter*

le cœur, *heart*

la composition, *composition*

la conquête, *conquest*

contenu, p. part., *contained*

la date, *date*

le devoir, *duty, exercise, lesson*

le dollar, *dollar*

écrire, *write*

égaler, *equal*

entourer, *surround*

l'Évangile, m., *gospel*

Guillaume, *William*

Luc, *Luke*

le nombre, *number*

le passage, *passage*

la planche, *board, plank*

le pouce, *inch*

la prise, *taking, capture*

le problème, *problem*

la retraite, *retreat*

le saint, *saint*

selon, *according to*

le siècle, *century*

suivant, *following*

le sujet, *subject*

la surface, *surface*

le verset, *verse* (e.g. Bible)

apprendre par cœur, *learn by heart;* à peu près, *nearly, about*

A. 1. Mon frère et moi nous faisons nos devoirs pour la semaine prochaine. 2. Nous sommes dans la bibliothèque de mon père, entourés de milliers de livres. 3. Premièrement nous apprendrons par cœur un passage de la Bible. 4. Ce passage se trouve dans le neuvième chapitre de l'Évangile selon saint Luc du onzième au dix-septième verset (*or* saint Luc, IX, 11–17; *read:* chapitre neuf, versets onze à dix-sept). 5. Deuxièmement, nous avons une composition à écrire sur un des sujets suivants: "La retraite des Dix-Mille," "La conquête de l'Angleterre en 1066 (*read:* mil soixante-six) par Guillaume I," "La prise de la Bastille en 1789" (*read:* dix-sept cent quatre-vingt-neuf). 6. Troisièmement, nous avons deux petits problèmes: (1) Calculer (cf. § 191) le nombre de mètres carrés contenus dans une surface longue de 6 m. 40 (*read:* six mètres quarante centimètres) et large de 4 m. 75; (2) Un centième de mètre s'appelle un centimètre et = (*read:* égale), à peu près, $\frac{2}{5}$ (*read:* deux cinquièmes) de pouce anglais. Combien de centimètres en 20 pouces?

B. (*Oral.*) 1. Qu'avez-vous fait ce matin? 2. Combien de livres y a-t-il dans la bibliothèque de votre père? 3. Qu'avez-vous appris par cœur? 4. Où se trouve ce passage? 5. Et ensuite qu'avez-vous fait? 6. Quel est le premier sujet qu'on vous a donné? 7. Et le deuxième? 8. Et le troisième? 9. Combien de problèmes avez-vous faits? 10. Quel était le premier? 11. Et le second? etc.

C. 1. Have you done your lessons (*devoirs*)? 2. I have done some of them. 3. I learned a passage in (*de*) the Bible by heart. 4. It was (a) part of the 15th chapter of the gospel according to St. John, verses 1 to 9. 5. We had already learned the 14th chapter. 6. What subject have you chosen for your composition? 7. The life of Napoleon III. 8. Why didn't you choose the life of William I, or the retreat of the Ten Thousand? 9. Those subjects were too difficult. 10. The date of the taking of the Bastille is 1789. 11. Napoleon I was born in 1769 and died in 1821.

D. *Read in French and write in full:* 1. Les $\frac{3}{10}$ d'un franc; la $\frac{1}{2}$ d'un dollar; $\frac{1}{6}$ de $\frac{3}{16}$; les $\frac{3}{4}$ du temps. 2. L'an 485; en 1616; l'an 1000; l'Amérique a été découverte (*discovered*) en 1492; Guillaume III est mort en 1702 et Louis XIV en 1715. 3. Le 15e (quinzième) verset du 20e chapitre. 4. Aux XVe, XVIe, et XVIIe siècles. 5. Nous vivons au XXe siècle.

E. 1. There are about 100 pupils in our school. 2. There are thousands of books in my father's library. 3. He bought 200 books last week. 4. John loses three quarters of his time. 5. This gentleman gives a third of his money to the poor. 6. Our cook saves half of her wages and spends the other half. 7. About thirty of our friends were at the station when the train arrived. 8. This room (*salle*) is 5 metres long by 4 metres wide. 9. That makes 20 square metres. 10. Edward (*Édouard*) VII, king of England, was born in 1841 and died in 1910. 11. Louis XIV was king of France in the XVII century. 12. This board is three centimetres thick. 13. We have a ladder four metres long.

LESSON XLV

132. Days of the Week. — They are as follows (all masculine):

dimanche, *Sunday*	mercredi, *Wednesday*	vendredi, *Friday*
lundi, *Monday*	jeudi, *Thursday*	samedi, *Saturday*
mardi, *Tuesday*		

133. Months. — The names of the months (all masculine) may be conveniently learned from the following rhyme:

> Trente jours ont septembre,
> Avril, juin, novembre;
> Trente et un ont mars et mai,
> Août, octobre, puis juillet,
> Et décembre et janvier;
> De vingt-huit est février.

134. Date of Month. — 1. Cardinal numerals are employed to denote days of the month, except the first = **premier**:

Le premier (deux, dix) mai.	(*On*) *the first* (*second, tenth*) *of May*
Ils sont arrivés le six.	*They arrived on the* 6*th.*
Ils arrivent toujours le lundi.	*They always come on Monday*(s).

(*a*) *On* in such expressions remains untranslated.

2. Observe the following date idioms:

Quel jour du mois est-ce (sommes-nous) aujourd'hui?	*What day of the month is it to-day?*
C'est aujourd'hui le dix.	*To-day is the tenth.*
Ce sera demain le onze.	*To-morrow will be the eleventh.*
D'aujourd'hui en huit.	*A week from to-day* (future).
D'aujourd'hui en trois semaines.	*Three weeks from to-day.*
Il y a quinze jours.	*A fortnight* (*two weeks*) *ago.*
Lundi prochain; lundi dernier.	*Next Monday; last Monday.*

135. Age. — Observe the following expressions denoting age:

Quel âge avez-vous (a-t-elle)?	*How old are you* (*is she*)?
J'ai vingt ans. Je suis âgé de vingt ans.	*I am twenty* (*years old*).
Elle a dix ans et son frère en a huit.	*She is ten* (*years old*) *and her brother is eight.*
Elle est plus âgée de deux ans.	*She is older by two years.*
À l'âge de dix ans.	*At ten years of age.*

(*a*) **An**(s) may not be omitted in specifying age.
(*b*) *By* = **de**, after a comparison.

136. Holidays. — The principal holidays (*jours de fête*) in France are: les dimanches, le jour de l'An (*New Year's Day*), le lundi de Pâques (*Easter Monday*), le lundi de la Pentecôte (*Whit Monday*), la Fête Nationale (14 juillet), la Toussaint (*All Saints' Day*), le jour de Noël (*Christmas Day*).

EXERCISE XLV

l'âge, m., *age*	fonder, *found, establish*
âgé, *old*	se marier, *marry, get married*
l'Atlantique, m., *Atlantic*	**Marseille**, *Marseilles*
le bureau, *office*	le navire, *vessel, ship*
le collège, *college, school*	la place, *position*
le congé, *leave, holiday*	le règne, *reign*
considérable, *considerable*	sortir, irreg., *go out, leave*
dernier, *last*	le succès, *success*
devenir, irreg., *become*	la traversée, *crossing, passage*
durer, *last*	voyager, *travel*

riche d'un million, *worth a million*

A. 1. Mon père est né à Lyon le lundi 8 mars 1825. 2. C'était sous (*in*) le règne de Charles X. 3. Quand il avait près de huit ans, en 1833, son père l'a envoyé au collège. 4. Il y a passé neuf ans. 5. Chaque semaine il avait deux jours de congé, — le jeudi et le dimanche. 6. Les autres jours il travaillait pendant dix heures. 7. Au sortir (*infin. as noun*) du collège il entre dans un bureau où il passe trois ans. 8. Un jour son père lui dit: "D'aujourd'hui en quinze tu partiras pour l'Amérique." 9. Il s'embarque à Marseille le mercredi 20 juin 1845. 10. Le navire a fait la traversée en six semaines. 11. Il arrive à la Nouvelle-Orléans au mois d'août. 12. En septembre il trouve une place dans un bureau. 13. Au bout de dix-huit mois il fonde un magasin à lui (*of his own*). 14. Il s'est marié en 1848. 15. Il a eu un succès considérable. 16. Il est devenu riche de deux millions et demi de francs. 17. Il a beaucoup voyagé. 18. Il a fait la traversée de l'Atlantique une trentaine de fois, la première fois en six semaines, la dernière fois en six jours. 19. Il est mort le vendredi 25 novembre 1910, à l'âge de 85 ans.

B. (*Oral.*) 1. En quelle année est né votre père? 2. En quel mois? 3. Quel jour du mois? 4. Sous le règne de quel roi? 5. Racontez-moi sa vie de collège. 6. Quand est-il parti pour l'Amérique? 7. Quel âge avait-il? 8. Combien de temps a duré la traversée? 9. Où a-t-il débarqué? 10. Qu'a-t-il fait ensuite? 11. Quand s'est-il marié? 12. Combien de fois a-t-il traversé l'Atlantique? 13. Quand est-il mort? 14. De combien était-il riche? etc.

C. (*Oral.*)   *Read the following aloud in French:* 1. Paris, le 2 février, le 15 janvier, le 6 avril, le 14 juillet, le 21 juin, le 25 mai, le 4 mars, le 17 octobre, le 25 décembre, le 8 novembre, le 5 août. 2. C'est aujourd'hui dimanche, ce sera demain lundi; c'est aujourd'hui lundi, ce sera demain . . . (*throughout the week*). 3. *Repeat the rhyme in* § 133.

D. 1. I was born on the 15th of May, 1873. 2. I began to go to school at the age of eight. 3. My brother, who was older than I by two years, went with me. 4. We had a holiday every Saturday. 5. [On] the other days we worked 6 or 7 hours. 6. When I was 17 my father found me a position in an office. 7. When I was 21 my brother and I set out for America. 8. The vessel left Havre on the 1st of August, 1894. 9. We arrived in New York in a week. 10. We found English very difficult. 11. But after a few months we spoke (*impf.*) it very well. 12. In the month of December we established a small store. 13. We have had considerable success, and we have become rich. 14. My brother has married, and has a house of his own. 15. He travels a good deal. 16. He has crossed the Atlantic a score of times.

E. 1. There are 12 months in a year (*année*). 2. The first is called January, the second February, etc. 3. The month of January has 31 days, the month of February has 28 days, etc. 4. The first day of the week is called Sunday, the second Monday, etc. 5. A year has 365 days, but a leap-year (*année bissextile*) has 366 days. 6. What day of the month is it to-day? 7. To-day is the 15th, to-morrow will be the 16th. 8. Last Saturday was the 17th. 9. Next Saturday will be the 24th, will it not? 10. Christmas day comes (falls) [on] the 25th of December, and New Year's day on the 1st of January. 11. It will come on a Sunday this year. 12. We shall go to see our relations a week from to-day. 13. We shall spend a week with them. 14. A fortnight ago my aunt fell ill. 15. She is more than 75 years old.

LESSON XLVI

137. Time of Day. — Observe the following expressions:

Quelle heure est-il?	*What time (o'clock) is it?*
Il est une heure.	*It is one o'clock.*
Il est deux heures et demie.	*It is half past two.*
Trois heures (et) un quart. } Trois heures et quart. }	*A quarter past three.*
Six heures moins un (*or* le) quart.	*A quarter to six.*
Trois heures trois quarts.	*A quarter to four.*
Trois heures dix (minutes).	*Ten minutes past three.*
Six heures moins cinq (minutes).	*Five minutes to six.*
Six heures quinze.	*Six fifteen.*
Il était midi et demi.	*It was half past twelve (noon).*
Il est minuit (et) un quart.	*It is a quarter past twelve (night).*
À huit heures du soir.	*At eight o'clock in the evening.*
À quelle heure?	*At what o'clock?*
À dix heures précises.	*At ten o'clock precisely (exactly).*
Vers (les) deux heures.	*About two o'clock.*

(*a*) Do not omit **heure(s)**.
(*b*) **Et** is essential only at the half hour.
(*c*) **Minutes** is usually omitted.
(*d*) Twelve o'clock is never **douze heures**.

EXERCISE XLVI

avancer, *be too fast*	**la messe,** *mass*
le déjeuner, *breakfast, lunch*	**la minute,** *minute*
l'emplette, f., *purchase*	**la montre,** *watch*
la journée, *day*	**préparer,** *prepare*
le mari, *husband*	**retarder,** *be too slow*
la ménagère, *housewife*	**la tasse,** *cup*

je l'ai vu le premier (la première), *I saw it first* or *I was the first to see it;* **se mettre à table,** *sit down (to dinner, etc.);* **faire des emplettes,** *make purchases, go shopping*

PRESENT INDICATIVE OF **mettre, sortir**

je mets	nous mettons	je sors	nous sortons
tu mets	vous mettez	tu sors	vous sortez
il met	ils mettent	il sort	ils sortent

A. (*La journée de la bonne ménagère*) 1. Je me suis levée à six heures moins le quart. 2. J'ai réveillé mes bonnes à six heures dix; je me lève toujours la première. 3. Je sors à six heures un quart pour aller à la messe de six heures et demie. 4. Je suis sortie de l'église à sept heures vingt. 5. J'arrive au marché à huit heures moins vingt. 6. Je rentre chez moi à huit heures précises. 7. La bonne, qui était sortie pour faire des emplettes, arrive dix minutes plus tard. 8. Je prends mon café un quart d'heure après. 9. À dix heures et demie nous commençons à préparer le déjeuner. 10. Mon mari arrive de la campagne par le train de onze heures trente-cinq. 11. Nous nous mettons à table à midi précis. 12. Mes filles rentrent de leur promenade vers quatre heures. 13. Nous prenons une tasse de thé à cinq heures. 14. Nous dînons à six heures trois quarts. 15. Nous allons au concert à huit heures et quart. 16. Nous rentrons à onze heures moins un quart. 17. Nous nous couchons une demi-heure plus tard.

B. (*Oral exercise on A.*)

C. (*Oral.*) *Read A aloud, substituting in each case a time five minutes later, except in sentence* 12.

D. Write out in words, in two ways where possible, e.g.: Trois heures et demie *or* trois heures trente; midi (minuit) un quart *or* midi (minuit) quinze.

1. 1 h. 30.	4. 2 h. 25.	7. minuit 30.	10. 5 h. 35.
2. midi 20.	5. 4 h. 50.	8. 1 h. 5.	11. 6 h. 48.
3. 1 h. 55.	6. 9 h. 3.	9. 11 h. 45.	12. 5 h. 15.

E. Write out the time in words, at intervals of five minutes, from 11 *o'clock* A.M. *to half past twelve* (*noon*).

F. 1. The good housewife rose at 6 o'clock precisely; she is always the first to rise. 2. The servant's day began at a quarter to seven. 3. What time is it by (*à*) your watch? 4. It is exactly noon. 5. Your watch is too slow by (*de*) two minutes. 6. Yours is too fast by a minute and a half. 7. Mine is right (*à l'heure*). 8. The concert begins at 8.25. 9. We shall be home, I hope, before 10.30. 10. My mother has gone to the seven o'clock mass. 11. Then she will go shopping. 12. The coffee will be ready in (*dans*) a quarter

of an hour.　13. Give me a cup of coffee, please.　14. My husband
is in the country; he will arrive by the 10.12 train.　15. The cook
is preparing the lunch.　16. The lunch is ready; we sit down.
17. At what time do you dine?

LESSON XLVII

138.　　　　　**Present and Perfect Participle**

	Giving	*Finishing*	*Selling*
Pres.	donn**ant**	finiss**ant**	vend**ant**

	Having	*Being*
	ay**ant**	ét**ant**

Perf.　ay**ant donné** (fini, vendu, eu, été, etc.), *having given,* etc.
　　　　ét**ant arrivé(e)**, *having arrived.*

(*a*) For verbs in –**cer,** –**ger,** see Appendix, *D.*

139. Use of Present Participle. — 1. When used as an adjective it agrees like an adjective:

Une scène charmant**e**.　　　　　*A charming scene.*
Une soirée dansant**e**.　　　　　*A dancing party.*

2. With verbal force it is invariable:

Pleurant elle continue son récit.　*Weeping she continues her story.*
Une boîte contenant de l'argent.　*A box containing money.*
Généralement parlant.　　　　　*Generally speaking.*

3. After **en** it is used as in English, **en** = *in, on, by, while,
when,* etc., and is invariable:

(**En**) disant ceci elle est sortie.　(*While*) *saying this she went out.*
En rentrant j'ai trouvé la lettre.　*On returning I found the letter.*
En lisant on apprend à lire.　　*By reading one learns to read.*

(*a*) Thus used, the participle regularly refers to the subject, but: **L'appétit vient en mangeant,** lit. *One's appetite comes while eating,* i.e. *Desire comes
with success,* etc.

140. Perfect Participle. — The forms **ayant, étant** are invariable, but the past participle agrees like an adjective:

Étant arrivé**s** de bonne heure, nous　*Having arrived early, we rested a*
　　nous sommes reposés un peu.　　　*little.*

(*a*) **Étant** is often omitted, and the past participle becomes appositive or
absolute: **Arrivés de bonne heure,** etc., *Having arrived* (or *arriving*) *early,* etc.;
L'honneur perdu, que me reste-t-il? *Honour* (*being*) *lost, what remains to me?*

141. English *–ing*. — 1. After a preposition (except **en**, cf. § 139), an *–ing* form is regularly translated by an infinitive:

Il parle de **partir**.	*He speaks of going.*
Sans **dire** un seul mot.	*Without saying a single word.*
Après **avoir dîné**.	*After dining* (or *having dined*).
Jean a été puni pour **avoir perdu** ses livres.	*John has been punished for losing (having lost) his books.*

(*a*) The perfect infinitive is obligatory after **après** and after other prepositions when *having* is, or may be, expressed in English.

2. An *–ing* form as subject or object of a verb is rendered by an infinitive, a noun or a clause:

Voir c'est croire.	*Seeing is believing.*
J'aime **à pêcher** (*or* la pêche).	*I like fishing.*
Il est facile **de parler**.	*Talking is easy.*

3. After verbs of *seeing, hearing,* etc., the *–ing* form is commonly translated by a relative clause or an infinitive, sometimes by a participle:

Je les vois **venir** (or **qui viennent**, or **venant**).	*I see them coming.*
Je l'entends **parler** (or **qui parlait**).	*I heard him speaking.*

EXERCISE XLVII

l'**appétit**, m., *appetite*
assis, p. part. of **asseoir**, *seated*
le **bonheur**, *happiness*
causer, *chat*
cependant, *however*
craindre, irreg., *fear*
déréglé, *irregular*
dire, irreg., *say, tell*
l'**ennui**, m., *tedium, sorrow*
s'ennuyer, *be bored, be sad, be lonesome,* etc.
la **façon**, *fashion, way*
le **feu**, *fire*

la **fin**, *end*
fumer, *smoke*
le **goût**, *taste, liking*
jeune, *young*
lire, irreg., *read*
la **mort**, *death*
la **pipe**, *pipe*
le **plaisir**, *pleasure*
le **proverbe**, *proverb*
répondre, *reply, answer*
seul, *single, alone, only*
tromper, *deceive, beguile*
la **vieillesse**, *old age*

assis devant le feu, *sitting (seated) before the fire;* **couché dans son lit,** *lying (while lying) in bed;* **debout à la porte,** *standing at the door*

Note. — The imperfect indicative regularly has the same stem as the present participle, e.g. prendre, **pren**ant, je **pren**ais, etc., lire, **lis**ant, je **lis**ais, etc., dire, **dis**ant, je **dis**ais, etc.

A. 1. Les vieux amis, assis devant le feu, fument leur pipe. 2. S'amusant comme cela ils passent leur temps. 3. Ils trompent leur ennui en causant de leur vie passée. 4. À les écouter (*or* en les écoutant) on dirait qu'ils ont été des hommes remarquables. 5. Étant jeunes les plaisirs les intéressaient. 6. Arrivés à l'âge mûr ils trouvaient leur plaisir à travailler. 7. Ils réussissaient et en réussissant ils prenaient goût au succès. 8. Ils trouvaient que le proverbe dit vrai: "L'appétit vient en mangeant." 9. Après avoir eu beaucoup de succès la vieillesse leur arrive. 10. N'ayant pas mené une vie déréglée ils en voient venir la fin sans rien craindre. 11. Mais laissés presque seuls par la mort de leurs amis ils s'ennuient un peu. 12. Généralement parlant cependant ils sont heureux.

B. (*Oral.*) 1. Comment les vieux amis passent-ils leur temps? 2. De quelle façon (= comment) trompent-ils leur ennui? 3. Est-ce qu'ils aimaient les plaisirs? 4. En quoi trouvaient-ils leur plaisir plus tard? 5. Expliquez le proverbe qu'on trouve dans la leçon. 6. Est-ce qu'on voit venir la vieillesse avec plaisir? 7. Quand est-ce qu'on s'ennuie? etc.

C. 1. Sitting (seated) near the fire my old friend smokes his pipe. 2. He is chatting of his past life with another friend. 3. (While) listening to him you would say that he is a young man. 4. But he is old and he has seen remarkable men. 5. He amuses himself by chatting about them. 6. When he was young he beguiled the tedium of life in (*dans*) pleasures. 7. When he came (§ 140, *a*) to mature age he found his pleasure in working. 8. He found more pleasure in working than in amusing himself. 9. He used to say that the proverb *l'appétit*, etc., is true. 10. After working with much success, old age comes to him. 11. But he sees it coming without losing his happiness. 12. He has nothing to fear, not having led an irregular life. 13. He has lost his friends; however, he is not lonesome. 14. Generally speaking he leads a happy life.

D. 1. These books are very amusing. 2. Think well before (*avant de*) answering. 3. Being ill, my mother cannot go out to-day.

4. On rising I found that it was already nine o'clock.   5. Our friends
having arrived, we can now go on board [the ship].   6. While waiting
for the train, we shall take a cup of coffee.   7. One can't live without
eating.   8. I thank you for (*de*) showing me your library.   9. Fishing is an amusement which I like very much.   10. We found our
friends waiting for us (*rel. clause*).   11. I saw the children playing
in the garden.   12. Lying in (my) bed I was reading an amusing
book.   13. Standing at the window he looked (*impf.*) at the children
playing.

LESSON XLVIII

142.   Present Subjunctive of *donner, finir, vendre*

I (may) give, etc.	*I (may) finish, etc.*	*I (may) sell, etc.*
je donne	finisse	vende
tu donnes	finisses	vendes
il donne	finisse	vende
nous donnions	finissions	vendions
vous donniez	finissiez	vendiez
ils donnent	finissent	vendent

(*a*) Learn the subjunctive with **que**, e.g. **que** je donne, etc., since a subjunctive is usually preceded by **que** = *that.*

(*b*) The English meanings above are only approximate; observe that
the subjunctive corresponds to various English constructions, see examples
below.

143.   Present Subjunctive of *avoir* **and** *être*

I (may) have, etc.		*I (may) be, etc.*	
j' aie	nous ayons	je sois	nous soyons
tu aies	vous ayez	tu sois	vous soyez
il ait	ils aient	il soit	ils soient

(*a*) A past participle is added to form the perfect subjunctive (cf. § 45):
(que) j'aie donné, etc.; (que) je sois arrivé(e), etc.

144. Use in Noun Clauses. — The subjunctive is required in
a noun clause (introduced by **que**) after expressions denoting: —

1. Will, desire, command, consent, prohibition, etc.:

Je désire (veux) que vous **restiez**.   *I desire (wish) you to remain.*
Je consens à ce que vous **restiez**.   *I consent that you should remain.*

2. Necessity:

Il faut que vous **restiez**.   *You must remain.*
Il est nécessaire qu'il **soit** prêt.   *It is necesssary that he should be*
                                            ready.

3. Opinion (e.g. approval, etc., or the contrary):

J'approuve que vous l'**achetiez**.   *I approve of your buying it.*
Il est bon qu'il **soit** ici.   *It is well that he is here.*

4. Emotion (e.g. joy, sorrow, surprise, anger, fear, etc.):

Je regrette qu'il **soit** parti.   *I regret that he has gone.*

5. Doubt, denial, ignorance, improbability, etc.:

Je doute (nie) que cela **soit** vrai.   *I doubt (deny) that that is true.*

6. **Que** (= *that*) is never omitted in French:

Je suis content **qu'il** soit ici.   *I am glad (that) he is here.*

145. Tense Sequence. — If the verb of the governing clause is in the present, imperative, future, or future perfect, the governed subjunctive regularly has the following tenses: —

1. To denote incomplete action, the present subjunctive:

Il faut que vous **parliez**.   *You must speak.*
Il ne faut pas que vous **parliez**.   *You must not speak.*
Ordonnez qu'il **parte**.   *Order him to go.*
Il faudra que vous **partiez**.   *You will have to go.*

2. To denote completed action, the perfect subjunctive:

Je doute qu'il l'**ait vendu**.   *I doubt that he (has) sold it.*

3. A governing condition of deferential statement (cf. § 190, 1) commonly also follows the same rules:

Je voudrais (bien) qu'il **parte**.   *I should like him to go.*

EXERCISE XLVIII

approuver, *approve*	fâché, *angry, sorry*
le corsage, *waist, bodice*	garnir, *trim, adorn*
coudre, irreg., *sew*	la garniture, *trimming*
la coupe, *cut, cutting*	il importe, *it is important*
courir, irreg., *run*	la jupe, *skirt*
cousu, p. part. of coudre, *sewn*	nécessaire, *necessary*
la couture, *sewing*	richement, *richly*
la couturière, *dressmaker*	savoir, irreg., *know (how to), can*
doubler, *line*	simple, *simple, plain*
douter, *doubt*	tellement, *so much*

courir les magasins, *go shopping, shop;* tout de même, *all the same, also;* je veux bien, *I will (do so), very well, all right, etc.;* que voulez-vous que je fasse? *what shall I do? what am I to do?*

Present Indicative of savoir

je sais	nous savons
tu sais	vous savez
il sait	ils savent

Present Subjunctive of aller, partir, faire, savoir

j'aille	je parte	je fasse	je sache
tu ailles	tu partes	tu fasses	tu saches
il aille	il parte	il fasse	il sache
nous allions	nous partions	nous fassions	nous sachions
vous alliez	vous partiez	vous fassiez	vous sachiez
ils aillent	ils partent	ils fassent	ils sachent

A. Continue: 1. Il faut que j'arrive à midi, ... que tu ... 2. Il veut que je sois prêt. 3. Elle désire que j'aie une robe neuve. 4. Il est nécessaire que je choisisse l'étoffe. 5. Il sera bon que j'attende un peu. 6. Il ne faut pas que je fasse cela. 7. Il voudrait bien que j'y aille. 8. Il est content que je sache le français. 9. Il est fâché que je parte.

B. 1. Il faut que j'aille chez la couturière ce matin avec ma mère, et elle désire que tu m'accompagnes. — 2. Je veux bien. 3. J'aime tellement (à) courir les magasins. 4. À quelle heure veux-tu que nous partions? — 5. Il faut que nous soyons chez la couturière vers dix heures. 6. D'abord nous désirons que tu choisisses, avec nous, de l'étoffe pour ma robe. 7. Ma mère veut qu'elle soit très simple. 8. Elle n'approuve pas que les jeunes filles soient richement habillées. 9. Elle est contente que les jupes et même les corsages soient très simples cette année, mais il faut tout de même que nous ayons un peu de garniture sur nos robes, n'est-ce pas? — 10. Il est très important qu'une robe soit bien garnie et doublée. 11. Mais il importe surtout qu'elle soit bien coupée et bien cousue. 12. Il est nécessaire qu'une couturière sache bien la coupe et la couture. — 13. La nôtre sait bien couper et coudre. 14. Je doute qu'il y en ait de plus habiles.

C. (*Oral.*) 1. Où allez-vous ce matin? 2. Veux-tu que je t'accompagne? 3. Qu'est-ce que ta mère voudrait que je fasse? 4. À quelle heure faut-il que je sois chez la couturière? 5. Quelle espèce de robe ta mère veut-elle que tu aies? 6. Approuve-t-elle que les robes soient riches? 7. Est-elle contente que les corsages soient richement garnis? 8. Qu'y a-t-il d'important en faisant (*making*) une robe? (*answer with* il faut). 9. Sais-tu coudre? etc.

D. 1. We must go to the dressmaker's to-day. 2. I wish you to go with me. 3. Very well; I will (*fut.*) go with you. 4. Do you like to go shopping? 5. Very much; when shall we start? 6. The dressmaker desires us to be at her shop at nine. 7. First we must choose cloth for my dress. 8. I wish it to be good and not (*pas*) too dear. 9. My mother likes young girls to wear simple dresses. 10. I am glad that skirts are plain this year. 11. But one must have trimming on the waists. 12. It is important that dresses should be well cut and well trimmed. 13. Can you cut and sew? 14. Not (*pas*) very well. 15. Do you like sewing? 16. I do; my mother approves of young girls knowing how to sew.

E. 1. My father wishes the architect to make the plans. 2. I am sorry that they have gone. 3. I am glad that our neighbour's sons have come. 4. The fields must be sown. 5. We wish the harvesters to cut the wheat. 6. The baker must make the bread. 7. Little girls must not be richly dressed. 8. It is not necessary that you should go away to-morrow. 9. I should like my dress to fit me well. 10. Little children must not tease animals. 11. It is important that dresses should be well lined. 12. I wish you (*tu*) to do your exercises. 13. Children must always do their exercises. 14. We shall have to begin our lessons at once. 15. We are always the first to begin.

LESSON XLIX

146. Subjunctive in Adjectival Clause. — The subjunctive is used in such clauses (introduced by a relative pronoun): —

1. To express, regarding the antecedent, something which is implied as being still unattained or in doubt:

Je cherche un chapeau qui m'**aille**   *I am looking for a hat that will*
   bien.   *(may, such as will) fit me.*

(*a*) If the English can be turned by *may* + verb, or *such as*, etc., use the subjunctive; otherwise the indicative, e.g. J'ai trouvé un chapeau qui me **va** bien, *I have found a hat that fits me.*

2. After a negative:

Il n'y a personne qui **sache** cela.   *There is nobody who knows that.*

3. When the antecedent is qualified by a superlative, or by **seul, unique, premier, dernier:**

C'est le meilleur ami que j'**aie.**   *He is the best friend I have.*
C'est le seul ami que j'**aie.**   *He is the only friend I have.*

(*a*) But the indicative is used (1) if what is said is merely explanatory, e.g. Mon meilleur ami qui **était** malade, etc., or (2) states a fact unreservedly, e.g. C'est la seule chose qu'il **a** dite, or (3) if the superlative be used as a noun, e.g. C'est la meilleure des maisons que j'**ai** vues.

4. In clauses translating *whoever, whatever, however:*

Qui que tu **sois**, parle.   *Whoever you are, speak.*
Quoi que vous **fassiez.**   *Whatever you do.*
Quelles que **soient** vos raisons.   *Whatever (may) be your reasons.*
Quelque bons qu'ils **soient.**   *However good they are (may be).*

147. Subjunctive in Adverbial Clause. — It is thus used after many conjunctions, like the following, expressing:

TIME: **avant que** (. . . **ne**), *before*   CONDITION: **au cas que**, *in case*
PURPOSE: **afin que** or **pour que**,   *that;* **à moins que** . . . **ne**, *unless*
  in order that   CONCESSION: **quoique** or **bien que**,
FEAR: **de peur que** . . . **ne**, *for*   *although*
  fear that   NEGATION: **sans que**, *without* (*that*)

Parlez **avant qu'**il (ne) **parte.**   *Speak before he goes.*
De peur que vous **ne tombiez.**   *For fear that you should fall.*
Bien que je ne **sois** pas riche.   *Though I am not rich.*

(*a*) For the complete list, see § 224.

148. Subjunctive in Principal Sentence. — 1. Thus used, **que** + the third singular and third plural present subjunctive serves to complete the imperative, thus:

SINGULAR	PLURAL
	donnons, *let us give*
donne, *give*	donnez, *give*
qu'il donne, *let him give*	qu'ils donnent, *let them give*

(a) Similarly for all verbs; for word-order of pronouns, see § 68.

2. It is also sometimes used without **que** to denote what is wished or desired:

Ainsi **soit-il! Vive** le roi!	*So be it! Long live the king!*
Plût (*impf.*) à Dieu qu'il **fût** ici!	*Would to God he were here!*

EXERCISE XLIX

accepter, *accept*	**se mettre,** irreg., *dress* (intr.).
assister à, *be present at, attend*	**le mouchoir,** *handkerchief*
le bal, *ball, dance*	**la nacre,** *mother-of-pearl*
le bouton, *button, stud*	**s'occuper de,** *occupy oneself with,*
la famille, *family*	*see about*
frais, *fresh, unsoiled*	**quant à,** *as to (for)*
les gens, pl., *people*	**la redingote,** *frock coat*
le gilet, *waistcoat, vest*	**la soirée,** *evening*
l'habit, m., *dress coat*	**le tailleur,** *tailor*
l'invitation, f., *invitation*	**le veston,** *sack coat*
la jaquette, *morning coat*	

les jeunes gens, *young men;* **les jeunes filles,** *young ladies;* **en toilette de bal** (or **de soirée**), *in evening dress;* **une soirée dansante,** *a dancing party*

PRESENT SUBJUNCTIVE OF **pouvoir**

je puisse	nous puissions
tu puisses	vous puissiez
il puisse	ils puissent.

A. Continue: 1. Avant que je parte, . . . tu.   2. Quoique je sois malade, je partirai, . . . tu . . . tu.   3. Ce sont les seuls gants que j'aie. 4. Quoi que je fasse je n'y réussirai pas. 5. De peur que je ne tombe. 6. *Give in full the imperative of* finir, vendre, avoir, être.

B. 1. Mes sœurs, mon frère et moi (nous) sommes invités à une soirée dansante chez ma tante. 2. Toutes les jeunes filles seront en toilette de bal (*or* de soirée). 3. Bien que nous soyons presque tous de la famille, ma tante ne voudrait pas que les jeunes gens qui y assistent soient en veston ou en jaquette. 4. Il faut qu'on se mette en habit pour danser chez elle. 5. Mon frère, quoiqu'il ne soit pas beaucoup plus âgé que moi, a déjà un habit et une redingote. 6. N'en ayant pas moi-même, il faut que j'aille chez le tailleur avant qu'il soit trop tard. 7. À moins que je n'aie un habit, il faut que je refuse l'invitation. 8. Quant aux gants blancs j'en ai, mais quelque bons qu'ils soient ils ne sont plus frais. 9. La seule chose que je puisse faire c'est d'en acheter de neufs. 10. Et le gilet blanc, la cravate blanche, les boutons de nacre et le mouchoir de soie blanche, il faut que je m'en occupe tout de suite.

C. (*Oral on B.*)

D. 1. My aunt will give a dancing party next week. 2. Although I am invited, I don't know whether I can be present (there). 3. She does not wish us to wear our (the) sack coat[s]. 4. We must be in dress coat[s] if we wish to dance at her house. 5. The young ladies must be in evening dress. 6. My brother has a dress coat, though he is younger than I. 7. Before (*avant d'*) accepting the invitation I must go to the tailor's. 8. It is the only thing I can do. 9. I cannot go to my aunt's unless I have a dress coat and a white tie. 10. However good a frock coat may be, one can't wear it at the ball. 11. Although these gloves are good, they are no longer unsoiled. 12. I must buy others. 13. Though I have mother-of-pearl buttons, I have no white tie. 14. You must see about these things at once. 15. Let young men dress well, especially when they are going to a (the) ball.

E. 1. My brother knows how to swim, though he is still young. 2. Unless you know how to swim, don't bathe here. 3. Whatever you do, don't do that. 4. However large the Seine is (is the Seine), it is not so large as the St. Lawrence. 5. Let us begin our work

before it is too late. 6. Let the maid bring me a pocket handkerchief. 7. Let the children play now if they wish. 8. I am looking
for a house in which (*où*) I shall be comfortable (*bien*). 9. I have
found some gloves that fit me. 10. The only ship which leaves
Havre this week is "La Lorraine." 11. It is the only thing I can
offer you. 12. Unless I have a morning coat before Tuesday, I
cannot go to the reception. 13. Mr. L. is the best friend we have
in Paris. 14. As to our family, we never dance. 15. Let the tailor
bring me my white waistcoat when it is ready.

LESSON L

149. **Past Definite of *donner*, *finir*, *vendre***

I gave, etc.	*I finished, etc.*	*I sold, etc.*
je donn**ai**	fin**is**	vend**is**
tu donn**as**	fin**is**	vend**is**
il donn**a**	fin**it**	vend**it**
nous donn**âmes**	fin**îmes**	vend**îmes**
vous donn**âtes**	fin**îtes**	vend**îtes**
ils donn**èrent**	fin**irent**	vend**irent**

(*a*) The first and second plural have the circumflex accent in all verbs.
(*b*) Certain verbs (all irregular) have the endings –**us**, –**us**, –**ut**, –**ûmes**,
–**ûtes**, –**urent** (see **courir** below).
(*c*) For the past definite of verbs in –**cer**, –**ger**, see Appendix, *D*.

150. **Past Definite of *avoir* and *être***

I had, etc.		*I was, etc.*	
j'eus	nous eûmes	je fus	nous fûmes
tu eus	vous eûtes	tu fus	vous fûtes
il eut	ils eurent	il fut	ils furent

151. Past Anterior. — It is formed by adding the past participle to the past definite of **avoir** or **être**, thus:

j'eus donné, etc., *I had given, etc.*
je fus arrivé(e), *I had arrived, etc.*

152. Use of Past Definite. — 1. It is used to denote what happened (completed past action), or what happened next (successive events):

La guerre **dura** sept ans.	*The war lasted seven years.*
On **força** le palais, les scélérats n'**osèrent** pas résister et ne **songèrent** qu'à fuir.	*The palace was forced, the villains did not dare to resist and only thought of fleeing.*

(a) The past definite is almost wholly confined to literary or 'book' French narrative and formal public address (cf. Note to § 47).

(b) In such a narrative the past definite denotes the principal events, while the imperfect denotes accompanying events; or, as is sometimes said, the past definite *narrates* and the imperfect *describes*.

2. Observe the special force of the following:

Avoir; j'**eus**, *to have; I received* (*obtained, got, etc.*).
Savoir; je **sus**, *to know; I found out* (*learned, etc.*).

153. Pluperfect and Past Anterior. — Both these tenses are used to translate the English pluperfect, but the past anterior denotes only what had happened immediately before another event, and is rarely employed except after certain conjunctions of time:

Après qu'il **eut dîné**, il partit.   *After he had dined, he set out.*

(a) Such conjunctions are: **lorsque**, **quand**, *when*, **après que**, *after*, **aussitôt que**, *as soon as*, and others rarer.

EXERCISE L

arrêter, *arrest, stop*	**la hâte**, *haste,*
auprès de, *with, as regards*	**joindre**, irreg., *join*
bas, *low*	**lorsque**, *when*
le bâton, *stick, club*	**le paysan**, *peasant, countryman*
la boutique, *shop*	**remplacer**, *take the place of*
le bras, *arm*	**rude**, *severe*
casser, *break*	**saisir**, *seize*
le coup, *blow*	**à travers**, *through*
la devanture, *front (shop) window*	**le trou**, *hole*
la difficulté, *difficulty*	**violent**, *violent*
se disposer, *prepare, get ready*	**voler**, *steal*
dur, *hard*	**le voleur**, *thief*
emporter, *carry off (away)*	

en bas âge, *at an early age;* **joindre les deux bouts**, *make (both) ends meet*

PAST DÉFINITE OF **courir, mourir, faire, voir**

je courus	je mourus	je fis	je vis
tu courus	tu mourus	tu fis	tu vis
il courut	il mourut	il fit	il vit
nous courûmes	nous mourûmes	nous fîmes	nous vîmes
vous courûtes	vous mourûtes	vous fîtes	vous vîtes
ils coururent	ils moururent	ils firent	ils virent

IMPERFECT INDICATIVE OF **joindre:** je joignais, etc.

A. Continue: 1. J'emportai le pain. 2. Je saisis le voleur. 3. Je sortis en hâte. 4. J'entendis un coup violent. 5. Je fus arrêté par lui. 6. Je courus après lui. 7. Lorsque j'eus arrêté le voleur. 8. Aussitôt que je fus arrivé(e).

B. Jean Valjean était d'une pauvre famille de paysans. Il avait perdu en bas âge son père et sa mère. Il ne lui restait qu'une sœur qui était mariée et qui avait sept enfants. Mais un jour le mari mourut. Jean le remplaça auprès des enfants. Sa sœur et lui en travaillant dur joignaient les deux bouts avec difficulté. Mais il arriva qu'un hiver fut rude. Jean n'eut pas d'ouvrage. Les enfants n'eurent pas de pain. Un dimanche soir un boulanger du village se disposait à se coucher lorsqu'il entendit un coup violent dans la devanture de sa boutique. Il arriva à temps pour voir un bras passé à travers le trou fait dans la devanture. Le bras saisit un pain (*loaf*) et l'emporta. Le boulanger sortit en hâte, courut après le voleur et l'arrêta. C'était Jean Valjean.

Adapted from *Les Misérables* by VICTOR HUGO.

C. (*Oral.*) *Read Exercise XX, B, using past definite for past indefinite.*

D. 1. Jean Valjean's father and mother were peasants. 2. He lost them at an early age. 3. Then he had only his sister with her family. 4. When her husband died Jean took his place and began to work for her and the children. 5. He used to work hard, and he made both ends meet without difficulty. 6. A severe winter came. 7. Jean got no work. 8. One evening, as the baker was getting ready to go to bed, he heard a violent blow. 9. He saw an arm passing through the shop window. 10. Seizing a loaf the arm carried it off. 11. The baker and his wife came out of the shop in haste. 12. He ran after the thief and caught him.

E. 1. Jean Valjean struck the shop window with a stick and broke it. 2. He got a loaf of bread by passing his arm through the hole. 3. Did the baker see Jean taking the loaf? 4. No, he did not see him, but he heard the blow. 5. When he heard the blow he dressed in haste. 6. He called his wife and rushed into the shop. 7. He saw the hole in the window. 8. Then he rushed into the street. 9. He ran in haste after Jean Valjean. 10. Jean threw away the loaf he had stolen. 11. The poor children did not get the loaf. 12. They ate no bread that evening.

LESSON LI

154. Imperfect Subjunctive of *donner*, *finir*, *vendre*

I gave, might give, etc.	*I finished, might finish, etc.*	*I sold, might sell, etc.*
je donnasse	finisse	vendisse
tu donnasses	finisses	vendisses
il donnât	finît	vendît
nous donnassions	finissions	vendissions
vous donnassiez	finissiez	vendissiez
ils donnassent	finissent	vendissent

(*a*) The third singular in all verbs has the circumflex accent.

155. Imperfect Subjunctive of *avoir* and *être*

I had, might have, etc.		*I was, were, might be, etc.*	
j'eusse	nous eussions	je fusse	nous fussions
tu eusses	vous eussiez	tu fusses	vous fussiez
il eût	ils eussent	il fût	ils fussent

(*a*) A past participle is added to form the pluperfect subjunctive:

(que) j'eusse donné, etc.
(que) je fusse arrivé(e), etc.

156. Tense Sequence. — If the verb of the governing clause be in any other tense than those mentioned in § 145, the governed subjunctive regularly takes the following forms: —

1. To denote incomplete action, the imperfect subjunctive:

Je désirais qu'il le **vendît.**	*I wished that he might sell it* or *I wished him to sell it.*
J'ai désiré qu'il le **vendît.**	
J'avais désiré qu'il le **vendît.**	*I had wished him to sell it.*

2. To denote completed action, the pluperfect:

Je doutais qu'il l'**eût vendu**.   *I doubted that he had sold it.*

J'aurais douté qu'il **fût parti**.   *I should have doubted that he had gone.*

(*a*) For the sequence after conditional of deferential statement, see § 145, 3.

NOTES. — 1. An infinitive construction is often used instead of the subjunctive, even where the latter is possible, e.g. **Il nous ordonne de partir** (for **Il ordonne que nous partions**), *He orders us to go;* **Je le ferai avant de partir** (for **avant que je parte**), *I shall do it before I go.*

2. In ordinary language the present subjunctive is often used instead of the imperfect, particularly in the case of the first conjugation, e.g. Il désirait que nous **arrivions** à temps (*for* que nous **arrivassions**), *He desired us to arrive in time.* This tendency is less strongly marked, however, in the case of the third person singular imperfect.

3. Other exceptions to the general rules are beyond the scope of an elementary text-book.

EXERCISE LI

agréablement, *agreeably*	le mal de mer, *seasickness*
les bagages, m., *luggage, baggage*	la malle, *trunk*
la cabine, *cabin, stateroom*	ordonner, *order, prescribe*
la cale, *hold* (of a ship)	il prit, 3d sing. p. def. of prendre
le chemin, *way, road*	récemment, *recently*
Cherbourg, *Cherbourg*	remis, p. part. of remettre, *recovered*
complètement, *completely*	rouler, *roll*
descendre, tr., *take down, lower*	le roulis, *rolling*
empêcher, *hinder*	le vaisseau, *vessel, ship*
le fer, *iron*	la valise, *valise*
habitué, *accustomed* (*to*, à)	le voyage, *journey, trip*
lourd, *heavy*	le wagon-lit, *sleeping car*

chemin de fer, *railway;* en pleine mer, *in the open sea;* il fallut (p. def. of falloir), *it was necessary, had to, etc.;* il faudrait (condl. of falloir), *would have to, etc.*

IMPERFECT SUBJUNCTIVE OF **prendre, pouvoir, mettre, faire**

je prisse	je pusse	je misse	je fisse
tu prisses	tu pusses	tu misses	tu fisses
il prît	il pût	il mît	il fît
nous prissions	nous pussions	nous missions	nous fissions
vous prissiez	vous pussiez	vous missiez	vous fissiez
ils prissent	ils pussent	ils missent	ils fissent

NOTE. — For the u throughout in **pusse**, etc., see § 149, *b*.

A. Continue: 1. Il fallait que je vendisse ma maison. 2. Il faudrait que je finisse bientôt. 3. Bien que je fusse habitué(e) à voyager. 4. Avant que j'eusse débarqué. 5. Il désirait que je fisse un
voyage. 6. Il doutait que je pusse le faire.

(The following passage is given in literary style to afford practice in the
verb-forms.)

B. 1. Un de mes amis fit récemment un voyage en Europe. 2. Il
fallut qu'il allât d'abord à la gare et qu'il prît son billet de chemin
de fer. 3. Pour qu'il pût voyager agréablement il prit une place
dans le wagon-lit. 4. Arrivé à New York il fallut qu'il s'occupât de
ses bagages. 5. Il ordonna qu'on descendît sa grande malle, qui
était très lourde, dans la cale et qu'on mît ses valises dans la cabine.
6. En pleine mer le vent soufflait et le vaisseau roulait. 7. Bien
que mon ami fût assez habitué au roulis il fallut qu'il se couchât
pour empêcher le mal de mer. 8. Avant qu'on eût fait la moitié
de la traversée il était complètement remis. 9. Il débarqua à
Cherbourg d'où il partit pour Paris.

C. 1. My father recently had to take (make) a journey to
Europe. 2. He had to get (take) his railway ticket. 3. He went
early to the station. 4. He went (there) early in order that he
might have a good place in the sleeping car. 5. When he arrived at
New York he had to see after his trunk. 6. He had his other luggage
with him in the train. 7. But he ordered his trunk, which was
heavy, to be lowered (use *on*) into the hold. 8. Although the wind
was blowing the ship didn't roll much. 9. As he was not accustomed to travelling he had to lie down. 10. He lay down in order
not to be (*avoir*) seasick. 11. Before he arrived at Cherbourg he
had (was) completely recovered.

D. 1. Before my friend started he took his ticket. 2. He had to
take his ticket at the station. 3. He had to be there early in order
to do that. 4. Although he arrived there early, he hadn't much
time. 5. I wished him to get a ticket for me also. 6. I should like
you to see about my luggage. 7. We should like you to put our
valises into the stateroom. 8. Although our friends hadn't arrived
we couldn't (*impf.*) wait. 9. We regretted that they had been
hindered. 10. Although my uncle was ill, he was able to travel.
11. We had arrived before the train left for Paris.

LESSON LII

157. Principal Parts. — 1. The whole conjugation of any regular verb, and of most irregular verbs, may be known from five forms of the verb, called "principal parts," as shown below for **écrire**, *write*. These parts are the infinitive, the present participle, the past participle, the present indicative 1st singular and the past definite 1st singular; from each is formed the mood or tense in the column below.

1. Infin.	2. Pres. Part.	3. Past Part.	4. Pres. Ind. 1 Sg.	5. P. Def. 1 Sg.
écrire	écrivant	écrit	j'écris	j'écrivis
Future	*Impf. Ind.*	*Comp. Tenses*	*Imperative*	*Impf. Subj.*
j'écrirai, etc.	j'écrivais, etc.	j'ai écrit, etc.	écris, etc.	j'écrivisse, etc.
Conditional	*Pres. Subj.*			
j'écrirais, etc.	j'écrive, etc.			
Rule: Add to the Infinitive (dropping final –e)	Rule: Drop –ant and add the endings	Rule: Add the Past Participle to the proper auxiliary (§ 45) to form the Compound Tenses, and also the Passive Voice of transitive verbs (§ 118).	Rule: Form the Imperative by dropping the subject pronoun of the 2d singular, 1st and 2d plural of the Present Indicative (–s of the 2d singular 1st conjugation being also dropped, except before **en, y,** e.g. parles-en, vas-y).	Rule: Form the Imperfect Subjunctive by substituting –sse –ssions –sses –ssiez –ˆt –ssent for the final letter of the 1st singular Past Definite, placing a circumflex accent over the last vowel of the 3d singular.
–ai –ons –as –ez –a –ont to form the Future, and	–ais –ions –ais –iez –ait –aient to form the Imperf., and			
–ais –ions –ais –iez –ait –aient to form the Conditional.	–e –ions –es –iez –e –ent to form the Pres. Subjunct.			
	(a) The 1st and 2d Plural Present Indicative and Imperative may also be formed by changing –ant into –ons, –ez.			

2. A condensed form of the above is used in the Alphabetical List of the Irregular Verbs (see Appendix), thus:

écrire	écrivant	écrit	écris	écrivis
(*write*)	écrivais			écrivisse
écrirai(s)	écrive			

PRESENT INDICATIVE:

écris, écris, écrit, écrivons, écrivez, écrivent.

158. Remarks on Irregular Verbs. — 1. The infinitive stem of some verbs is phonetically modified in the future and conditional, e.g. venir, **viend**rai(s).

2. The stem-vowel of the present participle is phonetically modified in the present subjunctive of some verbs, where stressed (1st, 2d, 3d singular and 3d plural), e.g. v**e**nant, v**ie**nne, v**ie**nnes, v**ie**nne, v**ie**nnent; usually also in the same persons of the present indicative, e.g. v**ie**ns, v**ie**ns, v**ie**nt, v**ie**nnent.

3. Many verbs have the present indicative singular in –s, –s, –t, others in –x, –x, –t, e.g. sais, sais, sait (savoir), veu**x**, veu**x**, veut (vouloir); the –t is omitted after c, d, t, e.g. vainc (vaincre), vend (vendre), met (mettre).

4. Some verbs have the past definite in –us, –us, –ut, –ûmes, –ûtes, –urent, and the imperfect subjunctive in –usse, –usses, –ût, –ussions, –ussiez, –ussent, e.g. cour**us**, etc. (courir), cou**russe**, etc.

5. All verbs with the past definite in –is continue the tense like finis, e.g. pris, pris, prit, prîmes, prîtes, prirent.

6. Verbs in –oir (a separate conjugation in some grammars) are treated as irregular verbs.

7. Exceptions to the rules of § 157 will be indicated in the Alphabetical List; **avoir** and **être** are not included under the rules.

8. The present indicative of each verb should be learned in full.

159. Exercise Form. — For exercises and tests the following tabular form is suggested; the form may be ruled large enough to contain several verbs, the different verbs being indicated by numerals, as shown in the margin:

INFIN.	PRES. PART.	PAST PART.	PRES. IND. 1 SG.	P. DEF. 1 SG.
(1) savoir, *know*	sachant	su	je sais	je sus
(2) connaître, *know*	connaissant	connu	je connais	je connus
(3) naître, *be born*	naissant	né	je nais	je naquis

FUT. 1 SG.	IMPF. IND. 1 SG.	P. IND. 1 SG.	IMPVE. 2 SG.	IMP. SUB. 1 SG.
(1) je saurai	je savais	j'ai su	sache	je susse
(2) je connaîtrai	je connaissais	j'ai connu	connais	je connusse
(3) je naîtrai	je naissais	je suis né(e)	nais	je naquisse

CONDL. 1 SG.	PRES. SUBJ. (*in full, using abbreviations if necessary*)
(1) je saurais	je sache, tu saches, il sache, nous sachions, vous sachiez, ils sachent.
(2) je connaîtrais	je connaisse, tu –s, il –e, nous connaissions, vous –iez, ils –ent.
(3) je naîtrais	je naisse, tu naisses, il naisse, nous naissions, vous –iez, ils –ent.

PRES. INDIC. (*in full, underlining forms common to the Imperative*)

(1) je sais, t. sais,[1] i. sait, n. savons, v. savez, i. savent.
(2) je connais, t. <u>connais</u>, i. connaît, n. <u>connaissons</u>, v. <u>connaissez</u>, i. connaissent.
(3) je nais, t. <u>nais</u>, i. naît, n. <u>naissons</u>, v. <u>naissez</u>, i. naissent.

[1] *Imperative:* sache, sachons, sachez.

NOTE. — Printed forms, ruled as above, and with space for writing out five verbs, may be obtained from the Publishers for classroom use.

EXERCISE LII

NOTE. — Before doing this and similar exercises, study the verbs required in detail in the Alphabetical List.

Like **connaître** is **reconnaître**, *recognize.*

Distinguish **savoir**, *know* (what has been learned, or is realized by the mind), *know how to, can,* from **connaître**, *know* (be acquainted with, recognize by the perceptions):

Je **connais** cette dame de vue.   *I know that lady by sight.*
Je ne **sais** pas où elle demeure.   *I don't know where she lives.*

Usually *was born* = **est né**, of persons still living; otherwise **était né** or **naquit**, but with numerous exceptions.

A. (*Oral.*) *Continue:* 1. Je ne saurai (connaîtrai) pas. 2. Je connaîtrais (saurais). 3. Je n'en savais rien. 4. Je n'y connaissais personne. 5. Je suis né(e) au 19ᵉ siècle. 6. Je sais faire cela. 7. Je ne connais pas cet endroit. 8. Il est content que je sache ma leçon, ... tu ... ta. 9. Je ne les ai pas reconnus.

B. 1. What do you know of that affair? 2. I know nothing of it. 3. Do you not know me? 4. I do, but I didn't recognize you at first. 5. They didn't know the date. 6. Would you know my brother? 7. I am glad that you know your verses. 8. They didn't know the city very well. 9. It is necessary that we should know him. 10. In what year were you born? 11. I was born in the last year of the 19th century.

C. 1. I was acquainted with that lady. 2. My mother knew her very well. 3. They will not know where we are. 4. He would not know where to find us. 5. I wish you to know your lessons for to-morrow. 6. I knew nobody at the concert. 7. William I was born in 1027. 8. Do you know at what o'clock the train arrived? 9. My uncle knows America well. 10. I didn't know whether you would recognize me. 11. I was the first to recognize you. 12. He didn't know how to do his work. 13. The teacher was glad that we knew our lessons to-day.

LESSON LIII

160. Agreement of Verb and Subject. — Review § 4 and observe: —

1. The agreement of the verb with a simple subject:

Le peuple français est vif.	*The French people are lively.*
La plupart du monde le croit.	*Most people believe it.*
La plupart (des hommes) le croient.	*Most men believe it.*

(*a*) A collective noun singular requires a verb singular; so also for collectives in general, if limited by **de** + a singular.

(*b*) Otherwise the agreement is usually with the sense as in English, example 3.

2. The agreement of the verb with a compound subject:

Toi et moi (nous) le croyons.	*You and I believe it.*
Vous et lui (vous) l'avez vu.	*You and he have seen it.*
Sa sœur et lui sont venus.	*His sister and he have come.*
L'un ou l'autre l'aura.	*One or the other will have it.*
Ni l'un ni l'autre ne sont bons.	*Neither are good.*

(*a*) The verb is regularly plural, unless, as in Ex. 4, one subject excludes the other; for agreement when the subjects are of different persons observe Ex. 1 and 2, usually with redundant **nous, vous.**

161. Position of Subject. — Apart from interrogations (cf. § 8), the subject often follows the verb, as in the following:

Fais comme moi, dit-il.	*Do as I do, said he.*
Que veux-tu? demanda le fils.	*What do you wish? asked the son.*
À peine le jour fut-il arrivé.	*Hardly had the day arrived.*
Aussi mon ami est-il venu.	*Hence my friend came.*
Peut-être a-t-il raison. ⎫ Peut-être qu'il a raison. ⎭	*Perhaps he is right.*
Il fera ce que peut faire un homme qui se respecte.	*He will do what a man who respects himself can do.*
Je ne sais pas où est ma mère.	*I don't know where my mother is.*
C'est en lui qu'espère son ami.	*It is in him that his friend hopes.*
But: C'est en lui qu'elle espère.	*It is in him that she hopes.*

(*a*) In remarks explanatory of quotation, as in English, Ex. 1 and 2.

(*b*) Often when an adverb heads the clause, Ex. 3, 4 and 5; always so for **aussi,** *hence,* Ex. 4, but never for **peut-être que,** Ex. 6.

(*c*) A subject (not a personal pronoun) often follows the verb in a relative clause or after **c'est que,** Ex. 7, 8 and 9.

EXERCISE LIII

A. 1. The American people like winter sports. 2. A part of our family live in the country. 3. This kind of pears is always dear. 4. You and he are always together. 5. You and I have always been good friends. 6. Neither (the one nor the other) of the pictures has been sold. 7. Few people (*gens*) know Paris better than he. 8. If I do this, answered he, I shall lose my time. 9. Perhaps we shall catch the train; let us hasten. 10. He will do for (*pour*) me all that a good friend can do. 11. My mother is kind to everybody; hence she is loved by all. 12. This dealer makes large

profits; hence he is becoming rich. 13. Where is your hat? I asked.
14. I know where my hat is, he replied, but I don't know where my
gloves are.

B. 1. The French people love the theatre. 2. How is your
father? my mother asked him. 3. He is not very well, he replied.
4. The man was running very fast; perhaps he had stolen something.
5. Do you remember what they were doing? 6. Does not everybody
love his country? 7. The architect will oversee what the workmen
are doing. 8. You and he were present at the ball, were you not?
9. He and I were there and also many of our acquaintances. 10. Will
you and your friend not come to see us when you are in town?
11. Do you know what I wish? 12. Do you know what that man
wants who is knocking at the door? 13. Do you know where the
reading room is? 14. Is it in this house that your uncle and aunt
live?

LESSON LIV

162.   **Principal Parts of** *pouvoir*, 'be able,' etc.; *vouloir*,
       'wish,' 'will,' 'like,' etc.; *voir*, 'see'

pouvoir	pouvant	pu	peux *or* puis	pus
vouloir	voulant	voulu	veux	voulus
voir	voyant	vu	vois	vis

EXERCISE LIV

(The irregular verbs in this and following exercises should be written out
in full or practised orally according to the model at § 159.)

A. (*Oral.*) *Continue throughout the tense:* 1. Je pourrai (voudrai).
2. Je voudrais (pourrais). 3. Je verrai (verrais). 4. Je voulais
(pouvais, voyais). 5. Je peux (veux, vois). 6. Je pus (voulus, vis).
7. Que je pusse (voulusse, visse). 8. Que je puisse (voie).

B. 1. I am not able to do that. 2. If I (you, he, we) were able.
3. Have you been able? 4. He (you, they) would be able. 5. What
do they wish? 6. I (he, we, you, they) did not wish to travel.
7. He (they) would like to remain here. 8. What books have

you seen? 9. Shall I see you to-morrow? 10. What do you see? 11. I see nothing. 12. If they had been here, I should have seen them.

C. 1. He (you, they) would like to study. 2. What have you seen? 3. He wishes me to see his pictures. 4. I wish them to see my garden. 5. He would see you if he were not ill. 6. They will see you if they can. 7. I wished to start yesterday, but I was not able. 8. They will not be able to sell their house. 9. Shall we be able to catch the train? 10. Do what you wish (*fut.*). 11. The carpenter wasn't able to carry the board; it was too heavy.

LESSON LV

163. Auxiliary Function. — Several verbs, when followed directly by an infinitive, have a sort of auxiliary function, and serve to form *verb-phrases* of an idiomatic character.

164.   *Vouloir*, 'will,' 'wish (want, desire) to,' etc.

Il ne veut pas vous voir.	*He will not (doesn't wish) to see you.*
Il vous parlera demain.	*He will speak to you to-morrow.*
Il ne voulait pas partir.	*He was unwilling to (wouldn't) go.*
Il voudrait (bien) le savoir.	*He would like to know it.*
Il aurait voulu venir.	*He would have liked to come.*

(*a*) Distinguish *will* of futurity, Ex. 2, from *will* of purpose, Ex. 1.

(*b*) Distinguish *would* of the imperfect, Ex. 3, from *would* of the conditional, Ex. 4 and 5.

165. *Pouvoir*, 'can,' 'be able to,' 'be permitted to,' 'may,' etc.

Je peux faire cela moi-même.	*I can do that myself.*
Est-ce que je puis entrer?	*May I come (go) in?*
Je ne pouvais pas lire la lettre.	*I couldn't read the letter.*
Je n'ai pas pu le faire.	*I could not (was unable to) do it.*
Il pourrait venir s'il voulait.	*He could come if he would.*
Aurait-il pu venir ce soir?	*Could he have come this evening?*
Pourrais-je vous demander ceci?	*Might (could) I ask you this?*

(*a*) **Pouvoir** = *can* or *may*, Ex. 1 and 2.

(*b*) Distinguish *could* = *was able* in a past tense, Ex. 3 and 4, from *could* = *would be able* of the conditional, Ex. 5 and 6.

(*c*) Note the English rendering of the conditional in Ex. 7.

166.　　*Savoir,* 'know,' 'know how to,' 'can,' etc.

Il sait écrire.	*He can (knows how to) write.*
Il est malade et ne peut pas écrire ce soir.	*He is ill, and cannot write this evening.*
Je ne saurais le croire.	*I cannot believe it.*

(*a*) Distinguish *can = know how to, has learned how to,* Ex. 1, from *can* of physical ability, Ex. 2.

(*b*) Note the English rendering of the conditional in Ex. 3.

EXERCISE LV

aider, *help*	la fourchette, *fork*
l'armoire, f., *cupboard*	intelligent, *intelligent*
arranger, *arrange*	Jeanne, *Jane*
l'assiette, f., *plate*	le ménage, *household*
le couteau, *knife*	la nappe, *tablecloth* (white)
le couvert, *cover* (dishes, etc., for one person)	la peur, *fear*
	le tiroir, *drawer*
la cuiller, *spoon*	

de peur de, *for fear of;* mettre la nappe, *lay the table(cloth), set the table;* faire le ménage, *keep house;* café au lait, *coffee with milk;* arranger les couverts, *arrange the dishes* (in setting the table)

A. Continue: 1. Je sais compter jusqu'à cent, tu. 2. Je voudrais bien y aller. 3. J'aurais voulu y aller si j'avais pu, tu . . . tu. 4. Je pourrais y aller si je voulais, tu . . . tu. 5. Je ne pouvais pas sortir. 6. Je ferai ce que je voudrai, tu . . . tu. 7. Aurais-je pu faire cela? 8. Je ne peux pas écrire parce que je suis malade, tu . . . tu.

B. 1. Jeanne est une petite fille habile et intelligente. 2. Elle sait déjà lire et écrire, mais elle ne peut pas aller tous les jours à l'école. 3. Elle voudrait savoir faire le ménage. 4. Et sa mère voudrait aussi qu'elle sache cela. 5. Tous les matins elle se lève de bonne heure pour qu'elle puisse aider sa mère. 6. Elle sait mettre la nappe et arranger les couverts. 7. Elle sait dans quels tiroirs se trouvent les serviettes, les couteaux, les fourchettes et les cuillers. 8. Si elle était plus grande, elle pourrait prendre les assiettes et les tasses qui sont dans la grande armoire. 9. Sa mère ne veut pas qu'elle y touche de peur de les casser. 10. Son père lui dit quelquefois: "Jeanne, si tu savais me faire un bon café au lait, tu serais une bonne petite ménagère."

C. (*Oral.*) 1. Savez-vous parler français? 2. Savez-vous l'écrire aussi? 3. Pourriez-vous écrire une lettre en français? 4. Sauriez-vous me dire si votre frère est déjà levé? 5. Pourquoi Jeanne se lève-t-elle de bonne heure? 6. Que sait-elle faire? 7. Que pourrait-elle faire si elle était plus grande? 8. Pourquoi sa mère ne veut-elle pas qu'elle touche à la vaisselle? etc.

D. 1. I cannot go to school to-day. 2. I should like to go (there) every day. 3. I can read, but I cannot write yet. 4. If I could go to school every day, I should soon learn to write. 5. My mother would like me to know how to keep house. 6. I know how to lay the table. 7. I cannot get the cups and plates in the cupboard. 8. My mother doesn't want me to touch them. 9. But I can get the knives, forks and spoons. 10. I know in which drawer they are. 11. If I were older, I could make a cup of coffee for my father. 12. I can't make the coffee yet; I am too young. 13. My mother says that if I could make the coffee, I should be a good little house-wife. 14. I should like to learn to make it.

E. 1. My sister can sing very well. 2. But she is ill and can't sing this evening. 3. She would like to sing if she could. 4. She helps her mother to (*à*) arrange the dishes. 5. She can't get the dishes (*vaisselle*) in the cupboard for fear of breaking them. 6. We cannot always do what we should like. 7. But we shall do what we can (*fut.*). 8. I tried to learn my lesson, but I couldn't. 9. Could you tell me what time it is? 10. I cannot; my watch is broken. 11. If I had my dress coat, I could go to the ball. 12. But the tailor couldn't bring it; it wasn't ready. 13. He would have brought it if he had been able. 14. We should like to go to Europe this summer if we could. 15. Couldn't you go with us?

LESSON LVI

167.   *Aller*, 'go'; *devoir*, 'owe,' 'be obliged';
                          venir, 'come'

aller	allant	allé	vais	allai
devoir	devant	dû (*f.* due)	dois	dus
venir	venant	venu	viens	vins

EXERCISE LVI

A. (*Oral.*) *Continue:* 1. J'irai (irais) le voir. 2. J'allais et venais tout le temps. 3. Je ne lui dois (devais, devrai) rien. 4. Je viendrai les voir. 5. Je m'en suis allé(e). 6. Je suis venu(e) à pied. 7. J'y vais tout de suite. 8. J'irai[1] (irais) avec plaisir. 9. Vas-y. 10. Viens. 11. Il faut que j'y aille (vienne). 12. J'y allai. 13. Je vins ici tout seul. 14. Il fallait que j'y allasse (vinsse). 15. Il est fâché que je doive partir, . . . tu.

B. 1. Where are you going? 2. I am going home. 3. He owes me ten francs. 4. You owe me nothing. 5. Come (2d *sing.*) with me. 6. Do not go there. 7. We shall go to the concert. 8. They will come to see us. 9. I should go if I could. 10. Come next week. 11. Go there at once. 12. Go away (*s'en aller*). 13. I desired him to go to the market. 14. They came early. 15. They have come.

C. 1. We are going to have some friends to dinner. 2. Whom are you going to invite? 3. We shall owe them much money. 4. I owed you nothing. 5. When will they come? 6. When did they (*f.*) come? 7. Pay me what you owe me. 8. Come at once. 9. I must (use *il faut*) go away. 10. He must come to see us. 11. Owe nothing to anybody. 12. They (*f.*) have gone away. 13. They came in [a] carriage. 14. It was necessary for him to come. 15. He didn't owe me anything.

LESSON LVII

168. Devoir = *owe*, but observe also its force in various tenses when followed directly by an infinitive:

PRESENT:	Je dois parler.	*I am to (have to, must) speak.*
IMPF.:	Je devais parler.	*I was (had, was obliged) to speak.*
FUTURE:	Je devrai parler.	*I shall have (be obliged) to speak.*
CONDL.:	Je devrais parler.	*I ought to (should) speak.*
PAST INDEF.:	J'ai dû parler.	*I have had (been obliged) to speak, had to speak, must have spoken.*
PAST DEF.:	Je dus parler.	*I had (was obliged) to speak.*
CONDL. ANT.:	J'aurais dû parler.	*I ought to have (should have) spoken.*

[1] **Aller** regularly requires a complement, but **y** so used is omitted before **irai,** etc., **irais,** etc.

169. *Aller.* — The present and imperfect + a direct infinitive give a sort of immediate future, like *go*, etc., in English:

Il va l'acheter.	*He is going (is about) to buy it.*
Nous allions partir.	*We were (just) about to start.*
Il allait se noyer.	*He was on the point of drowning.*
Allez le voir demain.	*Go to (go and) see him to-morrow.*

170. *Venir.* — Observe its force when followed by an infinitive (1) without a preposition, (2) with **de**, (3) with **à**, the two latter in the present and imperfect:

Il est venu me voir.	*He came to see (came and saw) me.*
Je viens **de** les voir.	*I have just seen them.*
Je venais **de** les voir.	*I had just seen them.*
S'il venait **à** voir le livre.	*If he happened to see the book.*

EXERCISE LVII

après-demain, *the day after to-morrow*
avant-hier, *the day before yesterday*
boire, *irreg., drink*
car, *for*
s'enrhumer, *catch (take) cold*
l'entrée, *f., entrée*
la fête, *festivity, holiday*
la glace, *ice (cream)*
la grand'mère, *grandmother*
le grand-père, *grandfather*
le hors-d'œuvre, *side dish, relish*
Lucie, *Lucy*

le menu, *menu, bill of fare*
la noix, *walnut*
la personne, *person*
le potage, *soup*
les préparatifs, *m., preparations*
le radis, *radish*
le rôti, *roast*
la salade, *salad*
la sardine, *sardine*
servir, *irreg., serve*
la sorte, *sort, kind*
tôt, *soon*
la visite, *visit, call*

d'ici là, *from now till then*

A. Continue: 1. Je venais de dîner chez eux, tu. 2. Je dois m'occuper du menu. 3. J'aurais dû commencer plus tôt. 4. Je devais y aller mais je ne pouvais pas, tu . . . tu. 5. J'ai dû partir de bonne heure. 6. Je devrais faire mes préparatifs, tu . . . tes. 7. Je viens de leur parler. 8. Je vais m'occuper de cette affaire. 9. Je suis venu(e) le voir. 10. Si je venais à le voir.

B. 1. Nous venons de dîner chez mon grand-père et ma grand' mère. 2. Toute la famille devait y être, mais quelques-uns des parents ne pouvaient pas venir. 3. Mon père s'était enrhumé et a dû partir avant la fin. 4. Avant-hier ma tante Lucie, à qui nous devions une visite, a donné une réception. 5. Comme c'est la saison des fêtes de famille, tous nos parents viendront dîner chez nous mardi prochain. 6. D'ici là ma mère et mes sœurs vont avoir beaucoup à faire. 7. Demain ou après-demain elles doivent commencer leurs préparatifs. 8. Si on venait à oublier quelque chose, ma mère serait très fâchée. 9. Elles auraient dû peut-être commencer plus tôt, car il va y avoir (*to be*) une vingtaine de personnes au dîner. 10. Ma mère doit s'occuper du menu. 11. Pour un bon dîner on devrait servir d'abord un hors-d'œuvre de radis, de sardines ou quelque chose de la sorte, et puis un bon potage. 12. Après le potage on devrait avoir une entrée, des légumes, un bon rôti et de la salade. 13. Ensuite on devrait servir des glaces, des fruits, des noix, et une tasse de café noir.

C. (*Oral on B.*)

D. 1. My grandfather and grandmother have just dined with us. 2. It (*ce*) was to be a family dinner. 3. The sons, daughters and their children were to be there. 4. Some of our relatives had to refuse the invitation. 5. My uncle had caught cold and was obliged to stay at home. 6. We are all to go to my aunt Lucy's reception the day after to-morrow. 7. One should attend these family festivities, you know. 8. The whole family is to dine at my aunt's next Monday. 9. She is going to see about the menu at once. 10. My mother was to help her, but she can't. 11. She fell while taking a walk. 12. She ought to have gone to bed at once. 13. You ought to take a little of this salad, it is very good. 14. May I offer you some fruit or walnuts? 15. One shouldn't drink too much black coffee.

E. 1. We have invited twenty people (*personne*) to dinner. 2. We shall first have radishes or sardines and then a soup. 3. The roast will come after the entrée. 4. There will be several sorts of fruits. 5. The ices and coffee will be served at the end. 6. He ought to come sooner. 7. He ought to have come sooner. 8. Here is a twenty-five franc note which I have just found. 9. It must be yours. 10. Yes, it is mine, I must have lost it yesterday. 11. We

were to start for the country the day before yesterday. 12. Come
and dine with us next Sunday. 13. You owe us a visit. 14. You
ought not to have spoken of it. 15. You ought to begin your preparations at once. 16. What are we to do now? The train has gone.
17. It has just gone. 18. It had just gone when I arrived at the
station. 19. We shall have to wait for another train.

LESSON LVIII

171. *Dire*, 'say,' 'tell'; *faire*, 'do,' 'make'; *mettre*, 'put,'
'place'; *prendre*, 'take'

dire	disant	dit	dis	dis
faire	faisant	fait	fais	fis
mettre	mettant	mis	mets	mis
prendre	prenant	pris	prends	pris

EXERCISE LVIII

adieu or au revoir, *good-bye*

A. (*Oral.*) *Continue:* 1. Je mets (prends, dis). 2. Je disais
(faisais, mettais, prenais). 3. Je prendrai (mettrai, ferai, dirai).
4. Je fis (mis, pris, dis). 5. Je mettrais (dirais, ferais, prendrais).
6. Je me suis mis(e) à table. 7. Je lui ai dit adieu (au revoir).
8. Que je mette (dise, fasse, prenne). 9. Que je disse (fisse, misse,
prisse). 10. Prends. 11. Dis. 12. Mets. 13. Fais.

B. 1. What do you (will you, would you) say? 2. What have you
said (done, taken)? 3. The others will take (say) that. 4. Would
they say (do) the same thing? 5. I was taking a walk. 6. What was
he saying? 7. He has put [on] his overcoat. 8. Tell me what he
has said (done, taken). 9. What have you done? 10. Take my
stick; don't take John's. 11. We wish you to say (do, take) what
you wish (*fut.*). 12. Do you wish me to set the table?

C. 1. Say what you will (*fut.*). 2. They have said (done, taken)
that. 3. Have you put the plates on the table? 4. Saying that,
he went away. 5. I shall take some salad. 6. They would say the

same thing. 7. They were saying good-bye. 8. They wouldn't take any wine. 9. Take my pen. 10. Put the cups and plates on the table. 11. Let us take a walk. 12. Let us tell them that. 13. I wished him to tell me all (*tout*). 14. I wished him to take my place.

LESSON LIX

172. *Faire* causatively. — 1. This verb + an infinitive corresponds to a great variety of expressions in English which may be explained by the meaning *cause to do* or *be done:*

J'ai fait écrire les enfants.	*I have made the children write.*
Il les fera écouter.	*He will make them listen.*
La robe qu'elle s'est fait faire.	*The dress she got made for herself.*

(*a*) The past participle **fait** thus used is invariable.

2. A governed substantive follows the infinitive, but a governed conjunctive personal pronoun goes with **faire:**

Faites venir la domestique.	*Have the servant (get the servant to) come.*
Faites-la venir.	*Have her come (send for her).*

3. If the infinitive with **faire** has a direct object, its personal object must be indirect:

Je fis lire **mon fils.**	*I made my son read.*
Je fis lire ce livre **à mon fils.**	*I made my son read this book.*
Faites-le-lui lire.	*Make him (get him to) read it.*

(*a*) Possible ambiguity is sometimes avoided by **par**, e.g. Il fit porter le sac **par** le guide, *He had the sack carried by the guide.*

(*b*) The infinitive of certain reflexives (**s'asseoir, se souvenir, se taire,** etc.) regularly omits **se**, e.g. **Faites asseoir vos amis**, *Have your friends sit down.*

(*c*) **Laisser**, *let*, **entendre**, *hear*, **voir**, *see*, sometimes have the same construction as **faire**: Laissez-leur (*or* -**les**) faire cela, *Let them do that;* J'ai entendu dire cela **à** mon frère *or* **J'ai entendu mon frère dire cela**, *I heard my brother say that.*

EXERCISE LIX

blanchir, *whiten, wash* (linen)
brosser, *brush*
le coiffeur, *barber, hairdresser*
le complet, *suit (of clothes)*
le cordonnier, *shoemaker*
le faux col, *collar* (detachable)
le garçon coiffeur, *journeyman barber*
les habits, m., *clothes*
Julien, *Julian*
le linge, *linen*
la manchette, *cuff*
la mesure, *measure*

mis, p. part. of **mettre**, *dressed*
la mise, *dress, manner of dressing*
la négligence, *carelessness*
la paire, *pair*
le pourboire, *gratuity, tip*
la propreté, *cleanliness, neatness, tidiness*
respecter, *respect*
soigner, *take care of*
soigneusement, *carefully*
le soulier, *shoe*
le vêtement, sing., *garment, suit,* pl. *clothes*

faire payer, *charge;* faire voir, *show;* laisser à désirer, *leave* (something) *to be desired, not be satisfactory;* se laisser aller à, *yield to, give way to*

A. Continue: 1. Je me fais respecter. 2. Je ferai travailler les ouvriers. 3. Je vais me faire faire une robe, tu . . . te. 4. Je me suis fait faire un complet, tu . . . t'. 5. Je devrais me faire couper les cheveux, tu . . . te. 6. Je leur ai fait payer le prix. 7. Je me suis fait payer, tu . . . t'. 8. Fais-les (*impve.*) travailler. 9. Je vais leur faire voir les beautés de la ville.

B. 1. Tout jeune homme devrait être bien mis. 2. On ne se fait pas respecter en se laissant aller à la négligence. 3. Il faut qu'on fasse blanchir soigneusement son linge. 4. Les faux cols et les manchettes font voir tout de suite si on aime la propreté. 5. Mon frère Julien soigne assez bien ses vêtements. 6. Cependant sa mise laisse un peu à désirer, et sa mère lui a dit d'aller chez le tailleur se faire faire un complet. 7. Le tailleur lui a fait voir des étoffes, et puis il a pris sa mesure. 8. Le tailleur lui fera payer le complet cent dix francs. 9. Ensuite, chez le cordonnier, il s'est fait prendre mesure pour une paire de souliers. 10. Le cordonnier se la (*or* les) fera payer vingt francs. 11. Entrant chez le coiffeur il s'est fait couper les cheveux. 12. Il paie la coupe de cheveux dix sous. 13. Après s'être fait brosser ses habits il donne quatre sous de pourboire au garçon coiffeur.

C. (*Oral on B.*)

D. 1. That young man is not well dressed. 2. He is going to get himself a suit made. 3. He will have his measure taken at the tailor's. 4. Have you had your measure taken? 5. I have had (myself) a suit made. 6. I didn't like the materials the tailor showed me. 7. He is going to charge me 125 francs. 8. Here is the pair of shoes which I have had made (for myself). 9. You ought to get your hair cut; it is too long. 10. I shall get it cut to-morrow. 11. After having my clothes brushed, I shall give the barber a tip. 12. Everybody should be well dressed. 13. One must make oneself respected in this world. 14. Get these collars and cuffs washed. 15. I have had our linen washed.

E. 1. Take good care of (*soigner bien*) your clothes. 2. Your dress (*mise*) is not very satisfactory. 3. Go to the shoemaker's to get yourself a pair of shoes made. 4. How much am I to pay? 5. He will charge you 25 francs, but it (*ce*) is cheap. 6. I shall make them study. 7. I shall make them write their exercises. 8. Get the tailor to come. 9. Get these collars washed carefully. 10. Your cuffs are not clean. 11. Cleanliness causes a young man to be respected. 12. Show me some (*de*) of your best cloths. 13. How much will you charge me [for] the suit? 14. This dress which I got (myself) made in Paris doesn't fit me. 15. I shall get myself another made as soon as I arrive in New York.

LESSON LX

173. *Envoyer*, 'send'; *recevoir*, 'receive'; *mouvoir*, 'move'; *mourir*, 'die'

envoyer	envoyant	envoyé	envoie	envoyai
recevoir	recevant	reçu	reçois	reçus
mouvoir	mouvant	mû (*f.* mue)	meus	mus
mourir	mourant	mort	meurs	mourus

Like **recevoir: s'apercevoir** (**de**), *perceive.*

EXERCISE LX

le cadeau, *present, gift*	**la poste,** *post office*
les nouvelles, f., *news*	**la soif,** *thirst*

mourir de soif, *be very thirsty*

A. (*Oral.*) *Continue:* 1. Je m'en aperçois. 2. Je lui enverrai (enverrais) la lettre. 3. Je recevrai quelque chose. 4. Je meurs (mourais) de soif. 5. Je recevais de bonnes nouvelles. 6. Il veut que je reçoive de bons gages. 7. Il faudra que je meure. 8. Que je reçusse.

B. 1. I send (shall send) my son to school. 2. He (you, they) will receive a gift. 3. What news have you received? 4. My poor aunt died yesterday. 5. All men will die. 6. They (we) were very thirsty. 7. They (*f.*) would have died. 8. Do you wish me to send the letters to the post office? 9. They (we, I) perceive (of) nothing. 10. If he dies, his family will have nothing. 11. I wished him to receive good wages.

C. 1. They receive news every day. 2. Put the letters you have received into this drawer. 3. My father will send me money. 4. I shall receive it soon. 5. All men are born and die. 6. His family knew he was dying. 7. They said he would die. 8. Many persons have died. 9. Napoleon III died in 1873. 10. I wish him to receive this letter to-day. 11. I should like Mr. Liard to send me a good roast.

LESSON LXI

174. Additional Verb-Phrases. — Observe the following:

faire savoir, *inform, let one know*	**entendre parler de,** *hear (spoken)*
entendre dire, *hear (say* or *said)*	*of*
aller chercher, *go for, go and get*	**faire attendre,** *keep (one) waiting*
envoyer chercher, *send for*	**venir chercher,** *come for*
venir prendre, *come for, come and*	**faire venir,** *send for*
get	

EXERCISE LXI

l'accident, m., *accident*	**Marcel,** *Marcellus*
l'après-midi, f., *afternoon*	**le neveu,** *nephew*
aussitôt que, *as soon as*	**la nièce,** *niece*
changer, *change*	**Renée,** *Renée* (name, *f.*)
le courrier, *courier, post, mail*	**retard (en),** *late*
se demander, *ask oneself, wonder*	**télégraphier,** *telegraph*
exact, *exact, precise*	**téléphoner,** *telephone*

j'ai reçu de ses nouvelles, *I have heard from (received news of) him*

A. Continue: 1. Je reçois souvent de ses nouvelles.   2. Je vais le lui faire savoir.   3. J'en ai souvent entendu parler.   4. J'entends dire que le train est en retard.   5. Je me demande si c'est vrai.   6. Fais-les (*impve.*) attendre.   7. Je ferai venir une voiture.   8. J'enverrai chercher mes neveux, tu . . . tes.   9. Je suis venu(e) les chercher.   10. Je vais les chercher tout de suite.

B. 1. J'ai reçu des nouvelles de mon neveu Marcel il y a quelques semaines.   2. J'ai reçu encore de ses nouvelles par le courrier de ce matin.   3. Il me fait savoir par sa lettre, et il me télégraphie aussi, qu'il arrivera avec ma nièce Renée cette après-midi.   4. Mais on entend tellement parler d'accidents!   5. On ne sait jamais ce qui peut arriver.   6. J'entends dire que leur train, celui de 5 h. 45 du soir, est presque tous les jours en retard.   7. Je me demande s'il va arriver à l'heure exacte aujourd'hui.   8. Je ne voudrais pas qu'on me fasse attendre, car je vais les chercher à la gare.   9. J'ai entendu dire que Marcel et Renée sont beaucoup changés.   10. Je ne les reconnaîtrai plus peut-être.   11. Mais je téléphonerai à mon mari de venir nous chercher à la gare.   12. Il pourra envoyer chercher une voiture qui ira le prendre à son bureau.   13. Il m'aidera à les reconnaître.   14. Aussitôt que nous les aurons trouvés nous les amènerons chez nous et nous ferons venir leurs bagages plus tard.

C. (*Oral.*)   1. Quand avez-vous reçu des nouvelles de votre neveu et de votre nièce?   2. Avez-vous reçu de leurs nouvelles aujourd'hui?   3. Quand vont-ils arriver?   4. De quel train parlez-vous?   5. Arrive-t-il généralement à l'heure exacte?   6. Qui allez-vous chercher à la gare?   7. Votre nièce est-elle beaucoup changée?   8. La reconnaîtrez-vous sans difficulté?   9. Qui doit envoyer chercher une voiture?   10. Que ferez-vous quand vous aurez trouvé votre nièce?   11. Quand enverrez-vous chercher ses bagages? etc.

D. 1. We have just received news of my nephew and niece.   2. We don't often get (receive) news of them.   3. Their letter arrived by this morning's mail.   4. They inform us that they are going to arrive this afternoon.   5. If the train is not late, they will be here at 5.25 P.M.   6. I wonder if the train will arrive on time to-day.   7. I have heard that it is almost always late.   8. My husband and I (we) are going to get them at the station.   9. They have telegraphed us that they will be late.   10. If they are much

changed, we shall not recognize them perhaps. 11. I wonder if
they will recognize us. 12. Your father has gone to get a carriage.
13. It will come and get us here. 14. We shall start as soon as it
comes. 15. First we shall bring my niece here, and then we shall
send for her baggage.

E. 1. Our friends heard from their brother six weeks ago. 2. They
heard from him again by yesterday evening's mail. 3. He is going
to arrive by the 6.00 P.M. train. 4. His sister will come with him.
5. We have heard of a great many accidents, have we not? 6. The
trains are often late. 7. We were wondering whether their train
would be late. 8. We should not like to be kept (use *on*) waiting.
9. We are going to get our nephew and niece at the station. 10. We
have heard that they are much changed. 11. We can't (*fut.*) recognize them perhaps. 12. Let us telephone to our father. 13. He
will come and get us. 14. He will send for a carriage. 15. The
carriage will come and get us.

LESSON LXII

175.   *Croire*, 'believe,' 'think'; *lire*, 'read'

croire	croyant	cru	crois	crus
lire	lisant	lu	lis	lus

Like **lire**: **élire**, *elect*.

EXERCISE LXII

le journal, *newspaper*   **lentement**, *slowly*

A. (*Oral.*) *Continue:* 1. Je ne crois pas cette nouvelle. 2. Je ne
lis (lisais) pas bien. 3. Je serai élu. 4. Il faut que je lise d'autres
livres. 5. Je lirais plus si j'avais le temps, tu . . . tu. 6. Je ne croirais pas tout cela. 7. Les journaux que j'ai lus. 8. Crois-y (*believe
in it*). 9. Lis beaucoup. 10. Il voulait que je crusse cette histoire,
. . . tu. 11. Je lus la moitié du chapitre.

B. 1. Read more slowly. 2. They (you, we) read too fast.
3. By reading we learn to read. 4. What do you wish me (them,
him) to read? 5. I (we) shall read those newspapers. 6. They
would read better if they read more slowly. 7. Believe me. 8. Let

us not believe them.   9. Would you believe it?   10. You don't
believe what I say.   11. We (I) shall never believe that story.

C. 1. He read (*p. def.*) the whole chapter.   2. They read (*p. def.*)
the half of it.   3. I wished him to read good books.   4. What
books have you read?   5. Charles used to read badly.   6. He reads
much better now.   7. What were you reading when I came in?
8. I was reading the newspaper.   9. I think it is going to rain.
10. They thought we were not coming.   11. I thought they would
be elected.   12. You thought I had gone away, didn't you?

LESSON LXIII

176. Infinitive for Noun Clause. — After verbs of declaring,
intending, thinking, hoping, the verb of a *that* clause in English
may often be rendered in French by a direct infinitive, but only
when both verbs in the sentence have the same subject:

Je croyais le voir passer.	*I thought (that) I saw him pass.*
J'avoue l'avoir oublié.	*I confess (that) I forgot it.*
J'espère réussir.	*I hope (that) I shall succeed.*
J'ai cru devoir rester.	*I thought (that) I ought to stay.*
Je compte y être.	*I expect (that) I shall be there.*
But: Je crois qu'il est venu.	*I think (that) he has come.*

(*a*) Such verbs are: **affirmer, avouer, compter, croire, déclarer, espérer,**
etc.

EXERCISE LXIII

avouer, *declare, confess*
bonjour, *good morning, good day*
le bulletin (de vote), *ballot paper*
le candidat, *candidate*
le citoyen, *citizen*
la commune, *municipality*
compter, *count, reckon, purpose,*
  intend, expect
le conseiller, *councillor*
déposer, *deposit, cast* (vote)
l'électeur, m., *elector*

l'élection, f., *election*
l'examen, m., *examination*
la majorité, *majority*
municipal, *municipal*
occupé, *busy*
se passer, *be happening, be going on*
à propos (de), *with regard (to), by*
  the way
l'urne, f., *urn, ballot box*
le vote, *voting*
voter, *vote*

à moins d'être, *if one (etc.) is not;* **je l'espère,** *I hope so;* **être refusé,**
fail (to pass an examination); **il compte être reçu,** *he expects to pass*
(*at an examination*)

A. Continue: 1. J'avoue l'avoir oublié. 2. Je comptais partir ce soir. 3. J'ai cru l'avoir vu passer. 4. Je crois pouvoir passer l'examen. 5. J'espère y réussir cette fois. 6. Je n'ai pas cru devoir voter pour M. Liard. 7. Je ne compte pas être élu. 8. Je crois qu'il sera élu.

B. 1. Bonjour, Raymond, d'où viens-tu? — 2. Je viens du village. — 3. Je croyais t'avoir vu passer il y a une heure. 4. Qu'est-ce qui se passe au village? — 5. C'est le jour des élections. 6. On élit les conseillers municipaux. — 7. J'avoue avoir oublié cette affaire importante. 8. J'étais si occupé à me préparer pour mes examens. 9. À moins d'être bien préparé on n'y réussit pas. 10. J'y ai déjà été refusé. 11. J'espère y être reçu la prochaine fois. 12. Mais à propos des élections, est-ce qu'il y a beaucoup de candidats? — 13. Oui, il y en a plusieurs; mon père en est un, et il compte être élu cette fois. — 14. Je l'espère bien. 15. Est-ce que beaucoup des électeurs ont voté? — 16. Oui, la majorité des citoyens de la commune ont cru devoir déposer leurs bulletins de vote dans l'urne. 17. Alors Raymond dit "au revoir" et s'en va.

C. (Oral.) 1. D'où vient Raymond? 2. Quand l'avez-vous vu passer? 3. Qu'est-ce qui se passait au village? 4. Pourquoi aviez-vous oublié les élections? 5. Avez-vous réussi aux examens? 6. Pourquoi? 7. Combien de candidats y avait-il aux examens? 8. Y ont-ils réussi tous? 9. Avez-vous déjà voté aux élections? 10. Croyez-vous devoir toujours voter? 11. Où dépose-t-on son bulletin de vote? etc.

D. 1. I saw many citizens going to the village yesterday to (*pour*) vote. 2. We thought we saw you passing [by]. 3. We confess we had forgotten the elections. 4. We were preparing (ourselves) for our examinations. 5. If we are not well prepared (*see B,* 9), we shall fail. 6. My brother has failed twice. 7. I hope he will succeed this time. 8. He hopes he will succeed at his examinations. 9. Does your uncle expect that he will be elected? 10. He does. 11. I think I can vote to-morrow. 12. I think my uncle will have a considerable majority. 13. How many municipal councillors are there in this municipality?

E. 1. The thief confessed that he had stolen the money. 2. We were very busy yesterday. 3. While the electors were voting we were preparing (ourselves) for the examinations. 4. Vote for Mr. Liard if you think you ought to do so (*le*). 5. He expects to be elected. 6. I hope he will be elected. 7. I hope I shall be able to take a trip next summer. 8. I hope you can (*fut.*) go with me. 9. Where do you expect to embark? 10. I expect I shall embark at Havre. 11. With regard to your examinations, do you expect to pass? 12. I do. 13. I expected to pass the last time, but I failed. 14. I believe you will succeed this time. 15. Let us hope so (*le*).

LESSON LXIV

177. *Boire,* 'drink'; *coudre,* 'sew'; *moudre,* 'grind';
résoudre, 'resolve,' 'solve'

boire	buvant	bu	bois	bus
coudre	cousant	cousu	couds	cousis
moudre	moulant	moulu	mouds	moulus
résoudre	résolvant	résolu	résous	résolus

EXERCISE LXIV

le médecin, *doctor*   **le verre,** *glass*

A. (*Oral.*) *Continue:* 1. Je bois (j'ai bu) du lait. 2. Bois un verre d'eau. 3. Est-ce que je résoudrai les problèmes? 4. Je ne boirai (boirais) pas de vin. 5. Je buvais du thé ou du café au lait. 6. Je mouds (moulais) le blé. 7. Je coupe et couds bien. 8. J'ai résolu les problèmes. 9. Je bus un verre de lait. 10. Il faut que je couse la robe.

B. 1. We (you, they) drink water. 2. Let him drink a glass of milk. 3. What were they drinking? 4. He never drank any wine. 5. The doctor wished him to drink a little wine. 6. The miller grinds (has ground, will grind) the wheat. 7. Let him grind it.

8. He (I) was grinding it.   9. We (you, they) sew and cut well.
10. Solve your problems.   11. I have solved mine.   12. Let us
drink a cup of coffee and milk before starting.

C. 1. I (we) shall not drink wine.   2. It is not necessary for us
to drink wine.   3. I should not drink wine if I were not ill.   4. If
you drank wine, you would be ill.   5. Don't drink wine; don't
drink any.   6. The dressmaker sews (has sewn, will sew) all day.
7. She (I) was sewing while you were reading.   8. Have the pupils
solved their problems?   9. The problems that they have solved
were not easy.   10. The miller ground the wheat to make flour.
11. The wheat was ground by the miller.   12. The dressmakers
sewed (*p. def.*) the ladies' silk dresses.

LESSON LXV

178. Use of Infinitive. — 1. Review Lesson XXVI and observe
the following:

Il a fini **par** m'insulter.	*He ended by insulting me* or *He finally insulted me.*
Je commencerai **par** apprendre ma leçon de français.	*I shall begin by learning* (or *I shall first learn*) *my French lesson.*
Je suis venu (**pour**) le consulter.	*I came (in order) to consult him.*
Il est **trop** fâché **pour** écouter.	*He is too angry to listen.*
Il est **assez** riche **pour** voyager.	*He is rich enough to travel.*

(*a*) **Par** = *by* usually only with **commencer** and **finir**, Ex. 1 and 2.
(*b*) **Pour** emphasizes the purpose, with a verb of motion, Ex. 3 (cf. § 170).
(*c*) *To* = **pour**, regularly after **assez** and **trop**, Ex. 4 and 5.

2. The infinitive often stands after prepositional phrases, of
which the last word is **de** or **à**:

Je me dépêche **de peur** d'être en retard.	*I am hastening for fear of being late (for fear I shall, etc.).*
Agissez **de façon à** réussir.	*Act so as to succeed.*

3. Observe the idiomatic distinctions in the infinitive constructions at the head of the Exercise below.

EXERCISE LXV

afin de, *in order to*	**fatigué**, *tired*
l'algèbre, f., *algebra*	**la jambe**, *leg*
autant, *as much*	**latin**, *Latin*
boiter, *limp, be lame*	**manquer**, *fail, miss*
la cause, *cause*	**ordinairement**, *generally*
égal, *equal*	**précédent**, *preceding*
l'exemple, m., *example*	**probablement**, *probably*
faillir, *fail*	**le vers**, *verse, line* (of poetry)

à cause de, *because (on account) of;* **cela m'est égal**, *that is all the same to me, I don't care, etc.;* **aimer autant**, *like as well, just as soon;* **aimer mieux**, *like better* or *prefer* (*to do*), *rather* (*do*); **j'ai fini de lire**, *I have finished reading*

j'ai failli tomber
j'ai pensé tomber } *I came very near (was on the point of) falling*
j'ai manqué de tomber

A. Continue: 1. Je me suis dépêché afin de finir. 2. Je suis trop fatigué pour finir. 3. Je commençai par apprendre les vers. 4. J'aimerais autant partir tout de suite. 5. J'aimerais mieux rester à la maison. 6. Je n'ai pas manqué le train. 7. Je finirai par résoudre mes problèmes. 8. J'ai fini de travailler pour ce soir. 9. Dépêche-toi de peur d'arriver en retard. 10. J'ai pensé (*or* failli) tomber.

B. 1. À notre école les classes commencent à neuf heures. 2. Afin de pouvoir préparer tous nos devoirs nous en faisons une partie le soir précédent. 3. Quelquefois nous sommes trop fatigués pour les faire tous. 4. Nous commençons généralement par préparer la leçon de latin. 5. J'aimerais autant commencer par résoudre nos problèmes d'algèbre. 6. Mais mon frère aime mieux faire d'abord le latin. 7. Tout cela m'est égal si je prépare mes autres leçons. 8. L'autre jour par exemple nous n'avons pas pu terminer nos problèmes à cause du latin. 9. Nous finissons ordinairement par notre leçon d'anglais. 10. On finit de travailler chez nous à dix heures. 11. Mon père s'amuse quelquefois à lire les journaux jusqu'à onze heures. 12. Nous nous réveillons souvent tard. 13. Et de peur d'être en retard à l'école nous nous dépêchons. 14. L'autre jour je suis tombé en me dépêchant et j'ai failli me casser une jambe. 15. Je boite encore.

C. (Oral on B.)

D. 1. I am too tired this evening to do all the lessons. 2. Let us begin by preparing our Latin. 3. On account of my algebra, I would rather not do my Latin. 4. I generally do my problems first. 5. But my brothers like best to do the easy lessons first. 6. Let us finish by learning something easy, for example, our verses. 7. I don't care, but I would just as soon learn them first. 8. I missed my history lesson yesterday. 9. We must finish working at ten. 10. We must go to bed now for fear of wakening too late. 11. We were very near being late yesterday, you know. 12. Yes, and I came very near breaking my leg. 13. I was hastening in order not to be late. 14. You see I am limping yet.

E. 1. We are too tired to prepare all our exercises this evening. 2. Has your brother finished preparing his? 3. Yes, and he is amusing himself now reading the newspaper. 4. Let us hasten for fear of being late. 5. We have hastened in order not to be late at the station. 6. My father rose late, and (he) missed the train. 7. He had to wait for the next train. 8. He came near missing that one too. 9. Would you prefer to go to the concert or the theatre? 10. It is all the same to us. 11. As for me, I would rather see a good play. 12. We shall probably end up by staying at home. 13. Most people like best to begin by doing something easy. 14. Those who work will finally succeed.

LESSON LXVI

179. *Battre,* 'beat,' 'thresh'; *dormir,* 'sleep'; *servir,* 'serve'; *nettoyer,* 'clean'

battre	battant	battu	bats	battis
dormir	dormant	dormi	dors	dormis
servir	servant	servi	sers	servis
nettoyer	nettoyant	nettoyé	nettoie	nettoyai

Like **dormir** and **servir**: **s'endormir,** *go to sleep;* **se servir de,** *make use of, use.*

EXERCISE LXVI

le beurre, *butter*	**le (la) malade,** *sick person,*
cruel, *cruel*	*patient*
mal, *badly*	**la nuit,** *night*

battre le beurre, *churn*

A. (*Oral.*) *Continue:* 1. Je bats le blé dans la grange. 2. Je dors toujours bien. 3. Est-ce que je me sers d'un crayon bleu? 4. Je n'ai pas bien dormi cette (*last*) nuit. 5. Dors bien. 6. Je dormis (dormirai) longtemps. 7. Bats le beurre. 8. Je me suis endormi(e) avant minuit. 9. Sers-toi de ces livres-là. 10. Sers le dîner. 11. Je nettoie les souliers. 12. Je nettoierai la vaisselle.

B. 1. Good morning, have you slept well? 2. Very well, thank you; and you? 3. Oh, I always sleep well now. 4. I am glad you are sleeping better. 5. The maid is churning. 6. The harvesters are threshing the wheat. 7. Let us thresh the wheat. 8. Serve the lunch, if you please. 9. Madam, the lunch is served (*or* Madam is served). 10. I wish you to serve these ladies. 11. They are served already. 12. He was cleaning (would clean) the shoes.

C. 1. My father always slept badly. 2. At what time did you go to sleep? 3. I went to sleep before twelve. 4. I slept very badly last night. 5. The children haven't gone to sleep yet. 6. That cruel mother is beating her child. 7. George was beaten for stealing apples. 8. Let us make use of these books. 9. Use my pen if you wish. 10. I have been using it. 11. The doctor wishes the patient to sleep. 12. I should like the maid to clean the kitchen. 13. That is no use (use *servir à*).

LESSON LXVII

180. Government of Verbs. — 1. An English transitive verb is sometimes rendered in French by a verb with **de** or **à**:

Il s'approchait **de** la ville.	*He was approaching the town.*
Je me souviens **de** vous.	*I remember you.*
Il obéit **à** son père.	*He obeys his father.*
Je **lui** obéirai.	*I shall obey him.*

2. A French transitive verb sometimes has the force of an English verb + a preposition:

J'attends le train.   *I am waiting for the train.*

3. **De** and **à** are sometimes not translated literally:

Cela dépend **de** vous.   *That depends on you.*
Pensez **à** votre devoir.   *Think of your duty.*

4. Compare the French and English constructions:

Je paie le thé.   *I pay for the tea.*
Je le paie à l'épicier.   *I pay the grocer for it.*
Je le lui ai payé.   *I have paid him for it.*
Je lui prends le fusil.   *I take (away) the gun from him.*
Il demande du pain à son père.   *He asks his father for bread.*

(a) Further examples: **acheter quelque chose à quelqu'un,** *buy something from somebody;* **emprunter ... à ...,** *borrow ... from ...;* **ôter ... à ...,** *take away ... from ...;* **voler ... à ...,** *steal ... from ...;* **pardonner ... à ...,** *pardon somebody for ...*

5. In many verbs the meaning varies with the preposition:

Ils jouent **aux** cartes.   *They play (at) cards.*
Elle joue **du** piano.   *She plays (on) the piano.*

(a) Further examples: **penser à,** *think of, think about (turn over in one's mind);* **penser de,** *think of (have an opinion about);* **servir,** *serve;* **servir à,** *serve as or for;* **se servir de,** *make use of, use.*

EXERCISE LXVII

ainsi, *thus, so*
la baratte, *churn*
dépendre, *depend*
employer, *employ*
l'étable, f., *stable* (for cattle)
la faute, *fault*
former, *form*
les grands-parents, *grandparents*
la laiterie, *dairy*
marcher, *march, go, run*
Marguerite, *Margaret*
obéir, *obey*

pardonner, *pardon*
le piano, *piano*
poser, *place, put, ask* (question)
le pré, *meadow*
la qualité, *quality*
la question, *question*
sage, *wise, well-behaved, good* (of children)
le seau, *pail*
tirer or **traire,** irreg., *milk*
l'ustensile, m., *utensil*

et ainsi de suite, *and so forth, and so on;* **faire marcher,** *make* or *cause to go, work* (of machines); **battre des mains,** *clap one's hands*

A. Continue: 1. J'obéis à mon père, tu . . . ton.   2. Je lui obéis.
3. Je lui prends son livre.   4. Je me sers d'encre noire.   5. Je m'en
sers.   6. J'emploie de l'encre noire.   7. Je m'approche du feu.
8. Je lui demande de l'argent.   9. Je m'aperçois de cela.   10. Je
m'en suis aperçu(e).   11. Je pensais à elles.   12. Je ne m'en suis
pas servi.   13. Je n'y ai pas pensé.

B.   1. Paul et Marguerite sont chez leurs grands-parents à la campagne.   2. Ils sont sages et obéissent à leur grand'mère.   3. Elle leur
pardonne facilement leurs petites fautes.   4. Ils s'amusent beaucoup à la regarder travailler et l'aident aussi.   5. Quelquefois elle
leur dit d'aller au pré chercher les vaches.   6. Ils amènent les vaches
à l'étable et grand'mère les tire.   7. Grand-père lui prend les seaux
pleins de lait et les emporte à la laiterie.   8. Deux fois par semaine
on fait du beurre.   9. On se sert d'une baratte pour battre le beurre.
10. On nettoie soigneusement la baratte, car la qualité du beurre
dépend beaucoup de la propreté des ustensiles qu'on emploie.
11. Grand-père fait marcher la baratte et les enfants s'approchent
de lui pour voir.   12. Ils lui posent (*or* font) beaucoup de questions.
13. Ils lui demandent: "Grand-père, tu ne dis rien; à quoi penses-tu?
14. Combien le marchand te paie-t-il le beurre?   15. Combien as-tu
payé la baratte?"   16. Et ainsi de suite.   17. Bientôt on s'aperçoit
que le beurre se forme et les enfants battent des mains.

C. (*Oral.*)   1. Où étaient les deux enfants?   2. Comment s'ap-
pellent-ils?   3. À qui obéissaient-ils?   4. Que leur pardonnait-elle?
5. À quoi s'amusaient-ils?   6. Qu'est-ce que la grand'mère leur
disait quelquefois?   7. Qui tirait les vaches?   8. À qui le grand-père
prenait-il les seaux?   9. De quoi se servait-on pour faire le beurre?
10. À quoi sert la baratte?   11. Qui faisait marcher la baratte?
12. Dites-moi les questions que les enfants posaient à leur grand-
père.   13. Pourquoi battaient-ils des mains? etc.

D. 1. Children be good; obey your parents.   2. Obey them always.   3. These children go to the meadow for the cows.   4. They
have brought them to the stable.   5. Grandmother will milk the
cows.   6. Grandfather will take from her the pails of milk.   7. I
work the churn in the dairy.   8. Clean the churn.   9. The quality of
the butter will depend on cleanliness.   10. The dairy and the uten-

sils must be clean. 11. We ask our grandparents many questions. 12. What are you thinking of? 13. I am not thinking about anything. 14. How much did the dealer pay you for the butter? 15. The butter has come. 16. We clapped our hands because the work was finished. 17. What use is a churn?

E. 1. Did you perceive that he didn't obey his father? 2. I didn't perceive it. 3. What do you think of this book? 4. Use my pen, yours is bad. 5. I shall use it with pleasure. 6. He took the pail from me. 7. I took the pail from him. 8. Think of your lessons. 9. We were thinking of them. 10. Pay the tailor for your clothes. 11. I have paid him for them. 12. Ask your friend for some money. 13. I have borrowed some from him already. 14. My little brothers are playing marbles. 15. Can your sister play the piano? 16. It is very cold; draw near the fire. 17. Pardon me for this fault. 18. Twice two make four, twice three make six, and so forth.

LESSON LXVIII

181. *Partir*, 'set out,' etc.; *sentir*, 'feel,' 'smell,' etc.;
suivre, 'follow'

partir	partant	parti	pars	partis
sentir	sentant	senti	sens	sentis
suivre	suivant	suivi	suis	suivis

Like **partir**: *sortir*, *go out*.

EXERCISE LXVIII

le chien, *dog*	**le maître**, *master*
le facteur, *porter*	**se sentir**, *feel* (of health)
le froid, *cold*	**sortir**, tr., *take* (*get*) *out*

A. (*Oral.*) *Continue:* 1. Je ne sens (sentais) pas le froid. 2. Je pars (partirai) de grand matin. 3. Je partis sans dire adieu. 4. Pars avant midi. 5. Sens ces fleurs. 6. Sors d'ici. 7. Je suis mon maître, tu . . . ton. 8. Je les ai suivis. 9. Je suivais le colonel. 10. Que je suivisse (partisse, sentisse).

B. 1. She is leaving (has left) for France. 2. My sisters set out yesterday. 3. He is going out to take a walk. 4. Let him not go out now. 5. Let him stay at home if he doesn't feel well. 6. Do you feel the cold? 7. They didn't feel the cold. 8. These flowers smell sweet (*bon*). 9. The dog follows his master. 10. He was followed by his dog. 11. Let him follow us. 12. Don't follow me. 13. Let us not go out this morning. 14. Let the others go out if they wish.

C. 1. They (*f.*) have gone out. 2. Let us go out [for] a little. 3. Don't go away without saying good-bye. 4. Go away from here at once. 5. If I were to follow him he would be angry. 6. We followed (*p. def.*) our parents. 7. The parents were followed by their children. 8. They will not feel well to-morrow. 9. They felt well. 10. Don't you feel well? 11. Let the porter get out our luggage. 12. Porter, please get out our luggage. 13. When you have got it out, bring it to the carriage.

LESSON LXIX

182. *C'est* **and** *il est.* — Observe the following typical sentences:

C'est facile (clair, bien).	*It (that) is easy (clear, well).*
C'est à désirer.	*It (that) is to be desired.*
C'est facile à faire.	*It (that) is easy to do.*
Il est facile **de parler**.	*It is easy to talk.*
Il est clair **que** j'ai raison.	*It is clear that I am right.*
Il est à désirer **que** la guerre finisse bientôt.	*It is to be desired that the war should soon end.*

(*a*) In Ex. 1, 2 and 3, **ce** = *it* or *that*, is the real subject.

(*b*) But when the real subject follows **être** in such constructions it is expressed by **de** + infinitive, as in Ex. 4, or by a **que** clause, Ex. 5 and 6, and **il** = *it* regularly stands as anticipatory subject.

NOTE. — Colloquially, **c'est** is somewhat freely used for **il est**, e.g. **C'est** clair que j'ai raison, and is always found in certain phrases, e.g. **c'est** dommage, **c'est** pitié, etc.

183. *Ce* and *il*(*s*), *elle*(*s*), etc. — Care must be taken to distinguish constructions of the following types:

Elle est Française.	*She is French (a Frenchwoman).*
Ils sont Allemands.	*They are German (Germans).*
Sa femme est couturière.	*His wife is a dressmaker.*
C'est une Française.	*She is a Frenchwoman.*
C'est une couturière.	*She is a dressmaker.*
Ce sont des Allemands.	*They are Germans.*
Quel Français est-**ce?**	*What Frenchman is it?*

(*a*) Observe in Ex. 1, 2 and 3 that the noun of nationality, calling or description omits the article; in such case a personal subject must precede être.

(*b*) But if the predicate noun, as in Ex. 4, 5, 6 and 7, has **un, des** or any other determinative (definite article, partitive, possessive adjective, demonstrative, interrogative adjective), it becomes the real subject, and **ce** precedes être (cf. §§ 35, 80).

EXERCISE LXIX

agréable, *agreeable, pleasant*	**la médecine,** *medicine*
brave, *brave, worthy*	**nombreux,** *numerous*
la clientèle, *customers, practice*	**normand,** *Norman*
conséquent (par), *consequently*	**la Normandie,** *Normandy*
le dommage, *damage, pity*	**observer,** *observe*
se fournir, *buy* or *get one's provisions (supplies, etc.)*	**la réputation,** *reputation*
	le rez-de-chaussée, *ground floor*
heureux, *happy, fortunate*	**supérieur,** *superior, upper*

c'est pourquoi, *that is why;* **faire de bonnes affaires,** *do a good business (trade);* **à partir de deux heures,** *beginning at two o'clock;* **c'est dommage que** (+ subjunctive), *it is a pity that*

A. Complete by supplying **ce** *or* **il** *and the correct preposition:*
1. . . . est difficile . . . faire.   2. . . . sera difficile . . . faire cela.
3. . . . est à désirer qu'il parte bientôt.   4. . . . facile . . . apprendre.
5. . . . est clair que la leçon est difficile.   6. . . . est intéressant de voyager.   7. . . . serait mieux . . . ne rien dire.   8. . . . serait mieux.
9. . . . est très bon; j'aime cela.

B. Complete by supplying **c'est, ce sont, il (elle) est, ils (elles) sont,** *as required:* 1. . . . des Anglaises.   2. . . . cordonniers.
3. . . . une Française.   4. . . . Américains.   5. . . . couturières.

6. . . . médecin.   7. . . . un médecin habile.   8. . . . des Normands.
9. . . . une vieille Normande.

C. 1. Il est très intéressant d'observer les nombreux voisins que
nous avons dans cette maison.   2. Au rez-de-chaussée il y a un
épicier.   3. C'est chez lui que nous nous fournissons souvent.   4. Il
est Normand, et vend de bon beurre et de bon fromage qui lui
viennent de Normandie.   5. C'est un très brave homme.   6. C'est
pourquoi il a tant de clients.   7. Il est facile de faire de bonnes
affaires si on a une bonne réputation.   8. C'est facile à expliquer.
9. Notre voisin du premier (étage) est médecin.   10. C'est un
homme très agréable.   11. Il a une clientèle importante.   12. C'est
aujourd'hui mercredi et il va recevoir beaucoup de malades.   13. Il
n'est que neuf heures, mais on commence déjà à arriver.   14. C'est
jeudi qu'il fait son cours à l'école de médecine.   15. Par conséquent
il ne recevra demain qu'à partir de deux heures.   16. Il est heureux
que nous ayons deux si bons voisins.   17. C'est dommage que nous
en ayons de moins bons aux étages supérieurs.

D. (*Oral.*) 1. Qui est votre voisin du rez-de-chaussée?   2. Est-il
Français?   3. Qu'est-ce qu'il vend?   4. Est-ce un brave homme?
5. Pourquoi a-t-il une bonne clientèle?   6. Est-il facile d'avoir beaucoup de clients?   7. Qui est votre voisin du premier?   8. Est-ce un
bon médecin?   9. Quel jour de la semaine est-ce?   10. Quelle heure
est-il?   11. Quand est-ce que votre voisin fait son cours?   12. Quand
reçoit-il ses malades? etc.

E. 1. It is pleasant to have good neighbours.   2. Our neighbour
on (of) the ground floor is a Norman.   3. He is a grocer.   4. His
wife is a Norman also.   5. They are very worthy people.   6. Is it
at his shop that you get your provisions?   7. Why is it that he has
so many customers?   8. It is because he has a good reputation.
9. It is easy to have plenty (*beaucoup*) of customers if one sells
cheap.   10. That is very true.   11. Who is it who has just come in?
12. It is our neighbour of the first flat.   13. He is a clever doctor
who has a large practice.   14. It is to-day that he sees (receives)
his patients.   15. It is a pity that there are so many sick people this
winter.   16. It is fortunate that you have such (*de si*) good neighbours.

F. 1. That gentleman is one of our numerous neighbours. 2. His wife is French. 3. Are you an American, madam? 4. No, sir, I am an Englishwoman. 5. It is interesting to study medicine. 6. It is difficult to learn French. 7. It is easier to read it than to write it. 8. It is a very difficult language. 9. Should we not start now? 10. I don't know; it is a pity we didn't start yesterday. 11. That is true; it is raining so much to-day. 12. There is the lady who lives in one of the upper stories. 13. Yes, it is she. 14. It is easy to see that she is not a Frenchwoman. 15. What day is it to-day? 16. What time is it?

LESSON LXX

184. *Traduire*, 'translate'; *construire*, 'construct,' 'build'

traduire	traduisant	traduit	traduis	traduisis
construire	construisant	construit	construis	construisis

Like **construire: instruire**, *instruct, educate.*

EXERCISE LXX

le **poème**, *poem*   le **poète**, *poet*

A. (*Oral.*) *Continue:* 1. Je traduis (traduisais) de l'anglais en français. 2. Je construisais (construis) une maison. 3. Les morceaux que j'ai traduits. 4. Les maisons que j'ai construites. 5. Traduis ces vers en français. 6. Ne les traduis pas en anglais. 7. Je traduisis un gros livre. 8. Le maître voudrait que je traduise beaucoup, . . . tu. 9. J'instruisis mes neveux.

B. 1. We learn much by translating. 2. I wish you to translate this poem. 3. Let us translate our exercises. 4. Which verses have you translated? 5. Architects build houses. 6. What houses has this architect built? 7. He (they) built (*p. def.*) many houses in this city. 8. The children whom I was instructing have learnt much.

C. 1. The master has wished John to translate a piece of Latin. 2. What pieces have you translated? 3. That poet translated (*p. def.*) many poems into English. 4. Translate these verses for me. 5. Mr. Potin was building a fine castle in Normandy. 6. We were building fine houses. 7. Let him translate this French poem. 8. They (*m.*) are well educated. 9. She is a very [well] educated lady.

LESSON LXXI

185. Impersonal Verbs. — 1. Review § 114.

2. Many verbs may stand in the third person singular with impersonal **il** anticipating a real subject, singular or plural, following the verb:

Il était tombé **de la neige.**	*Some snow had fallen.*
Il en reste trois **livres.**	*There remain three pounds of it.*
Il est arrivé **des lettres.**	*Some letters have arrived.*
Il est arrivé **des accidents.**	*Some accidents have happened.*

(*a*) Observe that the past participle is invariable.

3. **Il est** (était, etc.) may be used for **il y a:**

Il est des hommes qui le croient.	*There are some men who believe it.*

4. **Y avoir** is often used to form expressions of time reckoned backwards, or of distance:

Il y a trois ans (de cela).	*Three years ago.*
Combien **y a-t-il** d'ici à Paris?	*How far is it to Paris?*

5. Observe the following:

De quoi s'agit-il?	*What is the matter? etc.*
Il s'agit de l'acheter.	*It is a question of buying it.*
Il se peut qu'il vienne.	*It may be that he will come.*

EXERCISE LXXI

s'agir de, *be a question of*
l'aide-maçon, m., *mason's helper, hodman*
la chute, *fall*
la construction, *building*
se détacher, *get loose*
l'échafaudage, m., *scaffolding*
s'en falloir, *be near*
glissant, *slippery*
grave, *serious*
guérir, *get well, recover*
heureusement, *fortunately*

l'hôpital, m., *hospital*
les matériaux, m., *material(s)*
outre, *in addition to*
parmi, *among*
la pierre, *stone*
la pluie, *rain*
réparer, *repair*
la tête, *head*
le toit, *roof*
se tuer, *kill oneself, be killed*
la tuile, *tile*

se faire, *take place;* **faire glissant,** *be slippery;* **se faire mal,** *hurt oneself, get hurt;* **peu s'en est fallu . . . ne,** *came very near, almost happened*

A. Continue: 1. Je me suis fait mal, tu t'. 2. Peu s'en est fallu que je ne fisse cela, ... tu ... 3. Je m'en suis détaché(e), tu t'. 4. J'ai failli tomber.

B. Supply the proper past indefinite forms: 1. Il ...... (tomber) de la pluie. 2. La pluie ...... (tomber). 3. Il ...... (arriver) des lettres. 4. Des lettres ...... (arriver). 5. Il s'...... (détacher) une tuile. 6. Une tuile s'...... (détacher).

C. 1. On a construit cette maison il y a trois ans. 2. Il est arrivé un certain nombre d'accidents pendant la construction. 3. Il s'est fait plusieurs chutes parmi les ouvriers. 4. Un jour il était tombé de la neige et l'échafaudage était glissant. 5. À cause de cela deux aides-maçons, qui apportaient des matériaux aux maçons, sont tombés. 6. Heureusement ils ne se sont pas fait beaucoup de mal. 7. Un autre jour il a fallu qu'un ouvrier montât sur le toit. 8. Il s'agissait d'une tuile qui s'était détachée. 9. Mais il était tombé de la neige et en réparant la tuile l'ouvrier est tombé. 10. Peu s'en est fallu qu'il ne se tuât. 11. Il lui a fallu deux mois d'hôpital pour guérir. 12. Une autre fois un ouvrier a reçu sur la tête une tuile qui tombait. 13. Il a failli en mourir. 14. Outre ces trois cas il n'y a pas eu d'accidents graves.

D. 1. This house was built (use *on*) five years ago. 2. Many accidents happened (there happened, etc.). 3. Several falls occurred. 4. Many masons fell who were working on the scaffolding. 5. Some of the masons hurt themselves [very] much. 6. One day a workman was to repair the roof. 7. What was the trouble (use *s'agir*)? 8. It was a matter of a tile which had fallen. 9. Snow had fallen and it was slippery. 10. He fell and he had to stay three months in the hospital. 11. It may be that he will stay there four months. 12. Another workman got hurt also. 13. A stone fell (*see C,* 12) on his head.

E. 1. Fortunately not many serious accidents happened among the workmen. 2. Several tiles had become loose. 3. In repairing them a workman fell, and came near being killed. 4. It had rained. 5. Much rain had fallen that summer. 6. There were several accidents but no one was killed. 7. Amongst the workmen two hodmen hurt themselves. 8. They recovered, but they had to stay a month

in the hospital.   9. The building of that castle lasted ten years.
10. In addition to the masons, there were painters and other
workmen.

LESSON LXXII

186.   *Cuire*, 'cook,' 'bake,' etc.; *courir*, 'run';
            valoir, 'be worth'

cuire	cuisant	cuit	cuis	cuisis
courir	courant	couru	cours	courus
valoir	valant	valu	vaux	valus

EXERCISE LXXII

cuire (or **faire cuire**), *cook* (tr.); **cuire**, *cook* (intr.); **valoir la peine**, *be
worth while;* **valoir mieux**, *be better*

A. (*Oral.*) *Continue:* 1. Je fais cuire la viande. 2. Je cuis du
pain. 3. Je cuirai des poissons. 4. Cours vite. 5. J'ai couru.
6. Je vaux (valais, valus, vaudrai) autant que lui. 7. Je cours
(courais, courrai) en toute hâte. 8. Que je vaille (valusse). 9. Il
faut que je cuise les légumes. 10. Il fallait que je courusse.

B. 1. He was running. 2. We were cooking. 3. If they had
fish, they would cook them. 4. The horse ran fast. 5. That cow
will be worth five hundred francs. 6. That is no good (= is worth
nothing). 7. He wishes us to run. 8. Bake the bread. 9. That
was better. 10. They will (would) run. 11. He wished me to cook
the vegetables. 12. They have not run. 13. The blackboard was
no good.

C. 1. The horses will run. 2. That is not worth while. 3. If
you had baked the bread, it would be worth five cents a pound.
4. He wishes us not to run. 5. Do not run so fast. 6. It would
be better [to] go slowly. 7. The baker has baked the bread. 8. That
bread will not be worth six cents a pound. 9. I am sorry that that
is worth nothing. 10. You must cook the meat. 11. This meat is
not well cooked. 12. We did not wish them to run fast. 13. We
were running. 14. The vegetables were cooking.

LESSON LXXIII

[In §§ 187–191 are explained some uses of tenses and moods not dealt with in the more elementary lessons.]

187. Present Indicative. — 1. Observe its use with **depuis,** *since:* **depuis quand?** *since when?* **il y a . . . que, voici (voilà) . . . que,** to denote how long an action has been continuing:

Depuis quand **êtes**-vous ici?	*How long have you been here?*
Je **suis** ici depuis dix jours.	*I have been here for ten days (past).*
Il y a (*or* voici, voilà) deux mois que j'**attends** une lettre.	*I have been expecting a letter for two months.*

2. But if the action is denoted as being entirely past, a past tense must be used:

Combien de temps a-t-il attendu?	*How long did he wait?*
Il a attendu (pendant) dix jours.	*He waited for ten days.*

(*a*) **Pendant** emphasizes the duration of the time.

3. Observe:

C'est là que je l'ai vu.	*It was (is) there that I saw him.*

188. Imperfect Indicative. — Observe its use to denote what had been continuing (cf. § 187):

Depuis quand **étiez**-vous là?	*How long had you been there?*

(*a*) The imperfect stands occasionally for the conditional anterior in a result clause, e.g. Si je ne l'avais pas saisi, il **tombait** du train, *If I hadn't seized him, he would have fallen from the train.*

189. Future. — This tense, as also the future anterior, sometimes denotes probability, possibility, supposition, or the like:

Ce **seront** nos amis qui viennent d'arriver.	*Those are (I suppose, no doubt) our friends who have just come.*
Je me **serai** trompé.	*I must have made a mistake.*

190. Conditional. — 1. It is used in deferential statement or request:

Je le **croirais** du moins.	*I should think so at least.*
Auriez-vous la bonté de rester?	*Would you kindly stay?*

2. It sometimes denotes probability, etc. (cf. § 189):

Serait-il vrai?	*Can (could) it be true?*

3. It sometimes denotes concession (= *even, even if, though*), after **quand, quand même,** or with **que:**

Quand (même) il me **tuerait.**   *Even if he should kill me.*
Il me le **dirait** que je ne le croirais   *Even though he told me so, I should* pas.   *not believe it.*

4. It may denote implied futurity (cf. § 76):

Je prendrais ce qui **resterait.**   *I should take what remained.*

5. It is sometimes used in giving the substance of hearsay information, or the like:

À ce qu'on dit le roi **serait** malade.   *By what they say the king is ill.*

191. Infinitive. — Observe its exceptional uses:—
1. In brief phrases with imperative force:

S'adresser à côté.   *Apply next door.*
Répondre aux questions suivantes.   *Answer the following questions.*

2. With **de** = a finite verb (historical infinitive):

Et l'ennemi **de s'enfuir.**   *And the enemy fled (or flees).*

EXERCISE LXXIII

l'arrivée, f., *arrival*
la cuisson, *cooking, baking*
le four, *oven*
impatiemment, *impatiently*
le lendemain, *day after, next day*
le levain, *yeast*
lever, *rise*
oser, *dare*
la pâte, *paste, dough*
le pétrin, *kneading trough*
pétrir, *knead*
Pierre, *Peter*
rassis, *stale* (of bread)
la servante, *servant*
la tartine, *slice*
la veille, *evening before*

le **pain de ménage,** *homemade bread;* une **tartine de beurre,** *a slice of bread and butter;* **être en visite,** *be on a visit;* **être dans la joie,** *be in (great) glee;* **cela ne fait rien,** *that makes no difference, doesn't matter;* **au moins,** *at least;* **mais si,** *yes (it does, yes, yes, etc.)*

A. Continue: 1. J'attends depuis dix jours. 2. J'y étais depuis trois semaines. 3. Il y a (voici *or* voilà) un mois que j'attends une lettre. 4. J'ai travaillé pendant toute la soirée. 5. C'est à Londres que je l'ai vu pour la première fois, . . . tu. 6. Je me serai trompé(e), peut-être. 7. Je ne saurais le croire.

B. (*Pain de ménage*) 1. Pierre et Jacqueline sont en visite chez tante Julie depuis quelques jours. 2. Depuis le moment de leur arrivée ils sont dans la joie. 3. Le lendemain de leur arrivée ils ont vu faire du beurre. 4. Un jour ils ont assisté à la cuisson du pain. 5. Ils attendaient impatiemment depuis la veille. 6. Le moment arriva. 7. La vieille servante Célestine avait mis la farine et le levain dans le pétrin. 8. La pâte commençait à lever. 9. Les enfants voulaient tout voir. 10. "Laissez-nous approcher; nous n'y toucherons pas. — 11. Mais non, mes enfants. 12. Quand même vous n'y toucheriez pas je n'oserais pas vous laisser approcher. — 13. Je crois, dit Pierre, que cela ne ferait rien. — 14. Mais si, mon petit homme, cela ferait beaucoup. 15. Tu ne dois pas y regarder." 16. Plus tard Célestine pétrit la pâte. 17. Elle en fait des pains qu'elle met au four pour les faire cuire. 18. Et après cela elle les sort du four. 19. Les enfants en voudraient pour faire des tartines de beurre. 20. Mais le pain frais est moins bon que le pain rassis. 21. Il vaudrait mieux attendre au moins vingt-quatre heures.

C. (*Oral on B.*)

D. 1. The two children are on a visit at their aunt's. 2. They have been in [great] glee for several days. 3. Since their arrival they have been very happy. 4. They wanted to be present at the baking of the homemade bread. 5. The old servant had brought the kneading trough into the kitchen. 6. The flour and yeast had been in it since the evening before. 7. The next day the dough had begun to rise. 8. The children had waited impatiently. 9. Celestine, why won't you let us come near? 10. You may come near (*reflex.*), but you mustn't touch the dough. 11. That will make no difference, said Pierre. 12. We should like to have a slice of bread and butter. 13. Give us a piece when you take the bread out of the oven. 14. It will be too fresh; I shouldn't dare to give you it. 15. Yes, do; give it to us now. 16. No, no, not now. 17. Stale bread is better for children.

E. 1. They had long been saying that that would happen. 2. We have been wondering for some days where you were. 3. This castle has existed since the 14th century. 4. It was in that century that it was built. 5. It had been freezing for three days. 6. It froze for three days. 7. It had been snowing, which was very good for the sports. 8. How long had you been there when we came? 9. More than three weeks. 10. How long did your uncle remain in America? 11. He remained there more than ten years. 12. Could you tell me what time (*l'heure qu'*) it is?

F. Turn the following into the ordinary form of conditional sentence (cf. § 113): 1. Il le dirait que je ne le croirais pas. 2. La maison serait dix fois plus belle que je ne l'achèterais pas.

LESSON LXXIV

192. *Asseoir*, 'seat'; *suffire*, 'suffice,' 'be sufficient'

asseoir	asseyant	assis	assieds	assis
suffire	suffisant	suffi	suffis	suffis

Like **asseoir: s'asseoir**, *sit, sit down, be seated.*

EXERCISE LXXIV

le fauteuil, *armchair*	**suffisant**, *conceited*
prier, *pray, beg, ask*	

A. (*Oral.*) *Continue:* 1. Je m'assieds (assois). 2. Je me suis assis(e). 3. Assieds-toi près du feu. 4. Je m'assiérai près de la fenêtre. 5. Il désire que je m'asseye (assoie), . . . tu. 6. Je suffis (suffisais). 7. Je suffirai à cet ouvrage. 8. Il ne croit pas que j'y suffise. 9. Que je suffisse.

B. 1. How conceited he is! 2. That is sufficient (*pres.*). 3. Let that suffice. 4. That will be sufficient. 5. We shall be sufficient for everything. 6. Sit down (*or* be seated) if you please. 7. I used to sit there. 8. We often sit there. 9. They will not sit there. 10. He sat down in the armchair. 11. Let us sit down. 12. The ladies have not sat down. 13. She was sitting in an armchair.

C. 1. It was necessary that we should sit down. 2. We shall not sit down. 3. Two francs will be sufficient. 4. Mary sat down beside the fire. 5. That had to (use *fallait*) suffice. 6. The children will sit down on those chairs. 7. Ask the ladies to sit down. 8. We were asked to sit down. 9. When you (*tu*) are in the room you will sit down. 10. Let no one sit there. 11. Do not sit beside the window. 12. Everybody is seated.

LESSON LXXV

193. Remarks on Subjunctive. — 1. Review §§ 142–148, and note that many expressions, ordinarily followed by the indicative, require the subjunctive whenever doubt is implied (usually by interrogation, negation or condition):

Je ne crois pas que ce **soit** lui.	*I don't think it is he.*
Espérez-vous qu'il **réussisse?**	*Do you expect he will succeed?*
Si je prétendais qu'il **eût** tort.	*If I asserted that he was wrong.*
But: Je crois que c'**est** lui.	*I think it is he.*
J'espère qu'il **réussira.**	*I hope he will succeed.*

(*a*) Such are: **s'apercevoir, sentir, voir** (*perceiving*); **croire, espérer, penser, trouver** (*thinking*); **être certain, être probable, savoir** (*knowing*); **avouer, dire** (*declaring*), etc.

(*b*) After questions, the indicative usually stands if the answer *yes* is expected, and the subjunctive if *no* is expected.

(*c*) Also, when the statement of the subordinate clause is assumed to be a fact, the indicative is used, e.g. S'il savait que tu **es** ici, *If he knew that you are here;* Savez-vous qu'il **est** arrivé? *Do you know that he has come?*

2. **Il semble** (more or less doubt being implied) regularly requires the subjunctive, while **il me** (te, etc.) **semble** (= je crois, je pense) takes the indicative:

Il semble qu'elle **ait** tort.	*It seems that she is wrong.*
Il me semble qu'elle **a** tort.	*It seems to me she is wrong.*

(*a*) **Il me semble** also comes under 1, above.

3. The present subjunctive of **savoir** is sometimes used to denote deferential statement in a principal sentence:

Je ne **sache** rien de si bon.	*I know of nothing so good.*

4. The pluperfect subjunctive stands exceptionally for the pluperfect indicative in an *if* clause, and for the conditional anterior in a *result* clause (cf. § 113):

S'il **eût** (= avait) su cela, il ne   *If he had known that, he would not*
l'**eût** (= aurait) pas dit.   *have said it.*

5. The subjunctive is used after **que** replacing a conjunction requiring the subjunctive (cf. § 147), and also after **que** replacing **si** = *if:*

Venez **que** (= afin que, pour que)   *Come, in order that I may see you.*
je vous **voie**.
Si j'y vais et **que** je le **voie**.   *If I go, and if I see him.*

EXERCISE LXXV

la bibliothèque, *bookcase*	**la mode**, *fashion*
le (la) camarade, *comrade, companion*	**probable**, *probable*
commander, *order*	**le rideau**, *curtain*
la commode, *chest of drawers, bureau*	**serrer**, *press, put away*
l'ébéniste, m., *cabinet-maker*	**le store**, *(window) blind*
la gravure, *engraving*	**le tapis**, *carpet, tablecloth* (coloured)
le miroir, *mirror*	**la toilette**, *dressing table*
	le travail, *work*

à la mode, *in fashion, fashionable;* **faire visite à**, *to visit;* **de sorte que**, *so that*

A. Continue: 1. Je crois que cela est vrai. 2. Je ne crois pas que ce soit vrai. 3. Il est certain que j'en aurai besoin. 4. Est-il certain que j'en aie besoin? 5. Il croit que c'est moi, . . . toi. 6. S'il espère que je réussisse. 7. Il est probable que je partirai demain. 8. Est-il probable que je le sache? 9. Il semble que j'aie besoin d'un tapis. 10. Il me semble que j'en ai besoin.

B. Give the correct form of the verb in italics: 1. Je ne dis pas que ce *être* vrai. 2. Espérez-vous qu'ils y *être* demain? 3. J'espère qu'ils y *être*. 4. Je n'espère pas qu'il *venir*. 5. N'espérez-vous pas qu'il *venir?* 6. Il leur semble que cela *être* ainsi. 7. Il semble qu'il *avoir* besoin de meubles. 8. Attendez que je le *faire*.

C. 1. Paul croit avoir besoin de meubles pour sa chambre. 2. Sa mère et lui vont chez l'ébéniste en commander. 3. Paul croit qu'il lui faut un lit neuf. 4. "Mais, crois-tu, dit sa mère, que cela te soit nécessaire? — 5. Oui, maman, l'ancien n'est plus à la mode. 6. Il me semble aussi que j'ai besoin d'un fauteuil. — 7. Tu crois? Moi, je ne pense pas que tu en aies besoin. 8. Nous mettrons trois ou quatre chaises dans ta chambre, de sorte que tes camarades puissent s'asseoir quand ils te feront visite, et cela suffira. — 9. J'espère au moins que j'aurai une table de travail et une petite bibliothèque. — 10. Oui, mon enfant. 11. Il est clair que tu as besoin de ces choses-là. 12. Je crois qu'il te faudra aussi une commode pour serrer ton linge. 13. Mais je ne crois pas que tu aies besoin d'une toilette. 14. Il faut aussi que nous garnissions ta chambre de quelques gravures et d'un miroir. — 15. Ne trouves-tu pas aussi que j'ai besoin d'un tapis pour le parquet et d'un autre pour ma table? — 16. C'est vrai. 17. Il te faut aussi un store et des rideaux pour ta fenêtre."

D. (*Oral on C.*)

E. 1. We think we need new furniture. 2. These chairs are not fashionable now. 3. I do not think you need a new bed. 4. It seems to us that we need a bookcase to put our books in (use *y*). 5. I hope you will have an armchair. 6. We shall order one, so that you may sit down when you visit us. 7. It is not certain that we need a carpet for the floor. 8. Do you think you need a tablecloth for your table? 9. I hope my mother will adorn my room with a few engravings. 10. I think you will need a mirror. 11. I shall need a window blind and curtains also. 12. Put away your linen in the drawers. 13. We shall put our books in the bookcase.

F. 1. Sit down that I may be able to speak to you. 2. We hope our comrades will come by the first train. 3. I do not think they will come early. 4. Is it not probable that the train will be late? 5. All the trains have been late for several days. 6. Is it certain that you leave this afternoon? 7. It is probable that I shall. 8. But perhaps I shall not leave before to-morrow. 9. You don't think I need a dressing table, do you? 10. Yes, I do (*mais si*), and I think you need a bureau and a study table. 11. I must order them at the cabinet-maker's. 12. If they knew I was (am) here, they would pay me a visit. 13. Don't they know you have come? 14. Draw near that I may hear you better. 15. Do you know who has just come?

LESSON LXXVI

194. *Offrir*, 'offer'; *souffrir*, 'suffer,' 'endure'

offrir	offrant	offert	offre	offris
souffrir	souffrant	souffert	souffre	souffris

EXERCISE LXXVI

le malheur, *misfortune*   **souffrant**, *ailing, not (very) well*

A. (*Oral.*) *Continue:* 1. Je souffre (souffrais) beaucoup. 2. Je ne souffrirai pas cela. 3. Je lui offre de l'argent. 4. Il faut que je souffre cela. 5. Souffre que cela se fasse. 6. Il fallait que je lui offrisse la main. 7. J'en ai beaucoup souffert. 8. Offre-lui ce que tu as, ... nous. 9. Les malheurs que j'ai soufferts, ... tu.

B. 1. He is always ailing. 2. They have suffered a great deal. 3. We will not endure that. 4. Let us offer to (*de*) help them. 5. Suffer us to say that. 6. He had to endure it. 7. He offered (*p. def.*) me his hand. 8. We have offered them money. 9. Let them offer us that. 10. I have suffered a great misfortune. 11. We shall offer them what we have. 12. We offer you everything. 13. What place have you offered him?

C. 1. Nobody can suffer him. 2. I did not offer (*p. def.*) him any wine. 3. Have you offered them bread? 4. Offer him a cup of tea. 5. You had to suffer that, hadn't you? 6. Do not suffer him to speak. 7. Do not offer them what you have. 8. They suffer their misfortunes without saying anything. 9. Our friends suffered nothing. 10. We offered (*p. def.*) them all (that which) we had. 11. We used to suffer a great deal because of that. 12. You will never suffer for that. 13. If you knew the misfortunes I have suffered.

LESSON LXXVII

195. Infinitive or Subjunctive. — The subjunctive is often avoided by the use of an infinitive (cf. § 156, note 1), thus: —

1. With verbs taking an indirect personal object:

Je conseille à ma fille de lire ces livres-ci.	*I advise my daughter to read these books.*
Je lui défends de lire ceux-là.	*I forbid her to read those.*

(*a*) Such verbs are: **conseiller, défendre, demander, dire, écrire, ordonner, permettre, reprocher,** etc.

2. With verbs taking a direct personal object:

Je l'ai priée de monter.	*I asked her to go up.*
Cela les empêche de sortir.	*That prevents them from going out.*

(*a*) Such verbs are: **empêcher, prier, remercier,** etc.

3. Observe also the construction with two objects:

Je le lui reproche.	*I reproach him (her) for it.*
Je le lui demande.	*I ask him (her) for it.*
Je le remercie de sa bonté.	*I thank him for his kindness.*
Je l'en remercie.	*I thank him for it.*
Je vous en prie.	*I beg you to do (etc.) so.*

EXERCISE LXXVII

s'adresser, *apply*	**ennuyer,** *annoy, trouble*
l'ardeur, f., *ardour, warmth*	**le jeu,** *game, play*
l'attention, f., *attention*	**la loi,** *law*
attirer, *attract, call*	**méchant,** *bad, naughty*
le bien, *good* (noun)	**modérer,** *moderate*
se conduire, irreg., *conduct one-self*	**permettre,** irreg., *permit*
	peut-être, *perhaps*
la conduite, *conduct*	**la police,** *police*
conseiller, *advise*	**préférer,** *prefer*
corriger, *correct*	**protéger,** *protect*
défendre, *defend, forbid*	**reprocher,** *reproach, tax*
élever, *bring up*	**sinon,** *if not, otherwise*

mal élevé, *rude, impolite, ill-mannered;* **père de famille,** *father (of a family)*

A. Continue: 1. Le roi ordonne que je fasse cela. 2. Le roi m'ordonne de faire cela. 3. Elle me l'a conseillé. 4. La loi défend que je fasse cela. 5. La loi me le défend. 6. Il est défendu que je fasse cela. 7. Il m'est défendu de faire cela.

B. 1. Notre voisin a des enfants très mal élevés. 2. Je vais lui demander de les corriger. 3. Je devrais lui reprocher de manquer à son devoir. 4. Un bon père empêche ses enfants de se conduire mal. 5. Tout le monde devrait conseiller aux enfants d'être sages. 6. On ne devrait jamais permettre à personne d'être méchant. 7. Le bon père de famille ordonne à ses enfants de faire toujours le bien. 8. Si je disais à notre voisin de modérer l'ardeur de ses enfants dans leurs jeux, le ferait-il? 9. Peut-être. Sinon, dois-je écrire à la police de me protéger? 10. La police défend aux enfants d'ennuyer le public, mais je n'aime pas m'adresser à elle. 11. Je préfère prier encore une fois mon voisin de corriger ses enfants. 12. Il me remerciera peut-être d'avoir attiré son attention sur leur conduite.

C. (Oral on B.)

D. 1. Are your friend's children ill-mannered? 2. Yes, and we have often asked him to correct them. 3. We have taxed him with failing in his duty. 4. A good father does not permit his children to be naughty. 5. Everybody should advise them to do good. 6. Does not a good father always order his children to be good? 7. Does your friend moderate his children's ardour in their games? 8. Did you tell that little boy to be good? 9. Shall I write to the police to protect you? 10. I shall ask my friend to correct his children. 11. I beg you not to apply to the police.

E. 1. I thanked her for having called my attention to (*sur*) their conduct. 2. I thanked her for it. 3. It is forbidden to annoy the public. 4. You should not conduct yourself badly. 5. Ask your father to come with you. 6. Permit me to say to you that I do not like your conduct. 7. Do you advise your brother to go away? 8. No, I advise him to stay. 9. He has conducted himself badly, but he will not be naughty any more (*plus*). 10. If you are ill-mannered, you will attract (the) attention to yourself. 11. Take some of these pears, I beg of you. 12. I thank you for them.

LESSON LXXVIII

196. Agreement of Past Participle. — All cases of agreement of the past participle depend on the general principles already stated (§§ 49, 120), but observe the following:

La belle journée qu'il a **fait**!	*What a fine day we have had!*
La lettre que j'ai **voulu** écrire.	*The letter I wished to write.*
La dame que j'ai **entendue** chanter.	*The lady that I heard sing.*
La chanson que j'ai **entendu** chanter.	*The song that I heard sung.*
Les médecins qu'il a **fait** venir.	*The doctors he sent for.*

(*a*) The past participle of an impersonal verb is invariable, Ex. 1.

(*b*) In verbal phrases when an infinitive governs a preceding direct object, the past participle is invariable, Ex. 2; but note Il nous a **priés** d'y aller.

(*c*) **Entendu, vu, laissé** agree if the following infinitive has active force, but are invariable if it has passive force, Ex. 3 and 4.

(*d*) **Fait** + infinitive is invariable, Ex. 5 (cf. 172, 1, *a*).

Note. — When the direct object is an expression of quantity or a collective, the past participle regularly agrees with the prevailing sense (cf. § 160), but it has been thought unnecessary to include examples in an elementary text-book.

EXERCISE LXXVIII

la chanteuse, *singer*
embrasser, *embrace, kiss*
exquis, *exquisite, delicious*
femme docteur, *woman doctor, lady physician*
le gâteau, *cake*
s'informer (de), *inquire (about)*
la merveille, *wonder*
la pâtisserie, *pastry*
le pharmacien, *chemist, druggist*
le (la) pianiste, *pianist*
la pièce, *piece* (of money)
le pouls, *pulse*
ravissant, *charming*
le régime, *regimen, diet*
le remède, *medicine*
la santé, *health*
sonner, *ring*
tâter, *feel*
tirer, *put out* (the tongue)
la voix, *voice*

mettre au régime, *prescribe diet for, put on diet;* faire entrer, *show in;* à merveille, *marvellously, wonderfully;* comment trouvez-vous cela? *what do you think of that?*

A. Supply the proper form of the past participle of the infinitive in italics: 1. Voilà mes cousines; je les ai *prier* de venir.   2. La belle saison qu'il a *faire*.   3. Les morceaux qu'elle a *vouloir* jouer.   4. C'est ma sœur; nous ne l'avons pas *laisser* partir.   5. C'est la maison que j'ai *voir* bâtir.   6. Ce sont les personnes que j'ai *entendre* sonner.   7. La servante que j'ai *envoyer* chercher le remède.

B. 1. Geneviève est souffrante.   2. Elle s'est enrhumée au concert.   3. Sa cousine Denise vient la voir.   4. Geneviève l'a envoyé chercher ce matin.   5. La femme de chambre l'a entendue sonner, et elle l'a fait entrer.   6. Denise embrasse sa cousine et s'informe de sa santé.   7. "On a fait venir le médecin j'espère. — 8. Oh oui, c'est Mme Lecomte, la femme docteur, que ma mère a fait venir.   9. Elle m'a tâté le pouls et m'a fait tirer la langue.   10. Puis elle m'a ordonné un remède que la servante a pris (*got*) ensuite chez le pharmacien.   11. Outre cela elle m'a mise au régime.   12. Je ne dois prendre que du pain et du lait.   13. Pas de gâteaux, pas de pâtisserie pendant trois ou quatre jours. — 14. À propos, comment as-tu trouvé la chanteuse que nous avons entendue chanter au concert? — 15. Elle chante à merveille. — 16. Elle a une voix exquise, n'est-ce pas?   17. Et les deux morceaux que nous avons entendu jouer par le pianiste? — 18. Ils étaient ravissants."

C. (*Oral on B.*)

D. 1. We caught cold at the theatre.   2. We (*f.*) are not very well to-day.   3. Our cousins Denise and Jeanne have come to see us; we sent for them.   4. The housemaid heard them ring.   5. She has shown them in.   6. They inquired about our health.   7. They asked us if we had had the doctor.   8. It was a woman doctor that my mother sent for.   9. Did she feel your pulse?   10. Yes, and she made me show my tongue.   11. The old servant went to the chemist's to get the medicine.   12. The doctor has prescribed a diet for me (*f.*).   13. I am not to have either cakes or pastry for several days.   14. The singer whom you heard singing at the concert sang wonderfully, did she not?   15. Yes, and the pieces of music we heard played were charming.

E. 1. There are the houses that we saw being built last year.   2. By the way, where are the medicines you sent for?   3. Is it my cousin (*f.*) whom you have shown in? 4. It is (she); I have shown her upstairs (*faire monter*). 5. Who is the lady whom I heard sing at your house yesterday evening? 6. She is an Englishwoman with an exquisite voice. 7. What did you think of the songs she sang? 8. They were charming. 9. She and her sister are still here; we didn't let them go away. 10. We begged them to stay another week (still eight days). 11. My aunt has been put on diet because she has caught a cold. 12. Here is a two-franc piece which you dropped (let fall) when (*en*) going out. 13. I saw it fall, and I picked it up.

LESSON LXXIX

197.   *Écrire*, 'write'; *vivre*, 'live'

écrire	écrivant	écrit	écris	écrivis
vivre	vivant	vécu	vis	vécus

Like **écrire**: **décrire**, *describe*.

EXERCISE LXXIX

le mot, *word, note*   **le roman,** *novel*
la paix, *peace*   **le volume,** *volume*

A. (*Oral.*) *Continue:* 1. J'écris des lettres. 2. Je décrivais mon voyage, tu . . . ton. 3. Je lui écrirai un mot. 4. Je vis de peu. 5. Je ne lui écris pas. 6. Il faut que je leur écrive. 7. Décris ce que tu as vu. 8. Il fallait que je vécusse seul. 9. Je vivrai de mon travail. 10. Je vivais en paix. 11. J'écrivis des romans.

B. 1. That novel will live. 2. Describe the play to me. 3. I was writing a letter. 4. I wrote him a note. 5. They lived on little. 6. They have to write. 7. We live by (from) our work. 8. If he had a pen, he would write. 9. He had to write. 10. They will describe their travels. 11. Here are the letters I have written. 12. Victor Hugo wrote (*p. def.*) this poem in 1840.

C. 1. He lived almost ninety years. 2. He wrote seventy volumes. 3. She is still living (lives still). 4. You have to write. 5. I do not think he will live long. 6. He thinks that novel will live. **7.** He has described his travels. **8.** The poems that he wrote are exquisite. **9.** Let us live in peace. **10.** They were living in peace with everybody. **11.** I wish you may live a long time. **12.** Victor Hugo was still living when I was born.

LESSON LXXX

198. Partitives. — 1. Review §§ 25, 28, 29, and observe the following:

N'a-t-il pas **des** amis?	*Has he no friends?*
Pas **du** lait mais **du** thé.	*Not milk but tea.*
Il n'a que **des** dettes.	*He has nothing but debts.*
C'étaient **des** grands hommes.	*They were great men.*
Des petits-fils; **des** petits pois.	*Grandsons; green peas.*

(*a*) With negatives the article remains when the existence of the object referred to is implied, Ex. 1; in contrasts, Ex. 2; with **ne . . . que** = *only*, Ex. 3; and when adjective and noun form a real or virtual compound, Ex. 4 and 5.

2. When **de** forms part of a phrase governing a partitive, the partitive sign is wholly omitted:

Il **vit de** pain.	*He lives on bread.*
Il se **sert d'**encre noire.	*He uses black ink.*
Un arbre **couvert de** feuilles.	*A tree covered with leaves.*

199. Article with Titles. — 1. A title before the name of a person takes the definite article, except in direct address:

La reine Victoria fut aimée.	*Queen Victoria was beloved.*
Le docteur Ribot est arrivé.	*Doctor Ribot has come.*
But: Bonjour, docteur Ribot.	*Good morning, Dr. Ribot.*

2. If the title is preceded by a title of courtesy (e.g. **monsieur**, etc.), it keeps the article in all cases:

Bonjour, monsieur **le** docteur.	*Good morning, doctor.*
Son altesse **le** prince l'a dit.	*His Highness the prince said so.*

(*a*) For other titles, see § 211.

200. Apposition. — 1. Appositive nouns used in parenthetical explanation regularly take no article:

L'*Avare*, comédie de Molière.	*The* Avare, *a comedy by Molière.*
Paris, fils de Priam.	*Paris,* (the *or* a) *son of Priam.*

2. Apparent apposition is frequent in expressions like:

L'église (*sc.* de) Saint-Pierre.	*St. Peter's* (the church of, *etc.*).
Des meubles (*sc.* du temps de) Louis XV.	*Louis XV furniture.*

EXERCISE LXXX

l'appartement. m., *suite of rooms, flat*	déjeuner, *take lunch, lunch*
l'argenterie, f., *silverware*	le dessert, *dessert*
le beau-frère, *brother-in-law*	le (la) domestique, *servant*
le bœuf, *ox, beef*	à droite (*sc.* **main**), *to* or *on the right.*
la bonne chère, *good cheer, good living*	l'escalier, m., *stairway*
le bon vivant, '*jolly fellow,*' *etc.*	à gauche, *to* or *on the left*
le buffet, *sideboard*	meubler, *furnish*
le capitaine, *captain*	moderne, *modern*
le caviar, *caviare*	**Notre-Dame,** *Notre Dame*
le confort, *comfort*	rôtir, *roast*
le corridor, *passage, hall*	le siège, *seat, chair*
décorer, *decorate, adorn*	la verrerie, *glassware*

être en train de, *be occupied in, be busy* (Eng. + *–ing* form); **mettre le couvert,** *set (lay) the table;* (**en**) **robe de chambre,** *in their jackets* or *skins* (of potatoes); **les petits pains,** *breakfast rolls, rolls;* **les petits pois,** *green peas*

A. Continue: 1. Je me sers de farine pour faire du pain. 2. J'emploie de la farine. 3. Je le fais avec de la farine. 4. Je le fais de farine. 5. Je vis de pain. 6. Je ne mange que du pain. 7. N'ai-je pas des amis ici? 8. J'ai acheté des meubles Louis XVI.

B. 1. Ma sœur et mon beau-frère habitent un appartement, 125 rue Notre-Dame, à droite de l'église Saint-Pierre. 2. C'est une belle maison avec tout le confort moderne. 3. Même les escaliers et les corridors sont beaux à voir. 4. Mon beau-frère est capitaine et le capitaine Pictet lui fait visite de temps en temps. 5. Tous les deux (*or* l'un et l'autre) aiment la bonne chère, quoiqu'ils ne soient pas des bons vivants. 6. Le capitaine Pictet vient déjeuner aujourd'hui. 7. On est en train de mettre le couvert dans la salle à manger. 8. Cette pièce est meublée avec goût et décorée de jolies gravures du XVIIIe siècle. 9. Les sièges et le buffet sont des meubles Louis XVI. 10. Quand le buffet est garni de vaisselle, d'argenterie et de verrerie il est très beau. 11. Les assiettes et les verres sont sur la table. 12. On va servir du caviar, du bœuf rôti, des pommes de terre (en) robe de chambre, des petits pois et des petits pains. 13. Au dessert on aura du fromage et du café.

C. (*Oral.*) 1. Où habitez-vous? 2. Décrivez-moi votre appartement. 3. Qui est l'ami de votre beau-frère? 4. Sont-ils des bons vivants? 5. Qui vient déjeuner chez vous aujourd'hui? 6. Que fait-on dans la salle à manger? 7. Décrivez les meubles de cette pièce. 8. Qu'est-ce qu'on va servir au déjeuner? 9. Qu'est-ce que vous prendrez au dessert?

D. 1. We used to live [at number] 75 Lafayette Street. 2. The house was on the left of St. Paul's church. 3. We lived in a flat which hadn't all the modern comfort[s]. 4. The stairway wasn't beautiful. 5. My father was a colonel. 6. Colonel Henri used to visit him from time to time. 7. They are not 'jolly fellows,' but they like good living. 8. The servants are busy setting the table. 9. When the table is adorned with glassware and silverware it is very beautiful. 10. We have some Louis XVI chairs and a sideboard of the same century. 11. At the lunch they will have first a hors-d'œuvre. 12. They will be served (use *on*) with roast beef and green peas. 13. At dessert they will have good cheese and black coffee.

E. 1. We use flour to make bread. 2. Use my pen to write your letter. 3. The passages are adorned with engravings of the XVII century. 4. We have Louis XVI furniture in our dining room. 5. We are looking for a house which is well furnished. 6. Queen Victoria was born in 1819. 7. When Captain Lesage used to come to see us he would often lunch with us. 8. My brother-in-law and he liked good living. 9. People use glasses to drink wine. 10. They use cups to drink coffee. 11. Both rose early and took some rolls and coffee with milk. 12. Give me some of the black coffee. 13. This cup is full of coffee. 14. We didn't have any of the good cheese which we bought at Potin's.

LESSON LXXXI

201.   *Plaire*, 'please'; *rire*, 'laugh'

plaire	plaisant	plu	plais	plus
rire	riant	ri	ris	ris

Like **plaire**: **se plaire**, *be pleased, enjoy oneself, like it*, etc.

EXERCISE LXXXI

je vous demande pardon, monsieur, or **pardon, monsieur,** *I beg your pardon, sir*

A. (*Oral.*) *Continue:* 1. Je plais (plairai, plus) à tout le monde. 2. Je ne plaisais (plairais) à personne. 3. Je ne lui plais pas. 4. Je m'y plaisais beaucoup. 5. Il ne croit pas que je leur plaise. 6. Pourquoi est-ce que j'en ris? 7. Ne ris pas des malheureux. 8. Il faut que je rie. 9. J'ai beaucoup ri. 10. Je riais souvent en classe.

B. 1. That pleases (will please) him. 2. The play pleased (would please) nobody. 3. Do you like it in the country? 4. I do. 5. Come when it pleases you. 6. At what are you laughing? 7. I beg your pardon, I didn't laugh. 8. Don't laugh at the misfortunes of others. 9. They always laughed at us. 10. We shall laugh if it (that) pleases us. 11. They laughed very much at it.

C. 1. The architect desired the plan to please you. 2. We never liked it in the country. 3. I don't think you will enjoy it there. 4. He tries to please everybody. 5. He will please nobody. 6. That child was always laughing and singing. 7. Why do you laugh at that? 8. I don't wish you to laugh at it. 9. Why did you laugh a moment ago? 10. It wasn't necessary that he should laugh. 11. I always have to laugh when I see that.

LESSON LXXXII

202. Omission of Article. — 1. The article is omitted in many expressions made up of a verb + a noun:

J'ai soif; il a bien faim.	*I am thirsty; he is very hungry.*
Je vous demande pardon.	*I beg your pardon.*

(a) Examples are: **avoir besoin**, *need;* **avoir chaud (froid)**, *be warm (cold);* **avoir faim (soif, sommeil)**, *be hungry (thirsty, sleepy);* **avoir raison (tort)**, *be right* or *be in the right (wrong);* **faire chaud (froid)**, *be warm (cold);* **faire attention**, *pay attention;* **prendre garde**, *take care; very, quite,* are expressed commonly by **bien** (sometimes **très**).

(b) Compare also the omission of the article in prepositional phrases like **après (le) dîner**, *after dinner;* **avec plaisir**, *with pleasure,* and many others.

2. Contrary to English usage, **un** (une) stands before an abstract noun adjectivally modified:

Il montra **un** soin extrême.	*He showed extreme care.*
Une patience à toute épreuve.	*Patience equal to anything.*

(a) Compare also expressions like J'ai **une** soif ardente, *I have (a) burning thirst;* Il fait **un** froid terrible, *It is terribly cold.*

203. Article for Possessive Adjective. — 1. The definite article is frequently so used when no ambiguity results, but is not always obligatory:

Donnez-moi **la** main.	*Give me your hand.*
Il a perdu **la** vie.	*He has lost his life.*
Elle s'est déchiré **la** main.	*She has torn her hand.*
Son (le) bras lui fait mal.	*His arm hurts him.*

2. So also with **avoir mal (froid, chaud,** etc., cf. § 202), and in phrases of description with **avoir**:

J'ai mal à **la** tête (aux dents).	*I have a headache (toothache).*
Avez-vous froid **aux** mains?	*Are your hands cold?*
Il a **le** nez long (*or* un long nez).	*He has a long nose.*

3. When the object possessed is singular as regards each possessor, it regularly remains singular, even though more than one possessor is denoted:

Ils ont perdu la **vie**.	*They have lost their lives.*
Ils ont ôté leur **chapeau**.	*They took off their hats.*
Ils sont entrés, le **chapeau** sur la tête.	*They came in with their hats on their heads.*

204. Observe the constructions in the following:

Il fait froid.	*It (the weather) is cold.*
Il fait froid ce matin.	*It's a cold morning.*
Il fait froid dans cette salle.	*It is cold in this hall (this hall is cold).*
J'ai froid.	*I am cold.*
L'eau est froide.	*The water is cold.*
J'ai froid aux mains.	*My hands are cold.*
Vous avez les mains froides.	*Your hands are cold.*

EXERCISE LXXXII

ardent, *ardent, burning*
bonsoir, *good evening* (*night*)
le corps, *body*
la douleur, *pain*
élevé, *high*
éternuer, *sneeze*
garder, *keep*
la gorge, *throat*
gravement, *gravely*
la grippe, ' *grippe,' influenza*
humide, *damp*
le midi, *south*

l'ordonnance, f., *prescription*
le pore, *pore*
rétabli, *restored* (in health), *well again*
le rhume, *cold*
secouer, *shake*
le séjour, *sojourn, stay*
la température, *temperature*
terrible, *terrible*
le thermomètre, *thermometer*
tousser, *cough*
transpirer, *perspire*

cette dent me fait mal, *this tooth pains* (*hurts*) *me;* **j'ai un mal de dents terrible,** *I have a dreadful toothache;* **comment allez-vous?** *how are you?* **comment ça va-t-il?** (fam.), *how are you?* **ça va mal** (fam.), *I am not (very) well;* **prenez garde à vous,** *take care of yourself;* **faire une ordonnance,** *write (give) a prescription;* **qu'avez-vous?** *what is the matter with you?*

A. 1. Depuis quelque temps il fait trop froid et trop humide. 2. Beaucoup de gens ont des rhumes. 3. Moi j'ai pris la grippe. 4. J'ai mal à la tête et à la gorge. 5. Je tousse et éternue beaucoup. 6. J'ai des douleurs par tout le corps. 7. Les bras et les jambes me font bien mal. 8. J'ai un mal de dents terrible. 9. Je n'ai pas très faim, mais j'ai une soif ardente. 10. J'ai tellement chaud que je transpire par tous les pores. 11. Mon père a envoyé chercher le médecin. 12. Le voilà qui sonne. 13. "Bonsoir, monsieur le docteur. — 14. Bonsoir, Pierre, comment ça va-t-il? — 15. Ça va mal, docteur. 16. Je souffre partout." 17. En me tâ-

tant le pouls il me dit que j'ai les mains bien chaudes. 18. Il me
met un thermomètre sous la langue. 19. Il regarde son thermomètre
et secoue gravement la tête. 20. "Vous avez la température bien
élevée. 21. Prenez garde à vous. 22. Vous garderez le lit quelques
jours, n'est-ce pas? 23. Je vous ferai une ordonnance. 24. Quand
vous aurez pris le remède vous irez mieux. 25. Puis le temps
changera; il fera plus beau. 26. Vous serez bientôt complètement
rétabli. 27. Vous pourrez peut-être aussi faire un petit séjour dans
le Midi. 28. On guérit souvent en changeant d'air."

B. (*Oral on A.*)

C. 1. The weather has been very damp. 2. You have a cold,
haven't you? 3. Yes, and my head is aching. 4. My sister has a
sore throat. 5. Everybody is sneezing and coughing. 6. My father
is ill. 7. What is the matter with him? 8. He has taken the
'grippe.' 9. He has pains all over his body. 10. These children
are very cold. 11. They were playing in the yard and their hands
and feet are cold. 12. They are very hungry and very thirsty too.

D. 1. How are you? 2. What is the matter with you? 3. The
doctor will put a thermometer under your tongue. 4. Take care
of yourself. 5. You must keep to your bed. 6. You will be better
to-morrow. 7. Your hands are hot, but your temperature is not
very high. 8. Here is a prescription I have written (*faire*) for you.
9. This medicine will do you good (*du bien*). 10. Make a short
(*petit*) stay in the south and you will be completely restored [to
health]. 11. You are quite right; I shall do so (it). 12. I shall get
well by changing climate.

E. 1. It is warm in winter in the south of France. 2. When I
was skating my feet were very cold. 3. I suffered a great deal from
it. 4. But I am quite warm now. 5. I have a bad (use *bien*)
headache, and I have a toothache also. 6. Our professor has a sore
throat and must keep [to] the house. 7. Are you too warm? 8. No,
I am too cold. 9. When we are hungry we eat slices of bread and
butter. 10. If we are thirsty, we like water better than wine. 11. I
am terribly thirsty. 12. Give me a glass of water, if you please.

F. 1. It was so cold that I had to put on warmer clothes. 2. If
you are cold, take a cup of hot coffee. 3. You said it was warmer

to-day, but I think you are wrong. 4. It is colder. 5. I beg your pardon; I am right. 6. Monkeys have long arms and small heads. 7. Those bad boys entered the classroom with their hats on their heads. 8. My father almost lost his life in a railway accident. 9. He has (is) not completely recovered yet. 10. His arm hurts him still.

LESSON LXXXIII

205.   *Tenir*, 'hold'

> tenir   tenant   tenu   tiens   tins

(*a*) **Tenir** is conjugated precisely like **venir** (cf. § 167).

Like **tenir: appartenir**, *belong;* **obtenir**, *obtain;* **contenir**, *contain.*
Like **venir: devenir**, *become (of).*

EXERCISE LXXXIII

la **permission**, *permission*   **tenir de**, *take after*
le **porte-monnaie**, *purse*

A. (*Oral.*) *Continue:* 1. Qu'est-ce que je deviendrai (deviendrais)? 2. Je suis devenue heureuse. 3. Je devenais très riche. 4. Ma mère désire que je devienne plus sage, . . . tu. 5. J'obtiens (obtins) ainsi un bon prix. 6. J'obtiendrai (obtiendrais) la permission d'y entrer. 7. J'appartiens à cet endroit.

B. 1. The boxes contained pencils and pens. 2. A glass containing milk was on the table. 3. This purse contains all my money. 4. They have become very poor. 5. What has become of him (her)? 6. What has become of my pens? 7. To whom did that castle belong? 8. I ask [for] what belongs to me. 9. Some pictures belonging to this artist have been stolen. 10. What price will you obtain?

C. 1. This young man has become [a] doctor. 2. What will (would) become of us? 3. This field belonged to my father's property. 4. It will become my property when my uncle dies. 5. They say that living will become dearer. 6. We shall obtain (the) permission to stay. 7. He held the letter in his hand. 8. I wish that you may become happier. 9. The son takes after his father. 10. I hope the letter will contain money. 11. Don't hold your pen like that.

LESSON LXXXIV

206. Adjectives and Nouns. — 1. Review § 34, and observe:

caus**eur**, m., caus**euse**, f., *chatty* (adj.), *a chatty person* (noun)
flatt**eur**, m., flatt**euse**, f., *flattering* (adj.), *a flatterer* (noun)
cré**ateur**, m., cré**atrice**, f., *creative* (adj.), *a creator* (noun)

(*a*) When a corresponding present participle exists, –**eur** of nouns and adjectives becomes –**euse** in the feminine, Ex. 1 and 2 (cf. caus**ant**, flatt**ant**); otherwise –**teur** becomes –**trice** in the feminine, Ex. 3.

2. The feminine of many nouns is formed like that of adjectives of the same ending:

écoli**er**, –**ère**, *schoolboy*   institut**eur**, –**trice**, *teacher*
pays**an**, –**anne**, *peasant*   citad**in**, –**e**, *inhabitant of the town*

207. Agreement of Adjectives. — Review § 14, and observe the following special cases: —

1. Adjectives used as adverbs are regularly invariable:

Ces roses sentent **bon**.   *These roses smell sweet.*

2. Nouns serving as adjectives of colour are invariable:

Des robes **lilas** (citron).   *Purple (lemon-coloured) dresses.*

(*a*) But **rose, cramoisi, pourpre**, agree like adjectives.

3. A very few adjectives are always invariable:

Vingt livres **sterling**.   *Twenty pounds sterling.*

4. With **avoir l'air**, the adjective agrees either with **air** (m.), or with the subject (**d'être** being expressed or implied):

Elle a l'air **doux**.   *She has a gentle air (appearance).*
Elle a l'air (d'être) **douce**.   *She seems* or *looks gentle.*

(*a*) Either expression may be used without distinction.

5. The peculiar agreement with **gens**:

Les **vieilles** gens sont **positifs**.   *Old people are practical.*
Toutes les vieilles gens.   *All the old people.*
Tous les (ces) habiles gens.   *All the (those) clever people.*
Les gens sont **tous** ici.   *The people are all here.*

(*a*) All forms agreeing with **gens** are plural.

(*b*) An adjective is feminine before **gens** and masculine after it, Ex. 1 and 2, but cf. *c*.

(*c*) *All* = **toutes** only when separated from **gens** by an adjective variable for the feminine, Ex. 2; otherwise **tous**, Ex. 3 and 4.

Note. — Jeunes gens = *young men, young people*, is always masculine, and also **gens** used as an antecedent, e.g. Les gens **qui** sont **venus**.

208. Comparatives. — 1. Review § 56, and contrast the French and English forms of the following:

De plus en plus violent.	*More and more violent.*
Plus il devient riche moins il est généreux.	*The richer he becomes the less generous he is.*
Il en sera d'autant plus riche.	*He will be the richer for it.*
Le carnage fut d'autant plus grand qu'ils étaient plus nombreux.	*The carnage was the greater because they were more numerous.*

2. A finite verb completing a comparison is preceded by **ne**, unless the preceding verb is negative:

C'est meilleur que je **ne** croyais.	*It is better than I thought.*
Ce n'est pas si mal que je croyais.	*It is not so bad as I thought.*

3. When **aussi** (or **si**) is omitted, **comme** (not **que**) is used:

Un roi riche **comme** Crésus.	*A king as rich as Crœsus.*

EXERCISE LXXXIV

agricole, *agricultural*	**gai**, *gay, merry, cheerful*
l'air, m., *air, appearance*	**horticole**, *horticultural*
le bouquet, *bouquet, nosegay*	**l'instituteur**, m., f. **–trice**, *teacher*
la bouquetière, *flower girl*	**le lilas**, *lilac;* adj., *purple*
la boutonnière, *buttonhole*	**nouveau**, *new, novel*
charmant, *charming*	**le parterre**, *flower garden*
le citadin, f. **-e**, *townsman*	**le produit**, *product*
coiffer, *dress the hair* (*head*)	**promener**, *lead* or *take about*
le concours, *competition, show*	**la prospérité**, *prosperity*
doux, *gentle, mild*	**la rose**, *rose*
l'écolier, m., f. **–ère**, *schoolboy* (*girl*)	**sérieux**, *serious*
	le signe, *sign*
les environs, m., *neighbourhood*	**la tente**, *tent*

coup d'œil, *glance, prospect, sight, view;* **à la** (sc. **mode**) **française**, *in the French style* or *fashion;* **neuf**, *new* (not old), **nouveau**, *new, fresh, novel*

A. (*Concours agricole et horticole*) 1. Tous les braves gens des environs y arrivent à pied ou en voiture. 2. Les paysans y apportent les produits des champs, les paysannes ceux du verger et du parterre. 3. On y amène aussi les bœufs et les vaches. 4. Ils sont au parc à l'ombre. 5. Les vaches ont l'air très douces, n'est-ce pas? 6. Les paysans sont bons pour leurs bêtes et leur donnent à manger. 7. On met les fleurs et les fruits sous des tentes. 8. Les fleurs sentent bon et offrent un coup d'œil charmant. 9. Les pommes ont l'air d'être mûres. 10. Il fait beau et il y a beaucoup de monde. 11. Les citadins, hommes d'affaires, observent les signes de la prospérité du pays. 12. Les citadines cherchent de nouvelles espèces de fleurs ou de fruits. 13. Un instituteur et une institutrice promènent leurs écoliers et leurs écolières pour les instruire. 14. Une jolie bouquetière en robe lilas et coiffée à l'italienne vend des fleurs. 15. Tous les jeunes gens en achètent pour mettre à leur boutonnière. 16. Toutes les vieilles gens s'occupent d'affaires sérieuses.

B. (*Oral.*)   Read A aloud, *turning present tenses into the imperfect.*

C. 1. The country people of the neighbourhood are coming to the agricultural show. 2. They will bring to it the products of the fields. 3. The oxen and cows will be brought too. 4. And they do not forget the products of the orchard and flower garden. 5. The animals look so gentle. 6. Look at the flowers in (= under) the tents. 7. What a pretty sight! 8. And they smell so sweet! 9. Smell this bouquet. 10. These pears look ripe. 11. It is a new kind of pear. 12. These are business men. 13. They are townsmen. 14. The townswomen hope to find new kinds of roses or of fruits. 15. The teachers (*f.*) will bring their schoolgirls here. 16. All the young men will buy flowers from the flower girls. 17. Do you see that young countrywoman dressed in the Italian fashion? 18. I mean the young woman in [a] purple dress.

D. 1. All the young people are merry. 2. All the old people are more serious. 3. The older you are the more serious you become. 4. These worthy people are kind to everybody. 5. Everybody is kind to them. 6. We observed many signs of prosperity at the horticultural show. 7. The teachers (*m.*) were taking their scholars about (there). 8. They wanted to show them something new.

9. The schoolboys asked their teachers many questions. 10. The schoolgirls admired the flowers. 11. They have bought some pretty ones for their teachers (*f.*). 12. Old people are more serious than young people. 13. I am more serious than I used to be (*l'*). 14. This young countrywoman looks very intelligent. 15. She sold a good many flowers to the young men. 16. The younger one is the more one spends. 17. We become wiser and wiser as we become old. 18. My old friend has become as rich as Crœsus in South America.

LESSON LXXXV

209.　　*Cueillir*, 'pluck,' 'gather'; *ouvrir*, 'open'; *tressaillir*, 'start,' 'tremble'

cueillir	cueillant	cueilli	cueille	cueillis
ouvrir	ouvrant	ouvert	ouvre	ouvris
tressaillir	tressaillant	tressailli	tressaille	tressaillis

Like **ouvrir**: **couvrir**, *cover;* **découvrir**, *discover;* **s'ouvrir**, *open* (intr.).

EXERCISE LXXXV

Colomb, *Columbus*　　　　　**l'exposition**, f., *exhibition*

A. (*Oral.*)　*Continue:* 1. Je tressaille (tressaillais, tressaillis) de joie. 2. J'ouvre (ouvrais, ouvris) la malle. 3. Ouvre la porte. 4. Couvre-toi la tête, . . . nous. 5. Je cueille (cueillais, cueillis) des fleurs pour en faire un bouquet. 6. Les lettres que j'ai ouvertes. 7. J'ouvrirai les fenêtres. 8. Il faut que je les ouvre.

B. 1. She starts when she hears a noise. 2. They were trembling with fear. 3. Open the door, please. 4. I have opened it. 5. The door opens (*reflex.*). 6. I was opening my letters when he came. 7. I am (was) gathering flowers to make a bouquet. 8. Here are the flowers I have gathered for the exhibition. 9. Let her gather the prettiest flowers. 10. When will you pick your apples? 11. The fields were covered with snow.

C. 1. The windows are not open; open them. 2. I wish him to open his valise. 3. The king in person opened (*p. def.*) the exhibition. 4. On opening the letter she trembled. 5. Cover your head or you will catch cold. 6. The table was covered with papers.

7. She trembles (trembled) with joy. 8. They started at the noise of the train. 9. We are covering the apples with straw. 10. Where are the flowers that you were gathering? 11. Columbus discovered America in 1492.

LESSON LXXXVI

210. Personal Pronoun. — The following special cases of agreement should be noted: —

1. The invariable forms **il** (subject) and **le** (direct object) are used when the antecedent is indefinite or absent:

Y en a-t-il? — Je le crois.	*Is there any? — I think so.*
Je le ferai si vous le désirez.	*I shall do so if you wish (it).*
Nous l'avons emporté.	*We have carried the day.*

2. So also the pronominal adverbs **en** and **y**:

Voyons! où **en** étions-nous?	*Let me see! where were we?*
Quoiqu'il **en** soit.	*However it may be.*
Votre père **y** est-il?	*Is your father in (at home)?*

3. **Le** (**la, les**) sometimes has predicative force:

Êtes-vous sa mère? — Je **la** suis.	*Are you his mother? — I am.*
Êtes-vous Mme B.? — Je **la** suis.	*Are you Mrs. B.? — I am.*
Êtes-vous fatiguée? — Je **le** suis.	*Are you tired? — I am.*
Sont-ils soldats? — Ils **le** sont.	*Are they soldiers? — They are.*
Soyez braves et je **le** serai.	*Be brave and I shall be so.*

(*a*) If **le** refers to a determinate substantive (not partitive), it agrees, Ex. 1 and 2; otherwise it is invariable, Ex. 3, 4 and 5.

211. Possessives. — Review §§ 15, 16, 83–85, and observe: —

1. The use of the possessive adjective in polite address:

Bonjour **mon** père (**mon** colonel).	*Good morning, father (colonel).*
Mademoiselle votre sœur y est-elle?	*Is your sister at home?*

(*a*) In direct address **mon** (ma, etc.) commonly precedes a noun of relationship (but not **papa, maman**) or the title of a superior officer; **votre** (vos) is often preceded by **monsieur** (madame, etc.).

2. *Own* = **propre**, or is expressed by **à** + a pronoun:

Je l'ai fait de mes **propres** mains.	*I did it with my own hands.*
C'est mon opinion **à moi**.	*It is my own opinion.*
Il a une maison **à lui**.	*He has a house of his own.*

3. Ambiguity is sometimes avoided by using **à**, thus:

Son père **à lui** (à elle).	*His (her) father.*

4. The possessive pronoun may be used absolutely:

Je ne demande que **le mien**.	*I ask only what is mine.*
Les miens.	*My family (friends, party, etc.).*

212. Relative Pronoun. — 1. For the general rules, see §§ 92–98.

2. **Qui** without antecedent means *he who, the one(s) who, those who*, and when repeated *some . . . others*:

Qui s'excuse s'accuse.	*He who excuses himself accuses himself.*
Qui d'un côté **qui** de l'autre.	*Some on one side some on the other.*

3. Observe **de quoi** = "ce qui est nécessaire pour":

Il a de quoi vivre.	*He is well off.*
Donnez-moi de quoi écrire.	*Give me something to write with.*
Merci! — Il n'y a pas de quoi.	*Thanks! — Don't mention it (etc.).*

EXERCISE LXXXVI

l'achat, m., *purchase*	faible, *weak*
l'avoine, f., *oats*	la ferme, *farmhouse*
la basse-cour, *farmyard*	le foin, *hay*
la charrue, *plough*	l'hectare, m., *about 2½ acres*
comprendre, irreg., *understand*	le labour, *ploughing*
le cultivateur, *farmer*	la moissonneuse, *reaping machine*
le curé, *parish priest, curé*	nommer, *name, appoint*
le droit, *right*	l'orge, f., *barley*
l'écurie, f., *(horse) stable*	pareillement, *equally, likewise, also*
enchanté, *charmed, delighted*	le propriétaire, *proprietor, landlord*
l'existence, f., *existence*	le républicain, *republican*
exploiter, *exploit, work*	la terre, *earth, land*

ils se serrent la main, *they shake hands;* c'est là ma maison, *that is my house (there);* il m'en veut, *he has a grudge against me;* je n'y comprends rien, *I don't understand it at all;* où en êtes-vous de . . .? *how far are you on with . . .?* j'en ai pour . . ., *I have . . . worth of it;* ils l'ont emporté, *they have won, have carried the day;* il y va de ma vie, *my life is at stake;* c'en est fait de moi, *it is all over (all up) with me;* que voulez-vous que j'y fasse? *what am I to do? how can I help it? what can you expect?* etc.

A. Continue: 1. Je ne lui en veux pas. 2. Je n'y ai rien compris. 3. Où en suis-je de mes préparatifs? . . . tu . . . tes. 4. Est-ce que j'y comprends quelque chose? 5. Je l'emporterai sur eux. 6. C'en est fait de moi, . . . toi. 7. Il y va de ma vie, . . . ta. 8. J'ai une maison à moi, tu . . . à toi. 9. Je ne demande que le mien, tu . . . le tien.

B. (*Dans la basse-cour*) 1. "Bonjour, monsieur le curé. — 2. Bonjour, mon enfant. Monsieur votre père y est-il? — 3. Je vais l'appeler." 4. M. Legrand, gros cultivateur, arrive. 5. Le curé, récemment nommé, et lui se serrent la main. 6. "Vous êtes monsieur le curé? — 7. Et vous, monsieur Legrand? Je suis enchanté de faire votre connaissance. — 8. Moi pareillement, monsieur le curé. — 9. C'est là votre maison? — 10. Oui, c'est là la ferme. 11. Et plus loin c'est le château du propriétaire. 12. J'exploite quatre-vingts hectares dont la moitié est à lui et l'autre moitié à moi. 13. C'est de la bonne terre. 14. Les miens et moi sommes très heureux. 15. Mais depuis l'achat de mes quarante hectares notre propriétaire nous en veut. 16. Je n'y comprends rien. 17. Quoi! je n'aurais pas le droit d'acheter des terres? — 18. Mais où en êtes-vous de votre récolte, dit le curé. — 19. Nous en sommes aux trois quarts. 20. Le foin, l'avoine et l'orge sont très bons. 21. J'en aurai pour dix mille francs. 22. Voici l'écurie. 23. Les chevaux n'y sont pas. 24. Ils font marcher la moissonneuse dans les blés, et les bœufs sont au labour. 25. Nous labourons en ce moment avec trois charrues. 26. À propos, avez-vous des nouvelles des élections d'hier? — 27. Les républicains l'ont emporté sur les nôtres. 28. Quel dommage! 29. Il y va de l'existence de l'église, et peut-être de la France. 30. C'en est fait de nous. 31. Mais que voulez-vous que nous y fassions? 32. Nous sommes les plus faibles."

C. (*Oral on B.*)

D. Supply the proper form of **le**: 1. Êtes-vous Anglais? Nous . . . sommes. 2. Êtes-vous l'institutrice? Je . . . suis. 3. Sont-ils heureux? Ils . . . sont. 4. Sont-ce de braves gens? Il . . . sont. 5. Êtes-vous fatiguées? Nous . . . sommes. 6. Êtes-vous la femme du cultivateur? Je . . . suis.

E. 1. The new parish priest met the boy in the barnyard. 2. He asked him if his father was in. 3. He went to get his father. 4. The big farmer and the priest shook hands. 5. The priest was delighted to make his acquaintance. 6. That is the farmhouse behind the trees. 7. That is my landlord's castle. 8. The farmer had land of his own. 9. Half the land he worked belonged to him. 10. He and his [family] were well off. 11. But their landlord had a grudge against them. 12. They couldn't understand it at all. 13. The priest asked him how far he was on with his harvest. 14. The hay, oats and barley were already cut. 15. He had 5000 francs' worth of them. 16. Some of the harvesters were cutting the wheat (*plur.*). 17. We use reaping machines for that. 18. Other men are ploughing the fields with two ploughs. 19. To plough they use oxen. 20. The republicans won at the elections. 21. Our party (§ 211, 4) was beaten, said the priest. 22. But what can you expect?

F. 1. However it may be, I am not satisfied. 2. I shall accompany you if you wish (it). 3. I should be delighted if you did so. 4. He is wrong, but I will not tell him so. 5. I have made this bread with my own hands. 6. Have you a house of your own, or do you live with your relations? 7. You have been very kind to me and mine. 8. I thank you for it. 9. Don't mention it. 10. Our party will carry the day at the elections, I am certain (of it). 11. Are you republicans? 12. We are. 13. Good evening, aunt; are you ready to (*à*) go? 14. I am; let us go. 15. You seem to have a grudge against me. 16. We have read this work (*ouvrage*), but we don't understand it at all. 17. If you don't change [your] manner-of-living (*vie*), it is all up with you.

LESSON LXXXVII

213. *Craindre*, 'fear'; *joindre*, 'join'; *peindre*, 'paint'

craindre	craignant	craint	crains	craignis
joindre	joignant	joint	joins	joignis
peindre	peignant	peint	peins	peignis

(*a*) Note the similarity of these verbs in conjugation.

Like **craindre: plaindre,** *pity;* **se plaindre,** *complain.*

EXERCISE LXXXVII

l'artiste, m. or f., *artist*   le portrait, *portrait*
malheureux, *unfortunate*

A. (*Oral.*) *Continue:* 1. Je crains (craignais) de tomber. 2. Ne crains rien. 3. Ne te plains pas de cela. 4. Je peins (peignais) un paysage. 5. Les paysages que j'ai peints . . . que tu. 6. Il voudrait que je lui peigne un tableau, . . . tu. 7. Je joignis les bouts et les cousis ensemble. 8. Je peignis la boiserie. 9. Je plaignais les pauvres par (*in*) ce temps d'hiver.

B. 1. You paint very well. 2. Which (*plur.*) of the pictures have you painted? 3. Pity my misfortunes. 4. I pity you; you are very unhappy. 5. We do not complain. 6. Join the ends of this piece of cloth and sew them together. 7. They feared to miss the train. 8. Would you fear to arrive too late? 9. The fortunate do not always pity the unfortunate.

C. 1. Where is the portrait you were painting? 2. I should like you to paint my portrait. 3. Who painted this landscape? 4. That artist painted (*p. def.*) many landscapes. 5. Let us pity the unfortunate. 6. What does he fear? 7. He will fear to meet us. 8. We feared to say a single word. 9. They were always complaining.

LESSON LXXXVIII

214. *On.* — Review § 38, and observe further:

On est triste quand **on** a faim.	*A man is sad when he is hungry.*
On se demande si, etc.	*People wonder whether, etc.*
On perdrait **son** temps.	*You would lose your time.*
Lorsqu'**on** presse trop un poisson il **vous** échappe.	*When you hold a fish too tightly it escapes you.*

(*a*) **On** as subject is repeated if necessary, Ex. 1.

(*b*) The reflexive pronoun corresponding to **on** is **se** and the possessive is **son**, Ex. 2 and 3.

(*c*) Since **on** serves only as subject, the corresponding objective forms are borrowed from **vous**, etc., Ex. 4.

215. *Whoever, whatever.* Observe the following:

Qui que tu sois (vous soyez).	*Whoever you are* (= *may be*).
Quiconque parlera sera puni(e).	*Whoever speaks will be punished.*
Une plume **quelconque**.	*Any pen whatever* (*some, any kind of a pen, some pen or other*).
Quelques efforts qu'il fasse.	*Whatever efforts he makes* (*may make*).
Quelle qu'en soit la cause.	*Whatever* (*may*) *be the cause of it.*
Quoi que ce soit.	*Whatever it be* (*is, may be*).
Quoi que vous fassiez.	*Whatever you* (*may*) *do.*

(*a*) *Whoever* = **qui que** with **être** (subjunctive), Ex. 1, and elsewhere **quiconque**, Ex. 2; other equivalents are: **celui qui** (cf. § 82), or **qui** (cf. § 212, 2).

(*b*) *Any . . . whatever* = **quelconque**, which follows its noun and agrees like an ordinary adjective, Ex. 3.

(*c*) *Whatever*, preceding a noun = **quelque(s)** . . . **que** + subjunctive, Ex. 4.

(*d*) *Whatever*, preceding *to be* = **quel que** + subjunctive, Ex. 5.

(*e*) *Whatever*, absolutely = **quoi que** + subjunctive, Ex. 6 and 7.

(*f*) Observe also: **Lequel désirez-vous? — N'importe lequel,** . . . *Any one at all* (*whatever*); **Qui doit lire? — N'importe qui** . . . *Any one at all* (*whatever*).

EXERCISE LXXXVIII

allumer, *light, kindle*	**le fluide**, *fluid*
l'avenir, m., *future*	**le gaz**, *gas*
la bougie, *wax candle*	**l'habitation**, f., *habitation, dwelling*
brûler, *burn*	**l'huile**, f., *oil*
la chaleur, *warmth, heat*	**humain**, *human*
la chandelle, *candle*	**inflammable**, *inflammable*
le charbon, *coal*	**la lampe**, *lamp*
le chauffage, *heating*	**la lumière**, *light*
chauffer, *warm, heat*	**la manière**, *manner, way*
échapper (à), *escape (from)*	**mystérieux**, *mysterious*
l'éclairage, m., *lighting*	**l'obscurité**, f., *darkness*
éclairer, *light, illuminate*	**l'observation**, f., *observation*
l'électricité, f., *electricity*	**le pétrole**, *petroleum*
électrique, *electric*	

lampe à pétrole, *petroleum lamp;* **à l'avenir,** *in the future*

A. Continue: 1. Qui que je sois j'ai besoin d'amis, . . . tu . . . tu.
2. Quelques remèdes que je prenne je ne guéris pas, . . . tu . . . tu.

3. Quelle que soit mon habitation il faut la chauffer, . . . ton, etc.
4. Quoi que je fasse je ne réussirai pas, . . . tu . . . tu. 5. Je pourrai
me servir de n'importe quel livre, tu . . . te.

B. 1. Quelles que soient les habitations humaines, il faut les
chauffer et les éclairer. 2. Qui que vous soyez vous avez besoin de
chaleur et de lumière. 3. Dans l'obscurité il faut allumer quelque
chose d'inflammable. 4. Quoi qu'on fasse il faut un chauffage
quelconque par le temps froid. 5. Pour se chauffer on brûle du
bois ou du charbon. 6. De ce dernier on tire aussi le gaz dont on
éclaire les maisons et les rues. 7. On se sert aussi de lampes à
pétrole. 8. On peut se demander ce qu'on ferait si le pétrole venait
à manquer. 9. De quelle espèce d'huile se servirait-on dans ce
cas? 10. De n'importe quelle espèce, car toutes les espèces servent
à l'éclairage. 11. On pourrait employer aussi des chandelles et des
bougies. 12. Les unes et les autres ont souvent servi à éclairer les
maisons. 13. Il y a aussi la lumière électrique. 14. Qu'est-ce que
c'est que l'électricité? 15. C'est un fluide remarquable qui échappe
à notre observation. 16. De quelque manière qu'on l'emploie elle
reste toujours mystérieuse. 17. Nous ne savons pas ce que c'est
que l'électricité.

C. (*Oral.*) 1. Pourquoi faut-il que nos habitations soient chauf-
fées et éclairées? 2. Que nous faut-il pour cela? 3. Que nous faut-il
faire dans l'obscurité? 4. D'où tirons-nous le gaz? 5. Qu'est-ce que
nous faisons pour nous chauffer? 6. Qu'est-ce que nous faisons
du gaz? 7. À quoi servent les lampes à pétrole? 8. Que ferions-
nous s'il n'y en avait pas? 9. De quelle autre lumière nous servons-
nous? 10. Que dit-on ici de l'électricité? etc.

D. 1. One must heat the houses in cold climates. 2. Whoever
we are we must have light. 3. In darkness we must have some kind
of a lamp. 4. Whatever the dwellings of men may be they must
be lighted. 5. Whatever you do you must have fire in cold weather.
6. We use wood and coal to heat our houses. 7. We use coal to
make gas. 8. We light our houses with (*de*) gas. 9. Do you use
petroleum lamps in your house? 10. I wonder what people would do
without petroleum. 11. Could they use any sort of oil whatever?
12. Yes, and they could use electric light. 13. Do you know what

electricity is? 14. They call it a mysterious fluid, but nobody knows
what it is. 15. In whatever way it may be employed (use *on*), it
will probably remain mysterious.

E. 1. Heating is necessary in cold climates. 2. Lighting is
necessary everywhere. 3. The ancients used oil lamps or candles.
4. Light the gas. 5. Do not light the fire yet. 6. We used to burn
wood formerly, but we burn coal now. 7. In the future we shall
use electricity to give us heat. 8. We use it now to give us light.
9. Whoever you are, you must work in this country. 10. You can't
escape work here. 11. You can't use any wood whatever (use
n'importe) to make furniture. 12. Whoever comes to see me is well
received. 13. Whatever you have to say, say it at once. 14. Whatever be the cause of it, they don't come to see us now.

LESSON LXXXIX

216. Adverbs from Adjectives. — Adverbs of manner are
formed from many adjectives by adding –**ment**, thus: —

1. Added directly to adjectives ending in **e, é, i, u:**

> facilement, décidément, poliment, absolument

2. Otherwise added to the feminine of the adjective:

> pur, **pure**ment, doux, **douce**ment, actif, **active**ment

(*a*) Exceptionally –**e** changes to –**é** on adding –**ment**, e.g. énorme, énormé-
ment, précise, précisément.

(*b*) Most adjectives in –**ant**, –**ent** change –**nt** to –**m**, and add –**ment**,
e.g. constant, constamment, prudent, prudemment; but not lentement and
some others.

(*c*) Observe gentiment (gentil), brièvement (bref), impunément (impuni).

217. Adverbial Distinctions. — 1. **Si** = *yes* implies contra-
diction of or dissent from a negative assertion or question:

Je n'irai pas. — Si, si, venez. *I shall not go. — Yes, yes, come.*
Il ne s'en va pas? — Mais si. *He is not going? — Yes, certainly.*

2. Observe the following expressions:

Je dis que oui (non). *I say yes (no).*
Je crois que oui (non). *I think so (not).*

3. Autant = *as much (many)*; **tant** = *so much (many)*:

J'ai **tant** d'amis; j'en ai **autant** que n'importe qui.	*I have so many friends; I have as many as anybody.*

4. *Only* = **seulement** (1) when no verb is present, (2) when *only* refers to the subject, (3) or to the verb, (4) or to a **que** clause, and (5) it may be used to strengthen **ne . . . que**; otherwise *only* = **ne . . . que** or **seulement**:

Seulement les braves.	*Only the brave.*
Seulement mon frère le sait.	*Only my brother knows it.*
Écoutez **seulement**.	*Only listen.*
Il dit **seulement** qu'il vient.	*He only says he is coming.*
Il n'a **seulement** qu'à venir.	*He has only to come.*

But: Je **n'**ai **que** dix francs (*or* j'ai **seulement** dix francs); Il **n'a qu'à** demander (il a **seulement** à demander), etc.

(*a*) *Only* referring to the subject, may be turned also by **il n'y a que**, **ce n'est que**; *only* referring to the verb may be turned by the help of **faire**: Il **n'y a que** les morts qui ne reviennent pas, *The dead only do not come back;* Elle ne **fait que** pleurer, *She does nothing but weep.*

(*b*) Observe also the frequent use in modern French of **ne . . . pas que**, *not only*, e.g. Il **n'y a pas que** les pauvres qui aient besoin d'être aidés, *It isn't only the poor that need to be helped.*

5. Certain adverbs of place are used like **en, y** (cf. §§ 27, 39) as equal to a preposition + a pronoun (of things):

Voyez sur la table, cherchez **dessus** et **dessous**.	*Look on the table, search on it and under it.*

(*a*) Thus: dedans, dehors, dessus, dessous, devant, derrière, etc.

6. Que has adverbial force in exclamations:

Que vous êtes heureux!	*How happy you are!*

7. Tout used adverbially agrees like an adjective when immediately preceding a feminine adjective beginning in a consonant or **h** aspirate, but is elsewhere invariable:

Elles étaient **toutes** pâles et **tout** agitées.	*They were quite pale and very much excited.*

8. Observe the following renderings of *however, wherever, whenever:*

Quelque riche qu'il soit.	*However rich he is (may be).*
Quelque bien que vous parliez.	*However well you (may) speak.*
Toutes bonnes qu'elles sont.	*However kind they are (may be).*
Si (Pour) bonne qu'elle soit.	*However kind she is (may be).*
Partout où je le vois.	
En quelque lieu que je le voie. }	*Wherever I see him.*
Où que je le voie.	
Toutes les fois que je le vois.	*Whenever I see him.*

EXERCISE LXXXIX

l'aiguille, f., *needle*
aisé, *easy, comfortable, well-to-do*
le canard, *duck*
les ciseaux, m., *scissors*
le dé, *thimble*
dehors, *outside*
enseigner, *teach*
étrange, *strange*
le fil, *thread*
Hélène, *Helen*
l'occupation, f., *occupation*

oisif, *idle*
l'oisiveté, f., *idleness*
paraître, irreg., *appear*
la paresse, *laziness*
paresseux, *lazy*
la poule, *hen*
pourtant, *however*
la richesse, *wealth*
la tâche, *task*
utile, *useful*
le vice, *vice*
la volaille, *poultry*

je ne saurais qu'en faire, *I don't know what to do with it*

A. Continue: 1. Je crois que non. 2. J'ai autant d'amis que n'importe qui. 3. J'ai tant de foin que je ne saurais qu'en faire, tu . . . tu. 4. Je n'aurai qu'à demander. 5. Je n'avais que peu d'argent. 6. Je l'ai cherché sur la table et dessous. 7. Quelque habile que je sois. 8. Toute fatiguée que je parais. 9. Je ne suis pas paresseux.

B. 1. L'oisiveté est (la) mère de tous les vices. 2. Tout aisée qu'elle est Mme Legrand désire que sa fille Hélène apprenne à faire les choses utiles. 3. Il n'y a pas que les pauvres qui aient besoin d'apprendre à travailler. 4. Quelque étrange que cela puisse paraître les riches en ont autant besoin que les pauvres. 5. Les pauvres n'ont qu'à gagner leur vie. 6. Les riches ont une tâche encore plus difficile, — celle d'employer leur richesse pour le bien d'autrui. 7. Que la petite Hélène est heureuse! 8. Elle n'a pas que des amusements pourtant. 9. Elle a ses devoirs, son ouvrage. 10. Elle a déjà son dé, son aiguille, son fil et ses ciseaux. 11. Sa mère, si occupée qu'elle soit, trouve le temps de lui montrer à faire des vêtements. 12. Elle coupe, coud, garnit. 13. Elle a tant à faire qu'elle n'a pas le temps d'être oisive. 14. Non seulement elle a des occupations dans la maison, elle en a aussi dehors. 15. Elle s'occupe de la volaille de la basse-cour. 16. Elle donne à manger aux poules et aux canards. 17. Elle cherche des œufs partout où il y en a.

C. (*Oral.*) 1. Que dit-on ici de l'oisiveté? 2. Que désirait Mme Legrand? 3. La tâche des riches est-elle difficile? 4. Pourquoi dites-vous cela? 5. Que dit-on ici des pauvres? 6. La petite Hélène est-elle oisive? 7. Décrivez ses occupations. etc.

D. 1. The mother would like her daughter to learn useful things. 2. Laziness is a vice. 3. If we (*m.*) are idle we shall learn nothing useful. 4. It is not children only who need lessons. 5. However strange it may seem, everybody needs them. 6. You have as much need of them as I. 7. You and I have only to earn our living. 8. The task of the rich man is still more difficult. 9. He must work as much as we. 10. He must learn to use his wealth for the good of others.

E. 1. How fortunate we are! 2. He who has work to do is fortunate. 3. Little girls should have needles, thread, thimbles and scissors. 4. They must have plenty of duties and occupations. 5. However busy I am, I have time to teach my little sister. 6. I teach her [how] to make clothes. 7. We have so much to do that we haven't time to be idle. 8. We are busy not (*non*) only at school but at home. 9. We have tasks in the house and outside [of it]. 10. We feed the poultry every morning. 11. Whenever we feed the hens and ducks we look for eggs.

F. 1. Is it going to rain? 2. I think so. 3. I think not, for it is windy. 4. Mr. Legrand has as much land as his neighbour. 5. He has never had so much hay as he has (of it) this year. 6. If you need anything, you have only to ask [for it]. 7. Only ask for that and you shall have it. 8. The patient only said that he was tired and that he wanted to sleep. 9. He had been ill for a few days only. 10. I had only five francs, but I gave him the half of it.

G. 1. I looked for my pen on the table and under it, but without
finding it.   2. You haven't electric lighting in your house?   3. Oh
yes, we have had it for two years.   4. Those boys are lazy; they
will not work.   5. However well-to-do you are, you must work.
6. Whenever I meet Mr. Brunot he asks after your health.   7. Wherever you are, never forget that you are a Frenchman.   8. It isn't
only my Latin that I find difficult.   9. Only work, and you will
finally succeed.   10. I have done nothing but work all my life.

LESSON XC

218. Negation. — 1. Apart from a verb, *no, not* = **non:**

    L'avez-vous dit? — **Non** (pas).   *Did you say so? — No.*
    Non content de cela.   *Not satisfied with that.*
    Peut-être que **non.**   *Perhaps not.*

(*a*) Observe also **pas du tout,** *not at all.*

2. Along with a verb a negation consists regularly of two
parts, **ne** + some other word or words, thus:

ne . . . pas, *not*	ne . . . aucunement } *not at*	ne . . . rien, *nothing*
ne . . . point, *not*	ne . . . nullement } *all*	ne . . . ni . . . ni,
ne . . . guère, *hardly*	ne . . . aucun }	*neither . . . nor*
ne . . . jamais, *never*	ne . . . nul } *no, none*	
ne . . . plus, *no more*	ne . . . pas un }	
ne . . . que, *only*	ne . . . personne, *nobody*	

(*a*) **Point** is usually more emphatic than **pas,** and is less common in ordinary language.
(*b*) Negation is often denoted by **pas** without **ne,** in familiar language:
Ai-je **pas** dit cela? (= **n'ai**-je **pas** dit cela?).

3. **Ne** always precedes the verb, and **pas,** etc., regularly follows it:

    Je **ne** le leur ai **pas** dit.   *I did not tell them so.*
    Je **n'**en ai **guère** eu.   *I hardly had any of it.*

(*a*) But **pas** (**point**), usually, and **plus,** often, precede a simple infinitive;
they may precede or follow **avoir, être,** either when alone or in the infinitive perfect: Il parle de **ne pas** y aller; J'étais fâché de **ne** vous avoir **pas** vu
(*or* de **ne pas** vous avoir vu).

4. If the verb is omitted, but implied, **ne** is omitted:

Qui est venu? — Personne.   *Who has come? — Nobody.*
Est-il venu? — Pas encore.   *Has he come? — Not yet.*

(*a*) **Pas** (point) so used may not stand alone.

219. Omission of *pas*, etc. — Ne alone serves as a negative: —
1. In a **que** clause after negation:

Il n'y a rien qu'il **ne** sache.   *There is nothing he doesn't know.*

(*a*) So also after **prendre garde que**, *take care lest* (*that not*), and similar expressions.

2. Sometimes in an *if* clause with **si**:

Si je **ne** me trompe.   *If I am not mistaken.*

3. Sometimes in questions, such as:

Que **ne** ferais-je pour lui?   *What wouldn't I do for him?*
Que **n'**attendez-vous?   *Why don't you wait?*

4. Always in **je ne saurais**, etc., **je ne sais quoi**:

Ne sauriez-vous m'aider?   *Can't you help me?*
Un je **ne** sais quoi de noble.   *Something indefinably noble.*

(*a*) **Pas** is sometimes omitted with **pouvoir** and with other tenses of **savoir**.

5. In a few set expressions, such as:

N'importe; **n'**avoir garde.   *It matters not; not to care.*

220. Redundant *ne*. — In a **que** clause (subjunctive) **ne** is often redundant, as compared with English, thus: —
1. After expressions of fearing (but see *a*, *b*, below):

Je crains qu'il **ne** vienne.   *I fear he will come.*

(*a*) But after *not fearing*, expressed or implied, **ne** is omitted: **Je ne crains pas qu'il vienne**, *I do not fear he will come;* **Craignez-vous qu'il vienne?** *Do you fear he will come* (*surely not*)?
(*b*) When the *not happening* is feared, the full negative form stands in the **que** clause: Je crains qu'il **ne** vienne **pas**, *I fear he will not come;* Je ne crains pas qu'il **ne** vienne **pas**, *I do not fear he will not come.*

2. With compound tenses after **il y a**, etc.:

Il y a dix jours que je **ne** l'ai vu.   *I haven't seen him for ten days.*
Depuis que je **ne** vous ai vu.   *Since I saw you.*

3. After **s'en falloir**, negatively, interrogatively, or with **peu, guère**, etc.:

Peu s'en est fallu que je **ne** partisse.   *I came very near starting.*

4. After **empêcher, éviter, à moins que, avant que** (the latter optionally):

Empêchez qu'il **ne** sorte.	*Prevent him from going out.*
J'éviterai qu'on **ne** me voie.	*I shall avoid being seen.*
À moins qu'il **ne** soit malade.	*Unless he is ill.*
Avant qu'il (**ne**) parte.	*Before he goes.*

(*a*) This **ne** is not infrequently omitted after **empêcher** and **éviter**; after **empêcher** mostly when negative or interrogative.

5. After expressions of doubt or denial, used negatively or with implied negation:

Je ne doute pas que ce **ne** soit lui.	*I don't doubt that it is he.*
Niez-vous que ce **ne** soit lui?	*Do you deny, etc. (surely not)?*

(*a*) But: Je doute que ce soit lui; Doutez-vous que ce soit lui? (question as to a presumed fact).

NOTE. — Rules 4 and 5 are less strictly observed than 1–3, but always use **à moins que . . . ne**; for **ne** with comparatives, see § 208, 2.

EXERCISE XC

l'agent (de police), m., *policeman*	**éviter**, *avoid*
d'avance, *beforehand, too soon*	**la locomotive**, *locomotive, engine*
la bicyclette, *bicycle*	**le moyen**, *means, way*
le (la) bicycliste, *bicyclist*	**le pas**, *step*
caser, *put in place, settle*	**rarement**, *rarely, seldom*
la collision, *collision*	**sain**, *healthy, sound*
le compartiment, *compartment*	**sauf**, *safe*
dépasser, *exceed*	**siffler**, *whistle*
dérailler, *go off the track*	**timide**, *timid*
écraser, *crush*	**le tramway**, *tramway, tram(car)*
escorter, *escort*	**la vitesse**, *speed*

avoir peur de, *be afraid of;* **faire peur à**, *frighten;* **avoir peur que**, *be afraid that, fear that;* **de peur que**, *for fear that;* **faire collision**, *collide;* **sain et sauf**, *safe and sound;* **se faire écraser**, *get crushed (run over)*

A. 1. Tante Clémence habite la campagne. 2. Elle reçoit l'invitation d'aller voir ses amis de la ville. 3. Il y a des années qu'elle ne les a vus. 4. Ayant rarement voyagé elle est assez timide. 5. Elle a peur de tout. 6. En partant elle a peur de manquer le train et elle arrive à la gare une demi-heure d'avance. 7. Une fois casée dans le compartiment elle a peur que quelque accident n'arrive en route. 8. Il n'y a rien qui ne lui fasse peur. 9. Toutes les fois que siffle la locomotive elle tressaille. 10. Elle craint que le train ne déraille, qu'il ne fasse collision avec un autre, qu'il ne s'arrête pas à la gare où elle doit descendre. 11. Mais elle arrive saine et sauve. 12. Dans les rues ses amis l'accompagnent de peur qu'elle ne se fasse écraser par les tramways. 13. Elle ne sort guère à moins qu'une autre personne ne l'escorte. 14. En sortant seul on ne saurait toujours éviter qu'une voiture vous attrape. 15. Et les bicyclettes, n'y a-t-il pas moyen d'empêcher qu'elles marchent si vite? 16. Je doute qu'on puisse empêcher les bicyclistes de dépasser la vitesse permise par la police, à moins d'avoir des agents à chaque pas. 17. Il est défendu d'aller vite, mais que voulez-vous qu'on y fasse?

B. (*Oral on A.*) 1. *Read aloud sentences* 2–13, *turning the narrative into the past.* 2. *Give the rule for all cases where* **ne** *is used alone with a verb.*

C. 1. Our friends haven't seen us for a long time. 2. I haven't travelled much, but I am not timid. 3. I am not afraid of everything. 4. You are not afraid of anything. 5. We were afraid of missing the train. 6. We were afraid you would miss (*pres.*) the train. 7. I fear that an accident has happened. 8. There was nothing that frightened me. 9. Are you afraid the train will run off the track? 10. Do not go out unless your friends escort you. 11. Take care that you do not get run over by the tramway.

D. 1. We are bicyclists. 2. The police can't prevent us from going (*infin.*) fast. 3. It is against the law (*see A,* 17) to exceed a speed of more than five kilometres an hour. 4. Not satisfied with the speed allowed by the police, you want to go faster and faster. 5. Unless there is a policeman at every step, that can't be prevented (use *on*). 6. There is nobody who doesn't go fast sometimes. 7. What bicyclist obeys the police? — None. 8. There

was a collision on the railway, but nobody was killed. 9. Everybody arrived safe and sound.

E. 1. It is months since I was in the country; I rarely go there.
2. I shall pay you a visit to-morrow, unless the weather should be
bad. 3. In any (*tout*) case you must pay us a visit before you go.
4. If I am not mistaken, the engine of our train has just whistled.
5. I am afraid we shall not be comfortable in this compartment.
6. Let us find (*chercher*) another, no matter what one. 7. Do you
fear the train will not stop at your station? 8. I am not afraid it
will not stop. 9. Take care that your aunt doesn't get run over by
the tramway.

F. 1. The police can't prevent automobiles from running too
fast. 2. There is not one of them that doesn't exceed the speed
limit (*see A*, 16). 3. If we go too fast, we can't avoid the police
catching us now and then. 4. I do not doubt that the policemen
are in the right. 5. There is nothing that that young man cannot
learn. 6. Nobody doubts that he will finally succeed. 7. I am
afraid you are cold; draw near the fire. 8. It is years since we
had a winter like this one, if I am not mistaken.

LESSON XCI

221. Observe the use of **à**, **de**, **en**, **sur**, in forming adjectival
phrases, often rendered in English by compound nouns, or by
nouns used as adjectives: —

1. **De, en,** denoting material:

Une maison **en** (**de**) brique(s).	*A brick house.*
Une robe **de** (**en**) soie.	*A silk dress.*
Un collier **de** perles.	*A pearl necklace.*

2. **De** denoting source, purpose, destination, etc.:

La porcelaine **de** Sèvres.	*Sèvres porcelain.*
Les vins **d'**Espagne.	*Spanish wines.*
La salle **de** bains.	*The bathroom.*
Le train **de** Paris.	*The Paris train.*

3. **À** denoting purpose for which, or characteristic:

Une salle à manger.	*A dining room.*
Une tasse à thé.	*A teacup.*
Un coffret à bijoux.	*A jewel case.*
Un ver à soie.	*A silkworm.*
Une porte à deux battants.	*A folding door* (i.e. with two leaves).
Un bateau à vapeur.	*A steamboat.*
L'homme **au** chapeau noir.	*The man with a black hat.*

4. **À** and **sur** describing processes in art:

Une peinture à l'huile.	*An oil painting (painting in oils).*
Une gravure **sur** acier.	*A steel engraving (engraving on steel).*

222. Observe the following prepositional distinctions: —

1. **Environ** = *about* (of quantity); **vers**, *towards, about* (of time):
Environ dix kilomètres (cent francs); **vers** (les) dix heures; **vers** 1830.

2. **Entre**, *between, among* (also distributively and recipro-cally); **parmi**, *among* (in the midst of):
Une station **entre** Paris et Rouen; **entre** dix et douze heures; partagez-le **entre** vos amis; il fut trouvé **entre** les morts; **entre** (*in*) les mains de mon ami; ils parlaient **entre** eux; une brebis **parmi** les loups.

3. **Avant**, *before* (of time, order, rank); **devant**, *before* (in front of, in presence of):
Avant midi; mettez l'article **avant** le nom; **devant** le feu; **devant** le roi.

4. **Vers**, *towards* (physical tendency): **envers**, *towards* (moral tendency):
Levez les yeux **vers** le ciel; il est juste **envers** tous.

5. **Au-dessous de**, *under, underneath* (more specific than **sous**); **au-dessus de**, *over, above, higher than*:
Au-dessous du tableau; **au-dessous de** la valeur; **au-dessus de** la porte; les nombres **au-dessus de** cent.

6. **Près de**, *near* (physical): **auprès de**, *near, with, as regards, etc.* (moral):
Près du feu; **auprès de** sa famille.

EXERCISE XCI

l'acajou, m., *mahogany*

l'acier, m., *steel*

le battant, *part of a double* or *folding door*

le bijou, *jewel*

la brique, *brick*

le chêne, *oak*

le cocon, *cocoon*

le coffret, *casket, case*

le collier, *necklace*

le cuivre, *copper*

l'eau-forte, f., *aquafortis; etching*

forgé, *forged, wrought*

illustrer, *illustrate*

l'industrie, f., *industry*

l'ivoire, m., *ivory*

le marbre, *marble*

le mobilier, *furniture* (collect.)

le musée, *museum*

le noyer, *walnut*

l'objet, m., *object*

l'or, m., *gold*

la parure, *adornment*

le pastel, *pastel*

la peinture, *painting*

la perle, *pearl*

la porcelaine, *porcelain*

la princesse, *princess*

sculpter, *carve*

la soierie, *silk* (collect.)

la taille, *cutting*

le vase, *vase*

vaste, *vast*

Vénus, *Venus*

le ver, *worm*

il boit dans un verre, *he drinks from (out of) a glass;* je mange dans une assiette, *I eat from a plate;* je l'ai pris dans un tiroir (sur la table), *I took it from a drawer (from the table)*

A. 1. Hier nous avons visité un grand musée. 2. Il se trouve dans un ancien château bâti en brique et en pierre de taille (*freestone*). 3. Nous entrons par la belle porte en chêne à deux battants. 4. Au rez-de-chaussée on trouve les objets qui illustrent l'histoire de l'industrie. 5. Dans la salle des soieries on voit le cocon du ver à soie aussi bien que les belles robes de soie et les tapisseries des Gobelins. 6. Dans une autre salle se voient des tasses à thé et à café qui ont passé par des mains de reines. 7. Nous montons au premier par le bel escalier en marbre. 8. On entre dans la première pièce par une porte magnifique en fer forgé. 9. Cette salle s'appelle le "Salon des Fleurs." 10. Le gardien appelle notre attention sur le mobilier en acajou à tapisseries de Beauvais. 11. Il nous montre de beaux vases en porcelaine de Sèvres. 12. Nous admirons un coffret à bijoux en ivoire. 13. Le gardien prend dans le coffret un collier de perles, autrefois la parure d'une princesse. 14. Il y a ici en outre un beau tableau nommé "Vénus aux cheveux d'or."

15. Ensuite nous entrons dans la vaste ancienne salle à manger à boiseries sculptées en noyer. 16. On y voit beaucoup de tableaux: des peintures à l'huile et des portraits au pastel. 17. Il y a aussi des gravures sur cuivre (*copperplate*), sur acier et à l'eau-forte (*etching*).

B. (*Oral on A.*)

C. 1. My grandfather lives in an old stone house. 2. There is a beautiful oak table in his dining room. 3. The chairs and sideboard are also of oak. 4. Silk is the product of the silkworm. 5. The product of thousands of silkworms is required (use *il faut*) to make a silk dress. 6. In the museum we admired especially the Gobelin tapestries and the Sèvres porcelain. 7. The tapestries are to be seen in the silk room. 8. We use teacups to drink tea. 9. We don't drink (the) tea from coffee cups. 10. Kings and queens have drunk from these wineglasses. 11. Give me a wineglass. 12. Give me another glass of wine. 13. At the entrance to (of) the "Flower Hall" we observed a fine wrought-iron door. 14. My mother has a jewel casket of carved ivory. 15. Among the queen's jewels was a pearl necklace. 16. The London train arrived half an hour ago.

D. 1. We are going to have a brick house built. 2. The castle was built half in brick, half in freestone. 3. All the stairways are of marble. 4. The entrance doors are large folding doors of oak. 5. Permit me to call your attention to this fine mahogany furniture. 6. Don't you admire these Beauvais tapestries? 7. Frenchmen think that Sèvres porcelain is the finest in the world. 8. The vases of Sèvres porcelain are the finest objects in the museum. 9. I keep my jewels in a little casket of carved walnut. 10. The gentleman with the straw hat is Mr. Brunot. 11. The artist showed us the portrait of a charming little girl with golden hair. 12. This artist is very clever at (*à*) painting in oils. 13. Most people prefer oil paintings to steel engravings or etchings.

LESSON XCII

223. Conjunctions. — 1. **Que** = *that* is followed by the indicative or subjunctive according to the context:

Je vois **qu'il est** malade.	*I see that he is ill.*
Je suis fâché **qu'il soit** malade.	*I am sorry he is ill.*

2. **Que**, standing for another conjunction, regularly takes the same construction as the conjunction it replaces:

Quand vous **aurez** fini et **que** vous **aurez** le temps.	*When you have finished and (when you) have time.*
Venez **que** (= afin que, pour que) je vous **voie**.	*Come that I may see you.*

(a) For **que** = **si**, *if*, see § 193, 5.

3. *When* = **quand** or **lorsque** (the latter never interrogatively):

Quand (lorsque) je l'ai vu.	*When I saw him.*
Dites-moi **quand** il arrivera.	*Tell me when he will arrive.*

4. **Pendant que** = *while, whilst;* **tandis que** = *while, whilst, whereas, on the contrary:*

Lisez le journal **pendant que** j'écris ce billet.	*Read the newspaper while I am writing this note.*
Tandis que vous êtes ici.	*Whilst (while) you are here.*
Le père travaille, **tandis que** le fils est toujours oisif.	*The father works, while (whereas) the son is always idle.*

5. **Depuis que** denotes time; **puisque** denotes cause assigned:

Je suis bien seul **depuis que** mon frère est parti.	*I am very lonely since my brother went away.*
Il faut que je reste **puisqu'**il n'y a pas de train ce soir.	*I must remain, since there is no train this evening.*

6. Certain prepositions and prepositional phrases, governing an infinitive, correspond to conjunctional forms in **que**; the prepositional construction is usually employed when one subject is common to two verbs, but if not, the **que** form must be used:

Je partis **de peur de** le voir.	*I left for fear of seeing him.*
Je partis **de peur qu'**il ne me vît.	*I left for fear he might see me.*

(a) Other examples: afin de (afin que); de crainte de (de crainte que); à moins de (à moins que); avant de (avant que); après de (après que); de peur de (de peur que); pour (pour que); sans (sans que); jusqu'à (jusqu'à ce que), etc.

224. Reference list of conjunctions requiring the subjunctive:

à (la) condition que[1]	de (telle) sorte que[3]	pourvu que
afin que	en attendant que	quand même [5]
à moins que . . . ne	en cas que	que[6]
au cas où[2]	encore que	quoique
au cas que	en sorte que[3]	sans que
avant que	en supposant que	si[7]
bien que	jusqu'à ce que[4]	si bien que[3]
ce n'est pas que	loin que	si peu que
dans le cas où[2]	malgré que	soit que . . . soit que
de crainte que . . . ne	nonobstant que	soit que . . . ou que
de façon que[3]	non (pas) que	supposé que
de manière que[3]	pour peu que	tellement . . . que[3]
de peur que . . . ne	pour que	

[1] Also indic. or condl.   [2] More usually condl.   [3] Subj. of purpose, but not of result.
[4] Sometimes indic. of completed past event.   [5] Condl. ant. or plupf. subj.   [6] See § 223, 1,
above.   [7] See § 193, 5.

EXERCISE XCII

les ancêtres, m., *ancestors*	le laboureur, *ploughman*
augmenter, *increase*	la marche, *march*
le bâtiment, *building*	le marteau, *hammer*
le bûcheron, *woodcutter*	à mesure que, *in proportion as*
la civilisation, *civilization*	la moisson, *harvest, crop*
la consommation, *consumption*	moissonner, *harvest*
continuer, *continue*	le perfectionnement, *improvement*
défricher, *clear* (land)	le pont, *bridge*
l'enclume, f., *anvil*	pour que, *in order that, so that*
exagérer, *exaggerate*	la poutre, *beam*
la faucille, *sickle*	le procédé, *process*
la fonte, *cast iron*	réaliser, *realize, effect*
le forgeron, *blacksmith*	soit que . . ., *whether*
la hache, *axe*	tant que, *so (as) long as*
imaginer, *imagine, conceive*	utiliser, *utilize*
inventer, *invent, find out*	

cela va en augmentant, *that keeps increasing*

A. 1. Que la figure du forgeron est intéressante! 2. Depuis que
la civilisation existe il aide les hommes par ses travaux. 3. Jusqu'à
ce qu'il eût fait une hache le bûcheron ne pouvait pas couper les

arbres. 4. Après que le bûcheron eut défriché la terre le laboureur eut besoin de la charrue. 5. Aussitôt qu'il y eut une moisson il fallut faire une faucille pour la moissonner. 6. À mesure que la civilisation avançait on imaginait de nouveaux procédés d'utiliser le fer. 7. Pour que la hache et la faucille coupassent bien on inventa l'acier. 8. Puisqu'il fallait travailler vite et à bon marché on inventa la fonte. 9. Du moment qu'on a réalisé ces perfectionnements le fer a commencé à remplacer le bois et la pierre. 10. Dans les bâtiments nous employons des poutres d'acier tandis que nos ancêtres ne se servaient que de poutres de bois. 11. Les nouveaux chemins même sont des chemins de fer. 12. Mais soit qu'on fasse des routes ou des ponts ou des navires, la consommation du fer va en augmentant. 13. On pourrait dire sans exagérer que tant que continuera la marche de la civilisation elle sera accompagnée de la musique du marteau et de l'enclume.

B. (*Oral on A.*)

C. 1. What an interesting figure that (*que celle*) of the blacksmith! 2. His work has helped civilization very much. 3. The woodcutter could not cut trees until he had an axe. 4. The ploughman needs a plough as soon as the ground is cleared. 5. The harvester cannot cut his wheat until he has a sickle. 6. People invent new processes in proportion as civilization advances. 7. Steel is used to make axes. 8. Cast iron was invented so that people could work faster and cheaper. 9. Many improvements have been effected. 10. Iron must take the place of wood and stone. 11. Steel beams are used in our days, whilst formerly wooden beams were used. 12. The consumption of iron keeps increasing. 13. Whether we make ships or bridges, we need iron. 14. We shall need iron as long as civilization continues. 15. The march of civilization is accompanied by the music of the anvil. 16. Man cannot advance without new processes being invented.

D. 1. When Captain Pictet arrives I shall ask him to come in. 2. Since our relatives arrived we have been (*pres.*) very busy. 3. Since you need money I shall lend you some. 4. We started at eight o'clock in order not to be late. 5. I heard from my sister before she left (*quitter*) London. 6. Do not run for fear you may fall. 7. If he had ploughed the ground and if (*que*) he had sown the wheat, the crop would have been abundant. 8. Unless we are diligent we shall not succeed. 9. I shall be busy until you come. 10. They will not finish early without your helping them.

E. 1. Before we had electric light we used gas. 2. Our neighbours still have (the) gas, whilst we have electric light. 3. Wait until we have (the) time to see you. 4. He will wait until his brother comes. 5. While we were taking a cup of coffee the train started. 6. I work in order to become rich. 7. You work that your children may be rich. 8. Do not speak without thinking. 9. Do nothing without telling me what you are going to do. 10. We shall be glad when we have finished.

MATERIAL FOR CONVERSATION

NOTE. — This "Material for Conversation" is placed after the Lessons for the sake of convenience, and not to suggest that the Lessons should be mastered before conversation is begun. Conversation should begin early, and certain parts of the "Material," such, for example, as the "Fundamental Expressions," should be learned and used as soon as possible.

The classroom and its activities will naturally furnish the first topics for conversation. Hence the teacher should provide his class early with the vocabulary necessary for speaking about the objects, studies, etc., which pertain to the classroom. The vocabulary necessary for other topics should be furnished as the needs of the class demand.

1. Fundamental Expressions

(a) When pointing to objects:

Qu'est-ce que c'est que cela (ça)?	*What is that?*
C'est un crayon.	*It's a pencil.*
Comment appelle-t-on cela (ça)?	*What is that called?*
On appelle cela (ça) un livre.	*That's called a book.*

(b) When speaking of objects, actions, ideas, etc.:

Comment dit-on 'house' en français?	*How do you say 'house' in French?*
En français on dit 'maison.'	*You say 'maison' in French.*
Comment dit-on 'run' en français?	*How do you say 'run' in French?*
On dit 'courir' en français.	*You say 'courir' in French.*
Que veut dire le mot 'pain'?	*What does the word 'pain' mean?*
Le mot 'pain' veut dire 'bread.'	*The word 'pain' means 'bread.'*

(c) When speaking of spelling, pronunciation, etc.:

Comment écrivez-vous (écrit-on) le mot 'livre'?

Quelle est l'orthographe du mot 'livre'? } *How do you spell the word 'livre'?*

On écrit le mot 'livre' ainsi, l-i-v-r-e. — *You spell the word 'livre' thus.*

(For names of French letters, see Introd., A.)

Comment prononcez-vous (prononce-t-on) ce mot?

Quelle est la prononciation de ce mot? } *How do you pronounce this word?*

On prononce ce mot ainsi. — *You pronounce this word thus.*

2. Politer Forms

(a) In addressing people:

Monsieur, Madame, Mademoiselle.	*Sir, Madam, Miss.*

(b) In asking and receiving:

S'il vous plaît.	*If you please or please.*
Merci (*after accepting*).	*Thank you or thanks.*
Merci (*in declining*).	*No, thank you or no, thanks.*
Avec plaisir.	*With pleasure.*
Je vous remercie beaucoup (bien, mille fois, infiniment).	*I thank you very much.*

(c) When not understanding:

Monsieur? Madame? Mademoiselle?	*Excuse me Sir, Madam, Miss.*
Plaît-il? or Pardon? or Je vous demande pardon. (*More familiar:* Comment? or Vous dites?)	*I beg your pardon (What? What do you say?)*

(d) When desiring consent:

Voulez-vous (bien)...? or Veuillez.	*Will you kindly . . .?*
Ayez la bonté (l'obligeance) de ...	*Be kind enough to . . .*

(e) Politeness is often increased by the use of the conditional:

Pourriez-vous me dire, madame, l'heure qu'il est?	*Could you tell me, madam, what o'clock it is?*
Voudriez-vous (bien) me dire où nous en sommes aujourd'hui?	*Would you kindly tell me where we begin to-day?*

3. Model Conversation

On sonne (frappe) à la porte. J'ouvre moi-même et je dis:	*There's a ring (knock) at the door. I open the door myself and say:*
— Bonjour (bonsoir), mon cher ami. Entrez donc. Je suis enchanté (charmé) de vous voir.	*— Good day or good morning (good evening), my dear friend. Do come in. I am delighted to see you.*
— Merci, je ne vous dérange pas?	*— Thank you, I hope I am not disturbing you?*
— Oh non! pas du tout. Permettez-moi de vous débarrasser de votre chapeau.	*— Oh no, not at all. Allow me to take your hat.*
— Merci, vous êtes trop bon.	*— Thanks, you are too kind.*

— Ayez la bonté (donnez-vous la peine) de vous asseoir (*less formal:* asseyez-vous donc); ici dans ce fauteuil.

— *Kindly be seated; here in this chair.*

— Merci beaucoup, mais j'ai peur de vous déranger.

— Pas du tout. Ne vous gênez pas. Et comment vous portez-vous depuis si longtemps? (*less formal:* Comment allez-vous? comment ça va-t-il? comment ça va?)

— *Thank you very much, but I am afraid of disturbing you.*

— *Not at all. Make yourself at home. And how have you been this long time?*

— Très bien (pas mal), merci, et vous(-même)?

— *Very well, thanks, and how are you?*

— J'ai été un peu souffrant.

— *I have not been very well.*

— J'en suis désolé! Qu'est-ce que vous aviez?

— *I am very sorry. What was the matter?*

— C'était une espèce de neurasthénie. Mais ça va déjà mieux.

— *It was a sort of nervous exhaustion. But I am better now.*

— Tant mieux. J'espère que ça passera vite.

— *I am glad to hear it. I hope it will soon disappear.*

— Mais vous n'êtes pas bien; ce fauteuil n'est pas bon (commode, confortable).

— *But you're not comfortable; that chair doesn't suit you.*

— Si! si!

— *Oh yes, it does.*

— Mais non, permettez-moi. Je vais vous donner ce coussin. Levez-vous, s'il vous plaît. Là! maintenant, asseyez-vous. Vous êtes mieux, n'est-ce pas?

— *No, no, allow me. I'll give you this cushion. Rise, please. Now then, sit down. That's better, isn't it?*

— Oh, oui! mais vous êtes trop aimable.

— *Yes, indeed, but you are too kind.*

Après avoir causé un peu, mon ami s'excuse. Il faut qu'il s'en aille. Il dit:

After chatting a little my friend begs to be excused. He must go. He says:

— Mes compliments à monsieur votre père et à madame votre mère.

— *Remember me to your father and mother.*

— Merci, je n'y manquerai pas. Bien des choses (de ma part) à votre frère.

— *Thanks, I shall (will). Remember me to your brother.*

Nous nous disons: 'au revoir,' 'à ce soir,' 'à demain matin,' 'à lundi (mardi, etc.) prochain.' Nous nous serrons la main, et le voilà parti.

We say to one another 'good-bye,' 'good-bye till this evening,' 'till to-morrow morning,' 'till Monday (Tuesday etc.), next.' We shake hands and he's gone.

REVIEW EXERCISES

NOTE. — These sentences have been selected for the most part from Harvard, Yale and other College Entrance Papers, and are grouped so as to illustrate important points of grammar.

I. The Article

A. 1. I have no friends. 2. I have a great many flowers and will give you some. 3. He has neither father nor mother. 4. They haven't any money. 5. There were many houses in the town. 6. Here are some fine pears; do you wish any? 7. Are there any pencils in that box? There are none now. 8. Here are some fine apples. 9. They are all going to France to-morrow. 10. If you are thirsty you may drink some cold water. 11. He wanted to buy some apples but he didn't have any money. 12. You are wrong in thinking so. 13. Have you any books? Give me some. I have no books now. 14. We had a good deal of snow last winter. 15. There are many things we can learn by reading good books. 16. I beg your pardon; I am right and you are wrong. 17. I am always cold [on] the days when it is cold. 18. Are you warm? Yes, and I am thirsty also. 19. Is there any water here? Yes, here is some good, cool water. 20. There are white hens and black ones in the barn.

B. 1. Don't you need your hat when you go out? 2. Won't you buy her some good red apples? 3. Have you good friends? 4. We saw pebbles and sand in the water of the river. 5. In Canada people eat a great deal of fruit in autumn. 6. I am sure he asked for ripe apples; these are green ones. 7. The weather has been very warm and the flowers need water. 8. The little bird said, "Open the window for me, I am very hungry." 9. When horses are thirsty they need water and they go to the river. 10. There are good books and bad ones. 11. I have no friends in this country, but I have some in America. 12. He has potatoes, cabbage(s) and onions. He planted them on the second of May. 13. There were some very pretty flowers at the market this morning. 14. Perhaps you are right, but certainly I am too warm. 15. That pupil likes history better than grammar. 16. Children sometimes have wonderful courage. 17. The boys rushed in with their hats on their heads. 18. I had my hair cut this morning. 19. Mrs. Brown is a Frenchwoman. 20. Queen Victoria was born in 1819.

II. Numerals

1. I shall be eighteen years old in nineteen hundred and seventeen. 2. What time was it? It was half past ten. 3. When did your brother return from Europe? He arrived last night at a quarter past eight. 4. Write out in French 21, 63, 177, 46th, $\frac{1}{2}$, $\frac{3}{4}$. 5. What day of the month is it? It is the fifteenth of May, 1911 (*write date in full*). 6. They were born on the same day, the 17th of July, 1893 (*write date in full*). 7. I was born on the 15th of August, 1895 (*write date in full*). 8. What time was it when the train left? 9. It was twenty minutes to eleven. 10. Can you tell me the time? It is half past two. 11. I have here a box full of cherries. How many are there? Ninety-one. 12. I have been in Toronto a fortnight and I like the city. 13. We did not go there yesterday at ten o'clock. 14. You say that he is twenty years old. 15. Is his oldest brother not ten years older? 16. Does the train start for Boston at a quarter to nine? 17. We have been here three weeks. 18. My grandfather is eighty years old. 19. During the first two years he did not study. 20. Fifteen cents make seventy-five centimes. 21. Victor Hugo was born in 1802 (*write date in full*). 22. He died in 1885 (*write date in full*). 23. It is half past eleven; we must go home.

III. Personal Pronouns

1. Will you introduce me to her? 2. Are you angry with me? 3. Give it to me. 4. I took him there a week ago. 5. We have given the books back to them. 6. Show them to us, please. 7. Don't send them to him. 8. Hide yourself behind the door. 9. Will you kindly give me some? 10. Give it to us, do not give it to them. 11. They have made fun of us all day. 12. He lends it to me every Sunday. 13. Give us some, but do not give us so many. 14. John's watch is [made] of (*en*) gold. His father gave it to him. 15. I have your books, I shall finish one of them next week. 16. Did you sell that lady any sugar? 17. Yes, I sold her some, but I sold none to her sister. 18. Don't sell her any. 19. Where will he find a better neighbour than I? 20. We have none, but we should like to have some to-morrow. 21. His coat does not fit

him well; he has just been trying it on. 22. How many prizes have you? I have only one. 23. I have given them to my sister; they were hers. 24. Go away, we cannot be friends, but I have no grudge against you. 25. You have taken my pen. Please give it to her. 26. I saw him this morning, but I did not speak to him about it. 27. Here are some also; keep them for me. 28. I do not doubt it; he will win the day.

IV. Demonstratives

1. He who does not talk too much is wise. 2. Don't give me this pencil, give me that one. 3. These cakes are not as good as the ones we bought here yesterday. 4. It is easier to do this than that. 5. This house and the one in which our cousins live will be sold to-morrow. 6. This is worse than that. 7. Have you learned to-day's lesson better than yesterday's? 8. Which of these pears do you like the best? The one you have brought. 9. Is it you who told him so? 10. This book is mine, but that is my sister's. 11. Those who leave will never return. 12. These little children are the ones you met yesterday. 13. This pen and that one are mine. Where is your brother's? 14. It is easy to do. 15. Those are Germans. 16. Victor Hugo and Michelet are Frenchmen, the former is a poet, the latter an historian. 17. It was we who did the work. 18. Those who are not killed will fight. 19. Here are two books; give me this one and keep that one. 20. This man is my friend, that one is my enemy.

V. Possessives

1. Is that your umbrella? No, this one is mine, that one is yours. 2. This is my friend's watch. 3. Where do your parents live? In Montreal. 4. Here are my pens. Where are yours? 5. I don't know where mine are. 6. Didn't your parents see our friends and hers in England? 7. No, they saw only hers, because yours had already gone to Paris. 8. My watch and his are on the table, are they not? 9. Your party will not be stronger than ours. 10. This is my house; where is yours? 11. Mine is yonder behind the church. 12. A friend of mine has come from Chicago. 13. A relative of mine who lives in Chicago has become very rich. 14. An Englishman, a friend of mine, told me that. 15. Do you know the difference between mine and thine? 16. Is that watch yours? 17. No, sir, it is not mine, I think it is my brother's.

18. My dress is not ready yet, but yours was ready yesterday.
19. Your harvest is better than ours this year.   20. My book is
on the table, yours is under it.

VI. Relatives and Interrogatives

A. 1. Do not forget what I told you. 2. I do not like the flowers which she sold me. 3. Is the church of which you have spoken
near your house? 4. Here are two books, which is the more interesting? 5. Your father told me what your brother had done.
6. Take what you need and leave the rest beside my table.
7. What is the matter with that little boy? 8. What have you
given back to him? 9. This is the boy whose father is in England.
10. I don't know what you have just said. 11. Which of those
horses do you like best? 12. Whom did you see? 13. Who is
your neighbour? 14. What have you written? 15. What is that
beside you? 16. What kind of weather is it? 17. The gentleman
for whose farm I offered $10,000 has not sold it yet. 18. What is
there in that box? 19. There is the book I spoke of to you last
week. 20. Is that the house you spoke to me about? 21. He who
has never suffered does not know what joy is.

B. 1. The king asked whose was the field where they were
reaping. 2. I cannot express to you my gratitude for (*de*) what
you have done. 3. What are you doing now? Have you not begun yet? 4. There is the apple tree of which I have spoken so
often. 5. Why do people give the best things to those who do not
need them? 6. Have you finished the books I gave you last week?
7. Didn't you buy the pictures I saw in your room? 8. Tell me
what you want me to do. 9. Do you know what they thought?
They thought you had no friends. 10. He did not tell me what
the Louvre is. 11. Those are the flowers which I have bought.
12. There is a man whose son I know. 13. All that he has to do
is to tell you what he has seen. 14. What a big apple! Who gave
it to you? 15. What are you going to do to-day? I do not know
yet. 16. What is a pear tree? It is a tree which yields pears.
17. Whose is that house on the other side of the road? 18. My
brother owed me the half of what he had received. 19. Who is
she? Whose daughter is she?

C. 1. We are going to eat the fruit of the apple tree which is in
our garden. 2. You will send her a box of the coffee which I
brought from France. 3. What is a classroom? It is a room in

which we tell the teacher what we know. 4. Who is it? It is my father's friend, the general of whom I was speaking yesterday. 5. Tell me what you have been doing to-day. 6. Which of these two towns is the larger? 7. Has he read the letter which she has written him? 8. You see what it is to be a stranger. 9. Which of these gentlemen is the one I want to speak to? 10. A dictionary is a book which is used to explain the meaning of words. 11. Which of your friends has gone to Europe? 12. I met two men last week whose names I have forgotten. 13. That is the man whose son lives in the United States. 14. Whose son was Alexander? What did he do? 15. Can you tell me which is the largest lake in North America? 16. Has he all the money he needs? He has all I had. 17. My two brothers who live in Germany will remain with me until next Friday. 18. He would not tell me what he had said. 19. Do you need the books we have read this year? 20. We shall need those you read and others also.

VII. Indefinites

1. I will say nothing about it to any one. 2. Nothing is the matter with him. 3. Perhaps something better will be offered us. 4. I have seen no one to-day, but I saw everybody at church yesterday. 5. The old lady wishes to give the boy something good. 6. What do you need? I don't need anything. 7. You never saw any one so contented. 8. Everybody was hungry, and yet nobody wanted to make peace just to have bread. 9. Each of his fables is the story of a day. 10. If one has books enough, one can amuse himself reading. 11. There is never anybody at his house. 12. We were informed that his ship was to leave at noon on Saturday. 13. None of my friends has gone this year. 14. Give them something good to drink. 15. Has your father anything good in his garden? Nothing. 16. There is no fire in this room. How cold it is! 17. We were told not to come. 18. Did you see anybody you knew at the station? 19. I saw nobody there whom I knew. 20. What did you give him? I gave him nothing.

VIII. Irregular Verbs

1. Give the future indicative, first person singular of *valoir*, *faire* and *cueillir*. 2. Give the imperative, second person plural of *avoir*, *boire* and *conduire*. 3. Give the present subjunctive, first person singular of *lever*, *plaire* and *acquérir*. 4. Give the future

indicative, first person singular of *savoir, courir* and *venir*. 5. Give the present subjunctive, third person singular of *avoir, envoyer* and *jeter*. 6. Give the past participle of *prendre, dire* and *lire*. 7. Give the past definite in full of *voir, vivre* and *tenir*. 8. Give the imperfect subjunctive in full of *savoir, taire* and *écrire*. 9. Give the present indicative in full of *vouloir, se taire* and *s'en aller*. 10. Give the past definite in full of *craindre, devoir* and *boire*. 11. Give the principal parts of *suivre, plaindre* and *paraître*. 12. Give the principal parts of *aller, boire, venir* and *courir*. 13. I have sat down. 14. It has opened. 15. They are sleeping. 16. They were eating. 17. Let us run. 18. He will run. 19. They are drinking. 20. He is dying. 21. She died this morning. 22. Where was she born?

IX. Government of Verbs

1. Think of me when I am (*fut.*) not here. 2. I shall never be able to use them. 3. Do you ever think of England when you are in the United States? I never think of it. 4. I was going to ask my brother for some tickets. 5. He always has some and I shall ask him for two. 6. How much did you pay for the shoes you bought? 7. I paid twenty francs ninety-five centimes for them. 8. Will you buy me some paper to-morrow? 9. I cannot wait for you any longer; the breakfast is on the table. 10. Look in your dictionary for the meaning of all the words. 11. Listen to her, and when she makes mistakes, tell her. 12. I bought this hat at your hatter's and I paid ten francs for it. 13. She bought several hats in that shop and she paid very high for them. 14. He paid twelve thousand francs for the automobile (motor-car) he bought in London. 15. I have paid twenty-five francs for my hat. How much did you pay for yours? 16. The children are looking for the book. 17. How much did you pay for those beautiful red roses? 18. She has lost it, but I am going to look for it. 19. Did he approach the house? He did. 20. Did you remember what I told you? I didn't. I forgot it. 21. What do you use when you write? 22. I use paper and ink.

X. The Infinitive

A. 1. Tell your friend to come and see me. 2. I wish I were in France now. 3. The teacher makes the boys study their lessons. 4. Where can he be? 5. He won't be long in arriving. 6. I saw her leave the house half an hour ago. 7. Please send for him.

8. Are you going to have a house built this year? 9. The ladies I saw this morning have just set out for Paris. 10. I made him write a letter to his brother. 11. Make them send us another box of cakes. 12. Make them write slowly. 13. Make them write it slowly. 14. Their teacher made them write their exercises. 15. We have just given him what he wanted. 16. We heard them say that their friends had gone to Germany. 17. He stayed at home all day, but his friends could not come to see him. 18. It would be better to talk less and work more. 19. I still have several pages to read before (the) evening. 20. I had a house built for my son who has just married.

B. 1. I nearly fell on leaving your house. 2. You have only to bathe in the river. 3. You have only one thing to do, that is to confess everything to your father. 4. The king has just left the palace, but he will be back to-morrow. 5. Don't try to tell the whole story; it is too long. 6. How much water did I tell you to put in? 7. They have just arrived from France, and will return in the spring. 8. When are you coming to see us? 9. We shall not go to see you this week. 10. After reading the letter I gave it to him. 11. He has just left his friends in the street. 12. We do not want to return home, we want to stay here. 13. He amuses himself by describing to his family what he has seen. 14. I shall not fail to follow your advice. 15. It isn't worth doing (the trouble of being done). 16. Make him do his work before he goes away. 17. I see a gentleman at the door; will you be good enough to show him in? 18. Be good enough to give me what you have in your hand. 19. Could you tell me, sir, what the name of this street is? 20. We shall not go on foot to-day; we prefer to drive.

C. 1. Where are you going to spend your holidays? In the country. 2. Be good enough to tell me all you have seen and heard. 3. I am having my house painted. It will be finished a week from to-day. 4. We intended to go for a walk, but the weather was bad. 5. Show the ladies up and make the children be quiet. 6. Tell them to have it sent to her. 7. We cannot wait. Something must be done. 8. My neighbour told me that he was to leave [on] the next day. 9. I heard my name called three times. 10. Do you not see those two men coming? 11. They had the sick [man] carried into the other room. 12. Tell them to go away; they are making too much noise. 13. He has tried to do so twice already. 14. He is to set out for Germany to-morrow. 15. I was to meet my cousin here. She is to marry my friend to-morrow. 16. After the marriage, the newly married couple intend to live in Boston. 17. I had just visited my old friend who lives near the church. 18. I have had my boys read this book. 19. The young girls had (*ont dû*) to read it the day before yesterday. 20. He finally accepted the conditions.

XI. The Imperfect, Past Definite and Past Indefinite

1. My brother was reading when they entered the room. 2. Did they receive as much of them as you [did]? 3. We were translating our exercises when the professor entered the classroom. 4. Why did he go downstairs a few minutes ago? He went to send for the doctor. 5. When were you born? 6. On which chair did you place my valise? 7. I placed it on the one beside the window. 8. I didn't hear the man who was talking. 9. Many children have already gone to school, but there are some still at home. 10. Where did you go after breakfast? 11. Did you buy a pair of shoes when you went for a walk? 12. I did not see him at the station last night. 13. I did not buy (*prendre*) a ticket because my friends had not come. 14. There were many people who were going to take the train for Boston. 15. We drank some hot milk, we went to bed and we slept all night. 16. The river froze during the winter and we skated every Saturday. 17. With whom were they taking a walk when we met them? 18. I have not finished those books yet. 19. Did you buy some pears yesterday? 20. No, I didn't buy any, because I didn't have any money. 21. Didn't we sell you any tickets? 22. I bought the four pictures you saw, and my old aunt gave me the others. 23. Were there many boys in the country when you went there? 24. No, there were not many. 25. What were you doing when I entered? 26. When I told him who I was and what I wanted, he came at once. 27. How long has the king been reigning?

XII. The Future

1. When you come I will introduce you to them. 2. Come when you please and I will help you. 3. When we come to see you we shall tell you about it. 4. When I am in the country I shall have him work for me. 5. I shall wear my dress coat when I go to the theatre. 6. When I have no more money, I shall go and tell (it to) my father. 7. As soon as you have read the book tell me how you liked (= found) it. 8. Give it him when next (= the next

time) you see him. 9. After we have dined we shall go back to the town. 10. Will you go away when your brother arrives? 11. There are many interesting things which you will see when you go to Paris. 12. When you enter the church you will see your friend in front of the window. 13. I will give it to him when I see him this evening. 14. When they have seen all the pictures in the museum they are going to leave the town. 15. When you come to Toronto, come and see me. 16. As long as I live I shall not forget you. 17. When you have been there a year or two, you will know better what you should do. 18. As long as iron lasts civilization will last. 19. I shall go when my father comes. 2). Come when you will.

XIII. The Conditional

A. 1. If I had met him I should have spoken to him. 2. Would you not have sold it to them if they had offered you more money? 3. If I go, who will remain? if I remain, who will go? 4. That (young) girl could write if she wished. 5. If I should say so, would you believe me? 6. If I had been you (*say:* in (*à*) your place) I would not have given him anything. 7. We shall take a long walk to-morrow if it is pleasant (= fine). 8. He would speak to me if he were here. 9. He would have spoken to me ten days ago if he had been here. 10. If they worked they would not be poor. 11. If you need money, will you not work for me? 12. If the door opens, shut your book at once. 13. If that house were larger and (if it) had more rooms I would buy it. 14. He would lend it me if I asked him for it. 15. If he spoke more slowly I could understand him. 16. A friend of mine told me that he would come to see me at five o'clock, if it was not raining. 17. If he comes, I shall go for a walk with him after dinner. 18. If they should give you some white roses would you give them to your sister? 19. Perhaps that man will give you some milk, if you ask him for it. 20. If he had gone home with me, I should have given him his dinner.

B. 1. If you had called me, I should have got up at six o'clock. 2. If you have no money, how can you buy anything to eat? 3. If I were he (*see XIII, A*, 6), I should tell them what I think of them. 4. I should be very much obliged to you if you would tell me what you are thinking of. 5. You could have come earlier if you had wanted to. 6. If people tried to learn that language they would not find it difficult. 7. Should you have been able to see us if we had come here on Thursday? 8. If we had a great deal of money we should not be much happier. 9. If he had seen his friend he would have told us so. 10. If you will kindly lend me your pencil I shall write all the words. 11. I asked him if he would come to-day, but he would not answer. 12. If you give men what they desire they are happy. 13. These children would have gone to school if it had not rained. 14. Would his brother give him the money if he were to ask for it? 15. The other could have done so, if she had tried. 16. If I had spoken to him he would have fallen. 17. Come if you wish. 18. Come if you please. 19. I should have been very thankful to them if they had prevented me from doing that. 20. If he should be there tell him to come at once.

XIV. The Imperative

1. Ask him whether he has bought them. 2. Do not be afraid. 3. Don't talk to me about it. 4. Help yourself (*2d sing.*) and Heaven will help you. 5. Sit down here, you must be tired. 6. Let us not go there at once. 7. Don't go there, John, you will hurt yourself. 8. Don't send it to me yet. 9. My brother is not here yet, but don't wait for him. 10. Permit me to thank you for it (*en*). 11. Let him not go away, we need him. 12. Tell them to come. 13. It is ten o'clock, let us write our letters. 14. Will you kindly lend me your pen? 15. Lend me your pen, but do not lend it to her. 16. Let them stay with us. 17. Let them not do what you have forbidden. 18. Go away, dog, you are disturbing us. 19. You have bread; give me some. 20. I have some, don't give me any.

XV. The Subjunctive

A. 1. Before you go I should like to see you. 2. I am sorry you could not come. 3. I took care that she did not fall. 4. Unless they come I shall be at home until five o'clock. 5. I am glad you are here. 6. They fear that you may believe it. 7. I am glad he has read this book. 8. Do you wish me to return without seeing him? 9. I was astonished that he did not get up earlier. 10. It would be a pity that that should happen. 11. I am anxious that (*à ce que*) he should read this book. 12. The doctor is at home; shall I send for him? 13. I am afraid they do not know the difference between him and me. 14. You must return before my father goes away. 15. I am afraid he is ill. 16. I did not think it would rain. 17. I am sorry that she did not come early. 18. I wish you would bring what I asked you to bring. 19. Whether the weather is good (= fine) or bad we accept it. 20. You must bring your books with you to-morrow.

B. 1. I am very much afraid your father is ill. 2. I am glad you will be able to come. 3. Do you think it will rain? 4. I think it will not rain to-day. 5. I do not know any one who is truly happy. 6. Whatever his reasons were, he has been obliged to change them. 7. Would you like me to speak to him or to write to him? 8. When did he come here? I want him to return home. 9. I don't want you to be unhappy. 10. Do you think he will come? 11. I think he will come. 12. He is looking for some one who may know him. 13. Take care that he does not see you. 14. He is very sorry that you have a grudge against him. 15. It is necessary that you should not do it. 16. There is nothing in these books which can interest you. 17. Do they want us to stay in the country till the autumn? 18. I should like you to show me the house which you have had built. 19. Your young friend has painted a large picture, but I don't think he has succeeded well this time. 20. He does not want you to tell him everything (*tout ce que*) you know.

C. 1. My brother said that he wished me to write to him often. 2. I am glad that you were so well during my absence. 3. I wish you to stay here until my return. I am not going far. 4. It is necessary that you put out this lamp. It does not burn well. 5. I am sorry that you did not both go away before he came. 6. I am not sure that I know what has become of him. 7. It is possible that we may see him when he comes. 8. He is the richest man I know. 9. Could you show me a grammar which has all the rules? 10. I am looking for a house which is large enough for seven people. 11. Do you know a man who can build a better wall than he? 12. Whatever the conditions are I cannot accept them without reflecting. 13. Whoever he is, I am sure that he is no gentleman. 14. Whenever we saw them they were always very busy. 15. Wherever one may be, one will always find that politeness is useful. 16. I am glad that you have found your blue necktie. 17. My brothers must go to Europe next summer. 18. I am afraid he will come before noon. 19. Wherever you go, remember that I shall be thinking of you. 20. You must not waste your money.

XVI. Reflexives and Passives

A. 1. His mother has hurt her arm.   2. He is well to-day.
3. Did you go for a drive yesterday morning? No, I took a ride
in the park. 4. Don't be mistaken. What we say is true. 5. My
mother did not hurt herself. 6. What is your name? 7. My name
is Henry. 8. The French were very brave, they let themselves be
killed (*se faire tuer*) by thousands. 9. He never complains of the
weather. 10. We will go for a walk and we shall have a good time
all afternoon. 11. At what time did you get up this morning?
12. He was followed by a small yellow dog. 13. He is not at all
well this morning; he ought to take a walk. 14. She has cut her
finger. 15. It is late; get up quickly if you want to see the sun
rise. 16. Go with them and you will enjoy yourself a great deal.
17. What is the name of the lake which he has discovered?
18. Don't be angry with me. 19. This was the question which
people were asking of one another almost every day. 20. My
two sisters have always written each other long letters.

B. 1. I think they are going to be married next week. 2. Which
amusement do you like best, to go riding on horseback or on (*à*) [a]
bicycle? 3. I went to the play last night, but I did not enjoy myself. 4. The two little girls bade each other good morning and
shook hands. 5. It is never hard to amuse oneself if one is well.
6. Come, make haste; it is half past nine and we are late. 7. When
they get up they wash their hands and face[s]. 8. These ladies
bowed to each other and shook hands. 9. Have you not washed
your face yet? I cannot wait for you. 10. How many letters
have these young men written to each other? 11. They have
written letters to each other, but they have not seen each other
yet. 12. Let us all sit down around this large table. 13. The two
armies fought well. 14. I do not like your conduct. Such things
are not done in (the) good society. 15. Men who build houses
and barns are called carpenters. 16. A robbery was committed in
the bank, but the thief was caught. 17. I remember all that he
said. 18. They will get up early to go to the station. 19. Have
these two (young) girls promised to write to each other? Yes,
every week. 20. Here are the two letters which they have written
to each other during ten months.

XVII. Impersonals

1. When the weather is bad, we remain at home. 2. If it is warm to-morrow we shall go into the forest. 3. It is very hot, but not so hot as yesterday. 4. I think it will be fine to-morrow. We are going for a drive. 5. It is impossible for you to know what I am thinking of. 6. How warm it is! I think it will rain. 7. It is very cold; it will snow perhaps before long. 8. Although it is windy it is warmer than yesterday. 9. It was easy to shut the gate when there was no wind. 10. What kind of weather is it now? 11. It was fine a moment ago, but now it is raining. 12. In winter it is dark at half past four. 13. It is not easy to read when people are chatting about you. 14. It will be fine weather to-morrow, and our celebration will take place. 15. When it is warm, horses and men are thirsty. 16. There has fallen much snow. 17. It froze last night; it is fine now. 18. There were many people at the ball. 19. You must not go away. 20. You must do what I tell you.

XVIII. Adverbs

1. I do not wish to read or write. 2. Perhaps he will remain at home to-day. 3. There are some pencils in the box and a few books under it. 4. Where do you live? I live opposite you. 5. In Paris there are many children who have never seen anything but poor people. 6. They have never been in France and they now say they will not go there. 7. It was only a small thing. 8. I have never seen such a fine picture. 9. It often happens that we promise to do what we can never do. 10. Neither you nor I sing. 11. We have no more paper, we cannot write any more. 12. I speak neither English nor German, but I understand both a little. 13. How tired I am! I have been working hard. 14. He has neither friends nor money. 15. She had only a few francs in her pocket. 16. Have you ever read that play by Labiche? 17. Does that woman sing as well as your sister? 18. He does not like the languages at all, nor I either. 19. The books are not on the table now. 20. Perhaps you are right, but one must go somewhere.

XIX. Conjunctions

1. Take him there yourself, that he may see what you are doing for him. 2. Although he is not very strong, he has travelled everywhere. 3. Although we get up rather late we never miss the train. 4. Tell it to him before you forget it. 5. Unless one is ill one

ought always to work. 6. I shall miss the train unless you arrive on time. 7. Some of his pupils came to see him before he went away. 8. It is a long time since I have seen you. 9. You should not have done that without asking my permission. 10. He missed his train because he would not get up early enough. 11. I shall not give it to her unless she asks for it. 12. In order to make grain grow, the farmer must plough the land. 13. The grandfather died six months before John was born. 14. Remain here until your brother returns. 15. I was wondering yesterday whether I should be able to speak to you. 16. He spoke in such a way that one could not understand him. 17. It is a long time since I spoke to him. 18. We shall not leave until our father comes. 19. They will not go away without speaking to you. 20. He went home for fear of catching cold.

XX. Miscellaneous

A. 1. He had not seen him for three years. 2. After looking at the two books I asked him which one he wanted. 3. I think he is right. 4. The more he works the more I will give him. 5. That poor little child must have been ill; he ought not to remain there any longer. 6. I am not going to Canada unless I can make more money there than at home. 7. I have a grudge against all those who do not like French. 8. How long have you been reading those old newspapers? For fifteen or twenty minutes. 9. Have you been in Paris long? No, we have been here only two weeks. 10. You ought to know how that is done. 11. Where is my sister? She has gone downstairs to get her books. 12. Although those children can't read yet, they can play a little on the piano. 13. That gentleman must have been in Paris, for he speaks French like a Parisian. 14. What is the matter with you? I have a terrible toothache. 15. These are the poems I heard read when I was in France. 16. He was sitting in front of the fire, thinking of all he had suffered. 17. Do not say that you do not remember it, for I told you about it two hours ago. 18. Have your friends come? Oh, yes! They have been here several weeks. 19. Nearly all Parisians are fond of the country and each Sunday every family is eager to go and spend the whole day in the woods and fields. 20. He is the best pupil in the school, because he works better than all the rest.

B. 1. One should sometimes read French newspapers to learn the language. 2. I hope you will accept the sixteen francs I offer you. 3. I think you are right; he is far too lazy. 4. Your sister is older than you, but she is not so tall. 5. We are Americans, but we have been living in France for ten years. 6. We came here in the spring, having brought with us only three trunks and little money. 7. Are we not to meet our friends here? 8. We are going to meet them to-morrow in London. 9. They must have been very stupid; they never saw us. 10. Most of the students are unhappy now. 11. It is the largest town in America. 12. She ought not to have taken them so far from home. 13. Can you tell me how long that man has been ill? 14. We enjoyed ourselves there; the songs we heard sung were excellent. 15. When I used to know Henry, he did not know how to write. 16. The poor fellow had not eaten for two days; he was weak and hungry. 17. What do you say when you ask for anything in French? 18. I like reading very much. Do you wish me to read as many books as you do? 19. It was last Saturday that I went to the theatre. 20. What a pity that it is so late!

C. 1. They say that he died a few days ago, but few people believe it. 2. This is the oldest tree in the whole country. 3. That gentleman had lived two years in France before he came to the United States. 4. We had been living for two years in that house at the time (*moment*, m.) of his arrival. 5. That boy is lazy; he will often sleep (*pres.*) till ten o'clock. 6. I have been working hard all day and I am tired. 7. The master tells the pupils that they should not be so idle. 8. We ought not to have gone away before the others arrived. 9. When do you begin? We begin as soon as my brother has finished. 10. Send for the doctor; my cousin has hurt himself. 11. Do not get angry, but pardon your enemies. 12. The doctor has gone out; he will return at a quarter to eleven. 13. We had to sell our house cheap. 14. Never mind, bring your sister if she wishes to come. 15. Take off your gloves and sit down. 16. I did not answer because I was afraid. 17. I like to go sleighing when the weather is fine. 18. Do you know where Mr. T. lives? I know his father very well. 19. He is in the country and will remain there. 20. My brother is rich and is very fond of me. 21. There is a window which is open; tell John to close it. 22. One ought not to sit down here; it is too cold. 23. She ought to have come yesterday; I was expecting her. 24. The train must have been two hours late. 25. I have been ill for a week and I wish them to stay until I am better.

APPENDIX

A. GENDER OF NOUNS

1. Gender by Derivation. — French nouns from Latin are regularly derived from the accusative form, and their gender may usually be determined thus: —

(*a*) Latin masculines and neuters give French masculines:

L. murum, *m.*	mur, *m.*	L. librum, *m.*	livre, *m.*
L. corpus, *n.*	corps, *m.*	L. ferrum, *n.*	fer, *m.*

EXCEPTIONS: Latin abstracts in –or, *m.* (acc. –orem) are all *f.* in French, except **honneur, labeur, amour**; many neuter plurals in –a give a French feminine singular, e.g. L. folia = **feuille**, L. opera = **œuvre**, etc.

(*b*) Latin feminines give French feminines:

L. libram, *f.*	livre, *f.*	L. mansionem, *f.*	maison, *f.*

2. Gender by Endings. — The following general rules apply to nouns denoting inanimate objects: —

Masculine endings are:	Feminine endings are:
(*a*) Vowels (not –**e** or abstracts in –**té**, –**tié**).	(*a*) –**e** following a vowel or double consonant; abstracts in –**té**, –**tié**.
(*b*) Consonants (not –**son**, –**ion** or abstracts in –**eur**).	(*b*) –**son**, –**ion** and most abstracts in –**eur**.
(*c*) –**acle**, –**age**, –**asme**, –**ège**, –**ème**, –**isme**, –**tère**.	(*c*) –**ace**, –**ade**, –**ance**, –**ence**, –**euse**, –**ière**, –**oire**, –**ude**, –**ure**.

EXCEPTIONS: Numerous, especially for masculine rules (*a*) and (*b*); six nouns in –**age** are feminine: **cage, image, nage, page** (book), **plage, rage**.

3. Double Gender. — In some words the gender is determined by the sense; in others the sense by the gender, thus: —

(*a*) Most nouns in –**e** (and adjectives so used) denoting persons may be masculine or feminine:

    un or **une** artiste   **un** or **une** malade   **un** or **une** enfant

(*b*) The meaning varies according to the gender:

un livre, *book*	**un** voile, *veil*	**un** manche, *handle*
une livre, *pound*	**une** voile, *sail*	**une** manche, *sleeve*

4. **Formation of Feminine**. — Most nouns denoting living beings distinguish the gender thus: —

(*a*) By means of a different word: **oncle, tante; bœuf, vache,** etc.

(*b*) By adding **–esse** to the last consonant: abbé, **abbesse,** prince, **princesse,** etc.

(*c*) A few by **–ine:** héros, héro**ine,** etc.

(*d*) Most nouns of professions, and a few others, lack a feminine form: **docteur, ange,** etc.

(*e*) Some nouns are feminine, whether denoting males or females: **une** personne, *a person*, etc.

(*f*) Some names of lower animals are masculine only, and some feminine only: **un** éléphant, **une** fourmi, etc.; **mâle** or **femelle** is added to avoid ambiguity: **un** éléphant **mâle, un** éléphant **femelle.**

(*g*) Most other nouns follow the analogy of adjectives.

B. PLURAL OF NOUNS AND ADJECTIVES

The following rules are given for reference; see also the general rules, §§ 2, 32: —

1. Seven nouns in **–ou** take **–x:** bijou(**x**), caillou(**x**), chou(**x**), genou(**x**), hibou(**x**), joujou(**x**), pou(**x**); other nouns in **–ou** are regular: clou(**s**), sou(**s**), etc.

2. Regular are: bal(**s**), carnaval(**s**), chacal(**s**) and rarer words.

3. The ending **–ail** becomes **–aux** in bail, b**aux,** corail, cor**aux,** tra**vail,** tra**vaux** and in rarer words; but détail(**s**), etc., are regular.

4. Most common adjectives in **–al** have a plural in **–aux;** for doubtful cases consult dictionary.

5. Adjectives in **–eu** have the plural in **–s,** but observe héb**reu,** hé**breux.**

6. Some nouns have two plurals, mostly with varying meaning; examples are: aïeul, *pl.* **aïeux,** *ancestors,* aïeuls, *grandfathers;* ciel, *pl.* **cieux,** *skies, heavens, climates,* but ciels, *bed-canopies,* etc.; œil, *pl.* **yeux** but œils in compounds, e.g. œils-de-bœuf, *oval windows;* trav**ail,** *pl.* tra**vaux,** *works,* but travails, *reports,* etc.; ail, *pl.* ails or a**ulx,** *garlic.*

7. In compound nouns, only a component which is a noun or an adjective may take the plural sign.

8. Compounds without hyphen follow the general rules: portemanteau(**x**), grand'mère(**s**); but exceptionally: bon(**s**)homme(**s**), gentil(**s**)homme(**s**) and compounds of **mon–, ma–:** **mon**sieur, **mes**sieurs, **ma**dame, **mes**dames, etc.

9. In compounds with hyphen, both components usually vary: grand(s)-père(s), chou(x)-fleur(s).

10. In compounds with preposition and hyphen, the first component is variable when the plural force belongs to it: chef(s)-d'œuvre, etc.; but tête-à-tête, singular or plural, where the plural idea belongs to the expression as a whole.

11. When the first component is invariable, the compound follows the general rule, but only when the plural idea belongs to the variable component: vice-roi(s); but abat-jour, singular or plural, where the plural idea belongs to the expression as a whole.

12. The word garde in compounds is variable only when denoting persons: garde(s)-malades, *sick-nurse(s)*, but garde-robes, *wardrobes*.

13. Names of persons are regularly invariable: les deux Racine, les Duval; but a few historic family names take a plural sign: les Césars, etc.; usage varies for names denoting 'persons like': les Corneilles, les Gœthe, sont rares.

14. Invariable words used as nouns take no plural sign: les on dit, etc.; so also foreign nouns, unless fully naturalized: les post-scriptum, etc.; but: les biftecks, etc.

15. A few Italian words retain their plural in –i: dilettante, *pl.* dilettanti, etc.

C. VERB PARADIGMS

1. THE REGULAR CONJUGATIONS

I	II	III

Infinitive Mood

PRESENT	PRESENT	PRESENT
donner, *give*	finir, *finish*	rompre, *break*

Participles

PRESENT	PRESENT	PRESENT
donnant, *giving*	finissant, *finishing*	rompant, *breaking*

PAST	PAST	PAST
donné, *given*	fini, *finished*	rompu, *broken*

Indicative Mood

PRESENT	PRESENT	PRESENT
I give, am giving, etc.	*I finish, am finishing, etc.*	*I break, am breaking, etc.*
je donne	je finis	je romps
tu donnes	tu finis	tu romps
il donne	il finit	il rompt
nous donnons	nous finissons	nous rompons
vous donnez	vous finissez	vous rompez
ils donnent	ils finissent	ils rompent

IMPERFECT	IMPERFECT	IMPERFECT
I was giving, used to give, etc.	*I was finishing, used to finish, etc.*	*I was breaking, used to break, etc.*
je donnais	je finissais	je rompais
tu donnais	tu finissais	tu rompais
il donnait	il finissait	il rompait
nous donnions	nous finissions	nous rompions
vous donniez	vous finissiez	vous rompiez
ils donnaient	ils finissaient	ils rompaient

PAST DEFINITE	PAST DEFINITE	PAST DEFINITE
I gave, etc.	*I finished, etc.*	*I broke, etc.*
je donnai	je finis	je rompis
tu donnas	tu finis	tu rompis
il donna	il finit	il rompit
nous donnâmes	nous finîmes	nous rompîmes
vous donnâtes	vous finîtes	vous rompîtes
ils donnèrent	ils finirent	ils rompirent

FUTURE	FUTURE	FUTURE
I shall give, etc.	*I shall finish, etc.*	*I shall break, etc.*
je donnerai	je finirai	je romprai
tu donneras	tu finiras	tu rompras
il donnera	il finira	il rompra
nous donnerons	nous finirons	nous romprons
vous donnerez	vous finirez	vous romprez
ils donneront	ils finiront	ils rompront

CONDITIONAL	CONDITIONAL	CONDITIONAL
I should give, etc.	*I should finish, etc.*	*I should break, etc.*
je donnerais	je finirais	je romprais
tu donnerais	tu finirais	tu romprais
il donnerait	il finirait	il romprait
nous donnerions	nous finirions	nous romprions
vous donneriez	vous finiriez	vous rompriez
ils donneraient	ils finiraient	ils rompraient

Subjunctive Mood

PRESENT	PRESENT	PRESENT
(That) I (may) give, etc.	*(That) I (may) finish, etc.*	*(That) I (may) break, etc.*
(que) je donne	(que) je finisse	(que) je rompe
(que) tu donnes	(que) tu finisses	(que) tu rompes
(qu')il donne	(qu')il finisse	(qu')il rompe
(que) nous donnions	(que) nous finissions	(que) nous rompions
(que) vous donniez	(que) vous finissiez	(que) vous rompiez
(qu')ils donnent	(qu')ils finissent	(qu')ils rompent

IMPERFECT	IMPERFECT	IMPERFECT
(That) I (might) give, etc.	*(That) I (might) finish, etc.*	*(That) I (might) break, etc.*
(que) je donnasse	(que) je finisse	(que) je rompisse
(que) tu donnasses	(que) tu finisses	(que) tu rompisses
(qu')il donnât	(qu')il finît	(qu')il rompît
(que) nous donnassions	(que) nous finissions	(que) nous rompissions
(que) vous donnassiez	(que) vous finissiez	(que) vous rompissiez
(qu')ils donnassent	(qu')ils finissent	(qu')ils rompissent

Imperative Mood

PRESENT	PRESENT	PRESENT
Give, etc.	*Finish, etc.*	*Break, etc.*
donne[1]	finis	romps
qu'il donne	qu'il finisse	qu'il rompe
donnons	finissons	rompons
donnez	finissez	rompez
qu'ils donnent	qu'ils finissent	qu'ils rompent

[1] This form becomes 'donnes' when followed by -y or -en.

2. THE AUXILIARY VERBS

Infinitive

PRES. avoir, *have*   PRES. être, *be*

Participles

PRES. ayant, *having*   PRES. étant, *being*
PAST, eu, *had*   PAST, été, *been*

Indicative

PRESENT   PRESENT
I have, am having, etc.   *I am, am being, etc.*

j'ai	nous avons		je suis	nous sommes
tu as	vous avez		tu es	vous êtes
il a	ils ont		il est	ils sont

IMPERFECT   IMPERFECT
I had, was having, etc.   *I was, was being, etc.*

j'avais	nous avions		j'étais	nous étions
tu avais	vous aviez		tu étais	vous étiez
il avait	ils avaient		il était	ils étaient

PAST DEFINITE   PAST DEFINITE
I had, etc.   *I was, etc.*

j'eus	nous eûmes		je fus	nous fûmes
tu eus	vous eûtes		tu fus	vous fûtes
il eut	ils eurent		il fut	ils furent

FUTURE   FUTURE
I shall have, etc.   *I shall be, etc.*

j'aurai	nous aurons		je serai	nous serons
tu auras	vous aurez		tu seras	vous serez
il aura	ils auront		il sera	ils seront

CONDITIONAL   CONDITIONAL
I should have, etc.   *I should be, etc.*

j'aurais	nous aurions		je serais	nous serions
tu aurais	vous auriez		tu serais	vous seriez
il aurait	ils auraient		il serait	ils seraient

Subjunctive

PRESENT

(That) I (may) have, etc.

(que) j'aie	(que) nous ayons
(que) tu aies	(que) vous ayez
(qu')il ait	(qu')ils aient

PRESENT

(That) I (may) be, etc.

(que) je sois	(que) nous soyons
(que) tu sois	(que) vous soyez
(qu')il soit	(qu')ils soient

IMPERFECT

(That) I (might) have, etc.

(que) j'eusse	(que) nous eussions
(que) tu eusses	(que) vous eussiez
(qu')il eût	(qu')ils eussent

IMPERFECT

(That) I (might) be, etc.

(que) je fusse	(que) nous fussions
(que) tu fusses	(que) vous fussiez
(qu')il fût	(qu')ils fussent

Imperative

PRESENT

Have, etc.

	ayons
aie	ayez
qu'il ait	qu'ils aient

PRESENT

Be, etc.

	soyons
sois	soyez
qu'il soit	qu'ils soient

3. THE COMPOUND TENSES

Infinitive

PERFECT

To have given
avoir donné

PERFECT

To have arrived
être arrivé(e)(s)

Participle

PERFECT

Having given
ayant donné

PERFECT

Having arrived
étant arrivé(e)(s)

Indicative

PAST INDEFINITE

I have given, etc.
j'ai donné
tu as donné
etc.

PAST INDEFINITE

I have arrived, etc.
je suis arrivé(e)
tu es arrivé(e)
etc.

PLUPERFECT
I had given, etc.
j'avais donné, etc.

PLUPERFECT
I had arrived, etc.
j'étais arrivé(e), etc.

PAST ANTERIOR
I had given, etc.
j'eus donné, etc.

PAST ANTERIOR
I had arrived, etc.
je fus arrivé(e), etc.

FUTURE ANTERIOR
I shall have given, etc.
j'aurai donné, etc.

FUTURE ANTERIOR
I shall have arrived, etc.
je serai arrivé(e), etc.

CONDITIONAL ANTERIOR
I should have given, etc.
j'aurais donné, etc.

CONDITIONAL ANTERIOR
I should have arrived, etc.
je serais arrivé(e), etc.

Subjunctive

PERFECT
(*That*) *I* (*may*) *have given, etc.*
(que) j'aie donné, etc.

PERFECT
(*That*) *I* (*may*) *have arrived, etc.*
que je sois arrivé(e), etc.

PLUPERFECT
(*That*) *I* (*might*) *have given, etc.*
(que) j'eusse donné, etc.

PLUPERFECT
(*That*) *I* (*might*) *have arrived, etc.*
(que) je fusse arrivé(e), etc.

4. THE PASSIVE VOICE

Infinitive

PRESENT
être aimé(e)(s), *to be loved*

PERFECT
avoir été aimé(e)(s), *to have been loved*

Participle

PRESENT
étant aimé(e)(s), *being loved*

PERFECT
ayant été aimé(e)(s), *having been loved*

Indicative

PRESENT
I am (being) loved, etc.

je suis   aimé(e)
tu es   aimé(e)
il (elle) est   aimé(e)
nous sommes aimé(e)s
vous êtes   aimé(e)s
ils (elles) sont   aimé(e)s

PAST INDEFINITE
I have been (was) loved, etc.

j'ai   été aimé(e)
tu as   été aimé(e)
il (elle) a   été aimé(e)
nous avons été aimé(e)s
vous avez été aimé(e)s
ils (elles) ont été aimé(e)s

IMPERFECT
I was (being) loved, etc.
j'étais aimé(e), etc.

PLUPERFECT
I had been loved, etc.
j'avais été aimé(e), etc.

PAST DEFINITE
I was loved, etc.
je fus aimé(e), etc.

PAST ANTERIOR
I had been loved, etc.
j'eus été aimé(e), etc.

FUTURE
I shall be loved, etc.
je serai aimé(e), etc.

FUTURE PERFECT
I shall have been loved, etc.
j'aurai été aimé(e), etc.

CONDITIONAL
I should be loved, etc.
je serais aimé(e), etc.

CONDITIONAL ANTERIOR
I should have been loved, etc.
j'aurais été aimé(e), etc.

Subjunctive

PRESENT
(That) I may be loved, etc.
(que) je sois aimé(e), etc.

PERFECT
(That) I may have been loved, etc.
(que) j'aie été aimé(e), etc.

IMPERFECT
(That) I might be loved, etc.
(que) je fusse aimé(e), etc.

PLUPERFECT
(That) I might have been loved, etc.
(que) j'eusse été aimé(e), etc.

Imperative
Be loved, etc.

soyons aimé(e)s
sois aimé(e)
soyez aimé(e)s
qu'il (elle) soit aimé(e)
qu'ils (elles) soient aimé(e)s

5. THE REFLEXIVE VERB

Infinitive

PRESENT	PERFECT
se couper, *to cut oneself*	s'être coupé(e)(s), *to have cut oneself*

Participle

PRESENT	PERFECT
se coupant, *cutting oneself*	s'étant coupé(e)(s), *having cut oneself*

Indicative

PRESENT

I cut (am cutting) myself, etc.

je me coupe
tu te coupes
il se coupe
nous nous coupons
vous vous coupez
ils se coupent

PAST INDEFINITE

I have cut (cut) myself, etc.

je me suis coupé(e)
tu t'es coupé(e)
il (elle) s'est coupé(e)
nous nous sommes coupé(e)s
vous vous êtes coupé(e)s
ils (elles) se sont coupé(e)s

IMPERFECT

I was cutting (cut) myself, etc.
je me coupais, etc.

PLUPERFECT

I had cut myself, etc.
je m'étais coupé(e), etc.

PAST DEFINITE

I cut myself, etc.
je me coupai, etc.

PAST ANTERIOR

I had cut myself, etc.
je me fus coupé(e), etc.

FUTURE

I shall cut myself, etc.
je me couperai, etc.

FUTURE PERFECT

I shall have cut myself, etc.
je me serai coupé(e)

CONDITIONAL

I should cut myself, etc.
je me couperais, etc.

CONDITIONAL ANTERIOR

I should have cut myself, etc.
je me serais coupé(e), etc.

Subjunctive

PRESENT

(That) I may cut myself, etc.
(que) je me coupe, etc.

PERFECT

(That) I may have cut myself, etc.
(que) je me sois coupé(e), etc.

IMPERFECT	PLUPERFECT
(*That*) *I might cut myself, etc.*	(*That*) *I might have cut myself, etc.*
(que) je me coupasse, etc.	(que) je me fusse coupé(e), etc.

Imperative

Cut thyself (yourself), etc.

	coupons-nous
coupe-toi	coupez-vous
qu'il se coupe	qu'ils se coupent

NOTE. — The reflexive verb **s'en aller**, *go away*, presents special difficulty in the arrangement of the pronoun objects as seen in the following examples; in practice, **partir** often takes its place.

Present Indicative

AFFIRMATIVE	NEGATIVE
I go away, etc.	*I do not go away, etc.*
je m'en vais	je ne m'en vais pas
tu t'en vas	tu ne t'en vas pas
il s'en va	il ne s'en va pas
nous nous en allons	nous ne nous en allons pas
vous vous en allez	vous ne vous en allez pas
ils s'en vont	ils ne s'en vont pas

INTERROGATIVE	INTERROGATIVE NEGATIVE
Do I go away? etc.	*Do I not go away? etc.*
m'en vais-je?	ne m'en vais-je pas?
t'en vas-tu?	ne t'en vas-tu pas?
s'en va-t-il?	ne s'en va-t-il pas?
nous en allons-nous?	ne nous en allons-nous pas?
vous en allez-vous?	ne vous en allez-vous pas?
s'en vont-ils?	ne s'en vont-ils pas?

Past Indefinite

NEGATIVE

I have not gone away, etc.

je ne m'en suis pas	allé(e)
tu ne t'en es pas	allé(e)
il (elle) ne s'en est pas	allé(e)
nous ne nous en sommes pas	allé(e)s
vous ne vous en êtes pas	allé(e)s
ils (elles) ne s'en sont pas	allé(e)s

Interrogative Negative

Have I not gone away? etc.

ne m'en suis-je pas	allé(e)?
ne t'en es-tu pas	allé(e)?
ne s'en est-il (elle) pas	allé(e)?
ne nous en sommes-nous pas	allé(e)s?
ne vous en êtes-vous pas	allé(e)s?
ne s'en sont-ils (elles) pas	allé(e)s?

Imperative

Affirmative

Go away, etc.

va-t'en
qu'il s'en aille
allons-nous-en
allez-vous-en
qu'ils s'en aillent

Negative

Do not go away, etc.

ne t'en va pas
qu'il ne s'en aille pas
ne nous en allons pas
ne vous en allez pas
qu'ils ne s'en aillent pas

D. ORTHOGRAPHICAL PECULIARITIES — FIRST CONJUGATION

1. Verbs ending in –**cer**, e.g. **avancer** [avãse], *advance*, must preserve the [s] sound of **c** throughout their conjugation, and hence **c** becomes **ç** when it precedes **a** or **o** of an ending, but not elsewhere; for the sounds of **c** and **ç**, see Introduction, p. xviii.

Pres. Part.	Pres. Indic.	Impf. Indic.	Past Def.	Impf. Subj.
avançant	avance	avançais	avançai	avançasse
	avances	avançais	avanças	avançasses
	avance	avançait	avança	avançât
	avançons	avancions	avançâmes	avançassions
	avancez	avanciez	avançâtes	avançassiez
	avancent	avançaient	avancèrent	avançassent

Note. — Pronoun subjects are omitted to save space.

2. Verbs ending in –**ger**, e.g. **manger** [mãʒe], *eat*, must preserve the [ʒ] sound of **g** throughout their conjugation, and hence **g** becomes **ge** when it precedes **a** or **o** of an ending, but not elsewhere; for the sounds of **g** and **ge**, see Introduction, p. xviii.

Pres. Part.	Pres. Indic.	Impf. Indic.	Past Def.	Impf. Subj.
mangeant	mange	mangeais	mangeai	mangeasse
	manges	mangeais	mangeas	mangeasses
	mange	mangeait	mangea	mangeât
	mangeons	mangions	mangeâmes	mangeassions
	mangez	mangiez	mangeâtes	mangeassiez
	mangent	mangeaient	mangèrent	mangeassent

3. Verbs ending in –oyer and –uyer, e.g. **nettoyer**, *clean*, **essuyer**, *wipe*, change y to i whenever it comes before e mute in conjugation, but not elsewhere; verbs in –ayer, e.g. **payer**, *pay*, may retain y throughout, or change y to i before e mute; for e mute, see Introduction, p. xiii.

Pres. Indic.	Pres. Subj.	Future	Conditional
nettoie	nettoie	nettoierai	nettoierais
nettoies	nettoies	nettoieras	nettoierais
nettoie	nettoie	nettoiera	nettoierait
nettoyons	nettoyions	nettoierons	nettoierions
nettoyez	nettoyiez	nettoierez	nettoieriez
nettoient	nettoient	nettoieront	nettoieraient
essuie	essuie	essuierai	essuierais
etc.	etc.	etc.	etc.
paie } etc.	paie } etc.	paierai } etc.	paierais } etc.
paye	paye	payerai	payerais

4. Verbs having the stem vowel e, e.g. **mener**, *lead*, change this e to è wherever in conjugating the verb it is followed by a syllable containing e mute (but for verbs in –eler, –eter, see below).

Pres. Indic.	Pres. Subj.	Future	Conditional
mène	mène	mènerai	mènerais
mènes	mènes	mèneras	mènerais
mène	mène	mènera	mènerait
menons	menions	mènerons	mènerions
menez	meniez	mènerez	mèneriez
mènent	mènent	mèneront	mèneraient

NOTE. — The principle involved here is that if e mute occurs in two successive syllables, the first e takes the sound [ɛ], indicated above by è.

5. Verbs having the stem vowel **é** followed by a consonant, e.g. c**é**der, *yield*, change **é** to **è** in the present indicative and subjunctive, but retain **é** in the future and conditional when followed by a syllable containing **e** mute, **é** in the future and conditional having exceptionally the [ɛ] sound.

PRES. INDIC.	PRES. SUBJ.	FUTURE	CONDITIONAL
cède, etc.	cède, etc.	céderai, etc.	céderais, etc.

NOTE. — Verbs with stem vowel é + vowel are regular, e.g. créer.

6. Verbs in **–eler**, **–eter**, e.g. appeler, *call*, jeter, *throw*, usually double **l** or **t** before an **e** mute syllable in conjugation (but with some important exceptions, see below).

PRES. INDIC.	PRES. SUBJ.	FUTURE	CONDITIONAL
appelle	appelle	appellerai	appellerais
appelles	appelles	appelleras	appellerais
appelle	appelle	appellera	appellerait
appelons	appelions	appellerons	appellerions
appelez	appeliez	appellerez	appelleriez
appellent	appellent	appelleront	appelleraient

So also **jeter:**

jette, etc.	jette, etc.	jetterai, etc.	jetterais, etc.

NOTE. — The same principle is involved as that explained in the Note to 4, above, but here the [ɛ] sound of e is indicated by a doubled consonant.

7. A few verbs in **–eler**, **–eter** (the commonest being **acheter**, *buy*, **geler**, *freeze*) take the grave accent like **mener**, see 4, above.

PRES. INDIC.	PRES. SUBJ.	FUTURE	CONDITIONAL
achète, etc.	achète, etc.	achèterai, etc.	achèterais, etc.
gèle, etc.	gèle, etc.	gèlerai, etc.	gèlerais, etc.

E. LIST OF PRINCIPAL IRREGULAR VERBS

1. The rules for inferring the various moods and tenses from the principal parts are given in §§ 157, 158.

2. The pronoun subjects are omitted for brevity, but should be supplied in learning or reciting the verbs.

3. The future and conditional are combined for brevity, e.g. j'acquerrai(s) = j'acquerrai and j'acquerrais.

4. Compounds are usually to be found under the principal verb.

5. The more difficult tenses are given in full.

6. The auxiliaries **avoir** and **être** are not included.

7. For key to the list, see p. 259.

INFIN.	PRES. PART.	PAST PART.	PRES. INDIC.	PAST DEF.
Acquérir	acquérant	acquis	acquiers	acquis
(*acquire*)	acquérais			acquisse
acquerrai(s)	acquière			

PRES. IND.: acquiers, acquiers, acquiert, acquérons, acquérez, acquièrent.

PRES. SUBJ.: acquière, acquières, acquière, acquérions, acquériez, acquièrent.

conquérir, *conquer*   reconquérir, *reconquer*

Aller	allant	allé	vais[2]	allai
(*go*)	allais			allasse
irai(s)[1]	aille			

PRES. IND.: vais,[2] vas,[2] va,[2] allons, allez, vont.[2]

PRES. SUBJ.: aille, ailles, aille, allions, alliez, aillent.

[1] From Lat. ire.   [2] From Lat. vadere.

Assaillir	assaillant	assailli	assaille	assaillis
(*assail*)	assaillais			assaillisse
assaillirai(s)	assaille			

PRES. IND.: assaille, assailles, assaille, assaillons, assaillez, assaillent.

tressaillir, *start*   saillir, *jut out*

Asseoir	asseyant[2]	assis	assieds / assois	assis / assisse
(*seat*)	asseyais[3]			
assiérai(s)[1]	asseye			

PRES. IND.: {assieds, assieds, assied, asseyons, asseyez, asseyent. / assois, assois, assoit, assoyons, assoyez, assoient.}

PRES. SUBJ.: {asseye, asseyes, asseye, asseyions, asseyiez, asseyent. / assoie, assoies, assoie, assoyions, assoyiez, assoient.}

IMPVE.: {assieds, asseyons, asseyez. / assois, assoyons, assoyez.}

[1] or asseyerai(s) or assoirai(s).   [2] or assoyant.   [3] or assoyais

s'asseoir, *sit down*   rasseoir, *reseat, calm*   se rasseoir, *sit down again*

Battre	battant	battu	bats	battis
(*beat*)	battais			battisse
battrai(s)	batte			

PRES. IND.: bats, bats, bat, battons, battez, battent.

abattre, *fell*   débattre, *debate*   rabattre, *beat down*
combattre, *fight*   se débattre, *struggle*

INFIN.	PRES. PART.	PAST PART.	PRES. INDIC.	PAST DEF.
Boire	buvant	bu	bois	bus
(*drink*)	buvais			busse
boirai(s)	boive			

PRES. IND.: bois, bois, boit, buvons, buvez, boivent.

PRES. SUBJ.: boive, boives, boive, buvions, buviez, boivent.

reboire, *drink again*

Bouillir	bouillant	bouilli	bous	bouillis
(*boil*)	bouillais			bouillisse
bouillirai(s)	bouille			

PRES. IND.: bous, bous, bout, bouillons, bouillez, bouillent.

ébouillir, *boil away*   **rebouillir**, *boil again*

Conclure	concluant	conclu	conclus	conclus
(*conclude*)	concluais			conclusse
conclurai(s)	conclue			

PRES. IND.: conclus, conclus, conclut, concluons, concluez, concluent.

exclure, *exclude*   **inclure**,[1] *include*

[1] Past part. **inclus.**

Conduire	conduisant	conduit	conduis	conduisis
(*conduct*)	conduisais			conduisisse
conduirai(s)	conduise			

PRES. IND.: conduis, conduis, conduit, conduisons, conduisez, conduisent.

éconduire, *show out*   **induire**, *induce*   **reproduire**, *reproduce*
reconduire, *lead back*   **introduire**, *introduce*   **séduire**, *mislead*
déduire, *deduct*   **produire**, *produce*   **traduire**, *translate*
enduire, *plaster*   **réduire**, *reduce*

Confire	confisant	confit	confis	confis
(*preserve*)	confisais			confisse
confirai(s)	confise			

PRES. IND.: confis, confis, confit, confisons, confisez, confisent.

suffire (p. part. **suffi**), *suffice*

Infin.	Pres. Part.	Past Part.	Pres. Indic.	Past Def.
Connaître	connaissant	connu	connais	connus
(know)	connaissais			connusse
connaîtrai(s)	connaisse			

Pres. Ind.: connais, connais, connaît, connaissons, connaissez, connaissent.

méconnaître, *not to know*	**comparaître**, *appear*	**paître**,[1] *graze*
reconnaître, *recognize*	**disparaître**, *disappear*	**repaître**, *feed, feast*
paraître, *appear*	**reparaître**, *reappear*	**se repaître**, *feed, feast*
apparaître, *appear*		

[1] Lacks the past part., past def., and impf. subj.

Infin.	Pres. Part.	Past Part.	Pres. Indic.	Past Def.
Construire	construisant	construit	construis	construisis
(construct)	construisais			construisisse
construirai(s)	construise			

Pres. Ind.: construis, construis, construit, construisons, construisez, construisent.

déconstruire, *take apart*	**reconstruire**, *reconstruct*
instruire, *instruct*	**détruire**, *destroy*

Infin.	Pres. Part.	Past Part.	Pres. Indic.	Past Def.
Coudre	cousant	cousu	couds	cousis
(sew)	cousais			cousisse
coudrai(s)	couse			

Pres. Ind.: couds, couds, coud, cousons, cousez, cousent.

découdre, *rip, unsew*	**recoudre**, *sew again*

Infin.	Pres. Part.	Past Part.	Pres. Indic.	Past Def.
Courir	courant	couru	cours	courus
(run)	courais		cours	courusse
courrai(s)	coure			

Pres. Ind.: cours, cours, court, courons, courez, courent.

accourir, *run up*	**encourir**, *incur*	**secourir**, *help*
concourir, *concur*	**parcourir**, *run over*	
discourir, *discourse*	**recourir**, *apply*	

Infin.	Pres. Part.	Past Part.	Pres. Indic.	Past Def.
Craindre	craignant	craint	crains	craignis
(fear)	craignais			craignisse
craindrai(s)	craigne			

Pres. Ind.: crains, crains, craint, craignons, craignez, craignent.

contraindre, *constrain*	**plaindre**, *pity*	**se plaindre**, *complain*

INFIN.	PRES. PART.	PAST PART.	PRES. INDIC.	PAST DEF.
Croire	croyant	cru	crois	crus
(*believe*)	croyais			crusse
croirai(s)	croie			

PRES. IND.: crois, crois, croit, croyons, croyez, croient.
PRES. SUBJ.: croie, croies, croie, croyions, croyiez, croient.

Croître	croissant	crû	croîs	crûs
(*grow*)	croissais	(*f.* crue)		crûsse
croîtrai(s)	croisse			

PRES. IND.: croîs, croîs, croît, croissons, croissez, croissent.

Cueillir	cueillant	cueilli	cueille	cueillis
(*gather*)	cueillais			cueillisse
cueillerai(s)	cueille			

PRES. IND.: cueille, cueilles, cueille, cueillons, cueillez, cueillent.

accueillir, *welcome*   recueillir, *gather, collect*

Cuire	cuisant	cuit	cuis	cuisis
(*cook*)	cuisais			cuisisse
cuirai(s)	cuise			

PRES. IND.: cuis, cuis, cuit, cuisons, cuisez, cuisent.

recuire, *cook again*   reluire,[2] *glisten*   nuire,[3] *injure*
luire,[1] *shine*

[1] Past part. lui.   [2] Past part. relui.   [3] Past part. nui.

Devoir	devant	dû	dois	dus
(*owe, must*)	devais	(*f.* due,		dusse
devrai(s)	doive	*pl.* du(e)s)		

PRES. IND.: dois, dois, doit, devons, devez, doivent.
PRES. SUBJ.: doive, doives, doive, devions, deviez, doivent.

redevoir, *still owe*

Dire	disant	dit	dis	dis
(*say*)	disais			disse
dirai(s)	dise			

PRES. IND.: dis, dis, dit, disons, dites, disent.

contredire,[1] *contradict*   interdire,[1] *interdict*   prédire,[1] *predict*
dédire,[1] *retract*   médire,[1] *slander*   redire, *say again*

[1] The 2d pl. pres. indic. and impve. is –disez.

Infin.	Pres. Part.	Past Part.	Pres. Indic.	Past Def.
Dormir	dormant	dormi	dors	dormis
(*sleep*)	dormais			dormisse
dormirai(s)	dorme			

Pres. Ind.: dors, dors, dort, dormons, dormez, dorment.

endormir, *put to sleep*   redormir, *sleep again*   rendormir, *put to sleep again*
s'endormir, *fall asleep*   se rendormir, *go to sleep again*

Écrire	écrivant	écrit	écris	écrivis
(*write*)	écrivais			écrivisse
écrirai(s)	écrive			

Pres. Ind.: écris, écris, écrit, écrivons, écrivez, écrivent.

circonscrire, *circumscribe*   prescrire, *prescribe*   souscrire, *subscribe*
décrire, *describe*   proscrire, *proscribe*   transcrire, *transcribe*
inscrire, *inscribe*   récrire, *rewrite*

Envoyer	envoyant	envoyé	envoie	envoyai
(*send*)	envoyais			envoyasse
enverrai(s)	envoie			

Pres. Ind.: envoie, envoies, envoie, envoyons, envoyez, envoient.

Pres. Subj.: envoie, envoies, envoie, envoyions, envoyiez, envoient.

renvoyer, *send away*

Faire	faisant	fait	fais	fis
(*do, make*)	faisais			fisse
ferai(s)	fasse			

Pres. Ind.: fais, fais, fait, faisons, faites, font.

Pres. Subj.: fasse, fasses, fasse, fassions, fassiez, fassent.

contrefaire, *imitate*   parfaire, *complete*   satisfaire, *satisfy*
défaire, *undo*   * redéfaire, *undo again*   surfaire, *overcharge*
méfaire, *harm*   refaire, *do again*

Falloir (*impers.*)	——	fallu	il faut	il fallut
(*must*)	il fallait			il fallût
il faudra(it)	il faille			

Fleurir	florissant[1]	——		——
(*flourish*)	florissais[1]			——

[1] Has these irreg. forms when used of persons or collections of persons; impf. **fleurissais**, etc., is used of things; literally = *blossom, bloom*, it is regular throughout.

INFIN.	PRES. PART.	PAST PART.	PRES. INDIC.	PAST DEF.
Fuir	fuyant	fui	fuis	fuis
(*fly, flee*)	fuyais			fuisse
fuirai(s)	fuie			

PRES. IND.: fuis, fuis, fuit, fuyons, fuyez, fuient.
PRES. SUBJ.: fuie, fuies, fuie, fuyions, fuyiez, fuient.

s'enfuir, *escape*

Gésir	gisant	——	il gît	——
(*lie buried*)	gisais			——
——				

PRES. IND.: ——, ——, gît, gisons, gisez, gisent.

Haïr	haïssant	haï	hais	haïs
(*hate*)	haïssais			haïsse
haïrai(s)	haïsse			

PRES. IND.: hais, hais, hait, haïssons, haïssez, haïssent.
PAST DEF.: haïs, haïs, haït, haïmes, haïtes, haïrent.
IMPF. SUBJ.: haïsse, haïsses, haït, haïssions, haïssiez, haïssent.

Joindre	joignant	joint	joins	joignis
(*join*)	joignais			joignisse
joindrai(s)	joigne			

PRES. IND.: joins, joins, joint, joignons, joignez, joignent.

adjoindre, *adjoin*	**disjoindre**, *disjoin*	**oindre**, *anoint*
conjoindre, *conjoin*	**enjoindre**, *enjoin*	**poindre**, *dawn*
déjoindre, *disjoin*	**rejoindre**, *rejoin*	

Lire	lisant	lu	lis	lus
(*read*)	lisais			lusse
lirai(s)	lise			

PRES. IND.: lis, lis, lit, lisons, lisez, lisent.

élire, *elect*	**réélire**, *reelect*	**relire**, *read again*

Maudire	maudissant	maudit	maudis	maudis
(*curse*)	maudissais			maudisse
maudirai(s)	maudisse			

PRES. IND.: maudis, maudis, maudit, maudissons, maudissez, mau-
dissent.

INFIN.	PRES. PART.	PAST PART.	PRES. INDIC.	PAST DEF.
Mettre	mettant	mis	mets	mis
(*put*)	mettais			misse
mettrai(s)	mette			

PRES. IND.: mets, mets, met, mettons, mettez, mettent.

se mettre, *begin*	**émettre**, *emit*	**remettre**, *put back, hand to*
admettre, *admit*	**s'entremettre**, *interpose*	**repromettre**, *promise again*
commettre, *commit*	**omettre**, *omit*	**soumettre**, *submit*
compromettre, *compromise*	**permettre**, *permit*	**transmettre**, *transmit*
démettre, *dismiss*	**promettre**, *promise*	

INFIN.	PRES. PART.	PAST PART.	PRES. INDIC.	PAST DEF.
Moudre	moulant	moulu	mouds	moulus
(*grind*)	moulais			moulusse
moudrai(s)	moule			

PRES. IND.: mouds, mouds, moud, moulons, moulez, moulent.

émoudre, *whet*	**remoudre**, *grind again*	**rémoudre**, *sharpen*

INFIN.	PRES. PART.	PAST PART.	PRES. INDIC.	PAST DEF.
Mourir	mourant	mort	meurs	mourus
(*die*)	mourais			mourusse
mourrai(s)	meure			

PRES. IND.: meurs, meurs, meurt, mourons, mourez, meurent.

PRES. SUBJ.: meure, meures, meure, mourions, mouriez, meurent.

se mourir, *be dying* (usually pres. indic. and impf. only)

INFIN.	PRES. PART.	PAST PART.	PRES. INDIC.	PAST DEF.
Mouvoir	mouvant	mû	meus	mus
(*move*)	mouvais	(*f.* mue,		musse
mouvrai(s)	meuve	*pl.* mu(e)s)		

PRES. IND.: meus, meus, meut, mouvons, mouvez, meuvent.

PRES. SUBJ.: meuve, meuves, meuve, mouvions, mouviez, meuvent.

émouvoir, *arouse* (past part. ému)   **promouvoir**, *promote* (past part. promu)
se mouvoir, *move* (intr.)

INFIN.	PRES. PART.	PAST PART.	PRES. INDIC.	PAST DEF.
Naître	naissant	né	nais	naquis
(*be born*)	naissais			naquisse
naîtrai(s)	naisse			

PRES. IND.: nais, nais, naît, naissons, naissez, naissent.

renaître, *revive*

INFIN.	PRES. PART.	PAST PART.	PRES. INDIC.	PAST DEF.
Offrir	offrant	offert	offre	offris
(*offer*)	offrais			offrisse
offrirai(s)	offre			

PRES. IND.: offre, offres, offre, offrons, offrez, offrent.

souffrir, *suffer*

Ouvrir	ouvrant	ouvert	ouvre	ouvris
(*open*)	ouvrais			ouvrisse
ouvrirai(s)	ouvre			

PRES. IND.: ouvre, ouvres, ouvre, ouvrons, ouvrez, ouvrent.

couvrir, *cover*   entr'ouvrir, *open slightly*   rouvrir, *open again*
découvrir, *discover*   recouvrir, *cover again*

Partir	partant	parti	pars	partis
(*set out*)	partais			partisse
partirai(s)	parte			

PRES. IND.: pars, pars, part, partons, partez, partent.

départir, *distribute*   repartir, *set out again*   sortir, *go out*
se départir, *desist*   ressortir, *go out again*

Peindre	peignant	peint	peins	peignis
(*paint*)	peignais			peignisse
peindrai(s)	peigne			

PRES. IND.: peins, peins, peint, peignons, peignez, peignent.

astreindre, *subject*   enceindre, *gird*   repeindre, *paint again*
atteindre, *attain*   enfreindre, *infringe*   restreindre, *restrain*
ceindre, *enclose, gird, gird*   éteindre, *extinguish*   teindre, *dye*
   on (a sword, etc.)   étreindre, *draw tight*   déteindre, *fade*
dépeindre, *depict*   feindre, *feign*   reteindre, *dye again*
empreindre, *imprint*   geindre, *groan*

Plaire	plaisant	plu	plais	plus
(*please*)	plaisais			plusse
plairai(s)	plaise			

PRES. IND.: plais, plais, plaît, plaisons, plaisez, plaisent.

complaire, *humour*   déplaire, *displease*

Pleuvoir(*impers.*)	pleuvant	plu	il pleut	il plut
(*rain*)	il pleuvait			il plût
il pleuvra(it)	il pleuve			

Infin.	Pres. Part.	Past Part.	Pres. Indic.	Past Def.
Pourvoir	pourvoyant	pourvu	pourvois	pourvus
(*provide*)	pourvoyais			pourvusse
pourvoirai(s)	pourvoie			

Pres. Ind.: pourvois, pourvois, pourvoit, pourvoyons, pourvoyez, pourvoient.

Pres. Subj.: pourvoie, pourvoies, pourvoie, pourvoyions, pourvoyiez, pourvoient.

dépourvoir, strip, leave destitute

Infin.	Pres. Part.	Past Part.	Pres. Indic.	Past Def.
Pouvoir	pouvant	pu	peux *or* puis	pus
(*be able*)	pouvais			pusse
pourrai(s)	puisse			

Pres. Ind.: peux *or* puis, peux, peut, pouvons, pouvez, peuvent.

Pres. Subj.: puisse, puisses, puisse, puissions, puissiez, puissent.

Infin.	Pres. Part.	Past Part.	Pres. Indic.	Past Def.
Prendre	prenant	pris	prends	pris
(*take*)	prenais			prisse
prendrai(s)	prenne			

Pres. Ind.: prends, prends, prend, prenons, prenez, prennent.

Pres. Subj.: prenne, prennes, prenne, prenions, preniez, prennent.

apprendre, *learn*	entreprendre, *undertake*	rapprendre, *learn again*
désapprendre, *unlearn*	s'éprendre, *be taken with*	reprendre, *take back*
comprendre, *understand*	se méprendre, *be mistaken*	surprendre, *surprise*

Infin.	Pres. Part.	Past Part.	Pres. Indic.	Past Def.
Recevoir	recevant	reçu	reçois	reçus
(*receive*)	recevais			reçusse
recevrai(s)	reçoive			

Pres. Ind.: reçois, reçois, reçoit, recevons, recevez, reçoivent.

Pres. Subj.: reçoive, reçoives, reçoive, recevions, receviez, reçoivent.

apercevoir, *perceive*	décevoir, *deceive*	percevoir, *perceive, levy*
concevoir, *conceive*		

Infin.	Pres. Part.	Past Part.	Pres. Indic.	Past Def.
Résoudre	résolvant	résolu *or*	résous	résolus
(*resolve*)	résolvais	résous		résolusse
résoudrai(s)	résolve			

Pres. Ind.: résous, résous, résout, résolvons, résolvez, résolvent.

absoudre,[1] *absolve* (p. part. **absous**)   dissoudre, *dissolve* (p. part. **dissous**)

[1] Lacks past def. and impf. subj.

Infin.	Pres. Part.	Past Part.	Pres. Indic.	Past Def.
Rire	riant	ri	ris	ris
(*laugh*)	riais			risse
rirai(s)	rie			

Pres. Ind.: ris, ris, rit, rions, riez, rient.
Pres. Subj.: rie, ries, rie, riions, riiez, rient.

sourire, *smile*

Savoir	sachant	su	sais	sus
(*know*)	savais			susse
saurai(s)	sache			

Pres. Ind.: sais, sais, sait, savons, savez, savent.
Pres. Subj.: sache, saches, sache, sachions, sachiez, sachent.
Impve.:   sache, sachons, sachez.

Sentir	sentant	senti	sens	sentis
(*feel*)	sentais			sentisse
sentirai(s)	sente			

Pres. Ind.: sens, sens, sent, sentons, sentez, sentent.

consentir, *consent*   ressentir, *resent*   démentir, *contradict*
pressentir, *forebode*   mentir, *lie*   se repentir, *repent*

Servir	servant	servi	sers	servis
(*serve*)	servais			servisse
servirai(s)	serve			

Pres. Ind.: sers, sers, sert, servons, servez, servent.

se servir, *make use of*   desservir, *clear the table*

Suivre	suivant	suivi	suis	suivis
(*follow*)	suivais			suivisse
suivrai(s)	suive			

Pres. Ind.: suis, suis, suit, suivons, suivez, suivent.

s'ensuivre, *it follows* (impers.)   poursuivre, *pursue*

Taire	taisant	tu	tais	tus
(*be silent*)	taisais			tusse
tairai(s)	taise			

Pres. Ind.: tais, tais, tait, taisons, taisez, taisent.

Infin.	Pres. Part.	Past Part.	Pres. Indic.	Past Def.
Tenir	tenant	tenu	tiens	tins
(*hold*)	tenais			tinsse
tiendrai(s)	tienne			

Pres. Ind.: tiens, tiens, tient, tenons, tenez, tiennent.

Pres. Subj.: tienne, tiennes, tienne, tenions, teniez, tiennent.

Past Def.: tins, tins, tint, tînmes, tîntes, tinrent.

Impf. Subj.: tinsse, tinsses, tînt, tinssions, tinssiez, tinssent.

NOTE. — Compare conjugation of **venir**.

s'**abstenir**, *abstain*	**détenir**, *detain*	**obtenir**, *obtain*
appartenir, *belong*	**entretenir**, *entertain*	**retenir**, *retain*
contenir, *contain*	**maintenir**, *maintain*	**soutenir**, *sustain*

Traire	trayant	trait	trais	——
(*milk*)	trayais			——
trairai(s)	traie			

Pres. Ind.: trais, trais, trait, trayons, trayez, traient.

Pres. Subj.: traie, traies, traie, trayions, trayiez, traient.

abstraire, *abstract*	**distraire**, *distract*	**soustraire**, *subtract*
attraire, *attract*	**extraire**, *extract*	

Vaincre	vainquant	vaincu	vaincs	vainquis
(*conquer*)	vainquais			vainquisse
vaincrai(s)	vainque			

Pres. Ind.: vaincs, vaincs, vainc, vainquons, vainquez, vainquent.

NOTE. — The stem **c** becomes **qu** before any vowel except **u**.

convaincre, *convince*

Valoir	valant	valu	vaux	valus
(*be worth*)	valais			valusse
vaudrai(s)	vaille			

Pres. Ind.: vaux, vaux, vaut, valons, valez, valent.

Pres. Subj.: vaille, vailles, vaille, valions, valiez, vaillent.

équivaloir, *be equal to*	**revaloir**, *pay back*
prévaloir, *prevail* (pres. subj. **prévale**, etc.)	

Vendre	vendant	vendu	vends	vendis
(*sell*)	vendais			vendisse
vendrai(s)	vende			

Pres. Ind.: vends, vends, vend, vendons, vendez, vendent.

revendre, *sell again*

INFIN.	PRES. PART.	PAST PART.	PRES. INDIC.	PAST DEF.
Venir	venant	venu	viens	vins
(*come*)	venais			vinsse
viendrai(s)	vienne			

PRES. IND.: viens, viens, vient, venons, venez, viennent.

PRES. SUBJ.: vienne, viennes, vienne, venions, veniez, viennent.

PAST DEF.: vins, vins, vint, vînmes, vîntes, vinrent.

IMPF. SUBJ.: vinsse, vinsses, vînt, vinssions, vinssiez, vinssent.

NOTE. — Compare conjugation of **tenir**.

advenir, *happen*	**intervenir**, *intervene*	**se souvenir**, *recollect*
convenir, *agree, suit*	**parvenir**, *attain*	**subvenir**, *aid*
contrevenir, *violate*	**prévenir**, *prevent*	**survenir**, *occur*
circonvenir, *circumvent*	**provenir**, *proceed* (from, **de**)	**se ressouvenir**, *recollect*
devenir, *become*	**revenir**, *come back*	
disconvenir, *be discordant*	**redevenir**, *become again*	

Vêtir	vêtant	vêtu	vêts	vêtis
(*clothe*)	vêtais			vêtisse
vêtirai(s)	vête			

PRES. IND.: vêts, vêts, vêt, vêtons, vêtez, vêtent.

dévêtir, *divest*	**revêtir**, *invest*	**se revêtir**, *dress*
se dévêtir, *undress*		

NOTE. — Instead of **vêtir** use generally **habiller**.

Vivre	vivant	vécu	vis	vécus
(*live*)	vivais			vécusse
vivrai(s)	vive			

PRES. IND.: vis, vis, vit, vivons, vivez, vivent.

revivre, *revive*	**survivre**, *survive*

Voir	voyant	vu	vois	vis
(*see*)	voyais			visse
verrai(s)	voie			

PRES. IND.: vois, vois, voit, voyons, voyez, voient.

PRES. SUBJ.: voie, voies, voie, voyions, voyiez, voient.

entrevoir, *catch sight of*	**revoir**, *see again*	**prévoir**, *foresee* (fut. **prévoirai**)

INFIN.	PRES. PART.	PAST PART.	PRES. INDIC.	PAST DEF.
Vouloir	voulant	voulu	veux	voulus
(*will*)	voulais			voulusse
voudrai(s)	veuille			

PRES. IND.: veux, veux, veut, voulons, voulez, veulent.

PRES. SUBJ.: veuille, veuilles, veuille, voulions, vouliez, veuillent.

NOTE.— The regular impve. **veux, voulons, voulez** is rare; **veuillez**, *have the kindness to*, generally serves as 2d plur. impve.

F. KEY TO LIST OF IRREGULAR VERBS

[The references are to the pages of the Alphabetical List. For the orthographical irregularities of verbs of the first conjugation, see pp. 244–246.]

A

abattre	247
absoudre	255
abstenir	257
abstraire	257
accourir	249
accueillir	250
acquérir	247
adjoindre	252
admettre	253
advenir	258
aller	247
apercevoir	255
apparaître	249
appartenir	257
apprendre	255
assaillir	247
asseoir	247
astreindre	254
atteindre	254
attraire	257

B

battre	247
boire	248
bouillir	248

C

ceindre	254
circonscrire	251
circonvenir	258
combattre	247
commettre	253
comparaître	249
complaire	254
comprendre	255
compromettre	253
concevoir	255
conclure	248
concourir	249
conduire	248
confire	248
conjoindre	252
connaître	249
conquérir	247
consentir	256
construire	249
contenir	257
contraindre	249
contredire	250
contrefaire	251
contrevenir	258
convaincre	257
convenir	258

coudre	249
courir	249
couvrir	254
craindre	249
croire	250
croître	250
cueillir	250
cuire	250

D

débattre	247
décevoir	255
déconstruire	249
découdre	249
découvrir	254
décrire	251
dédire	250
déduire	248
défaire	251
déjoindre	252
démentir	256
démettre	253
départir	254
dépeindre	254
déplaire	254
dépourvoir	255
désapprendre	255

FRENCH–ENGLISH VOCABULARY

A

à, at, to, in; **— moi**, mine; **— demain**, good-bye (till to-morrow).

a, *see* **avoir**.

abeille, *f.*, bee.

abondant, abundant, plentiful.

abord, *m.*, approach; **d'—**, at first, firstly.

abri, *m.*, shelter; **à l'— de**, sheltered from.

acajou, *m.*, mahogany.

accident, *m.*, accident.

accepter, accept.

accompagner, accompany, go with, come with.

achat, *m.*, purchase.

acheter, buy.

acier, *m.*, steel; **gravure sur —**, steel engraving.

adieu, adieu, good-bye.

admirer, admire.

adresser, address; **s'—**, apply.

affaire, *f.*, affair, thing, business; **faire des —s**, do business.

afin, in order; **— de, — que**, in order to, in order that.

âge, *m.*, age.

âgé, aged, old.

agent, *m.*, agent, policeman.

agir, act; **il s'agit de**, it is about, it is a question of.

agréable, agreeable, pleasant.

agréablement, agreeably, comfortably.

agricole, agricultural.

ai, *see* **avoir**.

aide-maçon, *m.*, mason's helper, hodman.

aider, aid, help.

aigre, sharp, sour.

aiguille, *f.*, needle.

aille, *see* **aller**.

aimable, amiable, kind, nice.

aimer, love, like, be fond of; **— mieux**, prefer; **— autant**, like as well.

ainsi, thus, so; **et — de suite**, and so forth.

air, *m.*, air, look; **avoir l'—**, look, seem; **en plein —**, in the open air.

aisé, easy; at ease, well-to-do.

algèbre, *f.*, algebra.

aller, go, go on, fit; be; **comment allez-vous?** how are you? **s'en —**, go away; **y — de**, be at stake.

allumer, light, kindle.

alors, then, so.

amener, take, bring.

américain, American.

Amérique, *f.*, America; **— du Nord**, North America.

ami, -e, *m., f.*, friend.

amusement, *m.*, amusement.

amuser, amuse, interest, entertain; **s'—**, amuse (enjoy) oneself, have a good time.

an, *m.*, year.

ancêtre, *m. or f.*, ancestor.

ancien, ancient, old, former.

anglais, English.

Angleterre, *f.*, England.

animal, *m.*, animal.

animé, animated, lively.

année, *f.*, year.

août [u], *m.*, August.

apercevoir, perceive; **s'— de (que),** perceive, notice.

appartement, *m.,* suite of rooms, flat.

appartenir, belong.

appeler, call; **s'—,** be called, be named.

appétit, *m.,* appetite; **l'— vient en mangeant,** desire comes with success, etc.

apporter, carry to, bring.

apprendre, learn.

approcher, bring near; come near; **s'— de,** draw near, approach.

approuver, approve.

après, after, later; **— que,** after.

après-demain, the day after to-morrow.

après-midi, *m. or f.,* afternoon.

arbre, *m.,* tree.

architecte [arʃitɛkt], *m.,* architect.

ardent, burning.

ardeur, *f.,* ardour, warmth.

argent, *m.,* silver; money.

argenterie, *f.,* silverware.

armoire, *f.,* cupboard.

arracher, tear (out), tear off.

arranger, arrange, place.

arrêter, arrest, stop; **s'—,** stop.

arrivée, *f.,* arrival.

arriver, arrive, come; happen.

article, *m.,* article.

artiste, *m. or f.,* artist.

as, *see* avoir.

asperges, *f. pl.,* asparagus.

asseoir, seat; **s'—,** sit down.

assez, enough; rather, quite.

assiette, *f.,* plate.

assis, *p. part. of* **asseoir,** seated, sitting.

assister, be present (at = **à**).

Atlantique, *m. or f.,* Atlantic.

attacher, tie, tie up.

attendre, wait, wait for; **faire —,** keep waiting.

attention, *f.,* attention; **appeler l'— sur,** call attention to.

attirer, attract, call.

attraper, catch.

augmenter, increase.

aujourd'hui, to-day.

auparavant, before, formerly.

auprès de, with, as regards.

aurai, *see* avoir.

aussi, also, too; **— . . . que,** as . . . as.

aussitôt que, as soon as.

autant, as much, as many.

auteur, *m.,* author.

automne [otɔn], *m. or f.,* autumn.

automobile [ɔtɔmɔbil], *m. or f.,* motor-car, automobile.

autre, other; **l'un et l'—,** both.

autrefois, formerly, once.

autrui, others.

avance, *f.,* advance; **d'—,** beforehand, too soon.

avancer, advance, go on; be too fast.

avant, before; **— de, — que,** before.

avant-hier [avɑ̃(t)jɛːr], the day before yesterday.

avec [avɛk], with.

avenir, *m.,* future.

avidement, eagerly, greedily.

avoine, *f.,* oats.

avoir, have, get; **y —,** be; **il y a,** there is, there are; **qu'avez-vous?** what is the matter with you?

avouer, confess.

avril [avri(l)], *m.,* April.

ayons, ayez, *see* avoir.

B

bagages, *m. pl.,* luggage, baggage.

baie, *f.,* bay.

baigner, bathe; **se —,** bathe.

bain, *m.,* bath.

bal, *m.,* ball, dance.

balnéaire, bathing.

baratte, *f.*, churn.

bas, low; — âge, early age.

basse-cour, *f.*, farmyard, poultry-yard.

Bastille, *f.*, Bastille (taken July 14, 1789).

bateau, *m.*, boat.

bâtiment, *m.*, building.

bâtir, build.

bâton, *m.*, stick.

battant, *m.*, leaf (*of door*); porte à deux —s, folding door.

battre, beat, thresh, churn; — des mains, clap (their) hands.

beau, bel, fine, beautiful, handsome; il fait —, it is fine (weather).

beaucoup, much, very much, a great deal; many, very many.

beau-frère, *m.*, brother-in-law.

beauté, *f.*, beauty, fine sight, beautiful thing.

Beauvais, *m.*, Beauvais, a town some 50 miles n. w. of Paris, where there is a government tapestry manufactory.

bénéfices, *m. pl.*, profit.

besoin, *m.*, need; avoir —, have need, need.

bête, *f.*, beast, animal.

beurre, *m.*, butter.

Bible, *f.*, Bible.

bibliothèque, *f.*, library, bookcase.

bicyclette, *f.*, bicycle.

bicycliste, *m. or f.*, bicyclist.

bien [bjɛ̃], well, very well; very; much, many; really, indeed; comfortable; — que, although; *as n. m.*, good.

bientôt [bjɛ̃to], soon.

bijou, *m.*, jewel.

bille, *f.*, marble (*plaything*).

billet, *m.*, ticket.

biscuit, *m.*, biscuit.

blanc, white.

blanchir, whiten; wash (*linen*).

blé, *m. s. and pl.*, wheat.

bleu, blue.

bœuf [bœf], *m.*, ox; beef; *pl.* bœufs [bø].

boire, drink.

bois [bwɑ], *m.*, wood.

boiserie, *f.*, wainscoting.

boîte, *f.*, box.

boiter, limp.

bon, good, gentle; kind (to = pour); right, suitable; sentir —, smell sweet.

bonbons, *m. pl.*, sweets, candy.

bonheur, *m.*, good fortune, happiness.

bonjour, *m.*, good day, good morning.

bonne, *f.*, servant, maid.

bonsoir, *m.*, good evening.

bonté, *f.*, kindness.

bord, *m.*, bank, shore, edge, side.

botte, *f.*, bunch.

boue, *f.*, mud.

bougie, *f.*, wax candle.

boulanger, *m.*, baker.

bouquet, *m.*, bouquet.

bouquetière, *f.*, flower girl.

bout, *m.*, end; au — de, at the end of, after (*of time*).

boutique, *f.*, shop (*small*).

bouton, *m.*, button, stud.

boutonnière, *f.*, buttonhole.

branche, *f.*, branch.

branle, *m.*, swinging, moving, movement, going.

bras, *m.*, arm.

brave, brave; good, worthy.

brique, *f.*, brick.

brosse, *f.*, brush; — à dents, toothbrush.

brosser, brush.

brouter, browse, crop, eat.

bruit, *m.*, noise.

brûler, burn.

bûcheron, *m.*, woodcutter.

buffet, *m.*, sideboard.

bulletin, *m.*, list; **— de vote**, ballot(paper).

bureau, *m.*, office.

C

ça [sa], *see* **cela**.

cabine, *f.*, cabin (*on ship*).

cacher, hide.

cadeau, *m.*, present, gift.

café, *m.*, coffee, (first) breakfast; 'café'; **— au lait**, coffee with milk. **— -restaurant**, restaurant.

cahier, *m.*, exercise book, copybook.

calculer, calculate.

cale, *f.*, hold (*of ship*).

camarade, *m. or f.*, comrade, companion.

campagne, *f.*, country.

Canada, *m.*, Canada.

canadien [kanadjɛ̃], Canadian.

canard, *m.*, duck.

candidat, *m.*, candidate.

canne, *f.*, cane, walking-stick.

capitaine, *m.*, captain.

capitale, *f.*, capital.

car, *conj.*, for.

carotte, *f.*, carrot.

carré, square.

carte, *f.*, card, map.

carton, *m.*, cardboard, cardboard box, box.

cas, *m.*, case.

cascade, *f.*, cascade, waterfall.

caser, put in place, settle.

casino, *m.*, casino.

casser, break.

castor, *m.*, beaver.

cause, *f.*, cause; **à — de**, on account of.

causer, chat.

cave, *f.*, cellar.

caviar, *m.*, caviar(e).

ce, it, this, that, he, she, they, these, those.

ce, cet, cette, ces, this, that, these, those; **— ... -ci, — ... -là**, this, that.

ceci, this.

cela, that, this; **avec —?** what next? **comment ça va-t-il?** how are you? 'how goes it?'

célèbre, celebrated, famous.

celui, celle, ceux, celles, this (one), that (one), these, those; **—-ci ... —-là**, this one ... that one, the latter ... the former.

cent, (a) hundred.

centième, *m.*, one one-hundredth.

centime, *m.*, centime ($\frac{1}{100}$ of a franc, about $\frac{1}{5}$ of a cent or half-penny).

centimètre, *m.*, centimetre ($\frac{1}{100}$ of a mètre, about $\frac{2}{5}$ of an inch).

cependant, however, still, yet.

cerise, *f.*, cherry.

certain, certain.

chaise, *f.*, chair.

chaleur, *f.*, heat.

chambre, *f.*, room; **— à coucher**, bedroom.

chameau, *m.*, camel.

champ, *m.*, field.

chandelle, *f.*, candle.

changer, change; **— d'air**, change air, take a change of air.

chant, *m.*, singing, song.

chanter, sing.

chanteuse, *f.*, singer.

chapeau, *m.*, hat.

chapitre, *m.*, chapter.

chaque, each, every.

charbon, *m.*, coal.

chargé, loaded, laden.

charmant, charming.

charmé, charmed, delighted.

charrue, *f.*, plough.

chasser, chase, hunt.

chat, *m.*, cat.

château, *m.*, castle, mansion.

chaud, *adj.*, warm; *n. m.*, warmth;

avoir —, be warm; faire —, be warm (of *weather*).

chauffage, *m.*, heating.

chauffer, warm, heat; se —, warm oneself.

chemin, *m.*, road; — de fer, railway.

chêne, *m.*, oak.

cher, *adj.*, *adv.*, dear; le moins —, the cheapest.

Cherbourg [ʃɛrbuːr], *m.*, Cherbourg.

chercher, look for, seek, search; venir —, come for; aller —, go for, go and get, go to meet.

chère, *f.*, living, cheer.

cheval, *m.*, horse; chevaux de bois, merry-go-round; à —, on horseback.

cheveu, *m.*, (a) hair; *pl.*, hair.

chez, at the house (shop, etc.) of; — lui, at his house, with him.

chien [ʃjɛ̃], *m.*, dog.

choisir, choose, select.

chose, *f.*, thing.

chou, *m.*, cabbage.

chute, *f.*, fall.

cinq [sɛ̃k], five.

cinquante, fifty.

cinquième, *m.*, fifth.

ciseaux, *m. pl.*, scissors.

citadin, *m.*, townsman.

citoyen [sitwajɛ̃], *m.*, citizen.

civilisation, *f.*, civilization.

clair, clear.

Claire, *f.*, Claire, Clara.

classe, *f.*, class, classroom.

clef [kle], *f.*, key.

Clémence, *f.*, Clementina.

client [kliɑ̃], *m.*, client, customer, patient.

clientèle, *f.*, customers; practice.

climat, *m.*, climate.

clou, *m.*, nail.

cocher, *m.*, coachman, driver.

cocon, *m.*, cocoon.

cœur, *m.*, heart.

coffret, *m.*, casket.

coiffer, dress the head (hair).

coiffeur, *m.*, hairdresser, barber.

col, *m.*, collar; pass (*in mountains*).

collège, *m.*, college, school.

collier, *m.*, necklace.

collision, *f.*, collision.

Colomb [kɔlɔ̃], *m.*, Columbus.

colonel, *m.*, colonel.

combien [kɔ̃bjɛ̃], how much, how many.

commander, order.

comme, like, as.

commencer, commence, begin; — par, begin by, firstly.

comment, how.

commode, convenient, comfortable.

commode, *f.*, bureau, chest of drawers.

commune, *f.*, municipality.

comparaison, *f.*, comparison.

compartiment, *m.*, compartment.

complet, *m.*, suit (of clothes).

complètement, completely.

compliment, *m.*, compliment.

composition, *f.*, composition.

comprendre, understand.

compter [kɔ̃te], count; expect, hope.

comtesse, *f.*, countess.

concert, *m.*, concert.

concours, *m.*, competition; — agricole, agricultural show.

conduire, conduct; se —, conduct oneself, behave.

conduite, *f.*, conduct.

confort, *m.*, comfort.

confortable, comfortable.

congé, *m.*, leave, holiday.

connaissance, *f.*, acquaintance.

connaître, know.

conquête, *f.*, conquest.

conseiller, *m.*, councillor.

conseiller, counsel, advise.

conséquent, par —, consequently.
considérable, considerable.
consommation, f., consumption.
constamment [kɔ̃stamɑ̃], constantly, often.
construction, f., construction, building.
construire, construct, build.
contenir, contain.
content, satisfied, pleased, glad.
contenu, p. part. of contenir.
continuer, continue.
cordonnier, m., shoemaker.
corps, m., body.
corridor, m., corridor, hall, passage.
corriger, correct.
corsage, m., waist, bodice.
côté, m., side; à — de, beside.
coucher, put to bed; sleep; se —, lie down, go to bed, retire.
coudre, sew.
couler, flow, run.
coup, m., blow; — d'œil, glance, view, sight.
coupe, f., cutting, cut.
couper, cut, cut down.
cour, f., yard, court(yard).
courir, run.
courrier, m., courier; mail.
cours, m., course (of lectures), lecture; faire son —, (deliver) his lecture; — d'eau, stream.
court, short.
cousin, -e, m., f., cousin.
coussin, m., cushion.
cousu, see coudre.
couteau, m., knife.
coûter, cost.
couture, f., sewing.
couturière, f., dressmaker.
couvert, m., cover (dishes, etc., for one person); tablecloth; mettre le —, lay (set) the table.
couvrir, cover.
craie, f., chalk.

craindre, fear.
cravate, f., necktie.
crayon, m., pencil.
crier [krie], cry (out), shout, yell.
croire, believe, think.
cruel, cruel.
cueillir, gather, pluck, pick.
cuiller [kɥijeːr], f., spoon.
cuire, cook, bake; faire —, cook, bake.
cuisine, f., kitchen.
cuisinière, f., cook.
cuisson, f., cooking, baking.
cuivre, m., copper; gravure sur —, copperplate (engraving).
cultivateur, m., farmer.
curé, m., parish priest, 'curé.'

D

dame, f., lady.
dans, in, into.
danser, dance.
date, f., date.
davantage, more.
de, of, from.
dé, m., thimble.
débarquer, disembark, land.
débarrasser, rid of.
debout, upright, standing.
décembre, m., December.
décoration, f., decoration.
décorer, decorate.
découvrir, discover.
décrire, describe.
défendre, defend, forbid; il est défendu, it is forbidden, it is against the law.
défricher, clear (land).
dégeler, thaw.
dehors [dəɔːr], outside.
déjà, already, yet.
déjeuner, m., breakfast, lunch.
déjeuner, breakfast, lunch, take lunch.
demain, to-morrow.

demander, ask, ask for; **se —**, ask oneself, wonder.

demeurer, live, dwell.

demi, half.

demi-kilo, *m.*, pound, half-kilogram.

dent, *f.*, tooth.

dépasser, exceed.

dépêcher, dispatch; **se —**, hasten, make haste.

dépendre, depend.

dépenser, spend.

déposer, deposit; cast.

depuis, since; **— que**, since.

dérailler, go off the track.

déranger, disturb; **se —**, disturb oneself.

déréglé, irregular.

dernier, last.

derrière, behind.

descendre [desɑ̃:dr], descend, go down; get down, alight, get out; take down, put down.

désirer, desire, wish; **laisser à —**, not be satisfactory.

désolé, sorry.

dessert, *m.*, dessert.

dessous [dəsu], underneath.

détacher, detach, unfasten; **se —**, detach oneself, come loose.

deux, two; **tous les —**, both.

deuxième, second.

deuxièmement, secondly.

devant, before, in front of.

devanture, *f.*, front (shop) window.

devenir, become.

devoir, owe; be to; ought, be one's duty.

devoir, *m.*, duty; exercise (*school*).

dictionnaire, *m.*, dictionary.

différent, different.

difficile, difficult.

difficulté, *f.*, difficulty.

diligent, diligent, industrious.

dimanche, *m.*, Sunday.

dîner, *m.*, dinner.

dîner, dine.

dire, say, tell; **se —**, say to oneself (one another); be said; **vouloir —**, mean.

disposer, arrange; **se —**, get ready.

dix [dis], ten.

docteur, *m.*, doctor; **femme —**, woman doctor, lady physician.

dois, *see* devoir.

dollar, *m.*, dollar.

domestique, *m. or f.*, servant.

dommage, *m.*, pity; **c'est — que**, it's a pity that.

donc, then.

donner, give, give away; yield; **se — la main**, shake hands.

dont, of which, of whom, whose, with which, etc.

dormir, sleep.

dos, *m.*, back.

doubler, line (*clothing*).

douleur, *f.*, pain.

douter, doubt.

doux, sweet; soft, gentle, mild.

douzaine, *f.*, dozen.

droit [drwɑ], right; **à —e**, to the right.

dû, *see* devoir.

dur, *adj. or adv.*, hard.

durer, last.

E

eau, *f.*, water.

eau-forte, *f.*, aquafortis, etching; **gravure à l'—**, etching.

ébéniste, *m.*, cabinet-maker.

échafaudage, *m.*, scaffolding.

échapper (à), escape.

échelle, *f.*, ladder.

éclairage, *m.*, lighting.

éclairer, light, illuminate, enlighten.

école, *f.*, school.

écolier, **–ère** *m.*, *f.*, schoolboy, schoolgirl.

économiser, save.

écouter, listen (to).

écraser, crush; **se faire** —, get run over.

écrier (s') [ekrie], exclaim.

écrire, write.

écureuil, *m.*, squirrel.

écurie, *f.*, stable (*for horses*).

effet, *m.*, effect; **en** —, in fact, indeed.

égal, equal; **cela m'est** —, that's (all) the same to me, I don't care.

égaler, equal.

église, *f.*, church.

eh [e], — **bien!** well! well then!

électeur, *m.*, elector.

élection, *f.*, election.

électricité, *f.*, electricity.

électrique, electric.

éléphant, *m.*, elephant.

élève, *m.* or *f.*, pupil.

élevé, high.

élever, raise, bring up; **s'**—, rise, stand; **mal élevé**, rude, impolite, ill-mannered.

élire, elect.

elle, she, it, her.

elles, they.

embarquer, put on board; **s'**—, go (get) on board, take ship.

embrasser, embrace, kiss.

empêcher, hinder, prevent.

emplette, *f.*, purchase; **faire des** —s, buy things, go shopping.

employé, *m.*, employee, clerk.

employer, employ, use.

emporter, carry off, take away; **l'**— **sur**, win the day over.

emprunter, borrow.

en, of it, of them, some; from it, from them.

en, in, at; — **même temps**, at the same time; **de . . .** —, from . . . to.

enchanté, delighted.

enclume, *f.*, anvil.

encore, yet, still, again, more.

encre, *f.*, ink.

endormir, put to sleep; **s'**—, go to sleep.

endroit, *m.*, place.

enfant, *m.* or *f.*, child, boy, girl.

enfin, at last, finally; in short.

ennui [ãnɥi], *m.*, weariness, loneliness, tedium, sorrow.

ennuyer [ãnɥije], weary, annoy; **s'**—, grow weary, feel lonely, be bored, be sad.

enrhumer (s'), catch (a) cold.

enseigner, teach.

ensemble, together.

ensuite, then, next, afterwards.

entendre, hear; — **parler de**, hear of; — **dire**, hear said; — **chanter**, hear sing (*or* sung).

entourer, surround.

entrée, *f.*, entrance, admission; 'entrée.'

entrer, go in, come in, enter; **faire** —, show in.

environ, around, about; *n. pl.*, surrounding parts, neighbourhood.

envoyer, send; — **chercher**, send for.

épais, thick.

épi, *m.*, ear (*of grain*), head.

épicier, *m.*, grocer.

équestre [ekwɛstr *or* ekɛstr], equestrian.

es, *see* être.

escalier, *m.*, stairway.

escorter, escort.

espèce, *f.*, kind, sort, species.

espérer, hope.

essayer, try, try on.

et, and.

étable, *f.*, stable (*for cattle*).

établir, establish.

étage, *m.*, story, floor.

étais, *see* être.

état, *m.*, state, condition.

États-Unis [etaz yni], *m. pl.*, United States.

été, *m.*, summer.

été, *see* être.

éternuer, sneeze.

êtes, *see* être.

étoffe, *f.*, cloth, material.

étrange, strange.

être, be; en — de, the stage one is at; y —, be in, be at home.

étroit, narrow.

étudier, study.

eu, eus, eusse, *see* avoir.

Europe, *f.*, Europe.

eux, them, they.

Évangile, *m.*, Gospel.

éviter, avoid.

exact [ɛgzakt], exact; à l'heure —e, on time.

exagérer, exaggerate.

examen [ɛgzamɛ̃], *m.*, examination.

excellent, excellent.

excursion, *f.*, excursion.

excuser, excuse; s'—, excuse oneself, offer excuses.

exécuter, execute.

exemple, *m.*, example.

existence, *f.*, existence.

exister, exist, live.

expliquer, explain.

exploiter, work.

exposition, *f.*, exhibition.

exquis, exquisite, delicious.

F

fâché, sorry, angry, annoyed.

facile, easy.

facilement, easily.

façon, *f.*, way, manner.

facteur, *m.*, postman; porter.

faible, weak.

faillir, fail; be near(ly).

faim, *f.*, hunger; avoir —, be hungry.

faîne, *f.*, beechnut.

faire, do, make, take, cause; se —, be made, happen; se — —, cause to be made for oneself; il fait beau, it is fine; cela ne fait rien, that makes no difference.

fait, *p. part. of* faire; en être — de, be all over with.

falloir, be necessary, must, have to; il faut, it is necessary, we (you, etc.) must; il ne faut pas, we (you, etc.) must not; s'en —, be near.

famille, *f.*, family.

farine, *f.*, flour.

fasse, *see* faire.

fatigué, tired, weary.

fatiguer, fatigue, tire.

faucille, *f.*, sickle.

faut, *see* falloir.

faute, *f.*, fault, mistake.

fauteuil, *m.*, arm-chair.

faux col, *m.*, collar (*detachable*).

femme [fam], *f.*, woman, wife; — de chambre, housemaid.

fenêtre, *f.*, window.

fer, *m.*, iron.

ferai, *see* faire.

ferme, *f.*, farmhouse, farm.

fermer, close, shut.

fête, *f.*, holiday, festivity.

feu, *m.*, fire.

feuillage, *m.*, foliage, leaves.

feuille, *f.*, leaf.

février, *m.*, February.

figure, *f.*, figure; face.

figurer (se), imagine.

fil [fil], *m.*, thread.

fille [fiːj], *f.*, daughter, girl; jeune —, young girl, young lady.

fils [fis], *m.*, son.

fin, *f.*, end.

finir, finish, end; — par, finish by, lastly.

fis, fisse, *see* faire.

fleur, *f.*, flower, blossom, bloom.
fleurir, flower, bloom, blossom.
fleuve, *m.*, river (*falling into the sea*).
flocon, *m.*, flake.
fluide, *m.*, fluid.
foin, *m.*, hay.
fois, *f.*, time; une —, once; toutes les — que, whenever.
fond, *m.*, bottom, back part.
fonder, found, establish.
font, *see* faire.
fonte, *f.*, cast iron.
forêt, *f.*, forest.
forgé, wrought.
forgeron, *m.*, blacksmith.
former, form.
fort, *adj.*, *adv.*, strong; hard, sharp.
fosse [foːs], *f.*, ditch; grave; pit; — aux ours, bear pit.
four, *m.*, oven.
fourchette, *f.*, fork.
fournir, furnish, supply; se —, get one's supplies, buy (provisions).
frais, fresh, cool; unsoiled.
fraise, *f.*, strawberry.
franc, *m.*, franc (*about* 20 *cents or ten pence*).
français, French.
France, *f.*, France.
frapper, knock, strike.
frère, *m.*, brother.
froid [frwɑ], cold; faire —, be cold (*of temperature*); avoir —, be (feel) cold.
fromage, *m.*, cheese.
fruit, *m.*, fruit.
fumer, smoke.
fus, *see* être.

G

gages, *m. pl.*, wages.
gagner, earn, gain.
gai [ge], gay, merry, cheerful.
gant, *m.*, glove.

garçon, *m.*, boy, waiter, journeyman.
garde, *f.*, care; prendre —, take care.
garder, keep.
gardien [gardjɛ̃], *m.*, keeper, caretaker.
gare, *f.*, station (*railway*).
garnir, trim, decorate, adorn; fill, cover.
garniture, *f.*, trimming.
gâteau, *m.*, cake.
gauche, left.
gaz [gɑːz], *m.*, gas.
geler, freeze.
gêner, embarrass; restrain; se —, restrain oneself.
généralement, generally.
Geneviève, *f.*, Genevieve.
gens, *m. or f.*, people; jeunes —, young men.
gentil [ʒɑ̃ti], nice.
géographie, *f.*, geography.
George(s), *m.*, George.
gilet, *m.*, waistcoat, vest.
glace, *f.*, ice.
glacier, *m.*, glacier.
glissant, slippery.
Gobelins, *m. pl.*, Gobelins, government tapestry works in Paris.
gorge, *f.*, throat; gorge.
goût, *m.*, taste.
goûter (à), taste.
grammaire, *f.*, grammar.
grand, tall, large, great; de — matin, early in the morning.
grand'mère, *f.*, grandmother.
grand-père, *m.*, grandfather.
grange, *f.*, barn.
grands-parents, *m. pl.*, grandparents.
grave, grave, serious.
gravement, gravely.
gravure, *f.*, engraving.
grippe, *f.*, 'grippe,' influenza.

gros, big, large.

grossir [grosi:r], grow larger.

groupe, *m.,* group.

guère, ne . . . **—,** hardly, scarcely.

guérir, get well, recover.

Guignol, *m.,* Punch and Judy.

Guillaume, *m.,* William.

H

h aspirate is indicated thus: **'h.**

habile, clever.

habilement, cleverly.

habiller, dress, clothe; **s'—,** dress (oneself).

habit, *m.,* coat; dress coat; *pl.,* clothes.

habitation, *f.,* habitation, dwelling.

habiter, inhabit, live in.

habituer, accustom.

'hache, *f.,* axe.

'hâte, *f.,* haste.

'haut, high.

'Havre, *m.,* Havre.

hectare, *m.,* hectare (*about* $2\frac{1}{2}$ *acres*).

Hélène, *f.,* Helen.

herbe, *f.,* grass.

heure, *f.,* hour; o'clock; time; **de bonne —,** early.

heureusement, fortunately.

heureux, happy, fortunate.

hier [jɛ:r], yesterday.

histoire, *f.,* history; story.

hiver, *m.,* winter.

homme, *m.,* man.

hôpital, *m.,* hospital.

'hors de, out of.

'hors-d'œuvre, *m.,* side dish, relish.

horticole, horticultural.

huile, *f.,* oil.

'huit [ɥit], eight.

humain, human.

humide, damp.

I

ici, here; **d'— là,** till then.

il, he, it; (*with impers. verbs*), there.

illustrer, illustrate.

ils, they.

image, *f.,* image, picture.

imaginer, imagine, conceive.

impatiemment [ɛ̃pasjamɑ̃], impatiently.

important, important.

importer, import; be important; **n'importe quel,** no matter what, any . . . (whatever).

industrie, *f.,* industry.

infiniment, infinitely, very much.

inflammable, inflammable.

informer (**s'**), enquire about (**de**).

instituteur, *m.,* teacher (*primary*).

institutrice, *f.,* teacher.

instruire, instruct, teach.

intelligence, *f.,* intelligence; understanding.

intelligent, intelligent.

intention, *f.,* intention.

intéressant, interesting.

intéresser, interest.

intérieur, *adj., n. m.,* interior.

inventer, invent.

invitation, *f.,* invitation.

inviter, invite.

irai, *see* **aller.**

italien, Italian.

ivoire, *m.,* ivory.

J

jamais, ever; **ne** . . . **—,** never.

jambe, *f.,* leg.

janvier, *m.,* January.

Japon, *m.,* Japan.

jaquette, *f.,* morning coat.

jardin, *m.,* garden, gardens; **— des plantes,** Botanical Gardens.

jaune, yellow.

jaunir, become yellow.
je, j', I.
Jean [ʒɑ̃], *m.*, John.
Jeanne [ʒaːn], *f.*, Jane, Joan(na).
jeter, throw, throw away.
jeu, *m.*, game, play.
jeudi, *m.*, Thursday.
jeune, young.
joie, *f.*, joy, gladness, happiness.
joindre, join; **— les deux bouts**, make (both) ends meet.
joli, pretty.
jouer, [ʒwe] play.
jour, *m.*, day; **de nos —s**, in our day(s).
journal, *m.*, newspaper.
journée, *f.*, day.
joyeux, joyous, merry.
juillet [ʒɥijɛ], *m.*, July.
juin [ʒɥɛ̃], *m.*, June.
Julie, *f.*, Julia.
Julien, *m.*, Julian.
jupe, *f.*, skirt.
jusqu'à, as far as, to, up to; **— à ce que**, until.

K

kilogramme, *m.*, kilogram (*about 2 lbs.*).
kilomètre, *m.*, kilometre (*about ⅝ of a mile*).

L

là, there.
là-bas, yonder, over there.
labour, *m.*, ploughing.
labourer, plough.
laboureur, *m.*, ploughman, husbandman.
lac [lak], *m.*, lake.
lainage, *m.*, woollen goods.
laisser, leave, let; **se — aller**, yield.
lait, *m.*, milk.
laiterie, *f.*, dairy.

lampe, *f.*, lamp.
lancer, throw, cast, toss.
langue, *f.*, tongue, language.
large, wide, broad.
latin, Latin.
laver, wash; **se —**, wash oneself.
le, la, l', les, the.
le, la, l', les, him, her, it, them.
leçon, *f.*, lesson.
lecture, *f.*, reading.
légume, *m.*, vegetable.
lendemain, *m.*, day after, next day.
lentement, slowly.
lequel, laquelle, etc., who, which (one), what (one).
lettre, *f.*, letter.
leur, leurs, their; **le —**, theirs.
leur, to them, of them, them.
levain, *m.*, leaven, yeast.
lever, raise, lift up; rise; **se —**, rise.
libre, free.
lilas [lila], *m.*, lilac; *adj.*, purple.
linge, *m.*, linen.
lion, *m.*, lion.
lire, read.
lit, *m.*, bed.
livre, *m.*, book.
livre, *f.*, pound.
locomotive, *f.*, locomotive.
loge, *f.*, box (*theatre*).
loi, *f.*, law.
loin, far.
lointain, distant.
Loire, *f.*, Loire.
Londres, *m.*, London.
long, long.
longtemps, long, a long time, a long while.
lorsque, when.
Louis, *m.*, Louis, Lewis.
Louise, *f.*, Louise, Louisa.
lourd, heavy.
loutre, *f.*, otter.
Luc [lyk], *m.*, Luke.

Lucie, *f.*, Lucy.

lui, to him, to her, of him, of her, him, her, he.

lumière, *f.*, light.

lundi, *m.*, Monday.

lunettes, *f. pl.*, spectacles, glasses.

Luxembourg [lyksãbu:r], *m.*, Luxembourg, a palace and park in Paris.

Lyon, *m.*, Lyons.

M

M. *contr. of* Monsieur.

maçon, *m.*, mason.

madame, *f.*, madam, Mrs.

mademoiselle, *f.*, Miss.

magasin, *m.*, shop, store; courir les —s, go shopping, shop.

magnifique, magnificent.

mai [mɛ], *m.*, May.

main, *f.*, hand.

maintenant, now.

mais, but; — non, no, no; not at all.

maison, *f.*, house; à la —, at home, home.

maître, *m.*, master.

majorité, *f.*, majority.

mal, *adv.*, badly; *n. m.*, evil, pain, sickness; — de mer, seasickness; faire —, hurt; se faire —, hurt oneself; — à la tête, — de tête, headache.

malade, sick, ill; sick person, patient.

malheur, *m.*, misfortune.

malheureux, unhappy, unfortunate.

malle, *f.*, trunk.

maman, *f.*, mamma.

manche, *f.*, sleeve; la Manche, the English Channel.

manchette, *f.*, cuff.

manger, eat; donner à — à, feed.

manière, *f.*, manner, way.

manquer, miss, be lacking, fail; be near.

marbre, *m.*, marble.

Marc-Aurèle [mark ɔrɛːl], *m.*, Marcus Aurelius, Roman emperor (A.D. 121–181).

Marcel, *m.*, Marcellus.

marchand, *m.*, merchant, dealer.

marche, *f.*, march.

marché, *m.*, market; (à) bon —, cheap, cheaply.

marcher, march, go, run; faire —, drive, work.

mardi, *m.*, Tuesday.

Marguerite, *f.*, Margaret.

mari, *m.*, husband.

Marie, *f.*, Mary, Marie, Maria.

marier, marry (*of parents, clergyman, etc.*); se —, get married.

marronnier, *m.*, chestnut.

mars [mars], *m.*, March.

Marseille, *f.*, Marseilles.

marteau, *m.*, hammer.

matériaux, *m. pl.*, materials.

matin, *m.*, morning.

mauvais [mɔvɛ], bad.

me, m', me, to me.

méchant, bad, naughty, cross.

médecin, *m.*, doctor.

médecine, *f.*, medicine; école de —, medical school.

Médicis (de) [medisis], de' Medici, famous Florentine family, of which two members, Catherine (1519–1589) and Marie (1573–1642), were queens of France.

meilleur, *adj.*, better, best.

même, *adj.*, same, self; lui-—, himself; *as adv.*, even; tout de —, all the same; quand —, even if.

ménage, *m.*, household, housekeeping; pain de —, homemade bread.

ménagère, *f.*, housewife.

mener, lead, take, bring.

menu, *m.*, menu, bill of fare.
menuiserie, *f.*, woodwork.
menuisier, *m.*, joiner, carpenter.
mer, *f.*, sea; port de —, seaport;
bord de la —, seaside.
merci, thanks; no, thanks.
mercredi, *m.*, Wednesday.
mère, *f.*, mother.
mérite, *m.*, merit.
merveille, *f.*, wonder; à —, marvellously, wonderfully.
mesdames, *f. pl.*, ladies (*only in
address*).
messe, *f.*, mass (*religious*).
mesure, *f.*, measure; à — que, in
proportion as.
mètre, *m.*, metre (*about* 40 *in.*).
mettre, put, place; se — en
branle, begin to move; se — à
table, sit down to dinner (etc.);
se —, dress; mis, dressed; se
— en habit, put on dress coat.
meuble, *m.*, piece of furniture; *pl.*,
furniture.
meubler, furnish.
meunier, *m.*, miller.
midi, *m.*, noon; South.
miel, *m.*, honey.
mien (le), mienne (la), etc.,
mine.
mieux, *adv.*, better, best; être —,
be better (more comfortable).
mil, thousand (*in dates*).
mille [mil], (a) thousand.
millier [milje], *m.*, (a) thousand (*ap-
proximately*).
million [miljɔ̃], *m.*, million.
mince, thin.
minuit, *m.*, midnight.
minute, *f.*, minute.
miroir, *m.*, mirror.
mis, misse, *see* mettre.
mise, *f.*, dress.
Mississipi, *m.*, Mississippi.
Mme, *contr. of* madame.
mobilier, *m.*, furniture.

mode, *f.*, fashion; à la —, in fashion,
fashionable.
modérer, moderate.
moderne, modern.
moi, me, to me, I.
moins, less, least; — bon, worse;
à — que . . . ne, unless; à — de,
unless, except; au (du) —, at
least.
mois [mwɑ], *m.*, month.
moisson, *f.*, harvest.
moissonner, harvest.
moissonneur, *m.*, harvester.
moissonneuse, *f.*, reaping-ma-
chine.
moitié, *f.*, half.
moment, *m.*, moment, time; au —
où, when; en ce —, now; du —
que, as soon as.
mon, ma, mes, my.
monde, *m.*, world; people, com-
pany; tout le —, everybody.
mont, *m.*, mount; le — Blanc,
Mt. Blanc.
monsieur [məsjø], *m.*, sir, gentleman, Mr.
montagne, *f.*, mountain.
monter, mount, ascend, go up; get
in; put up.
montre, *f.*, watch.
montrer, show.
morceau, *m.*, bit, piece.
mort, *f.*, death.
mort, *see* mourir.
mot, *m.*, word; note.
mouche, *f.*, fly.
mouchoir, *m.*, handkerchief.
moudre, grind (*mill*).
mourir, die.
mouton, *m.*, sheep.
mouvoir, move, drive.
moyen [mwajɛ̃], *m.*, means, way;
il n'y a pas —, there is no way.
municipal, municipal.
mur, *m.*, wall.
mûr, ripe, mature.

mûrir, ripen.
musique, *f.*, music.
musée, *m.*, museum.
mystérieux, mysterious.

N

nacre, *f.*, mother-of-pearl.
nager, swim.
naître, be born.
Napoléon, Napoleon.
nappe, *f.*, tablecloth (*white*); mettre la —, lay the cloth, set the table.
navire, *m.*, ship.
ne, n', no, not; — ... pas, no, not; n'est-ce pas? aren't you? etc.
né, *see* naître.
nécessaire, necessary.
négligence, *f.*, negligence.
neige, *f.*, snow.
neiger, snow.
nettoyer, clean.
neuf, new.
neuf, nine.
neurasthénie, *f.*, nervous exhaustion.
neveu, *m.*, nephew.
ni, neither, nor; ne ... — ... —, neither ... nor.
nid, *m.*, nest.
nièce, *f.*, niece.
noir, black.
noix, *f.*, walnut.
nombre, *m.*, number.
nombreux, numerous.
nommer, name, call; appoint.
non, no, not.
nord, *m.*, north.
normand, Norman.
Normandie, *f.*, Normandy.
notre, nos, our.
Notre-Dame, *f.*, Notre Dame.
nôtre (le), nôtre (la), etc., ours; *pl.*, our party, etc.
nous, we, us, to us.

nouveau, –el, new.
nouvelle, *f.*, news; *also pl.*; j'ai reçu de ses —s, I have heard from him.
Nouvelle-Orléans, *f.*, New Orleans.
novembre, *m.*, November.
noyer, *m.*, walnut.
nu, naked, bare.
nuance, [nɥɑːs] *f.*, shade, colour.
nuit, *f.*, night.

O

obéir (à), obey.
objet, *m.*, object.
obligeance, *f.*, kindness.
obscurité [ɔpskyrite], *f.*, darkness.
observation [ɔpsɛrvɑsjɔ̃], *f.*, observation.
observer [ɔpsɛrve], observe, notice.
obtenir [ɔptəniːr], obtain.
occupation, *f.*, occupation.
occupé, busy.
occuper, occupy, make busy; s'— de, be busy with, see about, attend to.
octobre, *m.*, October.
œil [œːj], *m.*, eye; *pl.*, yeux [jø].
œuf [œf], *m.*, egg; *pl.*, œufs [ø].
offrir, offer.
oh [o], O, oh.
oiseau, *m.*, bird.
oisif, idle.
oisiveté, *f.*, idleness.
ombre, *f.*, shade.
omelette, *f.*, omelet.
on, one, people, they, we, you, some one, etc.
oncle, *m.*, uncle.
ont, *see* avoir.
onze, eleven.
or, *m.*, gold.
ordinaire, ordinary.
ordinairement, generally.
ordonnance, *f.*, prescription.
ordonner, order, prescribe.

orge, *f.*, barley.
orner, decorate, adorn.
orthographe, *f.*, orthography, spelling.
oser, dare.
ou, or.
où, where, in which; d'—, whence, from where.
oublier, forget.
ouest [wɛst], *m.*, west.
oui, yes.
ours [urs], *m.*, bear.
outil [uti], *m.*, tool.
outre, beyond, in addition to; en —, also, moreover.
ouvert, *see* ouvrir.
ouvrage, *m.*, work.
ouvrier, *m.*, workman.
ouvrir, open; s'—, open.

P

paille, *f.*, straw.
pain, *m.*, bread; loaf; petit —, roll.
paire, *f.*, pair.
paix, *f.*, peace.
palais, *m.*, palace; large (public) building; — des singes, monkey house.
panier, *m.*, basket.
papa, *m.*, papa.
papier, *m.*, paper.
paquebot [pakbo], *m.*, packet, steamer.
par, by, for, through, throughout, per, in.
paraître, appear, seem.
parc [park], *m.*, park.
parce que, because.
pardessus [pardəsy], *m.*, overcoat.
pardon, *m.*, pardon; je vous demande —, I beg your pardon.
pardonner, pardon, excuse.
pareillement, equally, also.
parent, *m.*, relation, relative, parent.

paresse, *f.*, laziness.
paresseux, lazy.
Paris, *m.*, Paris.
parler, speak, talk.
parmi, among, amongst.
parquet, *m.*, floor.
part, *f.*, share; de ma —, from me.
parterre, *m.*, flower garden.
parti, *m.*, party (*political, etc.*).
partie, *f.*, part; faire — de, be part of.
partir, depart, leave, go, go away, start; à — de, from . . . on (up).
partout, everywhere; — où, wherever.
parure, *f.*, adornment, ornament.
pas, *m.*, step.
pas, not; ne . . . —, no, not, not any, none.
passage, *m.*, passage.
passé, past, last; l'année —, last year.
passer, pass, go, run; spend (*time*); go by, disappear; se —, take place, go on.
pastel, *m.*, pastel.
pâte, *f.*, dough.
patin, *m.*, skate.
patiner, skate.
pâtisserie, *f.*, pastry.
Paul [pɔl], *m.*, Paul.
pauvre, poor.
payer, pay, pay for; faire —, charge.
pays [pei], *m.*, country.
paysage [peizaːʒ], *m.*, landscape.
paysan [peizã], *m.*, peasant.
pêche, *f.*, fishing.
peigne, *m.*, comb.
peindre, paint.
peine, *f.*, trouble; valoir (être) la —, be worth while.
peintre, *m.*, painter.
peinture, *f.*, painting.
pendant, during, for; — que, while.

penser, think; be near.

perdre, lose.

perdrix, *f.*, partridge.

père, *m.*, father; — de famille, father (of a family), citizen.

perfectionnement, *m.*, improvement.

perle, *f.*, pearl.

permettre, permit, allow.

permission, *f.*, permission.

personne, *f.*, person; *pl.*, people.

personne, anybody; ne . . . —, nobody.

perte, *f.*, loss.

petit, little, small, short; young.

pétrin, *m.*, kneading trough.

pétrir, knead.

pétrole, *m.*, petroleum.

peu, little, few; un —, a little.

peur, *f.*, fear; avoir —, be afraid, fear; faire — à, frighten; de — que, for fear that; de — de, for fear of.

peut-être, perhaps.

peut, peux [pø], *see* pouvoir.

pharmacien, *m.*, druggist, chemist.

pianiste, *m. or f.*, pianist.

piano, *m.*, piano.

pièce, *f.*, piece, room; play; la —, apiece.

pied, *m.*, foot; à —, on foot.

pierre, *f.*, stone.

Pierre, *m.*, Peter.

pin, *m.*, pine.

pipe, *f.*, pipe.

place, *f.*, room, seat, place, position, berth.

plage, *f.*, beach.

plaindre, pity; se —, complain.

plaire à, please; se —, be pleased, enjoy oneself, like it; s'il vous plaît, if you please, please; plaît-il? I beg your pardon.

plaisir, *m.*, pleasure.

plan, *m.*, plan.

planche, *f.*, plank, board.

plante, *f.*, plant.

plein, full; en —e mer, in the open sea.

pleuvoir, rain.

plonger, dive.

pluie, *f.*, rain.

plume, *f.*, pen.

plupart, *f.*, majority, (the) most, the most part.

plus, more; ne . . . —, no more, no longer, not now.

plusieurs [plyzjœːr], several, a good many.

poche, *f.*, pocket.

poème, *m.*, poem.

poète, *m.*, poet.

poire, *f.*, pear.

poirier, *m.*, pear tree.

pois [pwɑ], *m.*, pea; petits —, green peas.

poisson, *m.*, fish.

police, *f.*, police.

pomme, *f.*, apple; — de terre, potato.

pommier, *m.*, apple tree.

pont, *m.*, bridge.

porcelaine, *f.*, porcelain.

pore, *m.*, pore.

port, *m.*, port; wharf.

porte, *f.*, door.

porte-monnaie, *m.*, purse.

porter, bear, carry, wear; se —, be (*of health*).

portrait, *m.*, portrait.

poser [poze], place; ask (*questions*).

poste, *f.*, post, post office.

potage, *m.*, soup.

pouce, *m.*, thumb; inch.

poule, *f.*, hen.

pouls [pu], *m.*, pulse.

pour, *prep.*, for, in order to, to; en avoir —, have so much worth of; — que, in order to, so that.

pourboire, *m.*, gratuity, 'tip'.

pourquoi, why.

pourrai, *see* **pouvoir.**
pourrir, rot, decay.
pourtant, however.
pousser, grow.
poutre, *f.,* beam.
pouvoir, be able, can, may.
pré, *m.,* meadow.
précédent, preceding.
précipiter, hurl; **se —,** rush.
précis, precise, exact.
préférer, prefer.
premier, first.
premièrement, firstly.
prendre, take, take away, catch, get, buy.
préparatifs, *m. pl.,* preparation(s).
préparer, prepare; **se —,** prepare (oneself), get ready.
près (de), near, close by; **à peu —,** nearly, almost.
présent, present; **à —,** at present, now.
presque, almost, nearly; **— pas,** hardly any.
pressé, in haste.
prêt, ready.
prêter, lend.
prier [prie], pray, ask, beg (of).
princesse, *f.,* princess.
printemps, *m.,* spring.
pris, *see* **prendre.**
prise, *f.,* taking.
prix, *m.,* price.
probable, probable.
probablement, probably.
problème, *m.,* problem.
procédé, *m.,* process.
prochain, next; **l'année —e,** next year.
produit, *m.,* product.
professeur, *m.,* professor, teacher.
promenade, *f.,* walk, drive, etc.
promener, lead about; **se —,** take a walk (drive, etc.).
prononcer, pronounce.
prononciation, *f.,* pronunciation.

propos, *m.,* remark; **à — de,** with regard to; **à —,** by the way.
propre, clean.
propreté, *f.,* cleanliness.
propriétaire, *m.,* landlord.
propriété, *f.,* property, estate.
prospérité, *f.,* prosperity.
protéger, protect.
proverbe, *m.,* proverb.
public [pyblik], public; *n. m.,* public.
puis, then, next, afterward.
puis, puisse, *see* **pouvoir.**
puisque [pɥiskə], since.
pus, pusse, *see* **pouvoir.**

Q

qualité, *f.,* quality.
quand, when, whenever.
quant à, as to, as for.
quarante, forty.
quart, *m.,* quarter.
quatre, four.
que, qu', *pron.,* what, which, that, whom; **qu'est-ce — c'est — cela?** what is that?
que, qu', *conj.,* that, than, as; how! **ne . . . —,** only; **ne . . . pas —,** not only; **je crois — oui,** I think so.
quel, quelle, quels, quelles, which, what; **— que,** whatever.
quelconque, some, some or other.
quelque, some, any; **— . . . que,** however, whatever.
quelqu'un, some one, any one.
quelquefois, sometimes.
question, *f.,* question.
qui, who, which, that, whom; **de —?** whose? **ce —,** which, what; **— que,** whoever.
quinze, fifteen; **— jours,** a fortnight; **d'aujourd'hui en —,** a fortnight from to-day.
quoi, what; **— que,** whatever.
quoique, although, though.

R

raconter, relate, tell.

radis, *m.*, radish.

raison, *f.*, reason; avoir —, be (in the) right.

ramasser, gather, pick up.

rappeler, recall; se —, remember.

rarement, rarely.

rassis, stale (*of bread*).

ravissant, charming, delightful.

rayon, *m.*, shelf; department, counter.

réaliser, realize, effect.

récemment [resamã], recently.

réception, *f.*, reception.

recevoir, receive; être reçu, pass (*at examinations*).

récolte, *f.*, crop, harvest.

reconnaître, recognize.

redingote, *f.*, frock coat.

refuser, refuse; être refusé, fail (*at examinations*).

regarder, look (at).

régime, *m.*, regimen, diet; mettre au —, put on diet.

règne, *m.*, reign.

reine, *f.*, queen.

remarquable [rəmarkabl], remarkable.

remarquer, remark, notice, observe.

remède, *m.*, remedy, medicine.

remercier, thank.

remettre, restore; se —, recover (*from illness*); remis, recovered.

remplacer, take the place of.

rencontrer, meet.

rendre, render, make.

rentrer, go back, go (come) in again, return home.

réparer, repair.

répondre, reply, answer.

représenter, represent.

reprocher, reproach, tax.

républicain, *m.*, republican.

réputation, *f.*, reputation.

résoudre, resolve, solve.

respecter, respect.

ressembler [rəsãble], resemble.

restaurant, *m.*, restaurant.

restaurer, restore.

rester, stay, remain.

rétablir, restore.

retard, *m.*, delay; en —, late.

retarder, be too slow.

retraite, *f.*, retreat.

réussir, succeed; pass (*examination*).

réveiller, waken; se —, waken.

revendre, sell again.

revoir, see again; au —, good-bye.

rez-de-chaussée [retʃose], *m.*, ground floor.

rhinocéros [rinɔserɔs], *m.*, rhinoceros.

Rhône, *m.*, Rhone.

rhume, *m.*, cold.

riche, rich; — d'un million, worth a million.

richement, richly.

richesse, *f.*, wealth.

rideau, *m.*, curtain.

rien [rjɛ̃], anything; ne ... —, nothing, not anything.

rire, laugh.

rivière, *f.*, river.

robe, *f.*, dress, gown; — de chambre, dressing-gown.

roi [rwɑ], *m.*, king.

rôle, *m.*, rôle, part.

roman, *m.*, novel.

rose, *f.*, rose.

rôti [rɔti], *m.*, roast.

rôtir [rɔtiːr], roast.

rouge, red.

rouler, roll.

roulis, *m.*, rolling (*of ship*).

route, *f.*, road; en —, on the way.

rude, harsh, severe.

rue, *f.*, street.

rugissement, *m.*, roar.

ruisseau, *m.*, brook, stream.

S

sac [sak], *m.*, sack, bag.
sache, *see* savoir.
sage, well-behaved, good.
sain, healthy, sound.
saint, *m.*, Saint.
Saint-Laurent, *m.*, St. Lawrence.
sais [sɛ], *see* savoir.
saisir, seize.
saison, *f.*, season.
salade, *f.*, salad.
salle, *f.*, hall, room; — de classe, classroom; — à manger, dining-room; — de bains, bathroom.
salon, *m.*, drawing-room, parlour; — (salle) de lecture, reading room.
saluer, salute, bow to, take one's hat off to.
sans, without.
santé, *f.*, health.
sapin, *m.*, fir, spruce.
sardine, *f.*, sardine.
sauf [soːf], safe.
saurai, *see* savoir.
sauter, jump, leap.
sauvage, wild.
savoir, know, know how to; faire —, let one know; on ne saurait, one cannot.
savon, *m.*, soap.
scène, *f.*, scene.
scierie [siri], *f.*, saw mill.
sculpter [skylte], carve.
se, s', oneself, himself, herself, themselves.
seau [so], *m.*, pail
sec [sɛk], dry.
secouer, shake.
Seine, *f.*, Seine.
séjour, *m.*, stay.
selon, according to.
semaine, *f.*, week.
semblable, similar, alike, like.

sembler, seem, appear.
semer, sow.
sénat, *m.*, senate.
sentier, *m.*, path.
sentir, feel, smell; se —, feel (*health*).
séparer, separate.
sept [sɛt], seven.
septembre [sɛptɑ̃ːbr], *m.*, September.
serai, *see* être.
sérieux, serious.
serrer, press; put away; se — la main, shake hands.
servante, *f.*, servant.
service, *m.*, service.
serviette, *f.*, towel, napkin.
servir, serve; — à, be of use for; se — de, make use of.
seul, alone, only.
seulement, only.
Sèvres, *m.*, Sèvres, a town some five miles w. of Paris where there is a government porcelain manufactory.
si, if, whether.
si, so, such; however; yes (*emphatic*); mais —, yes, it would.
siècle, *m.*, century.
siège, *m.*, seat, chair.
sien (le), sienne (la), etc., his, hers, its.
siffler, whistle.
signe, *m.*, sign.
simple, simple, plain.
singe, *m.*, monkey.
sinon, if not, otherwise.
situé, situated.
six [sis], six.
sœur, *f.*, sister.
soie, *f.*, silk.
soieries, *f. pl.*, silks.
soif [swaf], *f.*, thirst; avoir —, be thirsty; mourir de —, be very thirsty.
soigner, take care of.

soigneusement, carefully.

soir, *m.*, evening, afternoon.

soirée, *f.*, evening, evening party; — dansante, dancing party.

sois, *see* être.

soit que, whether.

soixante [swasã:t], sixty.

soleil, *m.*, sun.

sommes, *see* être.

son, sa, ses, his, her, its, one's.

sonner, ring.

sont, *see* être.

Sorbonne, *f.*, Sorbonne (founded A.D. 1257), now part of the University of Paris.

sorte, *f.*, sort, kind; de — que, so that, in order that.

sortie, *f.*, going out, leaving.

sortir, go out, come out; bring out, take out.

sou, *m.*, cent, halfpenny.

souffler, blow.

souffrant, ailing, not very well.

souffrir, suffer, endure.

soulier, *m.*, shoe.

source, *f.*, spring.

souvenir (se), remember.

sous, under, beneath, below, in.

souvent, often.

soyons, *see* être.

sport [spɔ:r], *m.*, sport.

station, *f.*, station, stand; resort; — d'été, summer resort.

statue, *f.*, statue.

store, *m.*, (window) blind.

succès, *m.*, success.

sucre, *m.*, sugar.

sud [syd], *m.*, south.

suffire, suffice.

suffisant, conceited.

suis, *see* être.

suite, *f.*, sequel, what follows, continuation; tout de —, immediately, at once.

suivant, following.

suivre, follow.

sujet, *m.*, subject.

superbe, superb, very fine.

supérieur, upper.

sur, on, upon.

surface, *f.*, surface.

surtout, above all, particularly, especially.

surveiller, oversee.

T

table, *f.*, table.

tableau, *m.*, picture; — noir, blackboard.

tâche, *f.*, task.

tâcher, try.

taille, *f.*, cutting; pierre de —, free-stone.

tailleur, *m.*, tailor.

tambour, *m.*, drum.

Tamise, *f.*, Thames.

tandis que [tãdi *or* tãdis kə], whilst.

tant, so much, so many; — que, as long as; — mieux, so much the better, I am glad to hear it.

tante, *f.*, aunt.

tapis, *m.*, carpet; tablecloth (*coloured*).

tapisserie, *f.*, tapestry.

taquiner, tease.

tard, late; plus —, later, afterwards.

tartine, *f.*, slice; — de beurre, slice of bread and butter.

tasse, *f.*, cup.

tâter, feel.

te, t', thee, to thee, you, to you.

télégraphier, telegraph.

téléphoner, telephone.

tel, telle, tels, telles, such (a).

tellement, so, so much.

température, *f.*, temperature.

temps, *m.*, time; weather; à — pour, in time to; de — en —, now and then.

tendre, tender.

tenir, hold, keep; — **de**, take after.

tente, *f.*, tent.

terminer, end, finish, complete.

terrain, *m.*, ground, lot.

terre, *f.*, earth, land.

terrible, terrible.

tête, *f.*, head.

thé, *m.*, tea.

théâtre, *m.*, theatre.

thermomètre, *m.*, thermometer.

tien (le), **tienne (la)**, etc., thine, yours.

timide, timid.

tirer, draw, derive; milk (*cows*); put out (*of tongue*).

tiroir, *m.*, drawer.

toi, thee, to thee, thou, you, to you.

toilette, *f.*, toilet; dressing table; **faire sa** —, dress; — **de bal**, — **de soirée**, evening dress (*ladies*).

toit, *m.*, roof.

tomber, fall.

ton, ta, tes, thy, your.

torrent, *m.*, torrent, stream.

tort, *m.*, wrong; **avoir** —, be (in the) wrong.

tôt, soon.

toucher, touch; — **à**, come close to, meddle with.

toujours, always, still, yet.

toupie, *f.*, top (*plaything*).

tousser, cough.

tout, all, every(thing), every one; **tous les ans**, every year; — **ce que**, whatever; **pas du** —, not at all; *adv.*, quite; however.

traduire, translate.

train, *m.*, train; **en** — **de**, busy at.

traire, milk.

traîneau, *m.*, sleigh.

tramway [tramwe], *m.*, tramway, tram(car).

tranquille [trăkil], tranquil, quiet, peaceful.

transpirer, perspire.

transporter, transport, carry, bring.

travail, *m.*, work; **table de** —, study table.

travailler, work.

travers (à), through.

traversée, *f.*, crossing; passage, voyage.

traverser, cross, run across (through).

trentaine, *f.*, about thirty.

trente, thirty.

très, very.

tressaillir, start, jump, tremble.

trois [trwɑ], three.

troisièmement, thirdly.

tromper, deceive, cheat, beguile; **se** —, make a mistake, be mistaken; **si je ne me trompe**, if I am not mistaken.

trop [trɔ *or* tro], too, too much, too many.

trottoir, *m.*, sidewalk, pavement.

trou, *m.*, hole.

trouver, find, have; think; **comment trouvez-vous cela?** what do you think of that? **se** —, be.

truite, *f.*, trout.

tu, thou, you.

tuer [tɥe], kill; **se** —, kill oneself, be killed.

tuile, *f.*, tile (*for roof*).

Tuileries, *f. pl.*, Tuileries (lit. 'tile-field'), a royal palace in Paris, destroyed in 1871, of which the gardens still exist.

U

un, une, a, an, one.

université, *f.*, university.

urne, *f.*, urn, ballot box.

ustensile, *m.*, utensil.

utile, useful.

utiliser, utilize.

V

va, vas, *see* aller.

vache, *f.*, cow.

vais, *see* aller.

vaisseau, *m.*, vessel, ship.

vaisselle, *f.*, dishes.

valise, *f.*, valise.

valoir, be worth, be good; — mieux, be better; ne — rien, be no good.

vapeur, *f.*, steam; bateau à —, steamer, steamboat.

vase, *m.*, vase.

vaste, vast, large.

vaudrai, *see* valoir.

veau, *m.*, calf; veal.

veille, *f.*, day (evening) before.

vendre, sell; se —, sell, be sold.

vendredi, *m.*, Friday.

venir, come; — à, happen to; — de, have just; faire —, send for.

vent, *m.*, wind; il fait du —, it is windy.

venu, *see* venir.

Vénus [venys], *f.*, Venus.

ver, *m.*, worm; — à soie, silk-worm.

verger, *m.*, orchard.

verre, *m.*, glass.

verrerie, *f.*, glassware.

vers, towards; about (*of time*).

vers, *m.*, verse, line (*of poetry*).

verset, *m.*, verse (*of Bible*).

vert, green.

veston, *m.*, sack coat, sacque.

vêtement, *m.*, garment; suit; *pl.*, clothes.

veuillez (*see* vouloir), be so kind as to.

veux, veut, *see* vouloir.

viande, *f.*, meat.

vice, *m.*, vice.

vie, *f.*, life; living.

vieillesse, *f.*, old age.

viens [vjɛ̃], *see* venir.

vieux, vieil [vjø, vjɛːj], old.

village, [vilaʒ] *m.*, village.

ville [vil], *f.*, city, town; à la —, in (the) town.

vin, *m.*, wine.

vingt [vɛ̃], twenty.

vingtaine, *f.*, about twenty, score.

violent, violent.

visite, *f.*, visit; en —, visiting; faire — à, visit.

visiter, visit, inspect, examine.

vite, quickly, fast.

vitesse, *f.*, speed.

vivant, *m.*, living person; bon —, 'jolly fellow.'

vivre, live, exist.

voici, see here, here is, here are, this is.

voilà, see there, there is, there are, here is, this is, that is; nous —, here we are.

voir, see; se —, be seen; faire —, show; venir —, come to see; aller —, go to see, visit.

voisin, –e, *m.*, *f.*, neighbour.

voiture, *f.*, carriage.

voix, *f.*, voice.

volaille, *f.*, poultry.

voler, fly.

voler, steal.

voleur, *m.*, thief.

volume, *m.*, volume.

vont, *see* aller.

vote, *m.*, voting.

voter, vote.

votre, vos, your.

vôtre (le), vôtre (la), etc., yours.

vouloir, will, wish, want; je veux bien, very well, all right; je voudrais (bien), I should like; en — à, have a grudge against; que voulez-vous (que j'y fasse)? what can you expect? what can be done about it?

vous, you, to you.

voyage, *m.*, journey, trip.

voyager, travel.
vrai, *adj.*, *adv.*, true, truly.
vu, *see* **voir.**

W

wagon-lit, *m.*, sleeping car.

Y

y, there, in it, at it, in them, etc.;
   il — a, there is, there are; ago;
   il — en a, there is (are) some.
yeux [jø], *see* **œil.**

ENGLISH–FRENCH VOCABULARY

A

a, an, un, *m.*, une, *f.*

able, be —, pouvoir.

about, environ, vers, à peu près autour de; **think —,** penser à; **speak —,** parler de.

absence, absence, *f.*

abundant, abondant.

accept, accepter.

accident, accident, *m.*

accompany, accompagner.

according to, selon.

account, on — of, à cause de.

accustomed, accoutumé, habitué.

ache, *n.*, mal, *m.*, douleur, *f.*

ache, *v.*, faire mal, avoir mal; **my head aches,** j'ai mal à la tête.

acquaintance, connaissance, *f.*

acquainted, be — with, connaître.

addition, addition, *f.*; **in — to,** outre.

admire, admirer.

admission, entrée, *f.*

adorn, orner, décorer.

adornment, parure, *f.*

advance, avancer.

advice, conseil(s), *m.*

advise, conseiller.

affair, affaire, *f.*

afraid, be —, avoir peur, craindre; **be much —,** avoir grand'- (bien) peur, craindre beaucoup.

after, après; après que; **— some time,** au bout de quelque temps.

afternoon, après-midi, *m. or f.*

afterwards, après, puis, ensuite.

again, encore (une fois).

age, âge, *m.*

ago, il y a, voilà . . . que.

agreeable, agréable.

agreeably, agréablement.

agricultural, agricole.

ailing, be —, souffrir, être souffrant.

air, air, *m.*

Alexander, Alexandre.

algebra, algèbre, *f.*

Alice, Alice.

alike, semblable.

all, tout, tous, toute(s); **— that,** tout ce qui (que).

allow, permettre.

almost, presque, environ, près de; **— fall,** manquer de tomber.

alone, seul.

already, déjà.

also, aussi, pareillement.

although, bien que, quoique.

always, toujours.

America, Amérique, *f.*; **North —,** l'Amérique du Nord; **South —,** l'Amérique du Sud.

American, américain.

amiable, aimable.

among, parmi.

amuse, amuser; **— oneself,** s'amuser.

amusement, amusement, *m.*

amusing, amusant.

ancestor, ancêtre, *m. or f.*

ancient, ancien.

and, et.

angry, fâché, en colère; **be (get) — at,** se fâcher contre.

animal, animal, *m.*, bête, *f.*

animated, animé.

annoy, ennuyer.

another, un autre, encore un (autre), un deuxième.

answer, répondre, répliquer.

anvil, enclume, *f.*

anxious, inquiet; be — to, tenir beaucoup à; désirer beaucoup.

any, du, etc.; quelconque; en; — of them, en.

anybody, quelqu'un; not . . . —, ne . . . personne.

anything, quelque chose; not . . . —, ne . . . rien.

apiece, la pièce.

appear, paraître.

appetite, appétit, *m.*

apple, pomme, *f.*; — tree, pommier, *m.*

apply, s'adresser.

appoint, nommer.

approach, s'approcher (de).

approve, approuver.

architect, architecte, *m.*

ardour, ardeur, *f.*

are, *see* be.

arm, bras, *m.*

armchair, fauteuil, *m.*

army, armée, *f.*

around, autour de.

arrange, arranger.

arrival, arrivée, *f.*

arrive, arriver.

article, article, *m.*, objet, *m.*

artist, artiste, *m.* or *f.*

as, comme, puisque, aussi, si, que; — well —, aussi bien que; — for, quant à; — much —, autant que.

ask, demander (à), prier; — a question, poser (faire) une question; he has only to —, il n'a qu'à demander; — after, s'informer de; — for, demander; — of one another, se demander.

asparagus, asperges, *f. pl.*

astonished, étonné, surpris.

at, à; chez; not — all, pas du tout.

Atlantic, Atlantique, *m.* or *f.*

attend, assister à.

attention, attention, *f.*; call — to, appeler (attirer) l'attention sur.

attract, attirer.

August, août, *m.*

aunt, tante, *f.*

author, auteur, *m.* or *f.*

automobile, automobile, *m.* or *f.*

autumn, automne, *m.* or *f.*

avoid, éviter.

axe, 'hache, *f.*

B

back, fond, *m.*; dos, *m.*; be —, être de retour.

bad, mauvais; be — weather, faire mauvais (temps).

badly, mal.

baggage, bagages, *m. pl.*

bake, cuire, faire cuire.

baker, boulanger, *m.*

baking, cuisson, *f.*

ball, bal, *m.*

ballot, — box, urne, *f.*; — paper, bulletin (*m.*) de vote.

bank, banque, *f.*

barber, coiffeur, *m.*

bare, nu.

barley, orge, *f.*

barn, grange, *f.*; —yard, basse-cour, *f.*

basket, panier, *m.*

Bastille, Bastille, *f.*

bath, bain, *m.*; —room, salle (*f.*) de bains.

bathe, se baigner.

bay, baie, *f.*

be, *sign of the progressive form untranslated in French*; être, se porter, aller, y avoir, se trouver, faire (*of weather*), devoir; we

are to stay, nous devons rester;
— **better,** valoir mieux.

beach, plage, *f.*

beam, poutre, *f.*

bear, ours, *m.*; — **pit,** fosse (*f.*)
aux ours.

beast, bête, *f.*

beat, battre.

beautiful, beau.

beauty, beauté, *f.*

beaver, castor, *m.*

because, parce que; — **of that,** à
cause de cela.

become, aller, convenir; devenir;
what has — of her?, qu'est-elle
devenue?

bed, lit, *m.*; —**room,** chambre
(*f.*) à coucher; **go to —,** se
coucher.

bee, abeille, *f.*

beechnut, faîne, *f.*

beef, bœuf, *m.*

before, devant (*of place*), avant
(*of time*); auparavant; avant de,
avant que.

beforehand, d'avance.

beg, prier, demander; **I — of you,**
je vous (en) prie.

begin, commencer.

beguile, tromper.

behind, derrière.

believe, croire.

belong, être à, appartenir à.

beside, près de, à côté de.

best, *adj.*, le meilleur; *adv.*, le
mieux.

better, *adj.*, meilleur; *adv.*, mieux.

between, entre.

Bible, Bible, *f.*

bicycle, bicyclette, *f.*; **on a —,** à
bicyclette.

bicyclist, bicycliste, *m. or f.*

bid, — **good morning,** dire bonjour.

big, gros.

bird, oiseau, *m.*

biscuit, biscuit, *m.*

black, noir.

blackboard, tableau (*m.*) noir.

blacksmith, forgeron, *m.*

bloom, fleur, *f.*; **be in —,** être en
fleur(s).

blossom, *n.*, fleur, *f.*

blossom, *v.*, fleurir.

blow, *n.*, coup, *m.*

blow, *v.*, souffler.

blue, bleu.

board, planche, *f.*; **go on —** (*ship*),
s'embarquer; **go on —** (*train*),
monter.

boat, bateau, *m.*; **go boating,** se
promener en bateau.

bodice, corsage, *m.*

body, corps, *m.*

book, livre, *m.*

bookcase, bibliothèque, *f.*

bore, ennuyer.

born, be —, naître; **he was —,** il
est né, il naquit.

borrow, emprunter; — **from,**
emprunter à.

Boston, Boston, *m.*

Botanical, — Gardens, jardin (*m.*)
des plantes.

both, (tous) les deux, l'un (et)
l'autre.

bouquet, bouquet, *m.*

bow (**to**), saluer; — **to each
other,** se saluer.

box, boîte, *f.*; **pasteboard —,**
carton, *m.*; (*theatre*) loge, *f.*

boy, enfant, *m.*, garçon, *m.*

branch, branche, *f.*

brave, brave, courageux.

bread, pain, *m.*

break, casser.

breakfast, déjeuner, *m.*

brick, brique, *f.*

bridge, pont, *m.*

bring, apporter, amener, transporter.

broad, large.

brother, frère, *m.*; —-in-law, beau-
frère.
brush, *n.*, brosse, *f.*
brush, *v.*, brosser.
build, bâtir, construire, faire.
building, construction, *f.*, bâtiment, *m.*
bunch, botte, *f.*
bureau, commode, *f.*
burn, brûler.
burning, ardent.
business, affaires, *f. pl.*; — man,
homme d'affaires.
busy, occupé; en train de.
but, mais; que; ne . . . que.
butter, beurre, *m.*
button, bouton, *m.*; —hole, boutonnière, *f.*
buy, acheter; — oneself, s'acheter.
by, par, de; sur; en.

C

cabbage, chou, *m.*
cabinet-maker, ébéniste, *m.*
café, café, *m.*
cake, gâteau, *m.*
calculate, calculer.
call, appeler; attirer; be called,
s'appeler; what do you — that?
comment appelez-vous cela?
camel, chameau, *m.*
can, pouvoir, savoir.
Canada, Canada, *m.*
Canadian, canadien.
candidate, candidat, *m.*
candle, (*tallow*) chandelle, *f.*, (*wax*)
bougie, *f.*
candy, bonbons, *m. pl.*
cane, canne, *f.*
capital, capitale, *f.*
captain, capitaine.
capture, prise, *f.*
care, soin, *m.*; — for, soigner; I
don't —, cela m'est égal; take
—, prendre garde; avoir soin.

carefully, soigneusement.
carelessness, négligence, *f.*
carpenter, charpentier, *m.*, menuisier, *m.*
carpet, tapis, *m.*
carriage, voiture, *f.*
carrot, carotte, *f.*
carry, porter, transporter; — off,
emporter; — the day, l'emporter.
carve, sculpter.
case, cas, *m.*
casino, casino, *m.*
casket, coffret, *m.*
cast, jeter, déposer; (*of metals*)
fondre.
cast iron, fonte, *f.*
castle, château, *m.*
cat, chat, *m.*
catch, attraper, prendre; get (be)
caught, se laisser prendre, se
faire prendre.
cause, *n.*, cause, *f.*
cause, *v.*, faire.
caviare, caviar(e), *m.*
celebrated, célèbre, fameux.
celebration, fête, *f.*
Celestine, Célestine.
cellar, cave, *f.*
cent, sou, *m.*, cinq centimes, *m.*
centime, centime, *m.*
centimetre, centimètre, *m.*
century, siècle, *m.*
certain, certain.
certainly, certainement, sûre-
ment.
chair, chaise, *f.*, siège, *m.*, fauteuil,
m.
chalk, craie, *f.*
change, changer (de).
Channel, English —, la Manche.
chapter, chapitre, *m.*
charge, faire payer.
Charles, Charles.
charming, charmant, ravissant.
chat, causer.

cheap, (à) bon marché; **cheaper,** à meilleur marché.

cheaply, (à) bon marché.

cheese, fromage, *m.*

chemist, pharmacien, *m.*

Cherbourg, Cherbourg, *m.*

cherry, cerise, *f.*

chestnut, marronnier, *m.*

Chicago, Chicago, *m.*

child, enfant, *m. or f.*

choose, choisir.

Christmas, Noël, *m.*; — **day,** le jour de Noël.

church, église, *f.*

churn, *n.*, baratte, *f.*

churn, *v.*, battre le beurre.

citizen, citoyen, *m.*

city, ville, *f.*

civilization, civilisation, *f.*

clap, battre; — **hands,** battre des mains.

Clara, Claire, Clara.

class, classe, *f.*; —**room,** classe, *f.*, salle (*f.*) de classe.

clean, *adj.*, propre.

clean, *v.*, nettoyer.

cleanliness, propreté, *f.*

clear, *adj.*, clair.

clear, *v.*, défricher.

clerk, employé, *m.*, commis, *m.*

clever, habile.

cleverly, habilement.

climate, climat, *m.*

close, fermer.

cloth, étoffe, *f.*, drap, *m.*

clothes, habits, *m. pl.*, vêtements, *m. pl.*

coachman, cocher, *m.*

coal, charbon, *m.*

coal-oil, pétrole, *m.*

coat, habit, *m.*

cocoon, cocon, *m.*

coffee, café, *m.*; — **and** (**with**) **milk,** café au lait; — **cup,** tasse (*f.*) à café.

cold, *adj.*, froid; *n.*, rhume, *m.*;

catch —, s'enrhumer; be —, (*of weather*) faire froid, (*of living beings*) avoir froid.

collar, col, *m.*; (*detachable*) faux col, *m.*

college, collège, *m.*

collision, collision, *f.*

colonel, colonel, *m.*

comb, peigne, *m.*

come, venir, arriver; — **out,** sortir; —**home,** rentrer; —**in,** entrer; — **and (to) see,** venir voir; — **near,** approcher, s'approcher; **come!** voyons! — **with,** venir avec, accompagner.

comfort, confort, *m.*

comfortable, be —, être bien, être confortable.

commit, commettre.

comparison, comparaison, *f.*

compartment, compartiment, *m.*

complain, se plaindre.

complete, terminer, achever.

completely, complètement, tout à fait.

composition, composition, *f.*

comrade, camarade, *m. or f.*

conceited, suffisant.

conceive, imaginer.

concert, concert, *m.*

condition, état, *m.*, condition, *f.*

conduct, *n.*, conduite, *f.*

conduct oneself, se conduire.

confess, avouer.

conquest, conquête, *f.*

consequently, par conséquent.

considerable, considérable.

constantly, constamment.

consumption, consommation, *f.*

contain, contenir.

contented, content, satisfait.

continue, continuer.

cook, *n.*, cuisinière, *f.*

cook, *v.*, cuire, faire cuire.

cool, frais.

copper, cuivre, *m.*

coral, corail, *m.*
correct, corriger.
cost, coûter.
cough, tousser.
could, pouvais, pourrais; I — have, j'aurais pu.
councillor, conseiller, *m.*
count, compter.
countess, comtesse.
country, pays, *m.*, campagne, *f.*; — people, paysans; — man, paysan; — woman, paysanne.
courage, courage, *m.*
court, courtyard, cour, *f.*
cousin, cousin, *m.*, cousine, *f.*
'cover,' *n.*, couvert, *m.*
cover, *v.*, couvrir.
cow, vache.
Crœsus, Crésus.
crop, *n.*, récolte, *f.*, moisson, *f.*
crop, *v.*, brouter.
cross, *adj.*, méchant.
cross, *v.*, traverser.
cruel, cruel.
cuff, manchette, *f.*
cup, tasse, *f.*
cupboard, armoire, *f.*
curtain, rideau, *m.*
customer, client, *m.*
cut, cutting, *n.*, coupe, *f.*, taille, *f.*
cut, *v.*, couper, tailler; — down, couper.

D

dairy, laiterie, *f.*
damp, humide.
dance, danser; dancing party, soirée dansante.
dare, oser.
dark, obscur; it is —, il fait obscur.
darkness, obscurité, *f.*
date, date, *f.*
daughter, fille, *f.*
day, jour, *m.*, journée, *f.*; every —, tous les jours; in our —, de nos jours; all —, toute la journée.

deal, a great (good) —, beaucoup.
dealer, marchand, *m.*
dear, *adj.*, *adv.*, cher.
death, mort, *f.*
decay, pourrir.
deceive, tromper.
December, décembre, *m.*
decorate, décorer, orner.
decoration, décoration, *f.*
delighted, enchanté.
deliver (*a lecture*), faire.
department, rayon, *m.*
depend, dépendre.
deposit, déposer.
derive, tirer.
describe, décrire.
desire, désirer.
dessert, dessert, *m.*
dictionary, dictionnaire, *m.*
die, mourir; he died, il est mort, il mourut.
diet, régime, *m.*; prescribe a —, mettre au régime.
difference, différence, *f.*; that makes no —, cela ne fait rien.
different, différent.
difficult, difficile.
difficulty, difficulté, *f.*
diligent, diligent.
dine, dîner.
dining room, salle (*f.*) à manger.
dinner, dîner, *m.*
discover, découvrir.
dish, plat, *m.*; dishes, vaisselle, *f.*
distant, lointain.
disturb, déranger.
dive, plonger.
do, *sign of emphatic form, untranslated in French;* faire, rendre; be done, se faire.
doctor, médecin, *m.*, docteur, *m.*
dog, chien, *m.*
dollar, dollar, *m.*, piastre, *f.*
door, porte, *f.*
doubt, douter (de).
dough, pâte, *f.*

downstairs, en bas; **go —**, descendre (l'escalier).

dozen, douzaine, *f.*

draw near, s'approcher (de).

drawer, tiroir, *m.*

drawing-room, salon, *m.*

dress, *n.*, mise, *f.*; robe, *f.*

dress, *v.*, faire sa toilette; s'habiller, se mettre.

dressed, mis, habillé.

dress coat, habit, *m.*

dressing table, toilette, *f.*

dressmaker, couturière, *f.*

drink, boire.

drive, *n.*, promenade (*f.*) en voiture; **go for a —**, (aller) se promener en voiture.

drive, *v.*, se promener en voiture, aller en voiture.

drop, laisser tomber.

drum, tambour, *m.*

dry, sec.

duck, canard, *m.*

during, pendant.

duty, devoir, *m.*

dwelling, habitation, *f.*

E

each, chaque, chacun, tout, tous les; **— other**, l'un (à) l'autre.

eager, désirer beaucoup, tenir beaucoup à.

early, de bonne heure; **— in the morning**, de grand matin; **at an — age**, en bas âge; **earlier**, de meilleure heure, plus tôt.

earn, gagner.

earth, terre, *f.*

easily, facilement.

easy, facile.

eat, manger.

educated, instruit.

Edward, Édouard.

effect, *v.*, réaliser.

egg, œuf, *m.*

eight, huit.

eighteen, dix-huit.

eighty, quatre-vingts.

eighty-five, quatre-vingt-cinq.

either, ou; **— . . . or**, ou . . . ou; **not . . . — . . . or**, ne . . . ni . . . ni; **nor I —**, ni moi non plus.

elect, élire.

election, élection, *f.*

elector, électeur, *m.*

electric, électrique.

electricity, électricité, *f.*

elephant, éléphant, *m.*

eleven, onze.

embark, s'embarquer.

employ, employer.

end, *n.*, bout, *m.*, fin, *f.*

end, *v.*, finir.

endure, endurer, souffrir, supporter.

enemy, ennemi, *m.*

engine, locomotive, *f.*

England, Angleterre, *f.*

English, anglais; **—man**, Anglais; **—woman**, Anglaise.

engraving, gravure, *f.*

enjoy, **— oneself**, s'amuser; se plaire.

enough, assez; **time —**, assez de temps.

enter, entrer (dans).

entrance, entrée, *f.*

equal, *adj.*, égal.

equal, *v.*, égaler.

equestrian, équestre.

escape, échapper (à).

escort, escorter.

especially, surtout.

establish, établir, fonder.

etching, (gravure (*f.*) à) l'eau-forte.

Europe, Europe, *f.*

even, même.

evening, soir, *m.*; **— dress**, toilette (*f.*) de soirée (bal); **the — before**, la veille; **good —**, bonsoir.

ever, jamais.

every, tout, chaque; — **morning,** tous les matins.

everybody, tout le monde.

everything, tout.

everywhere, partout.

exact(ly), précis, exact.

exaggerate, exagérer.

examination, examen, *m.*

example, exemple, *m.;* **for —,** par exemple.

exceed, dépasser.

excellent, excellent.

exclaim, s'écrier.

excursion, excursion, *f.*

execute, exécuter.

exercise, devoir, *m.*

exercise book, cahier, *m.*

exhibition, exposition, *f.*

exist, exister.

existence, existence, *f.*

expect, espérer, compter, attendre, s'attendre à; **what can you —?** que voulez-vous qu'on (y) fasse?

explain, expliquer.

express, exprimer.

exquisite, exquis.

eye, œil, *m.; pl.,* yeux.

F

fable, fable, *f.*

face, figure, *f.*

fact, fait, *m.;* **in —,** en effet.

fail, manquer; (*at examination*) ne pas être reçu, être refusé, échouer.

fall, *n.,* chute, *f.*

fall, *v.,* tomber.

family, famille, *f.*

famous, célèbre.

far, loin; **as — as,** aussi loin que; **how — on is he?** où en est-il? **— too,** beaucoup trop.

farm, ferme, *f.,* propriété, *f.*

farmer, cultivateur, *m.*

farmhouse, ferme, *f.*

fashion, mode, *f.;* **in the Italian —,** à l'italienne.

fashionable, à la mode.

fast, vite; **be too —,** avancer.

father, père, *m.;* père de famille.

fault, faute, *f.*

fear, *n.,* crainte, *f.,* peur, *f.;* **for — of (that)** de crainte de (que).

fear, *v.,* craindre, avoir peur.

February, février, *m.*

feed, donner à manger à.

feel, sentir, tâter; (*of health*) se sentir.

fellow, garçon.

festivity, fête, *f.*

few, peu, quelques.

field, champ, *m.*

fifteen, quinze.

fifty, cinquante.

fight, se battre.

figure, figure, *f.*

finally, enfin, à la fin; finir par.

find, trouver.

fine, beau, bel, belle; **it is —** (*of weather*), il fait beau; **—-looking,** beau.

finger, doigt, *m.*

finish, finir, terminer, achever.

fire, feu, *m.*

first, premier; **(at) —,** d'abord; **I was the — to see it,** je l'ai vu le premier.

fish, poisson, *m.*

fishing, pêche, *f.;* **go —,** aller à la pêche.

fit, aller.

five, cinq.

flake, flocon, *m.*

flat, étage, *m.,* appartement, *m.*

floor, parquet, *m.;* étage, *m.*

flour, farine, *f.*

flow, couler.

flower, fleur, *f.;* **— garden,** parterre, *m.*

flower girl, bouquetière.

fluid, fluide, *m.*

fly, *n.*, mouche, *f.*

fly, *v.*, voler.

folding door, porte (*f.*) à deux battants.

foliage, feuillage, *m.*

follow, suivre; **following,** suivant.

fond, be — of, aimer.

foot, pied, *m.*; **on —,** à pied.

for, *prep.*, pour, par, depuis, pendant.

for, *conj.*, car.

forbid, défendre.

forest, forêt, *f.*

forget, oublier.

fork, fourchette, *f.*

form, former, se former.

former, ancien; celui-là.

formerly, autrefois, anciennement.

forth, and so —, et ainsi de suite.

fortnight, quinze jours, une quinzaine.

fortunate, heureux.

fortunately, heureusement.

forty, quarante.

four, quatre.

fourteen, quatorze.

fourth, quatrième; **a —,** un quart.

franc, franc, *m.*

France, France, *f.*

free, libre.

freeze, geler.

French, français; **—man,** Français.

fresh, frais.

Friday, vendredi, *m.*

friend, ami, *m.*, amie, *f.*

frighten, faire peur à.

frock coat, redingote, *f.*

from, de; **— them,** en; **a week — to-day,** d'aujourd'hui en huit.

front, in — of, devant.

fruit, fruit, *m.*

full, plein.

fun, make — of, se moquer de, rire de.

furnish, meubler.

furniture, meubles, *m. pl.*, mobilier, *m. s.*

future, avenir, *m.*

G

game, jeu, *m.*

garden, jardin, *m.*

garment, vêtement, *m.*

gas, gaz, *m.*

gate, porte, *f.*, barrière, *f.*

gather, cueillir; **— up,** ramasser.

general, général, *m.*

generally, généralement, ordinairement.

gentle, bon, doux.

gentleman, monsieur; homme (très) comme il faut; galant homme, homme de bonne société.

geography, géographie, *f.*

George, George(s).

German, allemand.

Germany, Allemagne, *f.*

get, avoir, prendre, recevoir, obtenir, faire; **— himself . . . made,** se faire faire; **— them to come,** faites-les venir; **go to (and) —,** aller chercher; **come to (and) —,** venir chercher (trouver, prendre); **— out,** sortir; **— up,** se lever.

gift, cadeau, *m.*

girl, fille, jeune fille.

give (away), donner; (*offer*) offrir; **— back,** rendre.

glacier, glacier, *m.*

glad, heureux, content.

glass, verre, *m.*; **glasses,** lunettes, *f. pl.*

glassware, verrerie, *f.*

glee, joie, *f.*

glove, gant, *m.*

go, aller, passer, marcher, partir; **— away,** s'en aller, partir; **— with,** accompagner; **— out,** sortir; **— in (into),** entrer (dans); **— home,** rentrer, aller chez soi; — **on,** avancer; — **down,** descendre; — **up,** monter; — **near,** s'approcher (de); — **to (and) see,** aller voir; — **on,** se passer; — **for,** aller chercher; — **back,** retourner.

Gobelin, Gobelins, *m. pl.*

going out, sortie, *f.*, sortir, *m.*

gold, or, *m.;* **golden,** d'or.

good, *n.,* bien, *m.*

good, *adj.,* bon, sage; **be no —,** ne valoir rien; **will you be — enough, be — enough,** veuillez, voulez-vous bien.

good-bye, adieu, au revoir.

gorge, gorge, *f.*

gospel, Évangile, *m.*

grain, grain, *m.*

grammar, grammaire, *f.*

grandfather, grand-père.

grandmother, grand'mère.

grandparents, grands-parents.

grass, herbe, *f.*

gratitude, reconnaissance, *f.*

gravely, gravement.

great, grand; **a — deal,** beaucoup.

greedily, avidement.

green, vert.

grind, moudre.

'grippe,' grippe, *f.*

grocer, épicier, *m.*

ground, terre, *f.*

ground floor, rez-de-chaussée, *m.*

group, groupe, *m.*

grow, pousser, croître; — **large(r),** grossir.

grudge, have a — against, en vouloir à.

H

hair, cheveux, *m. pl.;* **dress the —,** (se) coiffer.

half, demi; moitié, *f.;* — **past one,** une heure et demie.

hall, salle, *f.;* corridor, *m.*

hammer, marteau, *m.*

hand, main, *f.*

handkerchief, mouchoir, *m.;* **pocket —,** mouchoir de poche.

handsome, beau.

happen, arriver, se passer, avoir lieu.

happiness, bonheur, *m.*

happy, heureux, content.

hard, dur; difficile; fort.

harvest, *n.,* moisson, *f.,* récolte, *f.*

harvest, *v.,* moissonner.

harvester, moissonneur, *m.*

haste, 'hâte, *f.;* **make —,** se dépêcher.

hasten, se 'hâter, se dépêcher.

hat, chapeau, *m.*

hatter, chapelier, *m.*

have, avoir, être, faire; — **to,** falloir, devoir; **shall — to,** il faudra; **to — made,** faire faire; **you — only to,** vous n'avez qu'à.

Havre, le 'Havre.

hay, foin, *m.*

he, il, lui; celui.

head, tête, *f.;* (*of grain*) épi, *m.;* —-**ache,** mal (*m.*) de tête, mal à la tête.

health, santé, *f.*

hear, entendre; — **say (tell),** entendre dire; — **from,** recevoir des nouvelles de; — **of,** entendre parler de; **we have heard,** nous avons entendu dire *or* on nous a dit.

heart, cœur, *m.*

heat, *n.,* chaleur, *f.*

heat, *v.,* chauffer.

heating, *n.,* chauffage, *m.*

heaven, ciel, *m.*

heavily, fort.

heavy, lourd; épais.

Helen, Hélène.

help, aider; — **oneself,** s'aider.

hen, poule, *f.*

hence, aussi, par conséquent.

Henry, Henri.

her, son, sa, ses; la, lui, elle; **hers,** à elle, le sien (etc.).

here, ici; — **is,** voici, voilà; — **he is,** le voici, le voilà.

hide, cacher; se cacher.

high, haut, élevé; cher.

him, le, lui.

hinder, empêcher.

his, son, sa, ses; à lui, le sien (etc.).

historian, historien, *m.*

history, histoire, *f.*

hodman, aide-maçon, *m.*

hold, *n.,* cale, *f.*

hold, *v.,* tenir.

hole, trou, *m.*

holiday, fête, *f.,* (jour de) congé, *m.*; **holidays,** vacances, *f. pl.*

home, maison, *f.;* (**at**) —, à la maison, chez lui (etc.); **make yourself at** —, ne vous gênez pas.

homemade, — **bread,** pain (*m.*) de ménage.

honey, miel, *m.*

hope, espérer, compter.

horse, cheval, *m.;* **on** —**back,** à cheval.

horticultural, horticole.

hospital, hôpital, *m.*

hot, chaud.

hour, heure, *f.*

house, maison, *f.;* ménage, *m.;* **at the** — **of,** chez; —**maid,** femme de chambre; —**wife,** ménagère.

household, ménage, *m.*

how, comment? comme! que! — **many,** — **much,** combien?

however, cependant, pourtant; quelque . . . que; — **it may be,** quoi qu'il en soit.

human, humain.

hundred (**a**), cent; **about a** —, une centaine.

hunger, faim, *f.*

hungry, be —, avoir faim.

hunt, chasser.

hurt, faire mal à; — **oneself,** se faire mal.

husband, mari.

I

I, je, moi.

ice, glace, *f.*

idle, oisif, paresseux.

idleness, oisiveté, *f.*

if, si; (*before* il, ils) s'.

ill, malade.

ill-mannered, mal élevé.

illustrate, illustrer.

imagine, se figurer.

impatiently, impatiemment.

import, importer.

important, important; **it is** —, il importe, il est important.

impossible, impossible.

improvement, perfectionnement, *m.*

in, dans, en, à, de; — **it** (**them**), y; **to be** —, y être.

inch, pouce, *m.*

increase, augmenter; **keeps increasing,** va en augmentant.

indeed, bien, en effet.

industrious, diligent.

inflammable, inflammable.

influenza, grippe, *f.*

inform, informer, faire savoir.

inhabit, habiter.

ink, encre, *f.*

inquire, s'informer.

instruct, instruire.

intelligence, intelligence, *f.*

intelligent, intelligent.

intend, avoir l'intention de.

interest, intéresser.

interesting, intéressant.

interior, intérieur, *m.*

into, dans, en.

introduce, présenter.

invent, inventer, imaginer.

invitation, invitation, *f.*

invite, inviter.

iron, fer, *m.*
irregular, déréglé.
is, *see* be.
it, il, elle; le, la; cela; ce.
Italian, italien.
its, son, sa, ses.
ivory, ivoire, *m.*

J

James, Jacques.
Jane, Jeanne.
January, janvier, *m.*
jewel, bijou, *m.*
John, Jean.
join, joindre.
joiner, menuisier, *m.*
'jolly fellow,' bon vivant, *m.*
journey, voyage, *m.*
joy, joie, *f.*
Julian, Julien.
July, juillet, *m.*
jump, sauter.
just, seulement; **have —,** venir
de; **have — come,** venir d'arriver.

K

keep, tenir, garder; **— house,**
faire le ménage; **— to the house,**
garder la maison.
keeper, gardien, *m.*
key, clef, *f.*
kill, tuer.
kilo, *contr.* of kilogramme (*about*
2 *lbs.*).
kilometre, kilomètre, *m.*
kind, *n.*, espèce, *f.*, sorte, *f.*; **what
— of weather is it?** quel temps
fait-il?
kind, *adj.*, aimable, bon; **— to,**
bon pour.
kindly, **will you —,** veuillez (bien),
ayez la bonté de.
kindness, bonté, obligeance, *f.*
king, roi.

kiss, embrasser.
kitchen, cuisine, *f.*
knead, pétrir.
kneading trough, pétrin, *m.*
knife, couteau, *m.*
knock, frapper.
know, connaître, savoir; **— how to,**
savoir.

L

ladder, échelle, *f.*
laden, chargé.
lady, dame; **ladies,** dames, mesdames; **young ladies,** demoi-
selles, jeunes filles.
lake, lac, *m.*
lamp, lampe, *f.*
land, *n.*, terre, *f.*
land, *v.*, débarquer.
landlord, propriétaire, *m. or f.*
landscape, paysage, *m.*
language, langue, *f.*
large, grand, gros; **grow —,**
grossir.
last, *adj.*, dernier, passé; **at —,** à
la fin, enfin; **— year,** l'année
passée (dernière).
last, *v.*, durer.
late, tard, en retard; **later,** plus
tard.
Latin, latin, *m.*
latter, dernier; celui-ci.
laugh, rire.
law, loi, *f.*; **against the —,** défendu.
lay, placer, poser; **— the cloth,**
mettre le couvert.
laziness, paresse, *f.*
lazy, paresseux.
lead, mener.
leaf, feuille, *f.*; **leaves,** feuilles, *pl.*,
feuillage, *m.*
leap-year, année (*f.*) bissextile.
learn, apprendre.
least, *adj.*, moindre; *adv.*, moins;
at —, au (du) moins.
leave, laisser; partir (de); quitter.

lecture, cours, *m.*

left, gauche; **on the —,** à (la) gauche.

leg, jambe, *f.*

lend, prêter.

less, moins.

lesson, leçon, *f.,* devoir, *m.*

let, laisser, faire; (*with impve.*) que; **— us go,** partons; **— him go,** qu'il parte; **— us sit down,** asseyons-nous.

letter, lettre, *f.*

library, bibliothèque, *f.*

lie, être couché; **— down,** se coucher.

life, vie, *f.*

light, *n.,* lumière, *f.*

light, *adj.,* léger; **lighter,** plus léger, moins lourd.

light, *v.,* éclairer; (*kindle*) allumer.

lighting, *n.,* éclairage, *m.*

like, *v.,* aimer; vouloir, trouver, se plaire; **I should —,** je voudrais (bien); **— better (best),** aimer mieux.

like, *adv.,* comme.

likewise, pareillement.

limp, boiter.

line, *n.,* ligne, *f.*; (*of poetry*) vers, *m.*

line, *v.,* doubler.

linen, linge, *m.*

lion, lion, *m.*

listen (to), écouter.

little, *adj.,* petit; *adv.,* peu.

live, vivre; demeurer; **— (in),** habiter; **— on,** vivre de.

living, vie, *f.*; **good —,** bonne chère, *f.*

loaf (of bread), pain, *m.*

Loire, Loire, *f.*

London, Londres, *m.*

lonesome, be **—,** s'ennuyer.

long, long, longtemps; **a — time,** longtemps; **no longer,** ne . . . plus; **how —?,** depuis quand? **as — as,** tant que; **be —,** tarder.

look (at), regarder; **— for,** chercher; **they** (*f.*) **— gentle,** elles ont l'air douces.

loose, détaché; **become —,** se détacher.

lose, perdre.

loss, perte, *f.*

lot, terrain, *m.*

Louis, Lewis, Louis.

Louisa, Louise.

Louvre, Louvre, *m.*

love, aimer; **— one another,** s'aimer.

low, bas.

lower, *v. tr.,* descendre.

Lucy, Lucie.

luggage, bagages, *m. pl.*

Luke, Luc.

lunch, *n.,* déjeuner, *m.*

lunch, *v.,* déjeuner.

Luxembourg, Luxembourg, *m.*

Lyons, Lyon, *m.*

M

madam, madame.

magnificent, magnifique.

mahogany, acajou, *m.*

maid, bonne, *f.,* servante, *f.,* domestique, *f.*

mail, courrier, *m.*

majority, majorité, *f.*

make, faire, rendre; **have made for oneself,** se faire faire; **is made of,** fait de (en).

mamma, maman.

man, homme; **young men,** jeunes gens.

manner, manière, *f.*; **—-of-living,** vie, *f.*

many, beaucoup; **a great (good) —,** beaucoup de; bien des; **as — as,** autant.

map, carte, *f.*

marble, marbre, *m.*; (*for playing*) bille, *f.*

march, marche, *f.*

Marcus Aurelius, Marc-Aurèle.

Margaret, Marguerite.

market, marché, *m.*

marriage, mariage, *m.*

marry, marier (*of parents and officials*), épouser (*of contracting parties*); **be (get) married,** se marier.

Marseilles, Marseille, *f.*

Mary, Marie.

mason, maçon, *m.*

mass, messe, *f.*

master, maître, *m.,* professeur, *m.*

material, étoffe, *f.;* matériaux, *m. pl.*

matter, affaire, *f.;* **it is a — of,** il s'agit de; **what is the — with you?** qu'avez-vous? **no — which,** n'importe lequel.

mature, mûr.

May, *n.* mai, *m.*

may, *v.* pouvoir; **it — be,** il se peut.

me, me, moi.

meadow, pré, *m.*

mean, vouloir dire.

meaning, signification, *f.*

means, moyen, *m.*

measure, mesure, *f.*

meat, viande, *f.*

medicine, médecine, *f.;* remède, *m.*

meet, rencontrer; **— each other,** se rencontrer; **make (both) ends —,** joindre les deux bouts.

mention, mentionner, parler de; **don't — it,** il n'y a pas de quoi.

menu, menu, *m.*

merchant, marchand, *m.*

merit, mérite, *m.*

merry, gai, joyeux.

merry-go-round, chevaux (*m. pl.*) de bois.

metre, mètre, *m.*

midnight, minuit, *m.*

mild, doux.

milk, *n.,* lait, *m.*

milk, *v.,* tirer, traire.

miller, meunier, *m.*

mind, never —, n'importe.

mine, à moi, le mien; **a friend of —,** un de mes amis.

minute, minute, *f.,* moment, *m.*

mirror, miroir, *m.*

misfortune, malheur, *m.*

Miss, *n.,* mademoiselle.

miss, *v.,* manquer.

Mississippi, Mississipı, *m.*

mistake, erreur, *f.;* **make —(s),** se tromper.

mistaken, be —, se tromper; **if I am not —,** si je ne me trompe.

moderate, modérer.

modern, moderne.

moment, moment, *m.*

Monday, lundi, *m.*

money, argent, *m.*

monkey, singe, *m.*

month, mois, *m.*

Montreal, Montréal, *m.*

more, encore, plus, davantage; **any —,** encore; **no —,** ne . . . plus; **some —,** encore; **the — . . . the — . . .,** plus . . . plus.

morning, matin, *m.;* **— coat,** jaquette, *f.;* **good —,** bonjour.

most, le plus, la plupart de.

mother, mère, *f.*

mother-of-pearl, nacre, *f.*

motor-car, automobile, *m. or f.*

mountain, montagne, *f.*

move, remuer, mouvoir; se mettre en branle.

Mr., Monsieur (*contr.* M.).

Mrs., Madame (*contr.* Mme).

Mt. Blanc, le mont Blanc.

much, beaucoup; **very —,** beaucoup, bien; **as — as,** autant que; **so —,** tant, tellement.

mud, boue, *f.*

muddy, be —, faire de la boue.

municipal, municipal.

municipality, commune, *f.*

museum, musée, *m.*

music, musique, *f.*

must, falloir, devoir; we —, il nous faut, il faut que nous, nous devons; — not, il ne faut pas; — have been, a dû être.

my, mon, ma, mes.

myself, moi-même.

mysterious, mystérieux.

N

nail, clou, *m.*

name, *n.*, nom, *m.*; what is his —?, comment s'appelle-t-il? my — is, je m'appelle.

name, *v.*, nommer.

Napoleon, Napoléon.

narrow, étroit.

naughty, méchant.

near, près (de); be (come) —, manquer de, penser, faillir, s'en falloir de peu.

nearly, à peu près, près de, presque; I — fell, j'ai manqué de tomber.

necessary, nécessaire; be —, être nécessaire, falloir.

necklace, collier, *m.*

necktie, cravate, *f.*

need, avoir besoin de; il faut.

needle, aiguille, *f.*

neighbour, voisin, *m.*

neighbourhood, environs, *m. pl.*

neither, ni; — . . . nor, ne . . . ni . . . ni.

nephew, neveu.

nest, nid, *m.*

never, ne . . . jamais.

new, neuf, nouveau.

newly, récemment; — married couple, les nouveaux mariés.

New Orleans, la Nouvelle-Orléans.

news, nouvelle(s), *f.*

newspaper, journal, *m.*

New Year's Day, le jour de l'An.

New York, New-York.

next, ensuite, puis; prochain; what —? et avec ça? the — day, le lendemain.

nice, gentil, aimable.

niece, nièce.

night, nuit, *f.*; last —, hier au soir, cette nuit.

nine, neuf.

nineteen, dix-neuf.

ninety, quatre-vingt-dix.

no, non; mais non; ne . . . pas; — letter, pas de lettre; — one, personne.

nobody, ne . . . personne; personne.

noise, bruit, *m.*

none, ne . . . aucun (pas un); aucun; pas; there are — now, il n'y en a plus.

noon, midi, *m.*

nor, ni; — I either, ni moi non plus.

Norman, normand.

Normandy, Normandie, *f.*

north, nord, *m.*

not, ne . . . pas, non; is it —? n'est-ce pas? — one, pas un(e); — at all, pas du tout.

note, billet, *m.*, mot, *m.*

nothing, ne . . . rien, rien; — but, rien que.

notice, observer, remarquer.

Notre Dame, Notre-Dame.

novel, roman, *m.*

now, maintenant; à présent; — and then, de temps en temps; —adays, de nos jours; not —, ne . . . plus.

number, nombre, *m.*, numéro, *m.*

numerous, nombreux.

O

oak, chêne, *m.*

oats, avoine, *f. s.*

obey, obéir à.

object, objet, *m.*

obliged, obligé; **he was —,** il a dû.

observation, observation, *f.*

observe, observer, remarquer.

obtain, obtenir.

occupation, occupation, *f.*

occur, arriver, se faire.

o'clock, heure(s), *f.*

of, de; **— it (them),** en; **— the,** du (etc.).

offer, offrir.

office, bureau, *m.*

often, souvent.

oil, huile, *f.*; **— lamp,** lampe (*f.*) à huile; **— painting,** peinture (*f.*) à l'huile.

old, vieux, âgé; **she is more than three years —,** elle a plus de trois ans; **how — is he?** quel âge a-t-il? **— age,** vieillesse, *f.*

omelet, omelette, *f.*

on, sur, dans; de.

once, une fois; **at —,** tout de suite.

one, un, *m.,* une, *f.;* on; **the —,** celui (celle); **this —,** celui-ci; **that —,** celui-là; **the white ones,** les blancs.

onion, oignon, *m.*

only, ne . . . que, seulement; seul.

open, ouvrir, s'ouvrir; **— p. part.** ouvert; **in the — air,** en plein air.

opposite, en face de.

or, ou.

orchard, verger, *m.*

order, in — that, pour que, de sorte que, afin que; **in — to,** pour, afin de.

order, *v.,* commander, ordonner.

ordinary, ordinaire.

other, autre; **others,** les autres, d'autres.

otter, loutre, *f.*

ought, one —, on devrait; **he — not to have,** il n'aurait pas dû.

our, notre, nos; **ours,** à nous, le nôtre (etc.)

out of, hors de.

outside (of it), dehors.

oven, four, *m.*

over, par; au-dessus de.

overcoat, pardessus, *m.*

oversee, surveiller.

owe, devoir.

own, propre, à lui; **my —,** le mien.

ox, bœuf.

P

page, page, *f.*

pail, seau, *m.*

pain, douleur, *f.,* mal, *m.*

paint, peindre; **— in oils,** peindre à l'huile.

painter, peintre.

painting, peinture, *f.,* tableau, *m.*

pair, paire, *f.*

palace, palais, *m.*

papa, papa.

paper, papier, *m.*

pardon, *n.,* pardon, *m.;* **I beg your —,** je vous demande pardon.

pardon, *v.,* pardonner.

parent, parent, *m.*

Paris, Paris, *m.*

Parisian, parisien.

(parish) priest, curé.

park, parc, *m.,* jardin, *m.*

parlour, salon, *m.*

part, rôle, *m.,* partie, *f.;* **the most —,** la plupart, la plus grande partie.

partridge, perdrix, *f.*

party, soirée, *f.;* parti, *m.;* **our —,** les nôtres.

pass, *n.,* (*of mountains*) col, *m.*

pass, *v.,* passer; (*at examination*) réussir, être reçu.

passage, passage, *m.;* traversée, *f.;* corridor, *m.*

past, passé.

pastel, pastel, *m.*

pastry, pâtisserie, *f.*

path, sentier, *m.*

patient, malade, *m.* or *f.*

pay (for), payer; — a visit, faire une visite.

pea, pois, *m.*; green peas, petits pois.

peace, paix, *f.*

pear, poire, *f.*; — tree, poirier, *m.*

pearl, perle, *f.*

peasant, paysan, *m.*

pebble, caillou, *m.*

pen, plume, *f.*

pencil, crayon, *m.*

people, peuple, *m.*; personnes, *f. pl.*, gens, *m.* or *f.*; on, monde, *m.*

perceive, apercevoir, s'apercevoir de.

perhaps, peut-être (que).

permission, permission, *f.*

permit, permettre.

person, personne, *f.*

perspire, transpirer.

Peter, Pierre.

petroleum, pétrole, *m.*

pianist, pianiste, *m.* or *f.*

piano, piano, *m.*

pick, cueillir; — up, ramasser.

picture, image, *f.*, tableau, *m.*

piece, morceau, *m.*; (*of money*) pièce, *f.*

pine, pin, *m.*

pipe, pipe, *f.*

pit, fosse, *f.*

pity, *n.*, dommage, *m.*; pitié, *f.*; what a —, quel dommage.

pity, *v.*, plaindre.

place, *n.*, endroit, *m.*, place, *f.*, lieu, *m.*; take — of, remplacer; take —, avoir lieu.

place, *v.*, placer, poser, mettre.

plain, simple.

plan, plan, *m.*

plank, planche, *f.*

plant, planter.

plate, assiette, *f.*

play, *n.*, pièce, *f.*; go to the —, aller au théâtre.

play, *v.*, jouer; — on the piano, jouer du piano.

pleasant, agréable; (*of weather*) beau.

please, plaire à; if you —, please, s'il vous plaît.

pleased, content.

pleasure, plaisir, *m.*

plenty, assez de, beaucoup de.

plough, *n.*, charrue, *f.*

plough, *v.*, labourer.

ploughing, *n.*, labour, *m.*

ploughman, laboureur, *m.*

p.m., du soir.

pocket, poche, *f.*

poem, poème, *m.*

poet, poète, *m.*

police, police, *f.*; —man, agent (de police).

politeness, politesse, *f.*

poor, pauvre.

porcelain, porcelaine, *f.*

pore, pore, *m.*

port, port, *m.*

porter, facteur.

portrait, portrait, *m.*

position, place, *f.*, poste, *m.*

possible, possible.

postman, facteur.

post office, poste, *f.*

potato, pomme (*f.*) de terre.

poultry, volaille, *f.*

pound, livre, *f.*

practice, clientèle, *f.*

preceding, précédent.

precise(ly), précis.

prefer, préférer, aimer mieux.

preparation(s), préparatifs, *m. pl.*

prepare, préparer; se préparer.

prescribe, ordonner.

prescription, ordonnance, *f.*

present, cadeau, *m.*, présent, *m.*; at —, à présent; be —, assister, être présent.

pretty, joli.
prevent, empêcher.
price, prix, *m.*
priest, prêtre, curé.
princess, princesse.
prize, prix, *m.*
probable, probable.
probably, probablement.
problem, problème, *m.*
process, procédé, *m.*
product, produit, *m.*
professor, professeur, *m. or f.*
profit(s), bénéfices, *m. pl.*; **make —**, tirer des bénéfices.
promise, promettre.
property, propriété, *f.*
proportion, proportion, *f.*; **in — as**, à mesure que.
prosperity, prospérité, *f.*
protect, protéger.
proverb, proverbe, *m.*
provisions, vivres, *m. pl.*; **get —**, se fournir.
public, *n.*, public, *m.*
public, *adj.*, public.
pulse, pouls, *m.*
Punch and Judy, Guignol, *m.*
pupil, élève, *m. or f.*
purchase, achat, *m.*
purple, lilas.
purse, porte-monnaie, *m.*
put, mettre, placer; **— on**, mettre; **— away (in)**, serrer; **— in place**, caser; **— in**, y mettre; **— out**, éteindre.

Q

quality, qualité, *f.*
quarter, quart, *m.*; quinze minutes, *f.*; **at a — past one**, à une heure (et) un quart; **at a — to one**, à une heure moins le (un) quart.
queen, reine, *f.*
question, question, *f.*

quickly, vite.
quiet, tranquille; **be, become —**, se taire.
quite, assez, tout à fait, très, bien.

R

radish, radis, *m.*
railroad, **railway**, chemin (*m.*) de fer.
rain, *n.*, pluie, *f.*
rain, *v.*, pleuvoir.
rarely, rarement.
rather, assez; **I would —**, j'aimerais mieux.
read, lire.
reading, lecture, *f.*; **— room** (salle, *f.*) *or* salon (*m.*) de lecture.
ready, prêt; fait; **get —**, se disposer.
reap, moissonner.
reaping machine, moissonneuse, *f.*
reason, raison, *f.*, motif, *m.*
receive, recevoir.
recently, récemment.
reception, réception, *f.*
recognize, reconnaître.
recover, se remettre, se rétablir, guérir.
recovered, remis, rétabli.
red, rouge.
reflect, réfléchir.
refuse, refuser.
regard, **with — to**, à propos de.
regret, regretter.
reign, *n.*, règne, *m.*
reign, *v.*, régner.
relate, raconter.
relation, **relative**, parent, *m.*
relish, 'hors-d'œuvre, *m.*
remain, rester.
remarkable, remarquable.
remember, se rappeler, se souvenir de, retenir.
render, rendre.
repair, réparer.

reply, répondre, répliquer.
represent, représenter.
republican, républicain, *m.*
reputation, réputation, *f.*
required, is —, il faut.
resemble, ressembler (à).
resort, station, *f.*; **summer —**, station d'été.
respect, respecter.
rest, the —, le reste; les autres.
restaurant, restaurant, *m.*
restore, restaurer, remettre, rétablir.
retreat, retraite, *f.*
return, *n.*, retour, *m.*
return, *v.*, revenir (*come back*), retourner (*go back*); **— home**, rentrer (chez soi).
rhinoceros, rhinocéros, *m.*
Rhone, Rhône, *m.*
rich, riche.
richly, richement.
ride, go for (take) a —, se promener à cheval.
right, droit, *m.*; raison, *f.*; (*of time*) à l'heure; **on the —**, à (la) droite; **he is (in the) —**, il a raison.
ring, sonner.
ripe, mûr.
ripen, mûrir.
rise, se lever, s'élever; lever.
river, rivière, *f.*; (*falling into the sea*) fleuve, *m.*
road, chemin, *m.*, route, *f.*
roaring, rugissement, *m.*
roast, *n.*, rôti, *m.*
roast, *v.*, rôtir.
robbery, vol, *m.*
Robert, Robert.
rôle, rôle, *m.*
roll, *n.*, petit pain, *m.*
roll, *v.*, rouler.
rolling, *n.*, roulis, *m.*
roof, toit, *m.*
room, pièce, *f.*, salle, *f.*, chambre, *f.*
rose, rose, *f.*

rule, règle, *f.*
run, courir, marcher; (*of liquids*) couler; **— off the track**, dérailler; **get — over**, se faire écraser.
rush, se précipiter.

S

sack, sac, *m.*
sack coat, veston, *m.*
safe, sauf; **— and sound**, sain et sauf.
saint, saint, *m.*
salad, salade, *f.*
salute, saluer; **— each other**, se saluer.
same, même; **at the — time**, en même temps; **it is all the — to me**, cela m'est égal.
sand, sable, *m.*
sardine, sardine, *f.*
satisfactory, satisfaisant; **not be —**, laisser à désirer.
satisfied, satisfait, content.
Saturday, samedi, *m.*
save, économiser, épargner.
sawmill, scierie, *f.*
say, dire; **they —**, on dit.
scaffolding, échafaudage, *m.*
scene, scène, *f.*
scholar, écolier, –ère.
school, école, *f.*, collège, *m.*; **at —**, à l'école; **—boy**, écolier; **—girl**, écolière.
scissors, ciseaux, *m. pl.*
score, vingtaine, *f.*
sea, mer, *f.*; **—port**, port (*m.*) de mer; **be —sick**, avoir le mal de mer.
seashore, bord de la mer.
seaside resort, station (*f.*) balnéaire, bains (*m.*) de mer.
season, saison, *f.*
seat, place, *f.*, siège, *m.*, banc, *m.*
seated, be —, s'asseoir, être assis.
second, deuxième, second; deux.

see, voir; **be seen**, se voir; — **about** (after), s'occuper de; — **each other**, se voir.

seek, chercher.

seem, sembler, paraître.

Seine, Seine, *f.*

seize, saisir.

select, choisir.

sell, vendre, se vendre; — **again**, revendre.

senate, sénat, *m.*

send, envoyer; — **for**, envoyer chercher, faire venir.

separate, séparer.

serious, grave, sérieux.

servant, bonne, *f.*, servante, *f.*, domestique, *m. or f.*

serve, servir.

service, service, *m.*

set, mettre; — **out**, partir; — **the table**, mettre la nappe (le couvert).

seven, sept.

seventeen, dix-sept.

seventy, soixante-dix.

seventy-five, soixante-quinze.

several, plusieurs.

severe, rude.

sew, coudre.

sewing, couture, *f.*

shade, nuance, *f.*; ombre, *f.*; **in the —**, à l'ombre.

shake, secouer; — **hands**, se donner la main, se serrer la main.

shall, *sign of fut.;* **what — I do?** que voulez-vous que je fasse?

she, elle, ce.

sheep, mouton, *m.*

shelter, abri, *m.*; **sheltered from**, à l'abri de.

ship, navire, *m.*, vaisseau, *m.*

shoe, soulier, *m.*

shoemaker, cordonnier, *m.*

shop, magasin, *m.*, boutique, *f.*; **at the — of**, chez; **go shopping**, faire des emplettes, courir les magasins.

shore, bord, *m.*, côte, *f.*; **go on —**, débarquer.

short, court.

should, *sign of condl.;* **one —** devrait; **you — have**, vous auriez dû.

shout, crier.

show, *n.*, concours, *m.*

show, *v.*, montrer; faire voir; — **in**, faire entrer; — **up(stairs)**, faire monter.

shut, fermer.

sick, malade; — **people**, malades.

sickle, faucille, *f.*

side, côté, *m.*; **by the — of**, à côté de.

sideboard, buffet, *m.*

sidewalk, trottoir, *m.*

sight, vue, *f.*, coup (*m.*) d'œil; **fine sights**, beautés, *f. pl.*

sign, signe, *m.*

silk, soie, *f.*; —**worm**, ver (*m.*) à soie; — **dress**, robe (*f.*) de soie; — **goods**, soieries *f. pl.*; —**room**, salon (*m.*) des soieries.

silver, argent, *m.*

silverware, argenterie, *f.*

simple, simple.

since, depuis (que); que; puisque; **it is a long time —**, il y a longtemps que . . . ne . . .

sing, chanter.

singer, chanteuse, *f.*

singing, chant, *m.*

single, seul.

sir, monsieur.

sister, sœur.

sit (**down**), s'asseoir, se mettre à table.

sitting, assis.

situated, situé.

six, six.

sixteen, seize.

sixty, soixante.

skate, *n.*, patin, *m.*

skate, *v.*, patiner.

skirt, jupe, *f.*

sleep, dormir; coucher; go to —, s'endormir.

sleeping car, wagon-lit, *m.*

sleigh, traîneau, *m.*; go sleighing, aller (se promener) en traîneau.

slice, tranche, *f.*; — of bread and butter, tartine (*f.*) de beurre.

slippery, glissant.

slow, lent; be too —, retarder.

slowly, lentement, doucement.

small, petit.

smell, sentir; — sweet, sentir bon.

smoke, fumer.

sneeze, éternuer.

snow, *n.*, neige, *f.*

snow, *v.*, neiger.

so, si, ainsi; le; not —, pas si, moins; — much, — many, tant, tellement; — that, de sorte que, pour que.

soap, savon, *m.*

society, société, *f.*

solve, résoudre.

some, du, etc.; quelque; quelconque; quelques-uns; en.

somebody, some one, quelqu'un, on.

something, quelque chose (de).

sometimes, quelquefois.

somewhere, quelque part.

son, fils.

song, chanson, *f.*

soon, bientôt; sooner, plus tôt; as — as, aussitôt que; I would as —, j'aimerais autant.

sore, I have a — throat, j'ai mal à la gorge.

sorry, fâché; be —, regretter, être fâché.

sort, espèce, *f.*, sorte, *f.*

sound, *n.*, bruit, *m.*

sound, *adj.*, sain.

soup, potage, *m.*, soupe, *f.*

sour, aigre.

south, sud, *m.*, midi, *m.*

sow, semer.

speak, parler.

spectacles, lunettes, *f. pl.*

speed, vitesse, *f.*

spend, dépenser (*money*), passer (*time*).

splendid, superbe, magnifique.

spoon, cuiller, *f.*

sport, sport, *m.*

spring, printemps, *m.*; (*of water*) source, *f.*

spruce, sapin, *m.*

square, carré.

squirrel, écureuil, *m.*

stable, (*for cows*) étable, *f.*, (*for horses*) écurie, *f.*

stairway, escalier, *m.*

stale, rassis.

stand, se trouver, être debout, s'élever; standing, debout.

start, partir; tressaillir.

state, état, *m.*; —room, cabine, *f.*

station, gare, *f.*

statue, statue, *f.*

stay, *n.*, séjour, *m.*

stay, *v.*, rester.

steal, voler.

steam, vapeur, *f.*

steamer, bateau (*m.*) à vapeur, paquebot, *m.*

steel, acier, *m.*; — engraving, gravure (*f.*) sur acier.

step, pas, *m.*

stick, bâton, *m.*, canne, *f.*

still, encore, toujours.

St. John, saint Jean.

St. Lawrence, Saint-Laurent, *m.*

stone, pierre, *f.*

stop, arrêter; s'arrêter.

store, magasin, *m.*

story, étage (*of a house*), *m.*

story, histoire, *f.*

strange, étrange.

stranger, étranger, *m.*

straw, paille, *f.*; — hat, chapeau (*m.*) de paille.

strawberry, fraise, *f.*

stream, ruisseau, *m.*, cours (*m.*) d'eau.

street, rue, *f.*

strike, frapper.

strong, fort.

student, étudiant, *m.*

study, étudier.

study table, table (*f.*) de travail.

stupid, bête, stupide.

subject, sujet, *m.*

succeed, réussir; (*at examination*) être reçu.

success, succès, *m.*

such, tel; — a, un tel; si.

suffer, souffrir.

suffice, be sufficient, suffire.

sugar, sucre, *m.*

suit (of clothes), vêtement, *m.*, complet, *m.*

summer, été, *m.*

sun, soleil, *m.*

Sunday, dimanche, *m.*

sunny, be —, faire du soleil.

superintend, surveiller.

sure, sûr, certain.

surface, surface, *f.*

surround, entourer.

sweet, doux.

swim, nager.

T

table, table, *f.*; —cloth, nappe, *f.*, couvert, *m.*, tapis, *m.*; set the —, mettre la nappe (le couvert).

tailor, tailleur, *m.*

take, prendre; mener, conduire; — from, prendre à; — to, transporter à; — a walk, faire une promenade, se promener à pied; — away, emporter; — out, sortir; — after, tenir de; — about, promener; — off, ôter, quitter.

taking, prise, *f.*

talk, parler.

tall, grand.

tapestry, tapisserie, *f.*

task, tâche, *f.*, devoir, *m.*

taste, *n.*, goût, *m.*

taste, *v.*, goûter.

tax, reprocher.

tea, thé, *m.*; —cup, tasse (*f.*) à thé.

teach, enseigner, instruire, apprendre, montrer.

teacher, professeur, *m. or f.*; (*primary*) instituteur, *m.*, institutrice, *f.*

tear (out), arracher.

tease, taquiner.

tedium, ennui, *m.*

telegraph, télégraphier.

telephone, téléphoner.

tell, dire, raconter.

temperature, température, *f.*

ten, dix.

tender, tendre.

tent, tente, *f.*

terms, good —, bonne intelligence.

terrible, terrible.

Thames, Tamise, *f.*

than, que; (*before numerals*) de.

thank, remercier; thanks, merci, je vous remercie.

thankful, reconnaissant.

that, qui, que; ce, cet, cette; cela; celui(-là); que, de sorte que; — one, celui-là; — is, voilà, c'est; is — your book? est-ce là votre livre?

thaw, dégeler.

the, le, la, les,

theatre, théâtre, *m.*

thee, te, toi.

their, leur, leurs; theirs, à eux (etc.); le leur (etc.).

them, les, eux, elles, leur; of —, d'eux, en.

then, alors, puis, ensuite.

there, là, y; — (it) is, voilà; — is (are), il y a.

thermometer, thermomètre, *m.*

they, ils, *m.*, eux, *m.*, elles, *f.*; ce; on.

thick, épais.

thief, voleur, *m.*

thimble, dé, *m.*

thin, mince.

thine, à toi, le tien (etc.)

thing, chose, *f.*, affaire, *f.*; some— —, quelque chose.

think, penser, croire, réfléchir, trouver; what do you — of it? qu'en pensez-vous? comment le trouvez-vous? — of me, pensez à moi; what are you thinking of? à quoi pensez-vous?

third, troisième; tiers, *m.*

thirst, soif, *f.*; be thirsty, avoir soif; be very thirsty, avoir bien (très) soif, mourir de soif.

thirty, trente; about —, une trentaine.

this, ce, cet, cette; ce . . . -ci; ceci; — is, voici; — one, celui-ci.

thou, tu, toi.

though, bien que, quoique.

thousand (a), mille, mil, millier.

thread, fil, *m.*

three, trois.

thresh, battre.

throat, gorge, *f.*

through, par, à travers de.

throw, jeter, lancer; — away, jeter.

thumb, pouce, *m.*

Thursday, jeudi, *m.*

thy, ton, ta, tes.

ticket, billet, *m.*

tie, *n.*, cravate, *f.*

tie (up), *v.*, attacher.

tile, tuile, *f.*

till, jusque, jusqu'à.

time, temps, *m.*, fois, *f.*, heure, *f.*; moment, *m.*; three —s, trois fois; at what —? à quelle heure? on —, à l'heure, à l'heure

exacte; from — to —, de temps en temps; have a good —, s'amuser (bien).

timid, timide.

tip, pourboire, *m.*

tired, fatigué.

to, à, en, pour; chez; jusqu'à.

to-day, aujourd'hui.

together, ensemble.

to-morrow, demain; the day after —, après-demain.

tongue, langue, *f.*; show the —, tirer la langue.

too, aussi; trop; — much, trop.

tool, outil, *m.*

tooth, dent, *f.*; —brush, brosse (*f.*) à dents; —ache, mal (*m.*) aux dents.

top, toupie, *f.*

Toronto, Toronto, *m.*

torrent, torrent, *m.*

toss, jeter, lancer.

touch, toucher (à).

towards, vers.

towel, serviette, *f.*

town, ville, *f.*; in —, en ville; to —, à la ville.

townsman, citadin.

toy, joujou, *m.*

train, train, *m.*

tramway, tramway, *m.*

translate, traduire.

travel, *n.*, voyage, *m.*

travel, *v.*, voyager.

tree, arbre, *m.*

tremble, tressaillir.

trim, garnir.

trimming, garniture, *f.*

trip, voyage, *m.*, promenade, *f.*

trouble, peine, *f.*; what is the —? de quoi s'agit-il?

trout, truite, *f.*

true, vrai.

truly, vraiment, réellement.

trunk, malle, *f.*

try, tâcher; — (on), essayer.

Tuesday, mardi, *m.*
twelve, douze; — **o'clock,** midi, *m.*, minuit, *m.*
twenty, vingt.
twenty-five, vingt-cinq.
twice, deux fois.
two, deux.

U

umbrella, parapluie, *m.*
uncle, oncle, *m.*
under, sous; — **it,** dessous.
understand, comprendre; **not — at all,** n'y comprendre rien.
unfortunate, malheureux.
unhappy, malheureux.
United States, États-Unis, *m. pl.*
university, université, *f.*
unless, à moins de, à moins que . . . ne.
unsoiled, frais.
until, jusque, jusqu'à; jusqu'à ce que, que.
up, en haut; **be all — with,** en être fait de.
upper, supérieur.
upstairs, en haut; **show —,** faire monter.
us, nous.
use, *n.,* usage, *m.;* **make — of,** se servir de; **what — is that?** à quoi sert cela? **that is no —,** cela ne sert à rien.
use, *v.,* se servir de, employer; **I used to play,** je jouais.
useful, utile.
utensil, ustensile, *m.*
utilize, utiliser.

V

valise, valise, *f.*
vase, vase, *m.*
vast, vaste.
veal, veau, *m.*
vegetable, légume, *m.*
Venus, Vénus.

verse, verset, *m.;* (*line of poetry*) vers, *m.*
very, très, bien, fort; beaucoup.
vessel, vaisseau, *m.*
vice, vice, *m.*
village, village, *m.*
violent, violent.
visit, *n.,* visite, *f.;* **on a —,** en visite.
visit, *v.,* visiter, faire visite à, rendre visite à, aller voir.
voice, voix, *f.*
volume, volume, *m.,* tome, *m.*
vote, *n.,* voix, *f.;* **voting,** vote, *m.*
vote, *v.,* voter.

W

wages, gages, *m. pl.*
wainscoting, boiserie, *f.*
waist, corsage, *m.*
waistcoat, gilet, *m.*
wait (for), attendre; **keep waiting,** faire attendre.
waken, réveiller; se réveiller.
walk, promenade, *f.;* **go for a —,** (aller) faire une promenade.
wall, mur, *m.*
walnut, noix, *f.;* — **tree** (or **wood**), noyer, *m.*
want to, vouloir, désirer.
warm, *adj.,* chaud; **it is —,** il fait chaud.
warm, *v.,* chauffer.
warmth, chaleur, *f.*
wash, laver; se laver; (*linen*) blanchir.
waste, gaspiller.
watch, montre, *f.*
water, eau, *f.;* —**fall,** cascade, *f.*
way, façon, *f.,* manière, *f.;* chemin, *m.;* moyen, *m.;* **by the —,** à propos; **there is no —,** il n'y a pas moyen; **in such a — that,** de telle façon que.
we, nous; on.
weak, faible.

wealth, richesse(s), *f.*

wear, porter.

weather, temps, *m.*; **the — is fine,** il fait beau; **in cold —,** par le temps froid.

week, semaine, huit jours; **next —,** la semaine prochaine; **a — from to-day,** d'aujourd'hui en huit; **two weeks,** deux semaines, quinze jours, une quinzaine.

well, bien; **— then,** eh bien; **very —,** très bien, je veux bien; **not be very —,** être souffrant; **get —,** guérir; **— off (-to-do),** heureux, aisé; **be —,** se porter bien.

were, *see* be.

west, ouest, *m.*

what, que, quoi, ce qui, ce que; quel? qu'est-ce qui? qu'est-ce que?

whatever, quoi que; quel que; quelconque; quelque . . . que, n'importe quel.

wheat, blé, *m.*

when, quand, lorsque, où; à quelle heure?

whenever, quand, toutes les fois que.

where, où.

wherever, en quelque lieu que, partout où, où que.

whether, si; soit que, que.

which, qui, que, ce qui, ce que, lequel; quel; **of —,** dont.

while, whilst, pendant que, tandis que; en.

whistle, siffler.

white, blanc.

who, qui, lequel (etc.).

whoever, qui que, quiconque.

whole, tout, seule; **the — day,** toute la journée.

whom, qui, que, lequel (etc.).

whose, de qui, à qui, dont, duquel (etc.).

why, pourquoi.

wide, large.

wife, femme.

wild, sauvage.

will, *sign of fut.*; vouloir; **when you —,** quand vous voudrez; **— you kindly?** voulez-vous bien?

William, Guillaume.

win, gagner, l'emporter; **— the day,** l'emporter.

wind, vent, *m.*; **there is —,** il fait du vent.

window, fenêtre, *f.*; **(front) shop —,** devanture, *f.*

window blind, store, *m.*

windy, be —, faire du vent.

wine, vin, *m.*; **—glass,** verre (*m.*) à vin.

winter, hiver, *m.*

wise, sage, intelligent, raisonnable.

wish, désirer, vouloir; **I — (should like),** je voudrais.

with, avec, de, chez, contre, auprès de.

without, sans, sans que.

woman, femme; **— doctor,** femme docteur.

wonder, se demander.

wonderful, remarquable, étonnant, merveilleux.

wonderfully, à merveille.

wood, bois, *m.*

woodcutter, bûcheron, *m.*

wooden, de bois, en bois.

woollens, lainages, *m. pl.*

word, mot, *m.*

work, *n.*, travail, *m.*, ouvrage, *m.*

work, *v.*, travailler; faire marcher; exploiter; fonctionner.

workman, ouvrier, *m.*

world, monde, *m.*

worm, ver, *m.*

worse, *adj.*, pire, plus mauvais; *adv.*, pis, plus mal.

worth, be —, valoir; **— while,** valoir la peine; **have 5 francs —**

of, en avoir pour 5 francs; — **a million**, riche d'un million.

worthy, brave, digne.

would, *sign of condl. and of impf. ind.*; voudrais, voulais.

write, écrire; — **to each other**, s'écrire.

wrong, mauvais; tort, *m.*; **he is —**, il a tort.

wrought-iron, fer (*m.*) forgé.

Y

yard, cour, *f.*; mètre, *m.*

year, an, *m.*, année, *f.*; **every —**, tous les ans; **this —**, cette année.

yeast, levain, *m.*

yellow, jaune; **become —**, jaunir.

yes, oui, si.

yesterday, hier; **the day before —**, avant-hier.

yet, encore; déjà; cependant; **not —**, pas encore.

yield, donner.

yonder, là-bas.

you, vous; tu, te, toi; on.

young, jeune.

your, votre, vos; ton, ta, tes; **yours**, à toi, à vous; le tien (etc.), le vôtre (etc.).

yourself, vous, vous-même.

INDEX

313

ADVERTISEMENTS

FRENCH GRAMMARS, READERS, ETC.

Anecdotes Faciles (Super). 25 cts.

Blanchaud's Progressive French Idioms. 60 cts.

Bouvet's Exercises in French Syntax and Composition. 75 cts.

Bowen's First Scientific French Reader. 90 cts.

Bruce's Dictées Françaises. 30 cts.

Bruce's Grammaire Française. $1.15.

Bruce's Lectures Faciles. 60 cts.

Capus's Pour Charmer nos Petits. 50 cts.

Chapuzet and Daniel's Mes Premiers Pas en Français. 75 cts.

Clarke's Subjunctive Mood. An inductive treatise, with exercises. 50 cts.

Comfort's Exercises in French Prose Composition. 30 cts.

Davies's Elementary Scientific French Reader. 40 cts.

Edgren's Compendious French Grammar. $1.15. Part I, 35 cts.

Fontaine's Lectures Courantes. $1.00.

Fontaine's Livre de Lecture et de Conversation. 90 cts.

Fraser and Squair's Abridged French Grammar. $1.00.

Fraser and Squair's Complete French Grammar. $1.15.

Fraser and Squair's Elementary French Grammar. 90 cts.

Fraser and Squair's Shorter French Course. $1.10.

French Anecdotes (Giese and Cool). 40 cts.

French Verb Blank (Fraser and Squair). 30 cts.

Grandgent's Essentials of French Grammar. $1.00.

Grandgent's French Composition. 50 cts.

Grandgent's Materials for French Composition. Each, 12 cts.

Grandgent's Short French Grammar. 75 cts.

Heath's French Dictionary. Retail price, $1.50.

Hénin's Méthode. 50 cts.

Hotchkiss's Le Premier Livre de Français. 35 cts.

Kimball's Materials for French Composition. Each, 12 cts.

Mansion's Exercises in French Composition. 60 cts.

Mansion's First Year French. For young beginners. 50 cts.

Marcou's French Review Exercises. 25 cts.

Pellissier's Idiomatic French Composition. 00 cts.

Perfect French Possible (Knowles and Favard). 35 cts.

Prisoners of the Temple (Guerber). For French Composition. 25 cts.

Roux's Lessons in Grammar and Composition, based on *Colomba.* 18 cts.

Snow and Lebon's Easy French. 60 cts.

Storr's Hints on French Syntax. With exercises. 30 cts.

Story of Cupid and Psyche (Guerber). For French Composition. 18 cts.

Super's Preparatory French Reader. 70 cts.

ELEMENTARY FRENCH TEXTS.

Assolant's Aventure du Célèbre Pierrot (Pain). Vocabulary. 25 cts.

Assolant's Récits de la Vieille France. Notes by E. B. Wauton. 25 cts.

Berthet's Le Pacte de Famine (Dickinson). 25 cts.

Bruno's Les Enfants Patriotes (Lyon). Vocabulary. 25 cts.

Bruno's Tour de la France par deux Enfants (Fontaine). Vocabulary. 45 cts.

Daudet's Trois Contes Choisis (Sanderson). Vocabulary. 20 cts.

Desnoyers' Jean-Paul Choppart (Fontaine). Vocab. and exs. 40 cts.

Enault's Le Chien du Capitaine (Fontaine). Vocabulary. 35 cts.

Erckmann-Chatrian's Le Conscrit de 1813 (Super). Vocabulary. 45 cts.

Erckmann-Chatrian's L'Histoire d'un Paysan (Lyon). 25 cts.

Erckmann-Chatrian's Le Juif Polonais (Manley). Vocabulary. 30 cts.

Erckmann-Chatrian's Madame Thérèse (Manley). Vocabulary. 40 cts.

France's Abeille (Lebon). 25 cts.

French Fairy Tales (Joynes). Vocabulary and exercises. 35 cts.

Génin's Le Petit Tailleur Bouton (Lyon). Vocabulary. 25 cts.

Gervais's Un Cas de Conscience (Horsley). Vocabulary. 25 cts.

La Bedollière's La Mère Michel et son Chat (Lyon). Vocabulary. 30 cts.

Labiche's La Grammaire (Levi). Vocabulary. 25 cts.

Labiche's La Poudre aux Yeux (Wells). Vocabulary. 30 cts.

Labiche's Le Voyage de M. Perrichon (Wells). Vocab. and exs. 30 cts.

Laboulaye's Contes Bleus (Fontaine). Vocabulary. 35 cts.

La Main Malheureuse (Guerber). Vocabulary. 25 cts.

Laurie's Mémoires d'un Collégien (Super). Vocab. and exs. 50 cts.

Legouvé and Labiche's Cigale chez les Fourmis (Witherby). 20 cts.

Lemaître, Contes (Rensch). Vocabulary. 30 cts.

Mairêt's La Tâche du Petit Pierre (Super). Vocab. and exs. 35 cts.

Maistre's La Jeune Sibérienne(Fontaine). Vocab. and exs. 30 cts.

Malot's Sans Famille (Spiers). Vocabulary and exercises. 40 cts.

Meilhac and Halévy's L'Eté de la St. Martin (François) Vocab. 25 cts.

Moinaux's Les deux Sourds (Spiers). Vocabulary. 25 cts.

Müller's Grandes Découvertes Modernes. Vocabulary. 25 cts.

Récits de Guerre et de Révolution (Minssen). Vocabulary. 25 cts.

Récits Historiques (Moffett). Vocabulary and exercises. 45 cts.

Saintine's Picciola (Super). Vocabulary. 45 cts.

Ségur's Les Malheurs de Sophie (White). Vocab. and exs. 45 cts.

Selections for Sight Translation (Bruce). 15 cts.

Verne's L'Expédition de la Jeune Hardie (Lyon). Vocabulary. 30 cts.

Heath's Modern Language Series

INTERMEDIATE FRENCH TEXTS. (Partial List.)

About's Le Roi des Montagnes (Logie). 40 cts. With vocab. 50 cts.

About's La Mère de la Marquise (Brush). Vocabulary. 40 cts.

Balzac: Cinq Scènes de la Comédie Humaine (Wells). 40 cts.

Balzac's Eugénie Grandet (Spiers). Vocabulary. 00 cts.

Balzac's Le Curé de Tours (Super). Vocabulary. 30 cts.

Chateaubriand's Atala (Kuhns). Vocabulary. 35 cts.

Contes des Romanciers Naturalistes (Dow and Skinner). Vocab. 55 cts.

Daudet's La Belle-Nivernaise (Boielle). Vocabulary. 30 cts.

Daudet's Le Petit Chose (Super). Vocabulary. 40 cts.

Daudet's Tartarin de Tarascon (Hawkins). Vocabulary. 45 cts.

Dumas's Duc de Beaufort (Kitchen). Vocabulary. 30 cts.

Dumas's La Question d'Argent (Henning). Vocabulary. 40 cts.

Dumas's La Tulipe Noire (Fontaine). 40 cts. With vocabulary. 50 cts.

Dumas's Les Trois Mousquetaires (Spiers). Vocabulary. 45 cts.

Dumas's Monte-Cristo (Spiers). Vocabulary. 40 cts.

Feuillet's Roman d'un jeune homme pauvre (Bruner). Vocabulary. 55 cts.

Gautier's Voyage en Espagne (Steel). 30 cts.

Gréville's Dosia (Hamilton). Vocabulary. 45 cts.

Hugo's Bug Jargal (Boïelle). 40 cts.

Hugo's La Chute. From *Les Misérables* (Huss). Vocabulary. 30 cts.

Hugo's Quatre-vingt-treize (Fontaine). Vocabulary. 50 cts.

Labiche's La Cagnotte (Farnsworth). 30 cts.

La Brète's Mon Oncle et mon Curé (Colin). Vocabulary. 45 cts.

Lamartine's Graziella (Warren). 40 cts.

Lamartine's Jeanne d'Arc (Barrère). Vocabulary. 35 cts.

Lamartine's Scènes de la Révolution Française (Super). Vocab. 40 cts.

Lesage's Gil Blas (Sanderson). 45 cts.

Maupassant: Huit Contes Choisis (White). Vocabulary. 35 cts.

Michelet: Extraits de l'histoire de France (Wright). 35 cts.

Musset: Trois Comédies (McKenzie). 30 cts.

Sarcey's Le Siège de Paris (Spiers). Vocabulary. 45 cts.

Taine's L'Ancien Régime (Giese). Vocabulary. 65 cts.

Theuriet's Bigarreau (Fontaine). Vocab. and exercises. 35 cts.

Tocqueville's Voyage en Amérique (Ford). Vocabulary. 40 cts.

Vigny's Cinq-Mars (Sankey). Abridged. 60 cts.

Vigny's Le Cachet Rouge (Fortier). 25 cts.

Vigny's La Canne de Jonc (Spiers). 40 cts.

Voltaire's Zadig (Babbitt). Vocabulary. 45 cts.

Heath's Modern Language Series

INTERMEDIATE FRENCH TEXTS. (Partial List.)

Augier's Le Gendre de M. Poirier (Wells). Vocabulary. 35 cts.

Beaumarchais's Le Barbier de Séville (Spiers). Vocabulary. 35 cts.

Erckmann-Chatrian's Waterloo (Super). 35 cts.

Fleurs de France (Fontaine). 35 cts.

French Lyrics (Bowen). 60 cts.

Gautier's Jettatura (Schinz). 35 cts.

Guerber's Marie-Louise. 30 cts.

Halévy's L'Abbé Constantin (Logie). 30 cts. With vocab. 40 cts.

Halévy's Un Mariage d'Amour (Hawkins). Vocabulary. 30 cts.

Historiettes Modernes (Fontaine). Vol. I, 35 cts. Vol. II, 35 cts.

La France qui travaille (Jago). Vocabulary. 50 cts.

Loti's Pêcheur d'Islande (Super). Vocabulary. 40 cts.

Loti's Ramuntcho (Fontaine). 35 cts.

Marivaux's Le Jeu de l'amour et du hasard (Fortier). Vocab. 35 cts.

Merimée's Chronique du Règne de Charles IX (Desages). 30 cts.

Merimée's Colomba (Fontaine). 35 cts. With vocabulary, 45 cts.

Molière en Récits (Chapuzet and Daniels). Vocabulary. 50 cts.

Molière's L'Avare (Levi). 35 cts.

Molière's Le Bourgeois Gentilhomme (Warren). 30 cts.

Molière's Le Médecin Malgré Lui (Hawkins). Vocabulary. 30 cts.

Musset's Pierre et Camille (Super). 20 cts.

Pailleron's Le Monde où l'on s'ennuie (Pendleton). 30 cts.

Racine's Andromaque (Wells). 30 cts.

Racine's Athalie (Eggert). 30 cts.

Racine's Esther (Spiers). Vocabulary. 30 cts.

Renan's Souvenirs d'Enfance et de Jeunesse (Babbitt). 75 cts.

Sand's La Mare au Diable (Sumichrast). Vocabulary. 35 cts.

Sand's La Petite Fadette (Super). Vocabulary. 35 cts.

Sandeau's Mlle de la Seiglière (Warren). Vocabulary. 40 cts.

Sardou's Les Pattes de Mouche (Farnsworth). Vocabulary. 40 cts.

Scribe's Bataille de Dames (Wells). Vocabulary. 35 cts.

Scribe's Le Verre d'Eau (Eggert). 35 cts.

Septs Grands Auteurs du XIXe Siècle (Fortier). Lectures. 60 cts.

Souvestre's Un Philosophe sous les Toits (Fraser). 50 cts. Vocab. 55 cts.

Thiers's Expédition de Bonaparte en Egypte (Fabregou). 35 cts.

Verne's Tour du Monde en quatre-vingts jours (Edgren). Vocab. 45 cts.

Verne's Vingt mille lieues sous la mer (Fontaine). Vocab. 45 cts.

Zola's La Débâcle (Wells). Abridged. 60 cts.